CW00765539

Enforcement of a Judgment

Enforcement of a Judgment

Eleventh Edition

Claire Sandbrook LL.B (Hons),
F.I.C.M.
Solicitor of the Supreme Court

*Chief Executive Officer,
Shergroup Limited*

SWEET & MAXWELL

First Published 1948
Eleventh Edition 2011

Published in 2011 by
Thomson Reuters (Legal) Limited (Registered in England & Wales, Company No. 1679046. Registered office and address for service, 100 Avenue Road
London NW3 3PF)
Trading as Sweet & Maxwell for further information on our products and services, visit http://www.sweetandmaxwell.co.uk

Typeset by LBJ Typesetting Ltd of Kingsclere
Printed and bound in the Netherlands by Ten Brink, Meppel.

No natural forests were destroyed to make this product; only farmed timber was used and replanted.

A CIP catalogue record for this book is available from the British Library

ISBN—9780414043244

With Grateful Thanks to My Mentors

Alastair Black Esq., CBE, DL
Master Robert Turner

CONTENTS

Table of Cases

References are to para. number

Table of Statutes

References are to para. number

Table of Statutory Instruments

References are to para. number

Table of European Legislation

References are to para. number

Chapter 1

The Enforcement Debate

1–01 Since the 10th edition of this book was published in 2006 the subject of enforcing judgments has been gathering momentum culminating in the Royal Assent to the Tribunals Court and Enforcement Act which became law on the July 19, 2007.

The Act itself deals with a number of issues relating to enforcement including reform of the tribunal system in England and Wales as well as the Parts that relate specifically to enforcement methods available primarily in the civil court arena in Pts 3, 4 and 5. There is a small part relating to the enforcement of Compulsory Purchase Orders in Pt 7.

At the time of preparing this book Pts 3 and 4 are currently awaiting further regulations to create a working framework to enable the provisions of the Act to come into force. It is expected that these will be wholly or partly operational by 2012 but much depends on the appetite of the new Coalition Government to grasp the nettle in relation to enforcement matters. Budgetary considerations will no doubt also play a part in deciding whether there will be the necessary resources to bring in some of the more innovative thinking that resulted from over 10 years of consultation with stakeholders.

As this book goes to print the economic reality of hard times is all around us and the enforcement system has to brace itself for unchartered waters.

1–02 Statistically there are some shocking enforcement indicators which have led to the subject of enforcing a judgment climbing the charts in terms of political importance. These statistics (taken from the Credit Action charity) include:

- 2000 county court judgments were issued every single day for the first three months of 2009 against consumers and the question has to be asked how many of these had easily identifiable assets to enforce against.

- 238 landlord possession orders were made everyday leaving county court bailiff departments with eviction dates stretching into months rather than days.
- Every 51 seconds someone will be declared insolvent or bankrupt—where does the reliance on insolvency leave a judgment creditor who wants to be paid in full on the amount adjudged outstanding by the court?

It is a sobering thought that these are the kinds of facts and figures that an enforcement system must be able to respond to with workable remedies.

1–03 Turning to the Act in its constituent parts:

Part 3 of the Act deals with enforcement by taking control of goods which consolidates the law across England and Wales on the activities of both High Court Enforcement Officers, County Court bailiffs and to some extent certificated bailiffs and anyone wishing to operate an enforcement business.

Part 3 of the Act also provides a new procedure for recovering commercial rent arrears known in short as "CRAR". This procedure abolishes the old landlord's remedy of "distress for rent" and will in turn lead to a more court based form of remedy than is currently the case.

Under Pt 4 of the TCEA 2007 relating to court based methods of enforcement including attachment of earnings, charging orders, and information requests, some new ideas have found their way on to the statute book. How far these are likely to come into being actual processes within the legal system with an economic cloud of austerity on the way is difficult to say. There is no planned change to the third party debt order procedure.

Part 5 of the TCEA 2007 includes a number of new terms including Debt Relief Orders, Enforcement Restriction Orders, Debt Management Schemes and a revisit to Administration Orders. Judgment creditors need to be aware of the array of shelters that a person in debt can utilise to postpone paying what is owed.

1–04 The proposed new legislation is the culmination of the work and focus of successive Lord Chancellor's and their policy advisors. There have been numerous consultation processes since Lord Irvine announced his review of enforcement in 1998. The Government has sifted through the outcomes of its deliberations to achieve outcomes which are balanced and which assist creditors in the enforcement of their judgments but which also protect judgment debtors from unreasonable and unfair behaviour.

Even when regulations are made, whole chunks of the CPR will have to be rewritten to take account of the changes in both the RSC and CCR.

Underlying the legislation are the facts and figures around enforcement options. Judicial statistics which are published each year show the trends for enforcement choice in England and Wales. Statistics for January to March 2010 show a sea change by judgment creditors in their approach to enforcement choices.

- county court warrants of execution: 43,400 were issued which is a drop of 42 per cent on the same period in 2009;
- county court warrants of possession: 32,000—down 16 per cent;
- attachment of earnings order applications: 11,800—down 44 per cent;
- charging order applications: 31,000—down 7 per cent;
- third party debt order applications: 1,300—down 37 per cent;
- administration order applications: 300—down 44 per cent;
- order to obtain information applications: 6,300—down 26 per cent.

1–05 Statistics from Registry Trust Limited who are the keepers of the data on judgment information across the United Kingdom also show that in the first quarter of 2009 the value of consumer county court judgments actually decreased from the previous quarter and overall when combined with commercial county court judgment data the value in millions of county court judgments had reduced by 1.6 per cent.

So why is it that at a time of economic downturn we are seeing enforcement figures drop through the floor rather than rising as people look to liquidate their judgments? The answer is that court based enforcement costs the judgment creditor hard cash by way of an investment in the court fee. Judgment creditors will need to be much more discerning about how they "speculate to accumulate" when it comes to proceeding with any enforcement measure.

If one looks at the data which creates judgments, being the number of claims issued, one can instantly see a drop with 40,000 less claims being issued in the first quarter of 2010 and the indications are that figure is continuing to slide down.

1–06 The new Government has made noises about enforcement. It has said it will tackle "aggressive bailiffs" although nothing has actually been put forward as to what constitutes "aggressive" behaviour. Readers of this book will appreciate that the world of bailiffs goes far further than county court bailiffs or High Court Enforcement Officers. There is a whole world of parking fine, council tax, and non-domestic rate enforcement business which is handled by certificated and private bailiffs.

The Government has also pledged to raise the threshold on Charging Orders to £25,000 but then recently held another consultation paper on Orders for Sale which may mean the whole topic of thresholds and Charging Orders is melting away.

And amongst all the statistics and soundbites by politicians the public are having to cope with an enforcement system which is in flux with huge change hanging over it but with no one able to move forward.

For judgment creditors they deserve a flagship service both to litigate their claim and to enforce their judgment. Despite effort on so many levels successive governments have failed to deliver on this leaving the current systems in a state of limbo where neither the creditor or debtor can engage with the court or enforcement officer to see the current position.

For judgment debtors, they should now be engaging in an enforcement system which allows them to pay their judgment online, or in a range of other channels for payment. Instead they are buffeted in a system which fails to give them real time information on their situation or consistent advice on what to do next with the CCJ against them.

1–07 We all had high hopes of the consultation on enforcement when it started out in 1998. The best that has come out of the system is that the Sheriffs survived and were reformed into High Court Enforcement Officers. This has been a true success for Government, and judgment creditors. The system is still in many ways in its infancy, but HCEOs are responding to the needs of both creditor and debtor and through their private sector approach are investing in the systems which the public sector can only dream about. In saying this I would like to pay tribute to the policy officials and Minister at the time, Patricia Scotland. Through their hard work and attention to detail the Sheriffs were reformed and reborn as High Court Enforcement Officers. This small part of the enforcement industry reflects Government's commitment (which in many ways is a-political) to grow a branch of the enforcement profession which adheres to professional standards and which has the status to ensure that the public understand their responsibilities as citizens to meet their obligations.

As a result of the time taken to create a robust set of founding principles, with continuing input from the judiciary as well as government officials, HCEOs are seeing their profile and reputation rising as judgment creditors make a choice to use the High Court service. More of course can and should be done. The High Court Enforcement Officers Association has an opportunity to promote best practice on the application of its Miscellaneous Fees under the High Court Enforcement Officers Regulations 2004. HCEOs are developing their training programme for a new style of officer and we wait to see how far the training requirements will go if the SIA is scrapped.

In preparing this book, we look at the law as it is today, and we bring subtle changes to the 11th edition except in relation to execution against goods which takes the reader through the structure of Pt 3 of the TCEA 2007 and the all important Sch. 12. We anticipate what enabling regulations will be required to bring the Act into being as part of this edition.

And finally as the author and editor I would like to thank my assistant, Carrie Ockelford for her patience in helping me preparing the text for this book, along with the research and general editing carried out by my dedicated legal team, Sharon Housden and Graham Smith. As always I thank my husband, Steve and children for putting up with me and finally for my long suffering publisher, I thank him for being incredibly patient—but being a full time HCEO and trying to write about the day job never makes for easy deadlines.

Chapter 2

Enforceable Judgments, Orders & Awards

Introductory comments

2–01 In this book we look at the methods of enforcing the judgments and orders of the civil courts. The term "enforcement" is a collective one which relates to all the methods available to enforce the judgments and orders of the civil courts and magistrates' courts where necessary. Sometimes, it is interchangeable with the term "execution", but actually this really relates to the enforcement of the judgment or order where a warrant or writ of execution is issued to seize the judgment debtor's goods to compel payment.

In addition to the civil courts and magistrates' courts, a number of other bodies also create enforceable awards as part of their process.

For many practitioners and litigants in person, the need to be able to enforce the judgment or order successfully by compelling payment is one of the most frustrating parts of the litigation process, but without it the court's judgment or order is worthless if the judgment debtor decides not to co-operate and pay what is due—or worse still never had any assets against which to enforce.

Types of enforceable judgments

2–02 Broadly speaking, it is possible to enforce a money judgment in the following circumstances:

- when the time for compliance has arrived—see CPR Sch.1, RSC Order 46, r. 6 (4)(*b*);
- when it has not been satisfied;
- when it has not been stayed or when execution has not been stayed;
- when it has not become statute-barred.

The possible methods of enforcement of such judgments are set out below.

Enforcement definitions

2–03 In CPR 70.1(2) the Rules define a number of terms which apply to the enforcement of the court's judgment, and which are referred to in the enforcement rules at CPR Pt 71 to 73 (dealt with later in this book). This can be summarised as follows:

- "Judgment creditor" means the person who has obtained or is entitled to enforce the judgment or order;
- "Judgment debtor" means the person against whom a judgment or order has been given;
- "Judgment or order" includes an arbitral award, which the court registers for enforcement, and has ordered to be enforced or has given permission to enforce as if it were a judgment or order of the court. In these circumstances, the award made by the court will mean the court which registered the award or made the order;
- "Judgment or order for the payment of money" also includes a judgment or order for the payment of costs, but does not include a judgment or order for the payment of money into court.

Methods of enforcement in civil courts

2–04 Unless there is some contrary provision in a statute, rule or practice direction, a successful judgment creditor may use any of the available methods of enforcement to compel payment of what is owed from the judgment debtor. The judgment creditor can also use more than one method of enforcement either concurrently or consecutively to enforce payment, except where the method of enforcement chosen is an order for the attachment of earnings, in which case the other methods of enforcement cannot be pursued concurrently. A judgment given against a third party who is not a party for proceedings can be enforced as if that person were a party through the procedure known as "Third Party Debt Order (TPDO)".

For ease of reference, the methods in the High Court and county court are set out below.

Methods of enforcement in the High Court for the payments of money

2–05 These include:

- issuing a High Court Writ of fieri facias (the county court equivalent is a warrant of execution);
- issuing an application for a third party debt order;
- issuing an application for a charging order, stop order or stop notice;
- appointing a "receiver by way of equitable execution";
- issuing an application for committal, which is only available where it is specifically permitted by a rule or under the Debtors Act 1869 and 1878 (see CPR Sch. 1 RSC Order 45, r.5, CPR Sch. 1 RSC Order 52, PD52);
- issuing a writ of sequestration (where this is permitted) under CPR Sch. 1 RSC Order 45, r.5, where the nature of the judgment is in the form of an injunction.

It should be noted that attachment of earnings orders are not available in the High Court, other than to enforce a High Court maintenance order.

Turning away from judgments for the payments of money, where a judgment or order is for possession of land, this may be enforced in the High Court by a writ of possession. Where the judgment or order is for the delivery of goods, the successful claimant can issue a writ of delivery. If the judgment or order for possession or delivery is in the nature of an injunction, enforcement by committal proceedings or by writ of sequestration is also permissible.

In addition to the methods of enforcement, writs of execution in aid of a writ of fieri facias are available in the High Court and there is no equivalent in the county courts except for warrants of restitution.

Methods of enforcement in the county court

2–06 The methods of enforcement available in the county court are similar to the High Court, but there are one or two exceptions. County court orders may be enforced by:

- warrants of execution against the goods of the judgment debtor (see County Courts Act 1984 s.85 (as amended by SI 1991/724));
- warrants of possession of land (see CPR Sch. 2 CCR Order 26, r.17);
- a warrant for the delivery of goods (see CRP Sch. 2 CCR Order 26, r.16);

- an application for an attachment of earnings (see Attachment of Earnings Act 1971 s.1(2), CPR Sch. 2 CCR Order 27);
- an application for a charging order against any interest in land, as provided under s. 1 of the Charging Orders Act 1979 (as amended by the Administration of Justice Act 1982 s.34, 37, Sch. 3, County Courts Act 1984 s.148(1), Sch. 2 and the County Courts Jurisdiction Order 1981, (SI 1981/1123);
- a charging order against any security or funds in court or under any trust (this type of enforcement is very rare but does provide for enforcement against securities held by the judgment debtor);
- an application for a third party debt order;
- committal of the judgment debtor (see County Courts Act 1984 s.119 (as amended by Civil Procedure Act 1997 s.10, Sch. 2), CPR Sch. 2 CCR Order 29, r.1);
- by appointing a receiver (see County Courts Act 1984 s.107 and CPR Pt 69);
- in relation to maintenance orders and other debts owned to the Crown, a judgment summons (see s.5 Debtors Act 1869 (as amended by the Bankruptcy Act 1883 s.169(1), Sch. 5, Statute Law (Repeals) Act 2004, (SI 2002/439) (as restricted by Administration of Justice Act 1970 s.11, Sch. 4) and CPR Sch. 2 CCR Order 28, r.1));
- the making of an administration order (see County Courts 1984 s.112-117 and note that an administration order may also be made following an application for an attachment of earnings order pursuant to the Attachment of Earnings Act 1974 s.4 (as amended by the Insolvency Act 1976 s.13, Sch. 3, County Courts Act 1984, s. 148(1), Sch. 2 Para 40)).

Enforcement against one of several defendants

2–07 An order against several persons for payment of a sum of money, whether or not deemed joint and several, may be enforced against any one of them separately (*Land Credit Co of Ireland v Lord Fermoy* (1869–1870) L.R. 5 Ch. App. 323).

Enforcement by or against non-parties

2–08 Under CPR Pt 70.4 if a judgment or order is given or made in favour of a person who is not a party to proceedings, it may be enforced by or against that person by the same methods as if he were a party.

Such orders are rare but do arise (e.g. a "Wasted Costs" Order or an undertaking to pay a non-party's costs). A non-party who has the benefit of an order does not need permission to enforce the order and can enforce it against the party ordered to pay.

Solicitor's implied authority to commence enforcement

2–09 Having been retained in proceedings leading to a judgment, a solicitor has implied authority to commence enforcement on that judgment, without further instructions from his client (*Sandford v Porter & Waine* [1912] 2 I.R. 551). As this case is over 100 years old, it is suggested that the Professional Code of Conduct Rules may be limited by express agreement in the solicitor's retainer, which should have been included in the Client Care letter at the outset of instructions.

Information about costs, timescales and liability for charges should be fully explained, particularly in the case of enforcement through a High Court Enforcement Officer, where it is suggested the solicitor should warn the client of the client's liability to pay the High Court Enforcement Officer's charges, as such charges are a first charge on any monies recovered.

It is also suggested that solicitors need to be proactive with their clients in the area of advice when it comes to enforcing the client's judgment or order, as a failure to do so may amount to a failure to properly advise. If a client is not advised on the various methods of enforcement, and guided on the best chance of success or the availability of interest on a county court judgment that could have been transferred to the High Court for enforcement, then in the event of missing out on an opportunity to recoup the judgment debt, a solicitor can expect at worst a claim for negligence or at best a very disappointed client.

Enforcement of judgments where state immunity or diplomatic privilege arise

2–10 The immunity of sovereign states from the enforcement of domestic court judgments can be a minefield for the uninitiated. In English law the subject is dealt with under the State Immunity Act 1978, in which in s.1 there is general immunity from a state being sued—subject to limited exceptions.

These exceptions include either where the state has submitted to the jurisdiction of the English courts (s.2(1)) or where the transaction that is the subject of the lawsuit is a commercial one (s.3).

The enforcement of the judgment will usually arise against the state where it has been obtained under a commercial contract in which a state has agreed to the jurisdiction of the English court and submitted to its jurisdiction.

In deciding to enforce against a state, a practitioner must decide whether the state in question can be defined either as a unitary body with a legal personality or a separate entity within the definitions of the 1978 Act.

The answer to this preliminary point will determine how any judgment can be enforced.

2–11 Immunity also exists outside of the 1978 Act under the Diplomatic Privileges Act 1964. Under this legislation, diplomatic immunity is conferred upon a wide range of assets belonging to a state. As a result of claiming "diplomatic immunity", embassies can claim that their goods and chattels, including vehicles and money held in bank accounts, are subject to diplomatic immunity and therefore unavailable for enforcement purposes.

If, however, the embassy or some other organ of the state becomes involved in carrying out commercial activities, such as a tourist bureau or a property development subsidiary, then assets may not be immune. The problem here is establishing on evidence whether the assets are in fact used for commercial purposes. Here, a practitioner wishing to pursue a judgment against an embassy may find that the ambassador is prepared to issue a certificate that the goods are that of the embassy and are not available. If this happens, this is treated as evidence that the assets are not used for commercial purposes under s.13(5) of the Act, and so the burden will be on the judgment creditor to prove the contrary.

The property of a state cannot be subject to the enforcement of a judgment (s.13(2) (b)) unless consent has been given by the state. Such consent may have been given expressly in a commercial agreement giving consent to enforcement as well as submitting to the jurisdiction of the English courts. It requires some forethought into what can go wrong in a commercial relationship when entering into a contract with a state or any of its organs such as the embassy or commercial entities, to ensure it is possible for a judgment to be entered against that state. If no such express consent can be found in a contract, then it may still be possible to use the exception in s.13(4) of the Act, which provides that any property used for commercial purposes will be available for enforcement. Obviously, it is easier to rely on an express agreement rather than to construct this by using the exception.

2–12 In the case of *Societe Eram Shipping Co Ltd v Compagine Internationale de Navigation* [2003] UKHL 30; [2004] 1 A.C. 260 the issue surrounding the enforcement of a judgment against the state was examined. The case serves as a useful and modern precedent on the issues that need to be addressed by judgment creditors when faced with enforcement in what is a complex scenario. The enforcement method at the centre of this case was the third party debt procedure under CPR Pt 72. The basis of this procedure is that a bank as the debtor of the judgment debtor is served with an order to pay the judgment creditor and effectively "leapfrog" the judgment debtor to whom the bank owes the money in the bank account. The bank will be discharged from its obligation to pay the judgment debtor under the third party debt order when it pays the money owed to the judgment creditor under the terms of the final order. However, what the *Societe* case underlines is that for this enforcement method to work the debt must be owed within England and Wales and the bank owing the debt must also be within England and Wales. If this is not followed, a bank may risk paying the judgment creditor in England under the terms of the order, and then have to pay the judgment debtor in the jurisdiction where the judgment debtor's bank is situated.

Ultimately, when it comes to enforcing a judgment or order against a state or any part thereof, thought should be given at the outset of the commercial relationship as to what the contract should provide for. When contracting with a state, a "non-state party" should seek to protect itself through the contract that it draws up by including clauses which ensure that the state irrevocably appoints an agent who can accept service of process within the jurisdiction and submits to the jurisdiction of the English court, as well as consenting to the giving of any relief or the issue of any process including enforcement or execution against any property, irrespective of its use or intended use. If appropriate clauses are included in the contract, then should enforcement ultimately become necessary, such clauses will help lay the groundwork to ensure that the evidential burdens of jurisdiction, service and execution are met under English law. If it can be found that monies held in a bank account are owed to the state by a bank in the jurisdiction of England and Wales for commercial purposes, then the likelihood of successful enforcement improves—provided those monies can be identified. As with any third party debt enforcement, however, if there are no monies available, the enforcement method becomes fruitless.

Enforcement of judgments and orders of the Technology and Construction Court

2–13 The Technology and Construction Court (TCC) produces judgments and orders capable of enforcement, along with adjudicators' decisions and arbitrators' awards. The party wishing to make use of any provision of the CPR, especially if they are concerned with the enforcement of judgments and orders made in the TCC in London, can use the TCC registry in London or any convenient TCC district registry as listed in the rules. Outside London, where the judgment or order in respect of which enforcement is sought is made by a judge, the party seeking an enforcement procedure should use the registry of the court in which the judgment or order was made. Where orders are required or sought to support enforcement of a TCC judgment or order, the judge of the TCC is the appropriate judge for that purpose. If available, the judge who gave the relevant judgment or made the relevant order is the appropriate judge to whom all applications should be addressed.

A TCC county court judgment must be enforced in the county court (if less than £600) or in the High Court where the judgment amount is more than £5,000. A figure between £600 and £4,990 can be enforced in either court at the option of the judgment creditor.

Enforcement of orders made in the Court of Appeal

2–14 Under the Supreme Court Act 1981, s.15(4) any enactment authorising or requiring the taking of any steps for the enforcement of orders or judgments of the High Court applies similarly in relation to the orders or judgments of the Court of Appeal. In this book, reference to a High Court judgment normally includes a High Court order and a judgment or order of the Court of Appeal. Indeed, it is questionable whether there is any meaningful distinction between a "judgment" and an "order", as discussed in the note to CPR 40.1.1.

The County Courts Act 1984 contains no similar provision. Nevertheless, in *Ager v Ager* [1998] 1 W.L.R. 1074; [1998] 1 All E.R. 703 CA it was held that the jurisdiction conferred on the High Court by s.15(4) constituted a "general principle of practice" within the meaning of s.76 of the 1984 Act, which could be adopted and applied in proceedings in a county court.

Enforcement of orders made by the Supreme Court

2–15 The enforcement of orders made by the Supreme Court in England and Wales is dealt with in para. 13 of Practice Direction 40B, which supplements Pt 40 of the Civil Procedure Rules.

This provides for an application to be made in accordance with CPR Pt 23 for an order to make an order of the Supreme Court (or the House of Lords) into an order of the High Court.

The application needs to be made to the procedural judge of the division, District Registry or court in which the proceedings are taking place, and may be made without notice unless the court directs otherwise.

The Pt 23 application must be supported by the following:

- details of the order which was the subject of the appeal to the Supreme Court or the House of Lords;
- details of the order of the Supreme Court or the House of Lords, with a copy annexed, and
- a copy of the certificate of the Registrar of the Supreme Court or of the Clerk of Parliaments of the assessment of the costs of the appeal to the Supreme Court or the House of Lords.

The order to make an order of the Supreme Court or the House of Lords an order of the High Court should be in Form No. PF68.

An order made by the Supreme Court is a UK judgment, and enforcement of such an order in Scotland and Northern Ireland is dealt with in accordance with Sch.6 to the Civil Jurisdiction and Judgments Act 1982, which is dealt with in CPR Pt 74.

Interrelation of High Court with county court judgments for enforcement

2–16 Where the judgment creditor intends to enforce the judgment using execution against goods as his chosen method of enforcement, the following need to be borne in mind:

- a judgment must only be enforced in the High Court where the sum being recovered is £5,000 or more (and the proceedings are not under the Consumer Credit Act 1974);
- the judgment should only be enforced in the county court where the sum being recovered is less than £600;
- for judgments between £600 and £5,000 the judgment creditor has a choice in which court to enforce the judgment—a decision which should be driven by the likely success of the enforcement officer, and no doubt the cost and time involved in managing the enforcement;
- judgments obtained under an agreement regulated by The Consumer Credit Act 1974 (as amended) can only be enforced in the county court, regardless of the amount.

Where the county court judgment is over £600 (a figure that can be made up of the judgment debt, costs allowed and any interest running on the judgment), the judgment can be transferred to the High Court as a result of the limits imposed under the High Court and County Courts Jurisdiction (Amendment) Order (SI 1999/1014). This statutory instrument determines the value at which judgments can be transferred from the county court to the High Court. The initial statutory instrument was the High Court and County Courts Jurisdiction Order 1991, art. 8, which originally introduced a transfer level of £2,000. This figure then reduced to £1,000 and at the time of preparing this book stands at the £600 level. We wait to see whether in the next edition of this book the limit has been removed altogether, allowing judgment creditors freedom of choice when it comes to whether they want to enforce in the county court or High Court arena.

Enforcement of awards of bodies other than the High Court and county courts

2–17 Many tribunals are created by statute to deal with particular types of dispute. Hearings before a tribunal often result in an order for the payment of money. As most tribunals have no machinery for enforcement, CPR 70.5 provides the mechanism to allow the enforcement of the tribunal's award.

The Rules allow awards of certain tribunals to be enforced as if they were a judgment or order of the High Court or county court. The statute that creates the tribunal will be the relevant enactment for the purpose of CPR 70.5(3).

The rule does not apply, however, to:

- a foreign judgment to which CPR Pt 74 applies—and which is dealt with later in this book;
- arbitration awards;
- any order to which RSC Order 115 applies—this order provides for registration in the High Court for the purposes of the enforcement of certain orders made in connection with criminal proceedings and investigations;
- employment tribunal awards which now have their own specially created "Fast Track", which is dealt with later in this chapter;
- proceedings relating to traffic enforcement under CPR Pt 75, which are dealt with later in this book,

If enforcement of a tribunal award is permitted under the CPR, the following procedural points need to be noted:

- the application may be made without notice to the party who will become the judgment debtor, and the decision may be made by the court officer;
- the application must be made to the court for the district where the person against whom the award was made resides or carries on business, unless the court orders otherwise;

- the application notice must be in Practice Form N322A, which can be found on the HMCS website in the Forms and Guidance section;
- under CPR 70.5(6) a copy of the award must be filed with the application notice.

When making the application on Practice Form N322A (see above as to where to download a copy of this form), the application notice must state the name and the address of the person against whom it is sought to enforce the award, and how much of the award remains unpaid.

Under r.70.5(8), an application to the High Court to register a tribunal award for enforcement must be sent in writing to the Head Clerk of the Action Department of the Royal Courts of Justice, Strand, London WC2A 2LL.

The application must specify the statutory provision under which the application is made and state the name and address of the person against whom it seeks to enforce the decision. If the decision requires that person to pay a sum of money, then the amount which remains unpaid must be stated.

Different types of award of "other bodies" capable of enforcement

2–18

Arbitration Awards	An arbitration award is specifically excluded from CPR 70.5(2)(b). An application for permission under s.66 or s.101 (being a New York Convention Award) of the Arbitration Act 1996, s.26 of the Arbitration Act 1950 or s. 3(1)(a) of the Arbitration 1975 Act, to enforce an award in the same manner as a judgment or order may be made without notice in an arbitration claim form. The enforcement of an arbitration award is governed by CPR Pt 62 s.III in respect of enforcement proceedings commenced on or after March 25, 2002. CPR 62.20 deals with the enforcement of foreign awards.
Legal Aid	The enforcement of legal aid contribution orders is dealt with under the Legal Aid Act 1988 s.24. A Legal Aid certificate may, depending on its terms, cover proceedings to enforce an order made in proceedings to which it relates; if it does so, it will embrace proceedings to bankrupt the debtor or to wind up a debtor company

Legal Aid—*cont.*	(Civil Legal Aid (General) Regulations 1989, Reg. 46 (3)(f)). A contribution order in criminal proceedings may be enforced in the county court; see Para. 3 of Sch.3 to the Legal Aid Act 1988.
Judgments of The Supreme Court (House of Lords)	The judgments of The Supreme Court (also referred to as the House of Lords) are considered to be judgments "other than the High Court and county court". To convert a judgment from the highest court in England and Wales into a High Court judgment, an application must be made under CPR Pt 23, using Form No. PF68—see the notes above on the procedure.
VAT and Duties Tribunal	These decisions are enforceable as awards and can become enforceable as county court judgments.
Companies Act 1985	An order made by a competent court under the Companies Act 1985 is enforceable under the CPR according to the court in which it was made—see CPR Sch. 1, RSC Order 45, r. 5 and the note at sc45.5.4.
Commercial Court	Unless otherwise ordered, all proceedings for the enforcement of any judgment or order for the payment of money given or made in the Commercial Court will be referred automatically to a Master of the Queen's Bench Division or a District Judge (see CPR PD58 1.2(2)). Applications in connection with the enforcement of a judgment or order for the payment of money should be directed to the Registry, which will allocate them to the Admiralty Registrar or to one of the Queen's Bench Masters, as appropriate.
The Restrictive Practices Court	An order of the Restrictive Practices Court, which has jurisdiction to declare that certain agreements are contrary to the public interest and to restrain parties from enforcing them.
Tribunals Generally	A plethora of tribunals exist under various enactments—for a list of tribunals, see *http://www.trustonline.org.uk/understand-judgments-fines/tribunal-awards-and-the-register/* [Accessed October 14, 2010]. The judgments of these various tribunals are discussed on The Register of Judgments, Orders and Fines. The judgments made by such tribunals will be enforceable as a result of the provisions of CPR Pt 70.5

<table>
<tr>
<td>Magistrates' Courts Fines, Costs or Compensation</td>
<td>
By s.87 of the Magistrates' Courts Act 1980 fines, costs or compensation ordered by magistrates' courts may be enforced in the county court, on the application of the clerk but not by execution or attachment of earnings as if the sum were due to the clerk of the magistrates' court in pursuance of a judgment or order of the High Court or county court, as the case may be.
So far as the Central Office is concerned, the Senior Master issued a Practice Direction dated as far back as November 22, 1967, setting out the following procedure to be followed for this purpose:

1. The applicant will provide a witness statement affidavit, framed for the purpose of the particular type of execution desired and exhibiting the authority of the magistrates' court to take the proceedings. The authority will recite the conviction, the amount outstanding and the nature of the proceedings authorised to be taken. An extra copy of the exhibit will be required for filing in the Central Office.

2. Attendance will be made in the first place in the alphabetical section of the judgment department appropriate to the surname of the applicant. The copy of the exhibit will be lodged there and a reference number will be assigned to the matter, which will later be entered by the judgment clerk in a special register.

3. If the application is being made without notice (e.g. an interim charging order or third party debt order), the affidavit and original exhibit will then be taken to the Masters' Secretary's Office (Room E214) and lodged in the usual way.

4. Any other application will be initiated in the usual way after a reference number has been assigned. The clerk's application for a Charging Order or Third Party Debt Order should include a form of authority.

Such proceedings are not "a criminal cause or matter" for appeal purposes (see Gooch v Ewing [1986] Q.B. 791; [1986] 2 W.L.R. 445 CA (Civ Div)).
</td>
</tr>
</table>

Other Criminal Penalties	Equivalent provision is made for the recovery of fines, costs or compensation ordered by other Criminal Courts by the Administration of Justice Act 1970, s.41, Sch.9, as amended. A sum adjudged to be paid by a conviction of a magistrates' court, or a fine imposed or recognisance forfeited by the Crown Court and treated as a magistrates' fine, may be enforced by the High Court or a county court as if the sums were due to the clerk of the magistrates' court (Magistrates' Court's Act 1980, s.87). The magistrates' clerk is the notional judgment creditor and the magistrates must first inquire as to the offender's means. Enforcement through the High Court or county court is appropriate, for example where the offender is unable to pay immediately and enforcement needs to be effected by methods not available in the magistrates' court, e.g. third party debt orders (CPR Pt 72), or the Receiver (CPR Pt 69) is contemplated.
Costs or Compensation in Criminal Cases	An order for costs or compensation in a criminal case or by the Crown Court for the costs in the civil case are dealt with under the Administration of Justice Act 1970, s.41 (3), (4) and Sch.9, as amended, as well as the Magistrates' Courts Act 1980, s.58(1).
Matrimonial Awards	A maintenance order made by a magistrates' court and registered in the High Court under the Maintenance Orders Act 1958, Pt 1 can be enforced under the Family Proceedings Rules 1991 (SI 1991/1247) r.1.3 (and subject to specific provision of the FPR and any statute). The CPR including Schs 1 and 2, are applied in the Family Division with the necessary modifications. By virtue of CCR Order 27—set out in Sch.2 to the CPR—maintenance payments are to be treated as a judgment debt when it comes to enforcing payment. Therefore, an application for an attachment of earnings order to secure payments under a maintenance order made by a county court must be made to the county court which made the order. Any application under s.32 of the Matrimonial Causes Act 1973 for permission to enforce the payment of arrears that have become due more than 12 months before the application for an attachment of earnings order must also be made in that application.

Matrimonial Awards—*cont.*	An attachment of earnings order to enforce a maintenance order is a priority order, i.e. it ranks above non-priority orders. As such, arrears in the case of a priority order are treated differently in that they are carried forward and subject to the protected earnings rate and deducted from subsequent earnings—see Attachment of Earnings Act 1971, s.6.

Enforcement of employment tribunal awards

2–19 On April 6, 2010, Practice Direction 70 was further amended by the addition of para.4.1A for the purpose of enabling the use of a single form, Form N471, to cover all stages of the process by which a decision of an employment tribunal in England and Wales (which is, by virtue of the Employment Tribunals Act 1996 s.15(1), enforceable as if it were a judgment of a county court) may be enforced in the High Court by way of fieri facias.

The result of this amendment created a single-step process so that employment tribunal awards could be registered in the county court for enforcement and transferred to the High Court for enforcement by the enforcement officers of that court (referred to as "High Court Enforcement Officers").

It should be noted that the enforcement of these types of awards, although subject to a new procedure, can be complicated, primarily because the tribunals that issue the awards do so in a rather haphazard way across England and Wales. Care must therefore be taken to read the award carefully, to ensure the correct information is transferred from the paper award to the N471.

Successful applicants who have received the benefit of an award must also bear in mind the requirements of The Employment Protection (Recoupment of Jobseeker's Allowance and Income Support) Regulations 1996. These regulations, made under employment legislation, enable the state to recover from employers some or the entire amount of Jobseekers' Allowance and income support paid to employees who have subsequently been awarded compensation by an employment tribunal.

Enforcement of a compromise enforceable by statute

2–20 Similarly to the enforcement of a decision of a body other than the High Court or county court, the rules provide for the enforcement of a "compromise agreement". A party may enforce the compromise by applying for a specific method of enforcement under CPR Pt 71 to 73 or RSC Orders 45 to 47 and 52 or CCR Orders 25 to 29, all of which are dealt with later in this book.

The party must apply to the court for the district where the person against whom the order is sought resides or carries on business, unless the court has made an order to the contrary. The application must be in the prescribed form (N322A), and it must state:

- the name and address of the person against whom the order is sought to be enforced;
- the outstanding amount to be paid or details of the obligation which needs to be performed;
- where the application relates to a conditional compromise, further details about the agreement, and a copy of the decision or compromise must be filed with the application notice (see CPR 70.5(6)).

Where the application relates to a compromise, which requires a person to whom a sum of money is payable under the compromise agreement to do something in addition to discontinuing or not starting proceedings, then the application must be made on notice and will be determined by the court.

"Conditional compromises" involve a compromise that requires a person to whom a sum of money is payable to do something in addition to discontinuing or not starting proceedings (see CPR 70.5(7A)). In this situation the respondent of the application may oppose the application by filing a response within 14 days of service of the application notice. If this is done, the court will make an order as appears appropriate (and in default of a response in the time provided, the court will make the order sought by the applicant).

Where a compromise agreement includes the payment of a sum of money, and it requires no action by the creditor other than to discontinue or not start proceedings, the recovery of the sum of money may be enforceable under RSC Order 70.5(1) as if it were a sum payable under a court order.

Enforcement of other bodies and compromise agreements

2–21 There are a number of statutes that provide for the decision of a court, tribunal, or other body outside the traditional High Court or county court route that may be enforced as if it were a court order so that any sum that is ordered to be paid by a decision is recoverable as if it were a court order (see CPR 70.5(1)).

If the guiding statute provides that any decision is enforceable "if a court so orders", a party may apply for an order in the district where the person against whom the order is sought to be enforced resides or carries on business, provided there is nothing to the contrary ordered by the court which prevents this from happening (see CPR 70.5(3), (4)(b)).

An application to enforce in this way must be in the prescribed form on Form N322A (see CPR 70.5(5)(a) and CPR PD70 Para 4.2). The prescribed form must state:

- the name and address of the person against whom the order is sought;
- what remains outstanding as unpaid or what obligation needs to be performed.

The application can be made without notice and dealt with by a court officer.

If the statute provides that the decision be registered and enforced in the same manner as a High Court order, the applicant must apply in writing to the High Court to register the decision for enforcement (see CPR 70.5(8), CPR PD70 Para 5.5). The application should be made to the head clerk of the Action Department at the Royal Courts of Justice, Strand, London WC2A 2LL (see generally CPR PD70 Para 5.1). The application must state:

- the statutory provision under which it is made;
- the name and address of the person against whom it is sought to enforce the decision; and
- if the decision requires a person to pay a sum of money, the amount that remains unpaid (see CPR 70.5(8), CPR PD70 Para 5.2).

If the statute does not make the enforcement conditional on the "court so ordering", the party may choose the method of enforcement set out at the beginning of this chapter. The applicant will need to file with the court a copy of the decision to be enforced in the prescribed Form N322B, CPR PD70 Para 4.1(a).

In making the application, an applicant must state again:

- the statutory provision under which the enforcement or the recovery of money is sought;
- the name and address against whom the enforcement or recovery is sought;
- whether decision requires a person to pay a sum of money then the amount which remains unpaid.

Registration of judgments

2–22 A Register of County Court Judgments was created in 1852 and held by the Lord Chancellor's Department. The Register could be searched for a fee, for example to check whether a prospective borrower had previously been sued and judgment entered against them.

Since 1986, the Register has been held by Registry Trust Limited, which runs the very helpful website "Trust Online" at *http://www.trustonline.org.uk* [Accessed October 14, 2010].

As from April 6, 2006, the new enlarged Register of Judgments, Orders and Fines was created pursuant to the Register of Judgments, Orders and Fines Regulations 2005 (SI 2005/3595).

Subject to the regulations and exemptions in reg.9, the new Register records all county court judgments, administration orders and Child Support Agency liability orders, as well as High Court judgments and fine defaulters.

Chapter 3

Preliminary Steps

Introductory comments

3–01 Enforcement is a strategic step in litigation and, as such, court users should develop strategies for the successful enforcement of their judgment whether by default, after a full hearing or where a party fails to fulfill its obligations under a consent order.

The fundamental point that must be considered before any action is taken or money spent on court fees and advice is this: "Am I suing a person of straw?"

- If the answer to that question is "yes", then special care needs to be taken in advising on and carrying out a strategy for enforcement, even before litigation has begun, as ultimately all that the judgment creditor will end up with is a piece of paper confirming judgment in his favour, but with no money in the bank.
- If the answer to the question is "not sure", then before any enforcement action is taken, the judgment creditor can take steps to improve his chances of successful enforcement by asking questions, making enquiries and building a strategy before the claim form has even been issued.
- Finally, if the answer to the same question is "No", and the judgment creditor is sure that assets are available, the strategy should be to verify this information by independent means and to move quickly to ensure the assets are not dissipated before formal enforcement can begin.

This chapter is designed to ask some of the questions that may need to be answered before embarking on the enforcement process, to ensure there are no obstacles and a strategy is chosen to give the judgment creditor the best chance of success.

How strategic can a judgment creditor be about the enforcement of a money judgment?

3–02 Before looking at a number of technical areas within the court rules about the enforcement of judgments, the judgment creditor should try to develop a strategy—particularly where enforcement is a routine part of the judgment creditor's process. As the reader of this book, you may be working in a litigation department where enforcement is the next step after judgment and you have a number of clients to serve. Alternatively, you may be working within the litigation or credit control department of a company where the types of judgments which need enforcing are the same, but the type of judgment debtor is diverse or belongs to a specific group such as consumers in the home. Alternatively, you may be a judgment creditor who has a "one-off" judgment to enforce and you are reading this book as a guide on how to enforce a judgment that is very important to you.

In any given situation the matrix below should give a judgment creditor a basis from which to enforce a judgment using a combination of debtor type, type of situation—be it a home or trading address—and the methods of enforcement that fit best with the judgment debtor's assets:

Judgment Debtor Type	Judgment Debtor Situation	Method of Enforcement Available	Enforcement Technique
Individual	Home	Execution Against Goods	Try to visualise the "goods" in the form of assets that may be available, but bear in mind the judgment debtor can refuse entry to a bailiff or High Court Enforcement Officer to his or her private dwelling house.
		Attachment of Earnings	Is the judgment debtor employed? If so, the attachment of earnings procedure is one of the easiest methods of court-based enforcement. If on the other hand the judgment debtor is self-employed, go to the options for "sole trader" below.

Judgment Debtor Type	Judgment Debtor Situation	Method of Enforcement Available	Enforcement Technique
		Charging Order	Does the judgment debtor own their own home? Use HM Land Registry to check the position, and if so make enquiries to find out if there is any available equity in the property that can be charged.
		Third Party Debt Order	Does the judgment debtor operate a bank account or is the judgment debtor owed money from a third party? In either case it is possible to seek an order from the court ordering that any debt due to the judgment debtor is paid by the third party direct to the judgment creditor.
		Order To Obtain Information	Use this procedure if more information is needed about available assets, before embarking on a particular enforcement procedure.
		Insolvency procedures for personal insolvency	Use these procedures to achieve payment, provided the rules are followed.
Sole Trader	Business Trading Address	Execution Against Goods	Visualise the "goods" that may be available and remember a High Court Enforcement Officer does have the power to force entry to commercial premises (where necessary) to levy on any goods inside.

Judgment Debtor Type	**Judgment Debtor Situation**	**Method of Enforcement Available**	**Enforcement Technique**
		Charging Order	Does the judgment debtor own their own home? Use HM Land Registry to check the position.
		Third Party Debt Order	Does the judgment debtor have a bank account, or is he/she owed money by customers or the bank? Does the sales ledger of the business indicate the sole trader has outstanding invoices to be paid?
		Order To Obtain Information	Use this procedure if more information is needed about available assets or to ask for details of the books and accounts of the judgment debtor's business.
		Insolvency procedures for personal insolvency	Use these procedures if ultimately none of the above methods achieve payment, provided the rules are followed.
Partner	Home Address	Execution Against Goods	Visualise the "goods" that may be available, but bear in mind the judgment debtor can refuse entry to a bailiff or High Court Enforcement Officer to his or her private dwelling house.
		Charging Order	Does the judgment debtor own their own home? Use HM Land Registry to check the position.

Judgment Debtor Type	Judgment Debtor Situation	Method of Enforcement Available	Enforcement Technique
		Third Party Debt Order	Does the judgment debtor have a bank account or is the firm owed money? Does the firm's sales ledger indicate it has invoices to be paid?
		Order To Obtain Information	Use this procedure if more information is needed about the available assets or to call for the books and accounts of the judgment debtor's firm.
		Insolvency procedures for partnership or personal insolvency	Use these procedures if ultimately none of the above methods achieves payment, provided the rules are followed.
Partner	Business Trading Address	Execution Against Goods	Visualise the "goods" that may be available and remember a High Court Enforcement Officer does have the power to force entry to commercial premises (where necessary) to levy on any goods inside.
		Charging Order	Does the judgment debtor firm own its business premises? Use HM Land Registry to check the position.
		Third Party Debt Order	Does the judgment debtor have a bank account or is the firm owed money? Does the firm's sales ledger indicate it has invoices to be paid?

Judgment Debtor Type	Judgment Debtor Situation	Method of Enforcement Available	Enforcement Technique
		Order To Obtain Information	Use this procedure if more information is needed about available assets or to call for the books and accounts of the judgment debtor's firm.
		Statutory Demand/Bankruptcy Petition—	Use these procedures as necessary to achieve payment, provided the rules are followed
Company	Business Trading Address—remember many companies operate from the home address of a director	Execution Against Goods—	Visualise the "goods" that may be available—try not to use the "registered office" address as the address to send a bailiff or High Court Enforcement Officer—frequently, the registered office is the address of the company's accountant or solicitor—and remember a High Court Enforcement Officer will force entry to commercial premises where necessary to levy on any goods inside
		Charging Order—	Does the judgment debtor's company own their premises? Use HM Land Registry to check the position and act on the search result

Judgment Debtor Type	Judgment Debtor Situation	Method of Enforcement Available	Enforcement Technique
		Third Party Debt Order—	Does the judgment debtor have a bank account or are they owed money? Does their sales ledger indicate they have invoices to be paid?
		Order To Obtain Information—	Use this procedure to cross-examine the directors of the company on both the company's books and trading accounts
		Statutory Demand/Win ding Up of Company—	Use these procedures as necessary to achieve payment, provided the rules are followed

Naturally, this type of matrix can be adapted to fit the judgment creditor's requirements.

What follows next is a series of questions that may be pertinent before enforcement of the judgment is commenced.

Is leave required to commence the enforcement of a judgment?

3–03 No leave or other formality is necessary for the enforcement of a judgment, except as stated below. A judgment takes effect from the time when the judge pronounces it (see note in the White Book Service 2010 at CPR 40.2.1).

CPR 40.7 states that, except where a judgment is against a foreign state (in which case refer to CPR 40.10), the judgment takes effect from the day it is given or made, or any later date which the court may specify. The notes in the White Book Service 2010 discuss the possibility of a judgment being amended before it is entered or perfected, so court users should be aware of that potential hiccup in the smooth enforcement of a judgment!

When should any money be paid under a judgment?

3–04 The general rule is that where judgment is given or an order is made for the payment of money, including costs, the money should be paid at the expiration of 14 days from the date of the judgment or order (CPR, r.40.11). Obviously, if a day for payment is specified in the judgment or order, then the money should be paid on that date. The significance of subs. (1) of CPR 40.11 is that it makes it clear that the court has power to order that a money judgment or order can be paid, not only in a lump sum in 14 days or on a particular date, but also by instalments. Subsection (2) gives the court power to suspend or stay a money judgment or order against a party, whether requiring payment in a lump sum or by instalments, where the court is satisfied that the party is unable to pay.

County court judgments are registered immediately, which is a useful pressure point for ensuring a judgment debtor pays the amount due, in order to avoid registration on a credit reference agency database for six years. Since April 2004, High Court judgments have also been registrable as a result of changes introduced in the Courts Act 2003, and since 2006 these judgments have been added to the Register of Judgments Fines and Orders, which is maintained by Registry Trust Limited. For more information about the registration of court judgments, see *http://www.trustonline.org.uk.* [Accessed October 14, 2010]

The claimant must take some step or steps before starting enforcement and issuing execution. Leave is not required in routine cases and it is simple enough to issue a warrant of execution or a writ of fi fa, as well as commence an attachment of earnings application, issue an application for a charging order or third party debt order or seek an order to obtain information.

Where an order is made against several persons for payment of a sum of money, and whether or not they are deemed to be jointly and severally liable, the order may also be enforced against any one of them in separate enforcement applications (see *Land Credit Co of Ireland v Lord Fermoy* (1869-1870) L.R. 5 Ch. App. 323).

Of course, enforcement proceedings do require an application to be made to the court, with applications under CPR Pts 71, 72, and 73 requiring a Statement of Truth to be signed in accordance with the rules under CPR Pt 22. The proceedings are not started automatically on the issue of the judgment, which may be something that judgment creditors acting without the support of advice may fail to appreciate. Getting to judgment is only part of the litigation process, and if payment is not forthcoming, the judgment creditor will have to use the various methods of enforcement available to compel payment.

Does the judgment need to be served on the judgment debtor prior to enforcement?

3–05 Generally speaking, to enforce a judgment there is no express requirement within the CPR for the judgment creditor to serve a copy of the judgment on the judgment debtor.

However, there are a number of exceptions, which can be summarised as follows:

- Service of a copy of the judgment endorsed with a penal notice is necessary in the enforcement of a judgment through committal or sequestration proceedings, as discussed later on in this book.
- Where the claimant wishes to enforce a writ of possession, and the defendant is the only person in possession of the premises, the claimant must give the defendant notice of the judgment or order (see note to CPR Sch.1 sc 45.3.8 of the White Book Service 2010). A High Court writ of possession should not be issued without the defendant having been given the opportunity to apply to the court for relief (CPR Sch.1, RSC Order 45, r.3(3)(a)).
- A writ of fieri facias (or "writ of fi fa" as it is referred to throughout this book) may be issued by the court giving a judgment with an absolute right to recover money without any service of the judgment (see *Land Credit Co of Ireland v Lord Fermoy* [1870] L.R. 5 Ch. App. 323, and also see Winn L.J. in *T C Trustees Ltd v Darwen JS (Successors)* [1969] 2 Q.B. 296 and also *Re A Solicitor* [1884] 33 W.R. 131, where only the judgment debtor's solicitor had been served).

What happens if the judgment debtor makes an application to set judgment aside?

3–06 The High Court and Court of Appeal have discretion to stay execution (Supreme Court Act 1981, s.49(3)), but will only do so for good cause and not in order to give relief which, if allowable at all, should have been given in the action leading to the judgment (see *T C Trustees Ltd v Darwen J S (Successors)* [1969] 2 Q.B. 296). In Volume 2 of the White Book Service 2010, the accompanying commentary to s.49(3) of the Supreme Court Act 1981 sets out the scope of the court's ability to stay proceedings and execution, although since this legislation was first introduced the CPR is now applied across all civil courts including the Court of Appeal, High Court and county courts.

Applications to set aside judgment are often based on the failure of postal deliveries or lack of knowledge of the procedure to acknowledge service or serve a defence.

If there is to be an application for a stay of execution, for example under CPR Sch.1, RSC Order 47, r.1, it will probably be better if this is made before the judgment creditor goes to the expense of instructing a High Court Enforcement Officer (a term replacing former officer "the sheriff" and which is discussed fully later in this book).

It is worth noting that the fact that a warning letter has been sent to a judgment debtor will be a material factor in any consideration of an award of costs on any subsequent application to set aside judgment.

The effect of delay in applying to set aside the judgment

3–07 There is no doubt that the issue of delay in making an application to set aside the judgment does not help the judgment debtor in that application, which is underlined by decisions in recent cases.

In *Nolan v Devonport* [2006] EWHC 2025 (QB), Mr Nolan had obtained a judgment for a considerable sum against Mr and Mrs Devonport in 1995. Mr Devonport became bankrupt and five years later he died. The judgment creditor took no immediate steps to enforce the judgment. However, in 2002, Mr Nolan obtained permission to execute the judgment by way of a charging order. Mrs Devonport in response threatened to issue an application to set aside the judgment, which she then did by citing as one of her grounds in her application the delay by the judgment creditor to enforce the judgment. Judge Grenfell sitting as a judge in the High Court had no hesitation in striking out the application on the basis it was entirely a matter for the party who had a judgment in its favour to decide when and how to enforce it. Many judgments remain outstanding and unenforced for years while the judgment creditor waits for the right moment to enforce.

In these economically straightened times, many creditors with the benefit of a judgment may well feel it best to wait until the judgment debtor is better placed financially before seeking to pounce on available assets, which may have not been apparent when the judgment was originally obtained. It does appear in the case of third party debt orders and charging orders that the judgment creditor can be as patient as he wishes—and that can be for a very long time indeed.

Can enforcement action be taken on a Sunday?

3–08 This is only permissible in cases of urgency, and then with leave of the court. In the Practice Direction accompanying RSC Order 46 and CCR Order 26, unless the court orders to the contrary, a writ or warrant of execution to enforce a judgment or order of the court cannot be enforced on a Sunday, Good Friday or Christmas Day.

In *Templewood Aviation Ltd v Air Ceylon* Unreported February 16, 1978, the court gave leave to the Sheriff of Greater London to execute a writ of fi fa by seizing a Douglas DC-8 due in at Heathrow on a scheduled flight the following Sunday. Leave was granted by the Master ex parte on an affidavit as to the facts. It was suggested in the rules prior to the CPR that, although leave should be obtained in advance wherever possible, to act in an emergency without such leave would be an irregularity, which the court could cure by subsequent leave being given on appropriate terms. Under the present regime of the CPR, it could be argued that the court has power under its own initiative to cure any such defect.

What happens if the judgment is subject to an appeal?

3–09 If a judgment of the House of Lords or the Court of Appeal merely affirms the judgment appealed without any order for costs, enforcement may commence from the original judgment in the original court, without further steps.

An order of the Court of Appeal that varies or reverses the judgment appealed against is transmitted to the Central Office for amendment of the record, after which enforcement may take place. Independently of this practice, any judgment of the Court of Appeal may be enforced, as would a High Court judgment.

In the case of a House of Lords judgment varying or reversing that of the court below, or ordering the payment of costs, an application is necessary to make the order of the House an order of the High Court. Under CPR 40BPD.13 this application may be made without notice on evidence to a procedural judge. The order to make the order of the House of Lords an order of the High Court should be in Form No. PF68.

What steps can be taken to prevent a judgment debtor from dissipating assets?

3–10 If there is concern that a defendant or judgment debtor (as they may become) will dissipate the assets believed to be available to satisfy the judgment debt, the court has the power under its "Interim Remedies" provisions (found at CPR Pt 25) to make a broad range of orders to preserve the position and protect a party from another's attempt to dissipate assets.

An order for detention, custody or preservation may be made in relation to property which may become the subject matter of subsequent proceedings under CPR Pt 25.1(1)(c).

Under the Torts (Interference with Goods) Act 1977, s.4, the High Court may order delivery up of goods which are, or may become, the subject matter of proceedings for wrongful interference with goods. This power may be exercised before such proceedings have been commenced (see CPR 25.1(1)(e)).

A "freezing injunction" (formerly known as a *Mareva* injunction) under CPR Pt 25.1(1)(f) and (g) provides power to the court to restrain a party from removing assets located in the jurisdiction, or by restraining a party from dealing with any assets whether in the jurisdiction or outside of it which would interfere with the court's powers to grant interim relief.

The following table is designed to highlight key issues surrounding the use of freezing orders as an aid to the enforcement of an existing or, perhaps more importantly, a future judgment:

Can the claimant use a freezing order if there is no intention to issue proceedings?	The court has no jurisdiction to grant a injunction in circumstances where the applicant has no intention of issuing proceedings immediately or almost immediately (see *Fourie v Le Roux* [2007] UKHL 1; [2007] 1 W.L.R. 320)
Can a claimant make the application without notice to the defendant?	Yes, for obvious reasons. In the first instance the application for a freezing injunction is made without notice to a judge (see Practice Direction (Allocation of Cases to Levels of Judiciary) CPR PD2B at para 2.1).
What is the approach to take in framing the applicant's application to the court?	It is important to ensure that the application for a freezing order is framed to result in minimum interference with the respondent's rights. The purpose of the freezing order is not to punish the respondent but to protect the applicant (see *Flightwise Travel Service Ltd v Gill* [2003] EWHC 3082 (Ch), (Neuberger J.)
How does the applicant demonstrate to the court that assets are "at risk"?	It is not necessary to establish that the respondent is likely to act with the objective of putting his assets beyond reach; instead, what has to be shown is that there is, without the freezing order being made, "a real risk that a judgment or award in favour of the claimants would go unsatisfied" (see *RBS Invoice Finance Ltd v Karia* (2008) EWHC 1238 (QB)). In this case the court held that to draw the inference that there was a real risk of dissipation of assets by a company so that its financial obligations under a judgment would remain unsatisfied it was told there had to be good evidence of a real risk that the company would deal with assets in a manner distinct from the company's ordinary course of business; and see also (*Dean & Dean (A firm) v Grinina* [2008] EWHC 927 (QB)).

Can a respondent be permitted to trade despite a freezing order being made?	A respondent can be permitted to carry on trading by making payments of invoices in the course of trading, which may result in any judgment or award becoming unsatisfied wholly or partially had it not been for the trading and the payment of invoices (see *TTMI Ltd of England v ASM Shipping Ltd of India* [2005] EWHC 2666 (Comm), [2006] 1 Lloyd's Rep. 40 (Christopher Clarke J.), so the applicant should be aware of this and look to deal with it within the application
How strong does the "real risk" have to be in convincing the court to make the order?	Something more than a "real risk" that the judgment will go unsatisfied is required. The purpose of the injunction is to ensure that the court's judgment is not rendered valueless "by an unjustifiable disposal of assets" (see *Ketchum International Plc v Group Public Relations Holdings Ltd* [1997] 1 W.L.R. 4, CA *and Mobil Cerro Negro Ltd v Petroleus de Venezula SA* [2008] EWHC 532 (Comm); [2008] 2 All E.R. (Comm) 1034.).
Can a freezing order be made in county court proceedings?	The general rule is that a county court cannot grant a freezing injunction. The reason for this is that whilst the County Courts Act 1984 s.38 provides that in any proceedings in the county court the court can make any order similar in nature to the High Court, regulations made under s.38 impose certain restrictions on the jurisdiction of county courts in this respect. Where the jurisdiction of a county court to grant an injunction is restricted, a party may decide to invoke the jurisdiction of the High Court under the High Court and County Courts Jurisdiction Order 1991 art.3, which allows injunctions to be granted in the county court that are "incidental to and in support of" county court proceedings. Regulation 3(3) of the 1991 Regulations allows a county court to grant a freezing order where: ■ the purpose of the order is for the preservation, custody or detention of property which forms or may form the subject matter of proceedings and; ■ it is necessary to assist in the enforcement of a judgment or order in county court proceedings so as to preserve assets until execution could be levied upon them.
Can a county court revoke a High Court freezing order?	A county court may not vary or revoke a freezing order granted by the High Court but may vary the freezing order where all the parties are agreed on the terms of the variation (see reg. 3(1) and(4)(b) of the 1991 regs)

Can the High Court assist the county court in the granting of a freezing order?	Article 3 of the High Court and County Courts Jurisdiction Order 1991 provides for the High Court to have jurisdiction to hear an application for a freezing order made in the course or in anticipation of proceedings in a county court, where a county court may not, by virtue of regs under s.38(3)(b) of the County Courts Act 1984, grant the relief. The High Court therefore has jurisdiction to grant freezing orders incidental to, and in support of, county court proceedings. In *Schmidt v Wong* [2005] EWCA Civ 1506, [2006] 1 W.L.R. 561 CA, the Court of Appeal explained that in order to invoke the High Court's assistance, a claimant in county court proceedings would have to make an application to the High Court in accordance with CPR Pt 23 by issuing the application at the Royal Courts of Justice or the appropriate District Registry and paying the higher court fee. The application would then be made returnable before a judge. In the body of the application there should appear an explanation along the following lines: "This application is being made in the course of [in anticipation of] proceedings in the county court pursuant to article 3 of the High Court and County Courts Jurisdiction Order 1991. The county court has no jurisdiction to grant the relief sought by reason of regulation 3(1) of the County Court Remedies Regulations 1991." **NOTE:** The High Court's assistance should not be invoked by issuing a claim form in the High Court for the freezing order. This is because any freezing order which is then made can be extracted from the claim to which it relates and be treated as a free-standing remedy.
How is a freezing order applied for?	The forms of injunction available in both the High Court and county courts are set out in the notes to CPR Pt 25 in the White Book Service 2010. The application for a freezing order is made on an application notice in accordance with the provisions of CPR 23 (general rules about applications for court orders), as modified by the provisions of Practice Direction (Interim Injunctions) and the accompanying Practice Direction. The modifications are substantial. Applications for freezing orders must be supported by written evidence in the form of an affidavit (see Practice Direction (Interim Injunctions), para. 3.1). The claimant should depose to objective facts, from which it may be inferred that the defendant is likely to move assets or dissipate them. Unsupported statements or expressions of fear have little weight (see *O'Regan v*

	Iambic Productions (1989) 139 NLJ 1378 and *Rosen v Rose* [2003] EWHC 309 (QB)). Great care should be taken in the presentation of evidence to the court, so that the court can see not only whether the applicant has a good, arguable case, but also whether there is a real risk of dissipation of assets (as outlined above). A freezing order should not be granted unless the applicant has established an appropriately strong case showing, amongst other things, that the respondent owns the assets concerned or has some interest in them. It is for the applicant to make out his case.
How should the applicant deal with issues of the respondent's "dishonesty"?	Where the applicant believes that the respondent has been dishonest, the court should scrutinise with care whether what is alleged in this respect in itself really justifies the inference that the respondent is likely to dissipate assets, unless restricted (see *Thane Investments Ltd v Tomlinson* (No.1) Unreported [2003] EWCA Civ 1272 CA, and also *Renewable Power & Light Plc v Renewable Power & Light Services Inc* [2008] EWHC 1058 (Ch) in which the court found there was no evidence to suggest that an ex-director of a company had been trying to make himself judgment-proof by disposing of assets held in the United Kingdom, and therefore no cogent grounds justifying the continuation of undertakings thus giving effect to a freezing order made against him).
What must the applicant's evidence show on the issue of making the application without notice?	Where an application is made without notice to the respondent, the applicant's evidence must state why notice was not given (Practice Direction (Interim Injunctions, para. 3.4). It is essential that the respondent is given a proper opportunity to present his case with the notice hearing. He therefore has to be supplied with all the evidence on which the applicant is going to rely (see *Flightwise Travel Service Ltd v Gill* [2003] EWHC 3082 (Ch), *The Times* December 5, 2003 (Neuberger J.)).
Can the court vary or revoke a freezing order?	The court can vary or revoke a freezing order (r.3.1(7)), and a person who is not a party to the terms of the order but who is directly affected by such injunction may apply to have it set aside or varied (40.9)
What is the sanction for failing to obey the freezing order?	A person who disobeys a freezing order may be dealt with by contempt proceedings (see CPR 40BPD.9.1 and para 9.1). A party's contempt is not a complete bar to an application for a variation of the terms of a freezing order but in such circumstances, the court should exercise its discretion in the best interests of justice (see *Federal Bank of the Middle East v Hadkinson* (Stay of Action) [2000] 1 W.L.R. 1695; [2000] 2 All E.R. 395 CA).

Is there a time limit on enforcing a judgment?

3–11 The issues surrounding how long a judgment creditor has to enforce the judgment have continued to be the subject of developing case law. Under s.24(1) of the Limitation Act 1980 "an action" cannot be brought on any judgment after six years have expired from the date that the judgment became enforceable. It is possible to apply for leave to enforce the judgment after this six year period, and such an application is not "an action" on the judgment and therefore does not contravene s.24.

The right to sue on a judgment has always been regarded as a matter quite distinct from the right to issue further enforcement proceedings. The right to continue to enforce a judgment is seen by the courts as a matter of procedure, which was first tested in the case of *W T Lamb & Sons v Rider* [1948] 2 K.B. 331; [1948] 2 All E.R. 402 CA. The expiry of the six-year limitation period under s.24 of the Limitation Act does not therefore prevent the issue or renewal of enforcement proceedings (see *National Westminster Bank Plc v Powney* [1990] 2 W.L.R. 1084; [1990] 2 All E.R. 416 CA).

In seeking an order to allow a judgment to be enforced in these circumstances a judgment creditor will need to show that the facts of the case take it outside the general rule. Where a judgment creditor seeks permission to issue a writ of execution under CPR Sch.1 RSC Order 46 r.2(1)(a), the starting point for the court has to be whether the six-year gap on taking enforcement action is a sufficient ground for refusing permission.

3–12 The judgment creditor in the case of *Patel v Singh* [2002] EWCA Civ 1938 had failed to take any enforcement action on a judgment without any apparent good reason. The judgment creditor obtained a default judgment on September 8, 1992 and on May 1, 2002, nearly 10 years later, made an application for permission to issue a writ of execution under Order 46 r.2(1)(a). The basis of the judgment creditor's application was that the judgment debtor had moved to Germany shortly after the judgment had been entered and he had only just learnt that the judgment debtor had relocated back to this jurisdiction. The application was heard by the Master, who dismissed it on the grounds that the judgment creditor had not sufficiently explained the reasons for the delay in seeking to enforce the judgment. The Master's decision was upheld by the Court of Appeal, which agreed that the judgment creditor had failed to explain the delay. The court found that the judgment creditor had failed to take any steps to enforce the judgment debt or to instruct legal representatives or to seek to enforce the debt in Germany. She "simply appeared to have done nothing to enforce the debt".

It is therefore important that judgment creditors are proactive in their efforts to enforce any judgment in their favour, and are able to demonstrate to the court that they have just not simply "sat" on a judgment for six years. Efforts to enforce should be recorded so that if needs be they can form the basis of evidence to support an application to enforce a judgment outside of the time limit imposed by s.24 of the Limitation Act.

3–13 The application itself can be made without notice supported by evidence, usually in the form of a witness statement or affidavit of facts by the judgment creditor or his solicitor. Any evidence should state:

- the date of the judgment;
- the amount of the original judgment debt;
- the amount remaining due;
- the cause of any delay;
- that the applicant is entitled to execution, e.g. there must have been no change of parties or devolution of interest.

The Master or District Judge may decide not to deal with the application without notice being served on the judgment debtor. If the application is unsuccessful, it does not mean that there cannot be a second application, but any subsequent application should be founded on different evidence to that before the court on the first application (see *W T Lamb & Sons v Rider* [1948] 2 K.B. 331).

It is fair to say that the application to obtain permission to enforce by execution of a judgment over six years old is no mere formality. A judgment creditor will have to discharge the burden of proving that it is demonstrably just to grant such an order (see *Duer v Frazer* [2001] 1 W.L.R. 919; [2001] 1 All E.R. 249 QBD). The test is whether there are facts that take the case out of the general rule that execution would not be allowed after six years (see *Society of Lloyds v Longtin* [2005] EWHC 2491 (Comm)).

It is also worth noting that "an action" upon any judgment within the meaning of s.24(1) of the Limitation Act 1980 does not include insolvency proceedings, whether by winding up petition or bankruptcy petition (see *Ridgeway Motors (Isleworth) Ltd v ALTS Ltd* [2005] EWCA Civ 92; [2005] 2 All E.R. 304 CA (Civ Div)).

The corresponding rule in the county court is CPR Sch.2 CCR Ord. 26 r.5(1)(a) and again where six years have expired since the judgment (or from the date of some later part payment), leave to issue a warrant of execution is required. The requirement to obtain permission is mandatory where the judgment is more than six years old. It is also an abuse of process to issue a warrant without the requisite leave (see *Hackney LBC v White* (1996) 28 H.L.R. 219 involving the enforcement of a warrant of possession).

As in the High Court, the application may be made without notice, although the court can direct that notice is given, and evidence in support of the application follows the High Court rule.

What happens if there has been a change or death to one of the parties?

In the High Court under RSC Order 46, r.2(1)(b), where: **3–14**

- there has been a change in the parties (being either the judgment creditor or the judgment debtor); or
- that change has been caused by death or some other reason.

the permission of the court will be required before further enforcement action can be taken. However, the retirement of a partner in a judgment creditor firm has been held not to constitute such a change (see *Frank Hill Ex p. Holt & Co Re* [1921] 2 K.B. 831).

Where the judgment creditor has died, his or her personal representative will need to obtain the necessary leave to proceed with enforcement. This is done by making an application without notice and putting into evidence the grant of probate or, one presumes, the grant of letters of administration.

Where one of several judgment creditors dies after judgment has been obtained, the survivors are held entitled to issue a judgment summons without leave (see *Bundy v Motor-Cab Owner Drivers' Association* [1930] 143 LT 334).

The county court position under CCR Order 26 r.5(1)(b) relating to the death of one of the parties closely follows the High Court rule. Where there has been a change in the parties through death or some other circumstance, leave to issue a warrant of execution will be required.

In the county court, where one event involves a change of the person entitled to enforce more than one judgment, only one application is required (CCR Order 26, r.5(3)).

Can the court add or substitute a party?

The court has wide powers to add or substitute a party if it considers that it is desirable to do so under CPR 19.1. **3–15**

The court also has a similar power to order a party to cease to be a party. Special provisions are contained in CPR 19.5 in respect of the addition or substitution of parties after the relevant limitation period has expired, and CPR Pt 19 should be read in the context of the overriding objective (CPR Pt 1) and the court's case management powers (CPR Pt 3) where this becomes necessary.

What is the position on enforcement where the judgment debt has been assigned?

3–16 The assignment of part of a judgment does not amount to a change in the parties to enable the assignee to issue execution. The assignee of a judgment debt must apply for leave to issue execution under CPR Sch.1 Order 46 r.2. He does not need to obtain an order adding him as a party under CPR 19.2 (see *Bagley Re*, [1911] 1 K.B. 317 CA).

In an assignment situation, execution can only be levied in respect of the whole judgment (see *Forster v Baker* [1910] 2 K.B. 636 CA and a little more recently *Chung Kwok Hotel Co v Field No.1* [1960] 1 W.L.R. 1112; [1960] 3 ALL E.R. 143 at page 145).

Is leave required if goods are already in the custody of a receiver or a sequestrator?

3–17 Under rules for both High Court and county court business—RSC Order 46, r.2(1)(c) and CCR Order 26, r.5(1)(d), respectively—where any goods sought to be seized under a writ of execution are in the hands of a receiver appointed by the court or a sequestrator, leave is required before a writ or warrant of execution can be issued and enforced.

What is the practice for obtaining leave to enforce in the High Court or in the county court?

3–18 In the High Court an application for leave is made "without notice", as provided under CPR Sch.1, RSC Order 46, r.2, by issuing a general form of application under CPR Pt 23. The county court position under CPR Sch.2, CCR Order 26, r.5 mirrors the High Court rule.

In either court, the application for leave to enforce must be supported by a witness statement or affidavit which should:

- identify the judgment or order to which the application relates; and
- if the judgment or order is for the payment of money, state the amount originally due under the judgment and the amount due at the date the application notice is filed;
- state, where the case falls within RSC Order 46 r.2(1)(a), the reasons for the delay in enforcing the judgment or order;

- state, where the case falls within RSC Order 46 r.2(1)(b), the change which has taken place in the parties entitled to or liable to execution since the date of the judgment or order;
- state, where the case falls within r.2(1)(c) or (d), that a demand to satisfy the judgment or order was made on the person liable to satisfy it, and that he has refused or failed to do so;
- and give such other information as is necessary to satisfy the court that the applicant is entitled to proceed to execution on the judgment or order in question, and that the judgment debtor is liable to execution on that judgment.

Permission given by the court (under whatever authority it is granted) expires unless the writ is issued within one year after the date of the order, but without prejudice to the making of a fresh order (RSC Order 46, r.2(3)). A second application, after the first has been unsuccessful, is not barred as res judicata, but should be entertained only if founded on fresh material (*W T Lamb and Sons v Rider* [1948] 2 K.B. 331). If leave is granted on a second application, it may be on terms that the writ be issued within a certain time.

How should a partner be sued to ensure enforcement can commence immediately?

3–19 Under previous rules, the enforcement of a judgment or order against a partner in either his or her individual name and in their status as a partner was more complicated. The new rules under CPR Pt 70 simplify the position and the distinction is now between the partner and the partner's own assets, and the partner and their partnership assets.

This can be illustrated by considering the nature of a partner in a law firm. The partner is likely to own a partnership share in the law firm which includes the books, computers, desks, chairs and other office fixtures and fittings. This is the property of the partnership. The partner may also own his own home, car, shares and bank account, which are his own individual property. If a judgment was entered against the law firm, then the partners may well find creditors issue a writ of fi fa against the partnership at their offices, and also at their private home addresses.

A judgment or order made against a partnership can be enforced against any property of the partnership within the jurisdiction of the court (see para. 6A to the PD70).

A judgment or order made against the partnership *cannot be enforced* against a limited partner or a member of the partnership who is residing outside the jurisdiction when the claim form is issued.

Subject to these rules a judgment or order made against the partnership may be enforced against any person who:

- is not a limited partner;
- has acknowledged service of the claim form in his capacity as a partner.

If a partner who is served with a claim form in his or her capacity as a partner:

- fails to acknowledge service of the claim;
- admits in his or her statement of case that he or she is or was a partner at the time course of action arose;
- is found by the court to have been a partner at the time the course of action arose.

then that person can be subject to enforcement action in his capacity as a partner.

3–20 Further rules in relation to partnership property are made under CPR Pt 73 and its Practice Direction at CPR 73.4A, where a charging order or interim charging order is made against property belonging to a judgment debtor who is in a partnership. The rules require that documents must be served on a member of the partnership within the jurisdiction or a person authorised by a partner or some other person having control or management of the partnership business. Where an order requires a partnership to appear before the court, it will be sufficient for an individual partner to appear.

In relation to third party debt orders, where a debt is due to the judgment creditor from a partnership, any interim third party debt order (following CPR 72.4 (2)) must be served on a member of the partnership within the jurisdiction, a person authorised by a partner or some other person having control or management of the partnership business. Where an order is made under r.72.4 (2) which requires the partnership to appear before the court, it will be sufficient for an individual partner to appear.

How is a judgment enforced against a member of HM forces?

3–21 Special rules apply as to the enforcement of a judgment against a member of HM Forces. Although courts cannot make an attachment of earnings order against the pay or allowances of a member of the Armed Forces, arrangements can be made for compulsory deductions from pay through the Defence Council, whether the debtor is stationed in the UK or not, under:

- Section 151A of the Army Act 1955;
- Section 151A of the Air Force Act 1955; or
- Section 128E of the Naval Discipline Act 1957.

In suitable cases, the judgment creditor should first write to the judgment debtor requesting payment in the terms of the judgment. If payment cannot be made, the judgment creditor should invite proposals for settlement supported by a statement of means.

3–22 If the judgment debtor is willing to offer an acceptable instalment arrangement, then either of the following options is available:

- the judgment debtor should be asked to send payments as agreed, directly to the judgment creditor; or
- the judgment creditor can approach the paying officer of the judgment debtor to arrange for voluntary deductions from service pay to be made and sent to the judgment creditor.

Where the judgment debtor does not reply to this approach, or fails to make payments, the judgment creditor should send a further letter warning that if payment is not made, an approach will be made to the Service authorities for compulsory deductions from pay.

Where the failure continues, the judgment creditor should obtain a certificate of the judgment or order from the court. This should be sent with a letter to the appropriate service authority:

- including full details of the judgment debtor's rank and service number;
- indicating that the judgment creditor has made unsuccessful efforts to persuade the judgment debtor to comply with the court judgment or order;
- requesting that an order be made under the provisions of the appropriate Act for deductions from pay;
- giving the name and address of the court (and the claim number) to which payment(s) should be made.

3–23 The addresses for the Service authorities are set out below for ease of reference:

Service	**Address**
Army (officers—quote ref. 93A)	The Ministry of Defence (Army) SAA Mail Point 460 APC Kentigern House 65 Brown Street Glasgow G2 8EX
Army (regular other ranks—quote ref. 93)	The Ministry of Defence (Army) PPPA Mail Point 465 APC Kentigern House 65 Brown Street Glasgow G2 8EX
Royal Air Force (for officers quote ref. 5/1) (for airmen quote ref. 5/3)	The Ministry of Defence (RAF) EDS AFPPA AIS 22A1 RAF Pay and Support Centre Room 13 Building 250 RAF Innsworth Gloucester GL3 1EZ
Royal Navy and Royal Marines personnel (quote ref. 1)	The Ministry of Defence (Navy) NPP(ACS) 2D Room 023 Centurion Building Grange Road Gosport Hants PO13 3XA

If payment is not received within three months, enquiries should be made at the court office to see if payment has been received. If not, a further letter should be written to the Service address enquiring why payment has not been made.

What is the impact of human rights legislation on enforcement?

3–24 The Treaty on the European Convention on Human Rights and Fundamental Freedoms 1950 (ECHR) was incorporated into UK law by the Human Rights Acts 1998. The Convention rights—comprising certain Articles and Protocols which surround enforcement—include:

- Article 6: The right to a fair hearing.
- Article 8: The right to respect for private and family life, home and correspondence.

In addition, there are a number of Protocols to the Convention including Protocol 1, Art.1, which is the right to peaceful enjoyment of possessions, subject to matters of public interest and the state being able to enforce its laws.

The Human Rights Act 1998 confers rights on citizens, whether they are judgment debtors involved in paying a money judgment to the court or defendants being subjected to enforcement proceedings in relation to a possession order. Case law continues to develop on the various parts of the 1998 Act, and the CPR has a number of areas involving the combined effect of human rights considerations and enforcement law.

3–25 The table below highlights areas in the enforcement arena which have attracted comment on human rights:

Warrant of Possession	The issue of a warrant of possession was found to be no more than an administrative act to give effect to a judicial decision in the case of *Southwark London Borough Council v St Brice* [2001] EWCA Civ 1138; [2002] 1 W.L.R. 1537.
Writ of Possession	A local planning authority was granted an injunction to require the removal of gypsy caravans from land owned by gypsies where the siting of residential caravans on the land caused significant harm to the landscape and local amenities, and was in conflict with local planning policies. It was proportionate to grant an injunction in favour of the local authority and there was no breach of the defendant's rights under Art. 8 of the ECHR (see *South Cambridgeshire DC v Flynn* [2006] EWHC 1320 (QB)).
Order to Obtain Information	CPR 71.8 simplifies and clarifies the procedure if a judgment debtor fails to comply with the order to attend court, which overcomes concerns that the former rules in relation to oral examinations were incompatible with Art. 5 of the ECHR.
Charging Orders	In an order for sale application the court has to consider the provisions of Art. 8 of the ECHR, as set out in Sch.1 to the Human Rights Act 1998.
Judgment Summonses	In the case of *Mubarak v Mubarak* [2001] 1 F.L.R 698 the Court of Appeal held that the procedure was not compatible with the ECHR. As a result, the CPR was changed to make the procedure ECHR-compliant.
Recognition of Foreign Judgment	Where a defendant was unaware that a trial had been reactivated 12 years after it was stayed until even the time for an appeal had passed, he was manifestly denied a fair trial within Art.6 of the ECHR, and it was therefore contrary to public policy to enforce the claimant's judgment against him (*Marionier v Larmer* [2002] EWCA Civ 774, [2003] Q.B. 620.
Traffic Enforcement	In the congestion charge case of *R. (on the application of Walmsley v Lane* [2005] EWHC 896 (Admin); [2005] R.T.R. 28 it was held that the second defendant had a discretion to direct that penalty charge notices be cancelled in circumstances where there were grounds for

	mitigating the penalty or totally relieving the recipient of the penalty, even though the ground for resisting the charge under s.13 of the Regulations had not formally been established. The case involved an examination of the claimant's rights under Art.6 of the ECHR.
Freezing Orders	As might be expected, the making of this type of order may engage ECHR Art.8, although depending on the scope of the order, any interference may be justified under ECHR Art.8(2) as necessary "for the protection of the rights and freedom of others". The European Commission has held that ECHR Art.6(1) does not apply to the interlocutory proceedings in which such injunctions are granted, where the proceedings do not involve the "determination" of a civil right (see *Ewing v United Kingdom* (1988) 10 E.H.R.R. CD 141 and note to White Book Service 2010 at 39.2.1 and generally CPR Pt 39.2—General Rule—hearing to be in public).

How can risks be minimised in managing or handling an enforcement action?

3–26 As mentioned at the beginning of this chapter, it is important to find out what is achievable from the enforcement process before embarking on issuing any form of application or process. Time is not on the side of the judgment creditor, and procrastinating about the decision will only increase the likelihood that assets will dissipate. This is why it is so important to assess the options for enforcement before the claim form is even issued at court and to develop the idea of a matrix (as suggested at the outset of this chapter) to formulate a way forward once judgment is entered against the judgment debtor.

The litigation may be critical to a judgment creditor, either in business or as a personal issue, and of course the more important it is, then the more important it is to assess the potential risks before commencing litigation.

Realism

3–27 Judgment creditors can suffer from being unrealistic about the chances of successful enforcement. Those acting without advice have faith in the court system, which can be severely dented by an unsuccessful attempt at enforcement. All these issues were debated in the Lord Chancellor's Review of Enforcement, and certainly the government is keen to address the real concerns it unearthed in its findings about lack of confidence in the court system for enforcement.

It is important that judgment creditors and their advisors are realistic about the chances of success by looking into the financial circumstances of the would-be judgment debtor at an early stage and highlighting the shortcomings of any given method, for example that bailiffs cannot force entry to a private house, or that an attachment of earnings order is not available against a self-employed judgment debtor or a member of the Armed Forces.

Risk assessment

3–28 A risk assessment checklist at the start of each new enforcement action (or better still each new claim) can ensure it is being handled by a person with the correct competency, and who has sufficient time to devote to the case. If professional advisors are handling the matter, they should ensure they have procedures and systems to monitor any change in the circumstances of the judgment debtor which could lead to an unenforceable judgment.

Questions such as the financial solvency of the judgment debtor, the location of the judgment debtor and the assets available to satisfy the judgment are all important points to check and continue to check as the enforcement process continues. If steps need to be taken to stop assets being secreted away or dissipated, then these need to be looked at carefully in terms of timing, cost and accuracy of information as to the assets and the general situation.

Financial information about a judgment debtor, such as whether the property of the judgment debtor is up for sale, whether a judgment debtor business is still trading or whether the debtor's business has issued profit warnings, are all important indicators in the quest to enforce the judgment successfully.

It is all too easy to make assumptions about enforcement and not to check the facts carefully enough. If insurers are involved and could become liable to meet any judgment debt through the debtor's insurance, confirmation should be sought to check the insurer's interest. If the Motor Insurers Bureau is involved, if necessary take steps to ensure that any judgment will be met. If multiple parties are involved, one of which is insured, it should not be presumed that the enforcement of the judgment is a foregone conclusion. Instead, the credit worthiness of all the parties should be checked by using the power of the internet to make searches to check the solvency or creditworthiness of the judgment debtor.

Avoid delays

3–29 Once judgment has been obtained it is vital that delay is minimised and the risks again reassessed to see if there has been any change in the judgment debtor's circumstances. Enforcement should only be delayed if there is a good reason for doing so. Delays can lead to the debtor moving away, hiding any available assets or a change for the worst in the judgment debtor's fortunes. The most common problem is the judgment debtor seeking shelter from the judgment creditor's enforcement remedy through an insolvency procedure and, of course, in 2010 there are an increasing number of ways in which the debtor can achieve this course of action.

Interest

3–30 As interest runs on High Court judgments from either the date of the judgment, where it is a judgment of the High Court, or from the date of transfer to the High Court, it is important not to overlook the availability of interest which can be valuable to a judgment creditor, particularly if enforcement is going to be protracted for any reason.

Charging orders

3–31 Speed can be of the essence. If the debtor is selling a property and the judgment creditor fails to apply to register any interim charging order during the priority period of a pre-completion search as part of the conveyancing process of the judgment debtor's property, then it is likely that the new owner will take the title to the property free of any incumbrance, leaving the judgment creditor without a remedy (see *Howell v Montey The Times* March 17, 1990).

Reviews and checklists

3–32 Without regular reviews or a checklist to work from, it is all too easy to overlook individual matters, especially with new rules and procedures. A constant review of the enforcement process on a regular basis (at least once a week as a guide) should ensure that the desired outcome is achieved.

It is important to remember that enforcement work is equally as important as the work leading to judgment, as any delay can prejudice the success of enforcement. Therefore, designing a checklist which covers an enforcement strategy for either one case or an entire caseload will help keep a judgment creditor on top of developments, remind a judgment creditor to check salient points and allow changes in strategy to be made to meet the circumstances of the judgment debtor. A sample checklist for the enforcement of a judgment appears in the Appendix to this book.

Chapter 4

Stays of Execution

Introductory comments

4–01 Stays of execution become vitally important to parties in litigation when the judgment creditor or claimant wants to press to enforce the court's judgment or order and the judgment debtor/defendant wants to resist the inevitable consequences that execution will bring.

Stays of execution are often hurried affairs made by judgment debtors or defendants to protect assets or protect their right to stay in or on land. They will often be made without notice and need to be responded to quickly. Certainly from the point of view of execution against goods, High Court Enforcement Officers are well trained to respond immediately to stays of execution, as a failure to do so can leave them in a precarious position in relation to their duties to follow the command of the writ and also to obey any court order that is served upon them. Often stays will be handwritten by Masters in the Queen's Bench Division, and the advice to practitioners must be to tread carefully to ensure they are not dismissed out of hand for failing to appear more formal than perhaps the handwritten order may suggest.

General position on stays

4–02 In line with CPR r.3.1(2)(f) the court has general case management power to stay the whole or any part of any proceedings or judgment, either generally or until a specified date or event. This rule derives from the Supreme Court Act 1981, s.49(3).

The CPR glossary states a "stay" imposes a halt on proceedings, apart from taking any steps allowed by the CPR or the terms of the stay itself. Against the backdrop of legislation and Rules, case law over the last decade has embraced the overriding objective of the Civil Procedure Rules, with judges balancing the risks of granting a stay of execution against the risk of non-payment or repayment, depending on the circumstances (see *Total M and E Services Ltd v ABB Building Technologies Ltd* [2002] EWHC 248 (TCC) and *Wimbledon Construction Company 2000 Ltd v Vago* [2005] EWHC 1086 (TCC)), where the court was unimpressed by the arguments before it and refused to grant a stay of execution.

A judgment debtor who is unable to pay a judgment debt, or who alleges that it is otherwise inexpedient to enforce an order, may apply for a stay of execution under the CPR, the general rules for which are set out in Sch.1, RSC Order 47, r.1 and Sch.2, CCR Order 25, r.8.

Once a final judgment or order has been made, execution can be issued immediately, unless leave to issue execution is required or, as dealt with later in this chapter, the court orders a stay of execution. Parties must be alive to the possibility of a stay of execution coming late in the day in the proceedings, either as the judgment creditor, where an application for a stay of execution can be made at any time, or as the judgment debtor, whereby the stay can become a lifeline to preventing the removal of goods or the finalisation of a charging order, due to a serious oversight in responding to a claim form.

4–03 The court has wide powers to stay execution where the judgment or order is for the payment of money in both the High Court and county court. For a fairly recent case involving a stay of execution in connection with a writ of possession see *Hackney London Borough Council v Side by Side (Kids) Ltd* [2003] EWHC 1813 (QB); [2004] 2 All E.R. 373, which involved s.89 of the Housing Act 1980 and examined whether a stay could be maintained in the light of an agreement between the London Borough and the defendant company.

A judgment debtor, or the party being ordered to pay under the judgment or order, may apply to the court for a stay of execution of the court's judgment or order on the ground that, since the date of the judgment or order, there has been a change in circumstances which means that the execution of the judgment should be stayed.

Without prejudice to the terms of RSC Order 47, r.1, the court may grant a stay of execution for "such relief and on such terms as may be just" (CPR Sch.1, RSC Order 45, r.11).

Cases where a stay of execution is automatic

4–04 In certain proceedings, the making of an order, or issue of an application to the court, will automatically stay the proceedings. These include:

- the issue of an interpleader application by an enforcement officer which stays the execution of the writ of fi fa until the third party claim is dealt with by the court *(Re Ford, Ex p. Ford* [1887] 18 Q.B.D. 369); and

- an order for the payment of a judgment debt by instalments while the order allowing instalment payments is still in force; if the debtor defaults on making the instalment payments, an application for leave to issue execution must be made (see generally CPR Sch.1, RSC Order 47, r.1).

High Court business

4–05 Prior to the introduction of the CPR in 1999, applications in the High Court for a stay of execution were very common. However, CPR 40.11 now provides a mechanism which requires a party to comply with a judgment or order for the payment of a money judgment (including costs) within 14 days of the date of the judgment or order, unless there is a different date for compliance, the court has stayed proceedings or the Rules themselves provide another date for compliance.

If execution has already been issued, a judgment debtor may need to apply for a stay pursuant to RSC Order 47, r.1. If, however, execution has not yet been issued, it may be preferable to apply to vary the judgment to provide for payment by instalments (or lower instalments) using the provisions of either CPR 40.11 or CPR 13.4.

If an application for a stay of execution under CPR Sch.1, RSC Order 47, r.1 is needed, a judgment debtor will need to satisfy a High Court Master or district judge sitting in the District Registry that a stay of execution should be ordered, because:

- there are "special circumstances" which render it inexpedient to enforce the judgment or order (RSC Order 47, r.1(1)(a)); or
- the applicant is unable to pay the money (RSC Order 47, r.1(1)(b)), in which case the court will investigate the applicant's means and the applicant will need to disclose his income, the nature and value of any property and the amount of liabilities.

The order granting a stay may be absolute, on condition and/or for such period as the court thinks fit (RSC Order 47, r.1(1)).

The application for a stay is made in accordance with CPR Pt 23 and can be made despite the fact that the judgment debtor failed to acknowledge service of the claim form or serve a defence or take any previous part in the proceedings (RSC Order 47, r.2).

4–06 Grounds for the application for the stay of execution must be set out in the application notice, supported by evidence in the form of a witness statement or affidavit made by or on behalf of the applicant. The evidence must substantiate grounds for making the application. Where the judgment debtor's application is based on an inability to pay, then the evidence must disclose the judgment debtor's income and the nature and value of any property held, along with details of any liabilities.

The application notice and a copy of the supporting witness statement or affidavit must be served on the judgment creditor not less than four clear days before the hearing.

The usual form of order granting a stay of execution under this rule is as follows,

> "... stay of execution (under Order 47, r.1) so long as the defendant pays the judgment debt and costs by instalments at the rate of £[ ] per month on the [ ] day of each month, the first instalment to commence on the [ ] day of [ ] 20[ ], provided that if he should make default in the payment of the said instalments or any part thereof on the due date, the stay be forthwith removed in respect of the whole outstanding balance at the time of such default and the judgment creditor do have permission forthwith to issue execution by writ of fi fa on the said judgment and costs".

If the judgment debtor is the owner of premises, the court has power "there and then" to impose a final charging order on the premises, provided the judgment debtor agrees, so that the judgment creditor need not go through the machinery of obtaining a final charging order under CPR Pt 73. In the absence of an agreement, the Court should endeavour as far as possible to maintain a fair and proper balance between the needs of the judgment debtor to be granted a stay of execution and the needs of the judgment creditor to obtain due and prompt satisfaction of his judgment debt.

In any application for a stay of execution the starting point is that there has to be a good reason to deny the judgment creditor the immediate fruits of his judgment (*Winchester Cigarette Machinery Ltd v Payne* (No.2), *The Times*, December 15, 1993).

The terms of this rule give the court sufficiently wide discretion, if the circumstances of the case warrant it, to pierce the corporate veil and to look behind the incorporated companies involved in the dispute so as to ascertain the identity of the persons who control the companies. In a proper case, the court will grant a stay of execution (*Canada Enterprises Corp Ltd v MacNab Distilleries Ltd* [1987] 1 W.L.R. 813).

County Court business

4–07 By virtue of s.71(2) of the County Courts Act 1984, the district judge has power to stay the execution of the judgment if it appears at any time that the paying party in the proceedings is unable to pay any sum, whether in satisfaction of the claim or counterclaim, by way of costs or any instalment of these sums. In this situation the court may, in its discretion, suspend or stay any judgment or order that it gives or makes in the proceedings on terms and for a period that it believes is needed until the cause of inability has ceased.

The application is made on Form N245, which is a notice of application for suspension of warrant and/or variation of an instalment order.

By virtue of s.88 of the same Act, the court has power to stay the execution of any proceedings for such time and on such terms as it thinks fit, and with a similar breadth of discretion to s.71(2).

Under CPR Sch.2, CCR Order 25, r.8(1) power is devolved to court staff to suspend warrants of execution. The judgment creditor may object to the terms offered by the judgment debtor and either party may apply for the order to be reconsidered by the district judge at a hearing. Where, however, the judgment creditor objects to the warrant being suspended on any terms, the application will be listed for hearing before the district judge.

If a tenant or his solicitor attends at court to make an application to suspend a warrant and is wrongly turned away by court staff on the grounds that there is no judge available to hear the application, it is arguable that the application is made at this point and that when it is eventually heard there is jurisdiction to grant it, notwithstanding that the warrant has by the time of the hearing been executed (*Islington London Borough Council v Harridge* (1993) *The Times*, June 30, CA).

CCR Order 25, r.8(1) does not give the district judge independent power to suspend or stay a warrant of execution. It only enables him to exercise the powers conferred on the court by the relevant statutory provisions, being s.71(2), 88 and 103(5) of the County Courts Act 1984. It is not, however, necessary for the district judge to have the leave of the judge to exercise this jurisdiction.

The rules on granting a stay pending an appeal in the county court follow the High Court position. A stay will normally be granted where there is an appeal with some prospect of success and the defendant will be ruined if a stay is not granted (*Linotype-Hell Finance v Baker* [1993] 1 W.L.R. 321; [1992] 4 All E.R. 887 CA). The judgment in *Simonite v Sheffield City Council* [1992] 1 E.G.L.R. 105; [1992] 24 E.G. 134 suggested that the Linotype-Hell judgment should be treated with care, having regard to the 19th century cases of *Barker v Lavery* (1884–1885) 14 Q.B.D. 769, CA and *Atkins v Great Western Rly Co* (1886) 2 T.L.R. 400, CA.

Does an appeal act as a stay of execution?

4–08 Put simply, the answer is "No". An appeal does not operate as a stay of execution, although it is often a mistake that practitioners and litigants in person make, particularly when confronted with a determined judgment creditor intent on seeing a judgment enforced.

An application for a stay should be made at the conclusion of the trial or hearing to the judge who makes the decision that is to be appealed. The application should be made when the trial judge is asked to grant permission to appeal (see CPR 52.3(2)(a)). If a stay is refused or is not applied for in the lower court, a separate application for a stay supported by evidence may be made or included in any application for permission to appeal to the appeal court. An application made after the filing of an appeal notice is made in accordance with CPR Pt 23 (see CPR PD52, paras 5.5 and 11). The applicant must file with the notice of appeal the following:

- One additional copy of the application notice for the appeal court and one copy for each of the respondents;
- (Where applicable) a sealed copy of the order which is the subject of the main appeal; and
- The bundle of documents in support of the application, which includes the Pt 23 application notice and any witness statements or affidavits in support of the application notice.

Where the application to the Court of Appeal is urgent, it is essential that a note of the transcript of the judgment being appealed against be supplied, and that evidence in support of the application for a stay of execution is supported fully.

The court's discretion to grant a stay is unfettered. The court will not order a stay unless satisfied by cogent, full and frank evidence that there is a real risk of injustice (see *Hammond Suddard Solicitors v Agrichem International Holdings Limited* [2001] All E.R. (D) 258 (Dec)).

4–09 The common mistake by practitioners is to presume that the issue of the application for an appeal acts as a stay on any execution. As mentioned above, this is not correct. A separate application for a stay of execution must be made to ensure particularly that execution against goods is prevented from escalating towards the removal of any available goods. The mistake becomes apparent when the judgment debtor's solicitor, relying on the notice of appeal as a stay of execution, is telephoned by his client to say the enforcement officers are at the premises to remove goods. Frantic telephone calls and applications to the Practice Master or district judge then ensue to prevent the removal taking place.

A prospective appellant must show good cause as to why the respondent should be "denied the fruits of his judgment" (see *Winchester Cigarette Machinery Ltd v Payne (No. 2) The Times*, December 15, 1993 CA, which is also referred to above). A stay may then be ordered if the appellant would be ruined without it and has some prospect of success on the appeal (see *Linotype Hell Finance v Baker* [1992] 4 All E.R. 887, in which 19th century case law on the subject of when to grant a stay of execution was overturned by a single Lord Justice sitting in the Court of Appeal, on the basis they did not seem to reflect the current practice in the Court of Appeal. However, also see the comments above in which the judgment in this case was criticised).

In the case of *Sucden Financial Limited v Fluxo-Cane Overseas Limited* [2009] EWHC 3555 (QB) it was held by Teare J. that an order for a judgment debtor to attend court to provide information was not contrary to an order of staying enforcement of the judgment debt. The order to attend court was simply a step to enable the judgment creditor to enforce the debt that was not part and parcel of the enforcement process.

The judge held in that case that the making of an order under CPR Pt 71, which compelled the judgment debtor to come to court to disclose information, was not contrary to the original order and the enforcement of the judgment debt. CPR r.71.1 states expressly that the purpose of obtaining an order under Pt 71 is to enable a judgment creditor to enforce a judgment. This means that it is an order which puts the judgment creditor in a position where he might be able to enforce a judgment, but it is not part and parcel of the enforcement process. There also has to be a distinction between the steps taken to enable a judgment creditor to enforce a judgment and an action which is a species of execution such as a Third Party Debt Order. This case clearly fell into the category of a species of execution.

Sucden Financial Limited v Fluxo-Cane Overseas Limited [2009] EWHC 3555 (QB) is useful inasmuch that even if a judgment debtor obtains a stay of execution pending further enforcement, a judgment creditor can still apply to the court under CPR Pt 71, to seek to obtain further information about the judgment debtor's assets and general financial position, and such an application is not thwarted by the application for a stay of execution.

Appeal to the European Court of Human Rights

4–10 In *Westminster City Council v Porter* [2002] EWHC 2179 (CH); [2003] 2 W.L.R. 420 the defendant was ordered to pay a substantial sum of money and ultimately lost her appeal in the House of Lords. She then petitioned the European Court of Human Rights (ECHR), whilst in the meantime seeking a stay of execution in the UK courts. She argued that she had been denied due process and by a treaty to which the UK Government was a party, she was entitled to the right of petition to the ECHR. The judge refused a stay on the grounds that the European Court of Human Rights was not a court of appeal for domestic citizen litigants, and anyway due process had been accorded to the defendant in the domestic courts. Moreover, even if the ECHR were to find in favour of the defendant, it would only amount to a judgment against the UK Government and would give no rights to the individual citizen. Her only hope was that the UK would pass appropriate and perhaps special legislation, which was highly unlikely.

Stays of execution and insolvency

Bankruptcy proceedings

4–11 Under s.285 of the Insolvency Act 1986 the court may, at any time when proceedings under a bankruptcy petition are pending or a person has been adjudged bankrupt, "stay any action, execution or other legal process" against the property of the debtor.

The "court" means either the bankruptcy court or the court in which any action for execution or other legal process is being conducted.

Winding-up proceedings

4–12 Similar provisions apply in relation to companies under s.120 of the Insolvency Act 1986. Once a winding-up petition has been presented to the court in respect of a company registered under the Companies Act 1985, the court can stay "any action, suit or proceedings" against the company. In the case of a company registered under s.680 of the Companies Act, or an unregistered company, the court can order a stay to proceedings being brought by contributories in respect of company debts (see s.126(2) of the Insolvency Act 1986).

If a winding-up order is made, this will inhibit the commencement or continuation of any proceedings against the company including proceedings started in relation to execution, distress, attachment or sequestration. Any such proceedings will then be void (see s.128 of the Insolvency Act 1986).

Chapter 5

Transferring Judgments for Enforcement

Introductory comments

5–01 Within the two-tier system of civil courts in England and Wales there is a need for practitioners to understand how judgments can be moved from one tier of the system to another.

The rules on transfer of judgments are in many ways unsatisfactory because they can cause delay in the actual enforcement of a judgment, which can result in a loss of opportunity for the judgment creditor if the judgment debtor dissipates assets or becomes insolvent.

In the White Book Service 2010 the editorial introduction to CPR Pt 70 states quite bluntly that "the law on enforcement of judgments is unsatisfactory and in need of reform". Part 70 does not incorporate the remaining parts of the old Rules of the Supreme Court, or the County Court Rules, so practitioners must be able to follow where all the rules are situated within the CPR as a whole.

For the purposes of this chapter, however, the following areas of transfer of judgments are featured:

- transferring judgments for enforcement between county courts;
- transferring county court judgments to the High Court for enforcement;
- transferring High Court judgments to the county court for enforcement;
- transferring judgments both of the High Court and county courts outside of England and Wales for enforcement;
- transferring employment tribunal awards into the mainstream civil court system for enforcement.

Definitions

5–02 When it comes to enforcing a judgment, the terminology of claimant and defendant in the original proceedings changes so that the party entitled to enforce the judgment becomes the "judgment creditor" and the party against whom the judgment is to be enforced becomes the "judgment debtor". The definitions are set out in CPR r.70.1.

Payment of an award is included in the phrase "judgment or order", which then needs to be made into an enforceable judgment through the process of transferring it from the tribunal that made the award into a county court judgment, and perhaps then into a High Court judgment capable of enforcement in the higher court.

A judgment or order for the payment of money will include a judgment for the payment of costs, but these must have been decided before enforcement commences (see CPR 70.1.3). The successful party who wishes to obtain a payment prior to an assessment of costs should use the rule which provides the court with discretion under CPR 44.3(8) or CPR 47.15, and which gives the court power to issue an interim costs certificate which is then capable of being enforced.

The term "judgment or order for the payment of money" does not include a judgment or order for the payment of money into court. Rather, if the court has ordered that a payment into court be made and this is not complied with, then the remedy is to make an application for the imposition of a sanction, which may take the form of either striking out any claim or defence as the circumstances dictate.

Transferring judgments between county courts—CPR 70.3

5–03 Where a judgment creditor needs to transfer a judgment or order from one county court to another, the procedure is set out in the accompanying practice direction to CPR Pt 70 (see CPR 70PD.2).

The procedure is simple enough and can be set out as follows:

- The judgment creditor makes a request in writing to the court in which the case is proceeding, to seek a transfer of the case to another court. No fee is payable in seeking a transfer (see CPR PD70.2.1).
- On receipt of the judgment creditor's request, the court will transfer the proceedings to the other court unless the judge directs otherwise (see CPR PD70.2.2).
- As required by the practice direction, the court will give notice of the transfer to all the parties in the proceedings.

- After the proceedings have been transferred, the parties will then need to take any further steps in the new court—unless the Rules or practice directions provide otherwise (see CPR PD70.2.4).

Where a county court judgment has been obtained in either the Claims Production Centre (CPC) or the County Court Bulk Centre (CCBC), located in Northampton, then the judgment creditor should refer to practice direction 7C of the CPR, where special rules apply. More information about these two bulk centres can be found at *http://www.hmcourts-service.gov.uk/cms/cpc.htm* [Accessed October 14, 2010].

For CCBC users that request judgments electronically from the court, a request can be made to issue a warrant of execution overnight and details of the request will be sent to the judgment debtor's local court overnight.

Where the judgment creditor wishes to enforce a CCBC judgment through the High Court, the CCBC will deal with the request within a maximum of two days so that the transfer can take place and a writ of fi fa issued.

The reasons why a judgment creditor may wish to transfer a county court judgment from the lower to the higher court, are explained later in this chapter.

Transferring judgments from the High Court to the county court—CPR 70PD.3

5–04 A judgment creditor may wish to transfer a judgment obtained in the High Court to a county court to begin an application for an attachment of earnings order.

As attachment of earnings is not a method of enforcement available in the higher court to be able to use it as a way to enforce payment, a judgment creditor will need to go through the process of transferring the judgment for this purpose. One reason may be that a judgment debtor is in employment and it makes sense to deduct payment from his or her salary rather than executing against goods, or charging property.

If a judgment creditor wishes to therefore use the county court enforcement process in this way, the following documents will need to be filed in the county court with an application notice or request for enforcement:

- a copy of the judgment or order to be transferred;
- a certificate verifying the amount due under that judgment or order;

- if a writ of fi fa has previously been issued in the High Court to enforce a judgment or order by a High Court Enforcement Officer, a copy of the High Court Enforcement Officer's "return to the writ"; and
- a copy of the High Court order allowing the proceedings to be transferred to the county court.

Transferring judgments from the county court to the High Court

5–05 Perhaps the most common reason for transferring a county court judgment to the High Court for enforcement is to enable the judgment creditor to use the services of High Court Enforcement Officers which are referred to in the rules as "enforcement officers". These officers are authorised to act in that capacity under s.99 of the Courts Act 2003.

To enable a judgment creditor to transfer a judgment to the High Court for enforcement, and use the services of High Court Enforcement Officers, reference should be made to The High Court And County Courts Jurisdiction Order 1991 (SI 1991/724) (as amended), which was mentioned in Ch.3.

In wishing to transfer a judgment to the High Court for enforcement, the rules on transfer which need to be remembered are:

- Firstly, a judgment debt under £600 including any costs and interest cannot be transferred to the High Court—it has been felt for sometime by Government officials that High Court Enforcement Officers would not wish to enforce low value judgment debts, even though High Court Enforcement Officers have been saying they would like to be able to do so;
- Secondly, any judgment regulated by the Consumer Credit Act cannot be transferred to the High Court. The 1991 case of *Forward Trust Plc v Whymark* [1990] 2 Q.B. 670; [1989] 3 W.L.R. 1229 CA (Civ Div) highlighted the problem as it then was, of judgments being obtained under the Consumer Credit legislation which could carry interest at the Judgment Debt Act rate, as opposed to the county court rules on interest post judgment, where interest was not provided for (see art.8(1A) of the High Court and County Courts Jurisdiction Order 1991));
- Thirdly, judgment debts between £600 and £5,000 (which are not then regulated by the Consumer Credit Act) can be enforced by both High Court Enforcement Officers and county court bailiffs, and the choice is up to the judgment creditor to decide whether the judgment should be transferred to the High Court or if it should be left in the county court for enforcement;

- Fourthly, it is mandatory for judgments over £5,000 which are not regulated by the Consumer Credit Act to be transferred to the High Court for enforcement.

5–06 Once the judgment creditor has navigated the rules on transfer, and of course for many seasoned practitioners the office computer system is going to be making those decisions based on the above business rules, then the next step is for the judgment creditor to make request for a certificate of judgment under CPR Sch.2, CCR Order 22, r.8 (1). This certificate is issued for the purpose of enforcing a judgment or order in the High Court either by:

- executing against the judgment debtor's goods; or
- where the judgment or order to be enforced is an order for possession of land made in a claim for possession against trespassers.

The certificate is applied for on Form N.293a. When the certificate is granted by the county court, this takes effect as the order to transfer the proceedings from the county court to the High Court. The transfer becomes effective on the issue and sealing of the N.293a.

It should be noted that at the time of writing this text there can be delays in this procedure, and it is not something that county court staff are often prepared to do "over the counter". The CCBC centre in Northampton has a fast-track procedure for transfer, and enquiries should be made at the CCBC if the judgment creditor is a user of that system when issuing claims, so that any transfer procedure is carried out as quickly as possible.

Delays on transferring the judgment can have an adverse effect on the opportunity to enforce, particularly if the judgment debtor is deliberately dissipating assets or is becoming insolvent through the concerns of other creditors. There is, naturally, an argument that the 1991 Jurisdiction Order should be removed from the statute book, allowing judgments to be transferred more freely, although the court administration still has to track and check where any judgment is for enforcement in its two-tier system.

Therefore, until any reform of the jurisdictional position is achieved, judgment creditors and their advisors are encouraged to anticipate any delay in the enforcement of their judgment and calculate the impact on the opportunity to successfully enforce.

5–07 On the transfer of proceedings, the county court is required to give notice to the judgment debtor or the person against whom the possession order was made, that the proceedings have been transferred. An entry to that effect will be made in the court records. There are no published statistics as to how often notice is given to the judgment debtor that the judgment or order has been transferred. It would seem to be a very rare procedure, though, as many judgment debtors appear unaware that a judgment has been transferred when first visited by a High Court Enforcement Officer.

It should be noted that a certificate of judgment will not be granted to transfer the judgment or order if any of the following matters are pending in the county court:

- an application has been made by the judgment debtor for a variation in the date or rate of payment of money due under a judgment;
- an application by the judgment debtor under either CPR r.39.3 (3) (which relates to the situation where a party who failed to attend a hearing may apply for the judgment or order to be set aside) or CPR r.13.4 (where an application is made to set aside or vary judgment);
- a request by the judgment debtor for an administration order
- an application for stay of execution under s.88 of the County Court's Act 1984, where the District Judge exercises this jurisdiction under CPR Sch.2, CCR Order, r.8 to stay any proceedings where a party is unable to pay, and to stay those proceedings for such time and on such terms as the court thinks fit until the party's inability has "ceased".

Once the certificate of judgment has been issued, with the seal of the county court showing on the front, the N.293a is literally "turned over" to become a High Court form and the reverse is used as the "praecipe" to issue the High Court Writ of Execution, which will be either a writ of fi fa or a writ of possession, depending on the nature of the enforcement.

5–08 In 1998, the then Senior Master of the Queens Bench Division, Master Robert Turner, issued a Practice Direction relating to the procedure for the enforcement in the High Court of county court judgments (see *The Senior Master's Practice Direction of August 31, 1998* [1998] 4 ALL E.R. 63).

To assist judgment creditors and their advisors, High Court Enforcement Officers themselves created transfer centres to enable the smooth transfer of the judgment from the county court to the High Court.

It is worth setting out the very practical points contained in the Practice Direction at this juncture, because they continue to be an example of a judge taking an interest in the process in his court and ensuring that the process for transfer fits with the needs of judgment creditors and court administration. The Practice Direction provides the following:

Step 1—High Court counter staff check the certificate of judgment on the front to ensure it is been properly completed and sealed. A copy of the certificate also needs to be provided. No fee is payable on registration.

Step 2—The High Court counter staff then check that a certificate has been signed by an officer of the issuing court (a rubber stamp is not sufficient), and ensure that a certificate is dated and complies with the requirements of CCR Order 22 r.8 (1A). In particular, they will check that the certificate complies with the requirement, as stipulated on the face of the certificate, that it has been granted for the purpose of enforcing a judgment (or order in the High Court).

Step 3—Provided that steps 1 and 2 have been complied with, the court staff will:

- allocate a reference number, letter (according to the claimant's name) and year and endorse that on the top right hand corner of certificate and copy;
- date and seal the certificate and copy, return the original to the applicant and retain a copy for the court records; and
- enter the matter in a special register.

Step 4—The certificate then ensures that the county court judgment will now be treated for enforcement purposes as a High Court judgment, and interest at the appropriate rate will run from the date of the certificate. It should be noted that whilst the enforcement of the judgment has been transferred to the High Court, the main proceedings will remain within the jurisdiction of the county court and judgment creditors and their advisors can expect that judgment debtors will often make applications to the county court to stay or vary judgments from time to time.

Step 5—the title of all subsequent documents must be recited as follows:

IN THE HIGH COURT OF JUSTICE

High Court No. **5–09**
Queen's Bench Division
County Court Plaint No.
(Sent from the . . . . County Court by Certificate dated the . . . day of . . . . 19 . . .)

Between

AB Claimant

and

CD Defendant

Step 6—When the writ of fieri facias or writ of possession is issued, the certificate of judgment retained by the applicant must be date sealed by the High Court counter staff on the bottom left hand corner and endorsed with the designation of the High Court Enforcement Officer to whom the process is directed. Although any application for a stay of execution should be made by application notice in the High Court returnable before a Queen's Bench Master, all other applications for enforcement or ancillary relief must be made to the issuing county court.

Step 7—When dealing with transfers in district registries, Practice Direction needs to be followed to allow for variations as circumstances may require.

Interest payable on county court judgments which are transferred

5–10 Registration in the High Court means that a county court judgment which orders the judgment debtor to pay the outstanding judgment debt will now attract interest under the Judgments Act 1838 from the date of the certificate being on Form N.293a. The 1838 statute provides a regime for judgment interest which, from the judgment creditor's point of view, is more favourable than the interest provisions for judgments left to enforcement measures in the county court.

Under county court rules, no interest is payable on judgment debts of less than £5,000 from the date of judgment, except where The Late Payment of Commercial Debts (Rate of Interest) Order 1998 can be applied.

Furthermore, where interest is payable it "ceases" to be payable as soon as the judgment creditor commences enforcement proceedings in the county court. This would include any enforcement measure taken such as an application for an order to obtain information, a third party debt order or a judgment summons.

Interest on a charging order is not affected by the usual county court rules, as for the purposes of charging interest "enforcement" does not include an application for a charging order.

Where interest does run, then under The Judgment Act 1838, s.17 interest runs at 8 per cent per annum from either:

- the date of the High Court judgment; or
- the date of the certificate of judgment issued by the county court when transfer of the judgment to the High Court is permitted.

Once the judgment has been registered in the High Court, interest under the 1838 Act will continue to accrue even if, later, third party debt proceedings, or "equitable execution", are pursued in the county court (see County Courts Act 1984 s.42 (5)).

Transferring employment tribunal awards for enforcement

5–11 Research carried out by the Ministry of Justice (MoJ) in 2009 supported findings by the Citizens Advice Bureau in their report "Justice Denied", which highlighted the plight of applicants who had successfully won an employment tribunal action, only to find that the enforcement process in the civil courts let them down.

The MoJ research found that 39 per cent of people granted awards had not been paid and only 53 per cent had been paid in full. As a consequence of these findings, the then Justice Secretary, Jack Straw, stated he was "determined to ensure that employees awarded settlements following a dispute get their dues paid".

The research went on to show that 36 per cent of claimants who had not received payment had attempted to enforce the award through the county court and 40 per cent of unpaid or part paid claimants did not know that the award could be enforced through the county court. The MoJ moved relatively quickly to update the transfer rules regarding the enforcement of tribunal awards, to make it easier for successful claimants to enforce the award using the High Court enforcement process.

5–12 The CPR was updated to take account of the new procedure, and now ensures that a claimant who has not been paid a tribunal award can start enforcement proceedings through the county court of the district where the person(s) who has to pay the award lives or carries on business.

First, an advice form has been created on Form EX328 and circulated to all county courts across England and Wales. This form gives guidance on completing the application form to enforce a Tribunal's decision or ACAS settlement (see Form COT3).

An employment tribunal award does not require the permission of the court to begin proceedings, and no court fee is payable. A court fee will be payable, of course, when it comes to the enforcement of the award and a writ of fi fa or other court-based method of enforcement is chosen.

5–13 Once the claimant has identified the correct county court in which to file the application to transfer the award to the High Court, he or she will need to obtain and complete Form N322B. This is then returned to the county court with a copy of the Tribunal's decision. Form N322B can be downloaded from the Court Service website at *http://www.hmcourts-service.gov.uk* [Accessed October 14, 2010].

It may be that the successful claimant will be able to claim interest on the amount due, but each tribunal has its own rules and regulations regarding interest, and a successful claimant must make enquiries at the Tribunal as to whether interest can be claimed.

It should also be noted that specific regulations allow the Government to recoup jobseeker's allowance and income support paid to an employee who has won an award. The position on recouping any compensation should be checked when calculating the amount to be included in the court forms for enforcement.

5–14 Under CPR 70PD4.1A, where the decision to be enforced is the decision of the Employment Tribunal in England and Wales and the party seeking to enforce the decision wishes to enforce the award by way of a writ of fieri facias, the correct form to be used will be Practice Form N471.

This new form simplifies the process for a claimant and allows an application to be made to enforce a judgment by using the services of a High Court Enforcement Officer ("HCEO"). The award needs to be over £600 and not more than six years old.

The claimant simply needs to complete Form N471 and send it to either a named HCEO (a list of HCEOs can be found at the Association website at *http://www.hceoa.org.uk* [Accessed October 14, 2010]). The court fee to seal the writ of fi fa needs to be paid at the time of delivering the completed form. This amount will be added to the amount owed. The HCEO will then transfer the judgment and convert the Tribunal's award into a county court judgment.

As part of the discussions with the Ministry of Justice, it has been agreed that where an employment tribunal award claimant is unsuccessful in recovering the amount of the award using the services of a High Court Enforcement Officer, then no fee will be charged to the claimant in these circumstances. This initiative has been supported by the High Court Enforcement Officer's Association.

Transferring county court judgments outside England and Wales for enforcement

5–15 CPR Sch.2 CCR Order 22, r.8 is a self-contained and straightforward procedure for obtaining a certificate of judgment. In practice, such a certificate is required for the purpose of enforcing the judgment either elsewhere within the United Kingdom (i.e. outside England and Wales) or further afield.

Chapter 6

General Rules about the Enforcement of Judgments and Orders

Introductory comments

6–01 Ideally, this chapter would be limited to looking at CPR Pt 70, which should cover all the general rules about the enforcement of judgments and orders. Despite hoping in the 10th edition of this book that we would have a complete set of rules on enforcement in one place in our civil procedural code, we are still waiting for this to happen. So we carry on needing to know that the old rules are divided between High Court and county court business. These are contained in Sch.1 and Sch.2 of the CPR. In drafting CPR Pt 70 there are some gaps, and it is therefore a question of the practitioner being familiar with CPR Pt 70, along with CPR Sch.1, RSC Orders 45 and 46, as well as CPR Sch.2, CCR Orders 25, and 26.

The general rules relating to the enforcement of judgments and orders are therefore contained in:

- CPR Pt 70—General Rules About Enforcement;
- CPR Sch.1—RSC Order 45—Enforcement of Judgments and Orders: General;
- CPR Sch.1—RSC Order 46—Writs of Execution General;
- CPR Sch.2—CCR Order 25—Enforcement of Judgments and Orders: General;
- CPR Sch.2—CCR Order 26—Warrants of Execution, Delivery and Possession.

When the changes envisaged by the Tribunals Courts and Enforcement Act 2007 are brought into place by supporting legislation, and the Rules Committee make the necessary changes to the CPR, we should have a comprehensive enforcement code for practitioners to follow. Until then, we must soldier on!

What does CPR Part 70 cover?

6–02 CPR Pt 70 was added as part of a series of new rules published in March 2002 to the existing rules, to unify procedures between the county court and the High Court. The introduction of this new rule followed the Lord Chancellor's review of enforcement referred to in Ch. 1 of this book.

CPR Pt 70, along with CPR Pts 71, 72, and 73, was introduced by the Civil Procedure (Amendment) Rules 2001, (SI 2001/2792). The notes to the White Book 2006 refer in the opening paragraph of Pt 70 to enforcement rules which were "unsatisfactory" and "in need of reform". CPR Pt 70 certainly sets the scene for how the enforcement regime under the new rules will operate—both now and in the future. It covers in summary:

CPR 70.1	The scope and interpretation of this rule
CPR 70.2	Methods of enforcing judgments or orders
CPR 70.3	Transfer of proceedings for enforcement
CPR 70.4	Enforcement of judgment or order by or against a non-party
CPR 70.5	Enforcement of awards of bodies other than the High Court and county courts
CPR 70.6	Effect of setting aside a judgment or order
The accompanying Practice Direction deals in summary with:	
70PD.1	Methods of enforcing judgments
70PD.2	Transfer of county court proceedings to another county court for enforcement
70PD.3	Enforcement of a High Court judgment or order in a county court
70PD.4	Enforcement of awards of bodies other than the High Court or a county court
70PD.5	Registration of awards and decisions in the High Court for enforcement
70PD.6	Interest on judgment debts
70PD.7	Payment of debt after issue of enforcement proceedings

Definitions under CPR Part 70—CPR 70.1

6–03 CPR r.70.1 establishes these definitions, which are repeated here. It can be confusing as to which party is which, particularly in relation to what are termed "reverse actions". This is where the defendant in the main proceedings wins a judgment against the claimant, perhaps on a counterclaim or on a costs order, and the defendant becomes the judgment creditor as the successful party in the litigation. Consequently, a quick reminder on definitions includes the terms:

- "Judgment Creditor", which means the person who has obtained or is entitled to enforce a judgment or order.
- "Judgment Debtor", which means the person against whom the judgment or order was given or made—and it can include a person against whom a costs order has been made.

6–04 CPR 70.1(d) defines a "judgment or order for the payment of money" to include a judgment or order for the payment of costs, although this expressly does not include the payment of money into court, which is dealt with elsewhere within the Rules (see CPR Pt 36).

To enforce a costs order the amount of costs payable must have been decided before enforcement begins. A successful party who wishes to obtain a payment prior to the assessment of costs should either:

- seek an amount to be paid on account of costs before detailed assessment (CPR 44.3(8)); or
- seek an interim costs certificate once a request for a detailed assessment hearing has been filed (CPR 47.15).

An order under either of these rules can be enforced as a "judgment or order for the payment of money".

If the court has ordered a payment into court (see r.3.1(3)), but the sum has not been paid, it is not possible to enforce the payment by execution or enforcement. Instead, an application must be made to impose a sanction such as striking out the claim or defence as appropriate, as a way to ensure the return of the money held in the court.

Methods of enforcing judgments or Orders—CPR 70.2 and CPR 70PD.1

6–05 The Practice Direction accompanying CPR 70 sets out the methods of enforcing judgments or orders for the payment of money. These include:

- Writ of fieri facias—covered by RSC Orders 46 and 47 in Sch.1 to the CPR.
- Warrant of execution—covered by CCR Order 26, which appears in Sch.2 to the CPR.
- Third party debt order—which appears in Pt 72 of the CPR.
- Charging order, stop order or stop notice—which appears in Pt 73 of the CPR.
- Attachment of earnings—which appears in CPR Sch.2, CCR Order 27.
- Appointment of a receiver—which appears in CPR Pt 69.
- Committal—as set out in CPR Sch.1 RSC Order 45, r.5 and Order 52, CPR Sch.2, CCR Orders 28 and 29.
- Sequestration—which appears in CPR Sch.1 RSC Order 45, r.5.

Only the first two methods of enforcement—the writ of fi fa and warrant of execution—are wholly administrative processes requiring no judicial decision, although judicial decisions can be frequent once the execution of the writ or warrant actually begins.

6–06 Practitioners are encouraged to be innovative and strategic in their choice of enforcement method. Warrants of execution are still the biggest form of enforcement in the civil courts, and yet they serve only limited value where the judgment debtor has goods available.

In the era of case management and computerised systems it is too easy just to let warrants be printed out or emailed to the Bulk Centre in Northampton, without any real thought being given as to the best method of enforcement.

The cost of unsuccessful enforcement is not only the court fee in seeking an unsuccessful application, but also the cost of the entire litigation. More and more we see practitioners weighing up the cost against the benefit of enforcement. This type of thinking inevitably leads to far more incisive decisions being made.

Is simultaneous enforcement permissible?

6–07 The answer is "yes", and this is expressly permitted under CPR 70.2(2)(b). In fact, prior to 2002 the position was less clear and practitioners were often confused as to whether simultaneous enforcement was permissible. It was therefore rarely used as a strategy to bring about successful recovery against the most recalcitrant of judgment debtors.

Simultaneous enforcement can mean seeking a charging order over the judgment debtor's property, whilst at the same time instructing High Court Enforcement Officers to levy execution on all available goods. It may involve not only seeking enforcement against property and goods, but also seeking to freeze the judgment debtor's bank account under an application for a third party debt order where these assets are available and sufficient information is known to make the application.

The only exception to simultaneous enforcement is that an attachment of earnings order cannot be pursued in conjunction with any other method of enforcement. If a judgment creditor is unsure as to which method of enforcement to employ to achieve the recovery of a money judgment, he should consider using the order to obtain information application, as provided under CPR Pt 71.

What provisions govern the transfer from the High Court to the county court? CPR 70.3 and CPR 70PD.2

6–08 Under CPR 70.3 a judgment creditor wishing to enforce a High Court judgment or order in a county court must apply to the High Court for an order transferring the proceedings to the county court in question.

Under CCR Order 25, r.13 provisions regarding the transfer of county court proceedings to the High Court for enforcement are set out and follow the provisions of the High Court and County Court Jurisdiction Order 1991, art.8 (as amended).

Why transfer from the county court to the High Court for enforcement?

6–09 The most common reason for transferring from the county court to the High Court is to use the services of a High Court Enforcement Officer to take legal control of goods belonging to the judgment debtor. As explained earlier in the book High Court Enforcement Officers can only enforce county court judgments over £600 and which do not arise out of an agreement regulated by the Consumer Credit Act 1974.

By virtue of s.42 of the County Courts Act 1984 (as amended by the Courts and Legal Services Act 1990) provision is made for specific judgments of the county court to be transferred to the High Court for enforcement. When the judgment is transferred to the High Court it becomes a judgment—as if it had been issued in the High Court—and must be treated as a judgment or order of the High Court for all purposes except the power to set aside, correct, vary or caution the judgment or order or to appeal against it. In relation to these various applications, which can often occur, the judgment continues to be a county court judgment and not a High Court judgment or order.

How can a party to proceedings enforce a judgment or order against a non-party?—CPR 70.4

6–10 Orders in favour of or against a non-party are apparently "rare" according to the rules of the Supreme Court, but do arise for example where a wasted costs order is given against a solicitor, or a solicitor undertakes to pay a non-party's costs. A non-party who has the benefit of an order does not need permission to enforce that order against the party ordered to pay. The same methods of enforcement are available as for any other enforceable judgment or order.

What is the effect of a successful application to set aside a judgment or order?—CPR 70.6

6–11 If a judgment or order is set aside, then the enforcement of that judgment or order must cease immediately, unless the court directs otherwise.

Of course, the issue to take in to account in these circumstances is the issue of costs, which can be significant and include the cost for obtaining the judgment and issuing enforcement process. The issue of who pays these costs should be addressed at the hearing of the application to set aside judgment. The court, using its discretion, may decide to set aside the judgment on terms as to who pays the wasted costs. The possible outcomes include:

- costs to be paid by the judgment debtor (the usual order when setting aside a regular judgment);
- costs to be paid by the judgment creditor (the usual order when setting aside an irregular judgment); or
- costs in the cause.

What do the rules say about interest on judgment debts?—CPR 70PD.6

6–12 The accompanying Practice Direction under CPR Pt 70 deals partly with interest on judgment debts. The Practice Direction is not self-contained due to the plethora of information surrounding interest on judgment debts in other parts of the Rules.

However, if a judgment creditor is claiming interest on a judgment debt within the Practice Direction, he must include in his application or request to issue enforcement proceedings details of the following:

- the amount of interest claimed and the sum on which it is claimed;

- the dates from and to which interest has accrued;
- the rate of interest which has been applied, and where more than one rate of interest has been applied, the relevant days and dates.

What interest applies to a judgment debt?

6–13 Interest on High Court judgments runs from the date of the judgment (being the date when judgment is pronounced and not the date when judgment is finally entered Parsons v Mather & Platt Ltd [1977] 1 W.L.R. 855; [1977] 2 ALL E.R. 715, approved in *Erven Warnink BV v J Townend & Sons (Hull) Ltd (No. 2)* [1982] 3 ALL E.R. 312, CA)) under s.17 of the Judgment Act 1838. The current rate is 8 per cent per annum, which has been in place since April 1, 1993 by virtue of the Judgment Debts (Rate of Interest) Order 1993 (SI 1993/564).

The corresponding county court statutory provision is s.74 of the County Courts Act 1984. The County Courts (Interest on Judgment Debts) Order 1991 specifies when interest may be claimed on a county court judgment. Under this provision (as amended by various statutory instruments) county court judgments carry interest from the date of judgment for sums over £5,000.

The rules on interest post-judgment can be summarised as follows:

- interest on a county court judgment ceases at judgment, unless there is provision for interest under a contract or under statute;
- interest on county court judgments over £5,000 continues from the date of judgment until the judgment is satisfied;
- interest on county court judgments between £600 and £5,000 that are transferred to the High Court for enforcement enjoy interest from the date of the certificate of transfer issued by the county court on Form N293A;
- statutory interest on a judgment or order for the payment of costs runs from the date of the judgment or order, not from the date of the final costs certificate quantifying the costs to be paid, unless some other date is set by the court *Hunt v RM Douglas (Roofing) Ltd* [1990] 1 A.C. 398; [1988] 3 ALL E.R. 823 HL, overruling *K v K* [1977] Fam. 39 CA).

A worked example of how to calculate interest is set out in the Appendix to this book.

It is fair to say that the current situation regarding interest on judgments is unsatisfactory. Furthermore, an opportunity to reform the position and to clarify the rules was missed when the new rules on enforcement were introduced in March 2002.

The continuing reform of enforcement under the Tribunals Courts and Enforcement Act 2007 again fails to address the issue.

What happens if a judgment debt is paid after the issue of enforcement proceedings?—CPR 70PD.7

6–14 Part 70 covers the situation if the judgment debt is paid after enforcement proceedings have been issued.

If payment is made after the judgment creditor has issued any application or request to enforce the debt, but either:

- before any writ or warrant has been executed;
- or before there has been any hearing of an application to deal with the enforcement of the judgment such as the final hearing of a charging order

then the judgment creditor must notify the court in writing, unless para. 7.2 of the Practice Direction applies, in which case the judgment creditor must notify the relevant enforcement officer in writing.

What about the other provisions of the other orders?

6–15 Turning to Schs to the CPR, it is worth reviewing at this point the headings of the other orders relating to enforcement.

Enforcement in the High Court is still governed by RSC orders, which appear in Sch.1 to the CPR

RSC Order 17	Interpleader	An interpleader affects the execution of goods
RSC Order 45	General	References are made throughout this book to this chapter
RSC Order 46	Writs of Execution Including Writs of Possession/Delivery/ Restitution/In Aid	Again, references are made throughout this book,
RSC Order 47	Writs of Fieri Facias	
RSC Order 52	Committal	

RSC Order 45 deals with enforcement generally. A judgment or order for payment of money (other than into court) may be enforced by a writ of fieri facias, third party debt order, a charging order or the appointment of a receiver.

A judgment or order to do or abstain from doing an act may be enforced by a writ of sequestration (with the permission of the court) or an order of committal.

A judgment or order for possession of land may be enforced by a writ of possession, as well as a judgment or order for the delivery of goods without the alternative of paying their value by a writ of specific delivery.

In each case, where RSC Order 45, r.5 applies, enforcement may also be by a writ of sequestration or an order of committal.

RSC Order 46 deals with writs of execution generally. Rules 2 and 3 set out the circumstances when permission to issue a writ is necessary. Rule 4 contains provisions for making an application for permission. Rule 5 deals with applications for permission to issue a writ of sequestration.

RSC Order 47 contains provisions concerning writs of fieri facias, dealt with extensively in this book under "High Court Business".

Forms of writs of execution may be used as follows:

- writs of fieri facias — Form No. 53 to No 63
- writs of delivery — Form No. 64 and No 65
- writs of possession — Form No. 66 and No 66A
- writ of sequestration — Form No. 67
- writ of restitution — Form No. 68
- writ of assistance — Form No. 69

6–16 With certain exceptions, writs of execution issued in the Royal Courts of Justice are executed by either an Authorised High Court Enforcement Officer or are directed to the "Enforcement Officers of England and Wales", in which case they are then allocated amongst the Authorised High Court Enforcement Officers appointed within England and Wales on a cab rank system managed by the National Information Centre for Enforcement, which is owned and operated by Registry Trust Limited.

County court enforcement orders under the County Court Rules follow a similar pattern:

CCR Order 22	Judgments and Orders	See this Chapter and also the Chapter involving a Request for a Certificate of Judgment
CCR Order 24	Summary Proceedings For the Recovery of Land	See Chapter 16 Enforcement of Orders for possession to recover Land
CCR Order 25	Enforcement of Judgments and Orders: General	See various chapters including this chapter
CCR Order 26	Warrants of Execution, Delivery and Possession	
CCR Order 27	Attachment of Earnings	
CCR Order 28	Judgment Summons	
CCR Order 29	Committal For Breach of Order or Undertaking	
CCR Order 33—Part 1	Interpleader Proceedings —Under Execution	

References to these Schs are made throughout this book. The majority of topics are represented by a chapter dedicated to the particular form of enforcement.

Chapter 7

Orders to Obtain Information—CPR Part 71

Introductory comments

7–01 Since the 10th edition of this book was published in 2006, The Tribunals, Courts and Enforcement Act 2007 has arrived on the statute book. Part 4 of the Act provides for changes to the way information will be obtained from judgment debtors in future, as and when the provisions of the Act are finally put into workable Rules. We are not there yet, and so for the moment we are still working with the current form of CPR Pt 71. However, a review of how the Rules will change is useful, as it shows willingness by government to grasp the nettle in the enforcement arena by securing information about a person's assets from government data rather than waiting for a judgment debtor to co-operate with the court.

The new approach to obtaining information

7–02 The thread of this new approach can be traced back to the government's White Paper, "Effective Enforcement", published in March 2003. At that time in its review of enforcement procedures in England and Wales it was stated that one of the key principles of successful enforcement measures in any civil justice system would be served by improving the quality and quantity of information on which to base informed and responsible decisions about enforcement. Even at that time, the White Paper confirmed the government's intention to seek methods to improve the quality of information that would be available to identify the assets that a judgment debtor might have available to satisfy an outstanding judgment.

An initial set of reforms to the then enforcement rules were implemented in May 2002, when the old "oral examination" procedure was replaced with the new "order to obtain information" (OTOI) rule under CPR Pt 71.

At that time the format of the questions to be asked of a judgment debtor was codified into forms EX140 (where the judgment debtor was an individual) and EX141 (where the judgment debtor was the officer of a company).

These forms were designed to capture every conceivable piece of information required to be able to enforce a judgment. Copies of the questionnaires can be found on the Court Service website at *http://www.hmcourts-service.gov.uk/courtfinder/forms* [Accessed October 14, 2010].

7–03 It is worth taking a moment to look at these forms to understand the breadth of information they cover. It is also worth benchmarking the range of information requested against the average credit application form or litigation checklist used prior to issuing a court claim. We believe it is fair to say that the majority of questions asked on these forms could have been asked at the time the contract was entered into. With that in mind, it is of course far easier to elicit information from a would-be customer at the start of a trading relationship than it is by the time a judgment has been entered against them. Naturally, not every judgment that is entered is based on a contract claim; consequently, that approach will not be available in every case, but in many cases such an approach could be taken to avoid having to seek the information in a less collaborative relationship after judgment has been entered.

Practitioners also need to consider their approach to these applications. Some will see them as a waste of time and effort, but used properly, perhaps by taking a more relaxed approach on costs, orders to obtain information hearings can be an effective way to elicit information that would otherwise not be forthcoming.

As with every application it requires preparation. There is scope even within the standard forms to ask the debtor to bring papers, books, statutory books, supporting vouchers and statements to court to verify the information being given as part of the procedure. Indeed, going back to the dicta of the old authority of *Republic of Costa Rica v Strousberg* [1880] 16 Ch. D. 8, oral examinations (as they then were) were said to be "not only to be an examination but to be a cross examination and that of the severest kind".

7–04 If used as a mere form-filling exercise, one is likely to get back a form filled with unhelpful and incomplete answers. Used as structure to a cross examination where the judgment debtor can see that the judgment creditor and his advisors have done their homework, then it is likely a better outcome will be obtained. Unfortunately, the approach of treating an order to obtain information application as a cross examination of the judgment debtor as to the assets he or she has available to meet a judgment debt has in many ways been lost, and these applications are now seen merely as an administrative process. Taken as such, they will only produce inaccurate and unhelpful responses from judgment debtors who do not want to co-operate with the court.

A better strategy is for the judgment creditor to treat the procedure as a stringent cross examination, which may require an investment of time, preparation and attendance, outside any scale of fixed costs for professional representation. This will underline to the judgment debtor that the enforcement of the judgment is a serious matter. Of course, there are pros and cons for all these arguments, and a stringent approach may not be appropriate in every case. Nevertheless, every so often a judgment creditor will seek to enforce a judgment based on a principle, which is where a robust approach to gathering information by cross examination fits with this application.

It is also worth noting that Pt 71 is not confined merely to the enforcement of money judgments. For example, a judgment debtor who has not complied with an order for the return of specific goods can be questioned under this part of the rules as to the whereabouts of those goods and his intention on how to return them.

In essence, practitioners really need to focus on how to use this process to achieve the outcome they are looking for, which must be a better way to enforce the judgment.

How does the application begin?

7–05 Under CPR 71.2 the judgment creditor may apply for an OTOI requiring a judgment debtor or the officer of a judgment debtor company to attend court to provide information about:

- the judgment debtor's means; or
- any other matter about which information is needed to be able to enforce the judgment or order.

The application for the OTOI can be made without notice. It will need to be issued in the court where the judgment was obtained, unless the proceedings have transferred to a different court. If this is the case, then the application must be issued in this other court.

The application notice is made on Form N316 (where the judgment debtor is a non-company) or N316A where the judgment debtor is a company and an officer of the company is required to attend the hearing.

7–06 The application notice must set out the information required in the accompanying Practice Direction, which includes:

- the name and address of the judgment debtor;
- the identity of the judgment which the judgment creditor is seeking to enforce;
- if the application relates to a money judgment, the amount presently owed by the judgment debtor under that judgment;
- where the judgment debtor is a company, then the name and address of the officer of that company whom the judgment creditor wishes to be ordered to attend court, together with his position in the company;
- if the judgment creditor requires the questioning to be conducted before a judge he must give his reasons in the application form—if that request is not made, then the application will be dealt with by a court officer without a hearing;
- if the judgment creditor wishes the judgment debtor or any other person who is to be questioned to produce specific documents at court, then these must be identified in the application;
- if the application is to enforce the judgment or order which is not for a payment of money, then the judgment creditor must identify the issues he wishes the judgment debtor or the officer of the company to be questioned about;
- on receiving the application, the court officer may refer the matter to a judge, and will refer it to a judge for consideration if the judgment creditor requests the judgment debtor or officer of the judgment debtor be questioned before a judge.

Provided all the requirements of the application notice are satisfied, then an order to attend court will be issued in terms of CPR Pt 71.6.

Response from the judgment debtor

7–07 On receiving the order as set out above, the judgment debtor or any person served with an OTOI must attend the court on the date and time specified. At that hearing the judgment debtor or person served with the OTOI must produce any documents referred to in the order.

A judgment creditor has the opportunity to not only use the application to gather information using the questionnaires mentioned at the start of this chapter, but also to ask the judgment debtor to verify said information with original documentary evidence. This may be the statutory books and accounts of a company, or it may involve asking a judgment debtor who alleges being in receipt of state benefits to produce benefit books to confirm the amount and frequency of any such income.

There is no limit on the information that can be requested, and so it is really a question of the judgment creditor using the questionnaire as a structure for the cross examination on assets, and asking for that information to be verified with appropriate forms of proof.

The OTOI contains a notice in the following terms:

"You must obey this order. If you do not, you may be sent to prison for contempt of court".

This wording is referred to as a "penal notice". Its presence in the order is important if the order needs to be enforced because the judgment debtor fails to comply with the order to obtain information. It is the possibility of being found in contempt of court by failing to obey the court's order which gives the OTOI procedure its formidable sanction of imprisonment. A judgment creditor wishing to underline the seriousness of non-payment, or non co-operation with a court order, can use this sanction as a way of reinforcing the need for the judgment debtor to provide the necessary information without further delay.

Where does the hearing have to take place?

7–08 The venue of the court where the examination will be conducted is dealt with in PD71, Para. 2.1. The OTOI procedure provides that the judgment debtor or other person to be questioned should attend the county court within the district in which he resides or carries on business, unless the judge decides otherwise.

What happens if the judgment debtor refuses to answer questions?

7–09 A judgment debtor who does not answer the questions can be held in contempt of court. The OTOI application should therefore be seen as an important strategic arm of the enforcement regime for judgment creditors.

If the procedure is carried out in an administrative fashion then one can expect administrative type answers. If one takes it as a serious and formidable application which threatens a judgment debtor's liberty for non-compliance then the results from the preparation and questioning will result in meaningful answers which can be used to take further and appropriate enforcement action.

Does the judgment debtor have to give information about overseas assets?

7–10 A judgment debtor will be required to give information about any assets owing to him. This includes full information about his assets outside the jurisdiction as part of the examination process (*Interpool Ltd v Galani* [1988] Q.B. 738; [1987] 3 W.L.R. 1042 CA (Civ Div).

Can former officers of a company be examined?

7–11 In interpreting identical words in a previous rule, it was held that an "officer" included "former officers" of a company (*Societe Generale du Commerce et de L'industrie en France v Johann Maria Farina & Co* [1904] 1 K.B. 794).

Can the examination process be repeated?

7–12 Under the old oral examination regime was case law indicating that a further examination could be held in special circumstances. However, the new Rule places no restriction on repeat examinations and in so doing no doubt relies on modern-day CPR "case management and cost" powers to prevent abuse of the opportunity to re-question the judgment debtor about available assets.

Does the OTOI order have to be issued?

7–13 Despite the wording of the rule which requires an OTOI application to be issued, the court officer retains the power to refer any cases of doubt to the judge, who in turn can refuse to issue or require a further hearing where it is considered that the application is misconceived, e.g. because the time for payment has not yet expired (see *White Son & Pill v Stennings* [1911] 2 K.B. 418).

How does the OTOI have to be served?

7–14 The Civil Procedure (Amendment No. 4) Rules 2001 (SI 2001/2792) introduced new rules on the service of an OTOI application. The order must be served personally on the person ordered to attend the court, not less than 14 days before the hearing. If the order is to be served by the judgment creditor he must inform the court not less than seven days before the date of the hearing if he has been unable to serve it.

The new rule departs from the previous oral examination regime by requiring the judgment creditor to organise the service of the

OTOI instead of using the services of the county court bailiff service. Service is now only available through the county court bailiff service where the judgment creditor is a litigant in person. In all other cases, personal service must be made and paid for by the judgment creditor or someone acting on his behalf by virtue of para. 3 of PD71.

The obvious consequence of this is that it increases the cost of the OTOI because the cost of the process server must be met by the judgment creditor and the cost of this disbursement will not be recoverable from the judgment debtor.

Service by an alternative method of service is set out in CPR. r.6. Usually, there will have to be an attempt of personal service before the court can make an order allowing another form of service.

What costs are allowable on an OTOI?

7–15 Fixed costs for the application are prescribed by CPR Pt 45 In addition, CPR Pt 45.5 prescribes a fee of £15 for effecting personal service, which may go some way to reducing the cost of instructing a process server.

This figure is disproportionately low, as an enquiry agent/process server will usually charge more than this and the sum is small recompense for the judgment creditor's time in seeking service of the document.

Do travelling expenses have to be paid to the judgment debtor?

7–16 The judgment debtor or other person ordered to attend the OTOI hearing must, within seven days of being served with the order, ask the judgment creditor to pay him a sum reasonably sufficient to cover his travelling expenses to and from the court.

If this request is made, the judgment creditor must pay this sum (see CPR 71.4). This rule replaces the old rule on "conduct money" and was introduced again by the Civil Procedure (Amendment No. 4) Rules 2001 (SI 2001/2792).

The judgment creditor's affidavit in support of the application

7–17 The judgment creditor must file an affidavit, or more evidence if required by the person who served the order (unless it was served by the court, in which case the court bailiff prepares an affidavit), giving details of how and when the OTOI was served and confirming that:

- the person ordered to attend court had not requested payment of his travelling expenses; or
- the judgment creditor had paid a sum in accordance with such a request; and
- stating how much of the judgment debt remains unpaid.

The judgment creditor must either file the evidence as to the service and position on travelling expenses not less than two days before the hearing or produce the evidence at the hearing.

Proof that the judgment debtor has been served is essential to the success of the application.

Conduct of the hearing

7–18 The person ordered to attend court will be questioned on oath. Again, this point needs to be underlined to judgment debtors as a precursor to the application even being made. Many judgment debtors will not appreciate that they will be asked to stand in the court witness box and give their evidence on oath or make an affirmation. A judgment creditor who wants to avoid a full hearing should paint a very clear picture to a judgment debtor of the nature of this type of hearing.

The questioning will be carried out by a court officer, unless the court has ordered the hearing should be before a judge. Again, as part of a strategy one should consider whether the application should always be requested before a judge on the basis that without making the request the matter will be dealt with by a member of the court staff. It is far more intimidating for judgment debtors to have to state their affairs to a judge, who in turn will be recording their answers, than perhaps an administrative officer of the court staff.

7–19 More importantly, the judgment creditor or his representative may attend the hearing and ask the questions where the questioning takes place before a court officer. Once more, this is a way of strengthening the procedure to ensure that accurate and appropriate answers are given. The judgment creditor's representative or judgment creditor himself can attend court and conduct the questioning personally if the hearing is before a judge, which reinforces the seriousness of the application to a judgment debtor.

In the commentary to CPR 71.6 the White Book Service does state that all the questioning must be carried out by a court officer, and only if there is difficulty which requires the greater authority of a judge will the examination be heard by a judge (see para. 2.2 of PD71). The judgment creditor may attend before the court officer but must attend and conduct the questioning if the hearing is before a judge. The meaning of "judge" includes Masters, district judges and deputies, and of course what must be borne in mind are the dicta of the case of *Republic of Costa Rica v Strousberg* [1880], where the hearing is to be conducted as a "cross examination of the severest kind".

Questioning by a court officer follows the standard format of completing Forms EX140 or EX141, as prescribed by CPR PD71. These forms will not be used when questioning is conducted by the judgment creditor before the judge, although the judgment creditor is free to use these forms as a structure for the questions to be asked, which will reduce preparation time because of the forms' structure and comprehensive nature.

Adjournment of the hearing

7–20 If the hearing is adjourned for any reason, the court will give its directions as to the manner in which the notice of the new hearing is to be served on the judgment debtor.

The hearing may be adjourned because the judgment debtor needs to produce further documents or because there is some irregularity in the service of the order.

A good practice is to give the date and time of the new hearing to the judgment debtor before leaving court. Alternatively, the judgment debtor or person required to come to court to give any further information should be asked to agree to postal service of the notice of the new date, to prevent the expense of serving papers again by using a process server.

What happens if the judgment debtor fails to comply with the OTOI?

7–21 If a person subject to an OTOI application fails to attend court, and refuses at the hearing to take the oath or to answer any question, or indeed fails to comply with the order to give that information in any way, then the court will refer the matter to a High Court Judge or a circuit judge.

That judge, subject to certain provisions within the Rule, may make a committal order against that person for failing to obey the court's order to give the information.

A committal order for failing to attend court *cannot* be made unless the judgment creditor has complied with:

- CPR 71.4 in relation to travelling expenses; and
- CPR 71.5 in relation to filing the appropriate affidavit dealing with the issue of service of the OTOI application.

If the committal order is subsequently made, the judge will direct that the order be suspended *provided* the judgment debtor (or the person against whom the OTOI is made) attends court at the time and place specified and complies with all the terms of this subsequent OTOI and the original OTOI application.

7–22 The order will also state that if the person fails to comply with an OTOI which has been suspended, that person must be brought back before a judge to consider whether a committal order should be discharged.

The most common of the three types of non-compliance listed in CPR 71.8(1) is the judgment debtor's failure to attend court to be examined. The examination itself would have been before a court officer or district judge. That person certifies the judgment debtor's non-attendance as set out in PD71 para. 8. The High Court judge or circuit judge in reliance on that certificate then makes a committal order under CPR 71.8(2), but suspends that order *provided* the judgment debtor attends on a subsequent occasion. If the judgment debtor complies, then the examination takes place and the suspended committal order is discharged.

If, however, the judgment debtor fails to attend the suspended committal order, a warrant for his arrest will then be issued (see PD71 para. 8). Nonetheless, instead of being taken to prison to serve the committal sentence he will be brought before the court pursuant to CPR 71.8(4)(b). This hearing can be before a Master or district judge, as provided under PD71 para. 8.4. The judge's task is then to consider whether the committal order should be discharged, perhaps because of some irregularity, and in practice the order is invariably discharged because the debtor agrees to be examined there and then, thus completing the purpose of CPR Pt 71.

If for any reason the judge decides not to discharge the committal order because the judgment debtor refuses to answer any question or take the oath, then a warrant of committal is issued immediately (see PD71 Para. 8.6). The judgment debtor is then sent to prison to serve the sentence. The judge must be satisfied beyond reasonable doubt (as required under PD71 para. 8) that the judgment debtor has failed to comply with the original order to attend court and the terms of the suspended committal order, both of which have been served on the judgment debtor.

Human rights issues in relation to orders to obtain information

7–23 Some commentators have suggested that the new procedure is not compliant with the European Convention of Human Rights. There is nothing in European jurisprudence to prevent civil courts having proper machinery in place for the purpose of enforcing its orders.

The new procedure is clearly intended to be ECHR-compliant, and it is submitted to this effect. In practice, actual committal to prison is rare, as the bringing of the judgment debtor to court is invariably sufficient to complete the purpose of CPR Pt 71. It must be remembered that the sanction of a prison sentence is not in relation to non-payment of the debt; it is in relation to failing to obey the order of the court to give the necessary information.

The effect of the TCEA 2007 on Part 71

7–24 CPR Pt 71 and the procedure for obtaining an order to obtain information are not affected by the implementation of Pt 4 of the TCEA 2007.

What the new Act does do is to introduce two new procedures to assist the judgment creditor in enforcing the court's judgment. These are based on:

- an "information order", which is served on a third party;
- a "departmental information request", which is served on certain government departments.

These additional procedures will allow a judgment creditor to verify, via third parties, any information provided by a judgment debtor or, in the case of government departments, to go to those departments directly for the information.

What is the difference between the two new procedures?

7–25 In relation to information orders, these apply to the private sector. As such, once served, the organisation must respond with the information as part of the court process.

Departmental information requests are different in that the court is making a request to a government department or public sector body, rather than serving them with an order to comply.

The difference is subtle, but whilst the court can compel a private sector body to comply, it can only request a public sector body to supply the necessary information.

How will the procedures work in practice?

7–26 The new procedures will only apply where there is a judgment debt to enforce. In either case it is not the judgment creditor who actually makes the application, instead, and new to enforcement procedures, the procedure is initiated by the court (see s.96(2) TCEA 2007).

The judgment creditor would apply to the court under s.95 of the TCEA 2007 for one of the procedures to be followed, be it either a departmental information request or an information order. It is then for the court to decide (see s.96 (3) of the new Act) whether it needs to apply for a departmental information request or an information order to be able to fulfil the judgment creditor's application. The court therefore has to exercise its discretion one way or the other, and it will only do so if it is satisfied that it will help with the judgment creditor's application.

How will the information be used?

7–27 The court can use the information received under either the information order or the departmental information request to provide a judgment creditor with information about the most appropriate action to be taken in enforcing a judgment debt (see TCEA 2007 s.101(3)). However, the court will only have this power once regulations are drafted and implemented to control the way in which this will happen (see TCEA 2007 s.101(6). At the time of preparing this book, no such regulations appear to be even in preparation to support this purpose.

As and when information is supplied, the court actually responsible for the enforcement method will be able to use the information. Information can be passed to another court that is in control of the enforcement action if the action is proceeding elsewhere (see TCEA 2007 s.101(5)).

The court can use information from either type of application to make further applications, if so required (see TCEA 2007 s.101(2)).

How will the procedure be commenced?

7–28 To begin an application for either an information order or a departmental information request the judgment creditor will have to make an application to the court under s.95(1) of the TCEA 2007. This provides that a person who is the judgment creditor in relation to the judgment debt may apply to the High Court or a county court for information about what kind of action it would be appropriate to take to recover a particular debt. Again, at the time of writing this book the new Act leaves it open for the procedure to be set down by regulations which have yet to be introduced.

Once the judgment creditor has made the application, then s.96 of the new Act gives the court authority to make either a departmental information request or an information order.

In doing so, the court must notify the judgment debtor that it intends to make either a departmental information request or an information order—and it must inform the judgment debtor that they do not have the right to object (TCEA 2007 s.96(4)).

How much information can be disclosed to the judgment creditor?

7–29 In making either a departmental information request or an information order the court may disclose as much information as it feels necessary to aid the third party being asked for the information to respond to the application. This specifically includes disclosing the identity of the judgment debtor (see TCEA 2007 s.96(6)).

What is the nature of an information order?

7–30 Information orders are governed by s.98 of the new Act. The objective is to obtain information from third parties such as banks or building societies about available deposits which could be used to discharge a judgment debt.

These orders are more than likely to be used as an aid to the process of applying for a third party debt order (see CPR Pt 72). Information about an available deposit would make the outcome of a Third Party Debt Order that much more successful if it could be verified that a known deposit was available. At present, the judgment creditor has only a number of limited ways to ascertain if a judgment debtor's bank is in funds, from which a final Third Party Debt Order can be discharged.

The process will be that when the court sends the order through to the third party then the third party will be ordered to disclose the required information to the relevant court.

It is expected that information orders are only likely to be made by the court where the judgment debtor refuses to give any information about a deposit held by a third party or there is some doubt as to the usefulness of the information provided.

If the third party served with the information order does not have the information required, it will be protected from any breach of obligations under s.100 of the TCEA 2007.

7–31 It is hoped that the new regulations will impose a time limit on how quickly the third party must respond, and so we wait to see what the new regulations will look like in relation to this new form of enforcement.

It can be anticipated that on occasions there will be a failure to disclose some or all of the information that is required. The Act sets out in s.100(2) a number of "permitted reasons" as to when such a failure occurs. These include:

- the information discloser (i.e. the third party) does not have the information or hold the information;
- the information discloser is unable to ascertain whether the information is held because the identity of the judgment debtor is not clear;
- the disclosure of the information would involve a level of unreasonable effort or expense.

If an information discloser wishes to rely on a "permitted reason" under s.100(2), then a certificate must be filed at the court, which must state the reason why the information has not been disclosed as well as giving the permitted reason(s) for any failure to disclose the information.

How can information be used from an information order?

7–32 Under s.101(9) of the TCEA 2007 the,

> "use or disclosure of information in accordance with this section is not to be taken to breach any restriction on the use or disclosure of information (however imposed)".

Information disclosed under these provisions does not breach any confidentiality obligations, which in turn gives protection to the information discloser and the court, which can disclose the requested information without further repercussions.

We can expect when the supporting regulations are passed that these will indicate how judgment debtor information can be used or disclosed, in order to provide the judgment creditor with information about the kind of enforcement action it will be appropriate to take in court to recover the judgment debt. After all, that was the whole purpose of these new enforcement measures.

We can also expect the supporting regulations to prescribe the duties of information disclosers, who would appear to have a very onerous duty in the way in which they process information requests, so that this approach ties in with the obligations to process data fairly under the Data Protection Act 1998.

What happens if data is not handled with care?

7–33 Section 102 of the TCEA 2007 makes it an offence to use disclosed information under an information order, unless it can be shown it has been used in one of the following ways:

- The information has been used in accordance with an enactment or order of the court and is in accordance with regulations.
- The information has been used for the purposes of any proceedings before the court and is in accordance with regulations.
- The information has previously been lawfully disclosed to the public.
- The information has been used in accordance with the rules of court that comply with regulations which have yet to be published.
- The information has been used to provide the judgment creditor with information about what kind of enforcement action (if any) it will be appropriate to take in court to recover the judgment debt (see TCEA 2007 s.101).

TCEA 2007 s.102 also provides a defence for any person charged with the unlawful use or disclosure of information, to prove that he or she reasonably believed that the use or disclosure was lawful.

If this cannot be shown, then a person may be found guilty of an offence under this section, and risks:

- on indictment, imprisonment of up to two years and/or a fine; or
- on summary conviction, imprisonment up to 12 months and/or a fine not exceeding the statutory maximum.

Are these provisions retrospective?

7–34 Sections 95 to 104 of the TCEA 2007 are indeed retrospective and will apply to any judgment debt once the new Act is in force, regardless of when the judgment debt became payable or recoverable (see s.105(1) of the TCEA 2007).

How do departmental information requests differ from information orders?

7–35 Unlike information orders in which information has to be produced by the third party, a departmental information request is just that; it is a request. It will be made to "the Minister of the Crown or other person, who is in charge of the department" under s.97(2) of the TCEA 2007. Such a request, however, cannot be made to the Scottish Administration, Northern Ireland Office or the Welsh Assembly (see TCEA 2007 s.97(6)).

The recipient of the request being a government department "may" decide to disclose to the court any information it considers necessary to comply with the request.

Under s.99(2) of the TCEA 2007 it is implicit that a government department may exercise its discretion as to whether or not it will provide the information requested. We will have to see how government departments are resourced to be able to comply with the process for acting on departmental information requests. At present, though, there is no indication of the likely timescale in which such a request may need to be processed. Naturally, any delay as far as enforcement proceedings are concerned could be costly if a government department is not compelled to respond through internal service levels transparent to judgment creditors.

What will be the procedure?

7–36 Under s.97(3) and (4) the Minister of the Crown may provide the "prescribed information", but the extent of this information has yet to be set out in regulations.

The government body likely to be disclosing such information is Her Majesty's Customs and Revenue. We can anticipate that the prescribed information will probably include information about a taxpayer in terms of their employment, their annual pay, their level of tax and other matters which can be disclosed from their tax coding.

What duty is imposed on the information disclosure?

7–37 Under s.99(2) any information considered necessary to comply with the request can be disclosed by the information discloser.

The information discloser will have an opinion as to what is "necessary" to comply with the wording of the request. Of course, a government department may decide that it does not have to provide the information because it is not necessary.

It has been suggested that there may be no remedy against this sort of decision except by making an application to a body such as the local government commissioner.

Either way, the court cannot make a departmental information request to the Commissioners for HMRC until regulations have been put in place. Whatever regulations are made will mean that when information is provided, these will not breach the Data Protection Act (see s.101(3)) of the TCEA 2007.

If information is obtained from HMRC, then a judgment creditor will also have to obtain the consent of HMRC before that information can be used to recover a judgment debt. Yet again, the current wording of the Act is silent as to how that procedure will work in practice.

What offences can be committed?

7–38 The same offences as for information orders can be committed by any person who fails to handle the information disclosed under a departmental information request with the necessary care.

Is the departmental information request retrospective?

7–39 Transitional provisions for departmental information requests are the same as for information orders.

Chapter 8

Third Party Debt Proceedings—CPR Part 72

Introductory comments

8–01 The reforms of March 2002 swept away the familiar term "garnishee proceedings" and replaced it with the slightly more longwinded term "third party debt order", or "TPDO", as we shall refer to it throughout this chapter.

Although CPR Pt 72 is a replacement for the old garnishee procedure, both share the same basic purpose, which is to take a payment from any money owed to the judgment debtor by his own debtors, whether that be his bank or building society, trade debtors or his own judgment debtor.

Where the judgment debtor is owed money by a third party the judgment creditor can obtain the TPDO so that the judgment debtor's debtor, being the "third party", should pay the judgment debtor's judgment creditor instead of the judgment debtor. The order is obtained without notice on an interim basis. A hearing then follows when the court decides whether or not to make the TPDO into a final order.

8–02 The most popular use of this method of enforcement is against a bank account which is in credit (as the money in the account is, of course, a debt due by the bank to its customer). As a result, a judgment creditor who has the bank details of the judgment debtor (possibly as a result of obtaining information pursuant to CPR Pt 71) can obtain a TPDO against the bank. However, there are pitfalls to this and TPDOs remain an unpopular method of enforcement compared to other methods such as charging orders, attaching earnings and executing against goods.

The difficulties in successfully achieving a final order so far as the judgment creditor is concerned involve the gathering of precise information as to the debt or debts owed to the judgment debtor, to enable the court to make a final order. Data protection legislation means that the gathering of information through a one-off telephone call to the judgment debtor's bank is now not possible, and information must be gained from sources in the public domain, or volunteered by the judgment debtor either during proceedings or as part of the background to the incursion of the debt, say in a credit application form.

Is a debt due to the judgment debtor by a third party?

8–03 To enable a TPDO application to succeed, the relationship between the judgment creditor and judgment debtor must exist between the judgment debtor and the third party. If a judgment debtor can sue his debtor for an outstanding amount and recover it, then, on the face of it, there is a debt which can become the subject of a TPDO. Case law in this area has, of course, developed to define what is and is not an attachable debt. The old cases, which are numerous, remain relevant subject to the application of CPR Pt 1 to deal with any case justly. Therefore, the court can apply the case authorities to modern situations, provided it considers and applies the principles of the overriding objective of the CPR.

To succeed, the judgment creditor must establish there is a debt "due" to the judgment debtor by the third party. In the case of a bank account the situation appears clear. There are other types of debt which can be attached *provided* that certain conditions are met. For example, in the case of a building contract in a form published by the Royal Institute of British Architects, (RIBA) where the builder is paid on the issue of the certificate from the architect, money in the hands of the building owner cannot be attached until the architect issues the necessary certificate, as the "debt" is not due to the builder until that time, and then only for the amount mentioned in that certificate (*Dunlop & Rankin Ltd v Hendall Steel Structure Pitchers (Garnishees)* [1957] 1 W.L.R. 1102; [1957] 3 All E.R. 344).

Nor can a TPDO accelerate the time for payment of the debt. Where the money is not due, there is nothing to be attached (*Webb v Stenton* [1882–1883] L.R.11 Q.B.D. CA 518; *Re Greenwood* [1901] 1 Ch. 887 CA).

8–04 It is therefore essential that the debt should be in existence at the date of the interim TPDO (which is discussed below). The debt does not need to be payable immediately (see *O'Driscoll v Manchester Insurance Committee* [1915] 3 K.B. 499 at 515, CA), and in such a case the proper order is for "the debt to be attached forthwith", but for the payment to the judgment creditor to be postponed to the date when the debt would have been paid to the judgment debtor (see *Tapp v*

Jones (1874–1875) L.R. 10 Q.B. 591 at 593, per Blackburn J. and *Re Cowans' Estate, Rapier v Wright* (1880) L.R. 14 Ch. D. 638 at 643).

The sum which is the subject of the TPDO must also be recognised as a debt. In the case of *Israelson v Dawson (Port of Manchester Insurance Co Ltd))* [1933] 1 K.B. 301, CA, it was held that an agreement of an insurance company to indemnify the assured against liability for damages, for which judgment had been given against him, did not constitute a debt. The expression "debt . . . accruing due" in CPR 72.2(1)(a) does not include any sum which may become a debt, however probable and however soon it may be a debt (see *Webb v Stenton* (1883) L.R. 11 Q.B.D. 518 at 522 CA and *Howell v Metropolitan District Railway Co* (1881–82) L.R. 19 Ch. D. 508).

It has been held that money payable out of the proceeds of the sale of property, which then vests in trustees on certain trusts when it comes into their hands, is not a "debt accruing" within the meaning of the Rule. A trustee is not a debtor to the beneficiary of a trust unless he has, or but for some fault of his might have had, in his hands money which it is his duty to hand over to the beneficiary (per Lindley L.J. in *Webb v Stenton* (1883) L.R. 11 Q.B.D. 518 at 522 CA).

Salary accruing but not due is not a debt (see *Hall v Pritchett* (1877) L.R. 3 Q.B.D. 215 and *Mapleson v Sears* (1911) 105 L.T. 639). The only way to "attach" these assets before they have become "debts" is by applying for the appointment of a receiver.

A judgment creditor cannot use a TPDO to stand in a better position as regards a third party than the judgment debtor, as "he can only obtain what the judgment debtor could honestly give him" (see *Re General Horticultural Co Ex p Whitehouse* (1886) L.R. 32 Ch. D. 512).

What types of "debt" can be attached?

8–05

Rent	Rent due can be attached (*Mitchell v Lee* [1867] L.R. 2 Q.B. 259), but although rent accrues from day to day under the Apportionment Act 1870, it is not attachable until it becomes payable by the tenant (*Barnett v Eastman* (1898) 67 L.J. Q.B. 517). Subject to the amount of the judgment debt and the rent payable, the more usual way to attach rent is the appointment of a receiver under CPR Pt 69, but these applications are so rare that judicial statistics do not even recall the number of applications for the appointment of a receiver, which are made in the courts.
Joint judgment against two or more persons	A judgment creditor with a judgment against two or more persons can attach a debt owing to any of his judgment debtors (see *Miller v Mynn* [1859] 23 L.J. Q.B. 324).

Debt of unascertained amount	The fact that the amount of a debt or accruing debt is not ascertainable will not prevent an interim TPDO from being made (*Lucy v Wood* [1884] W.N. 58; *De Pass v Capital & Industries Corporation* [1891] 1 Q.B. 218). In *O'Driscoll v Manchester Insurance Committee* [1915] 3 K.B. 499, money payable to a doctor by the Insurance Committee was held to be attachable after receipt by the committee of funds received by them to pay the doctor even though the precise sum due to the doctor had not been ascertained.
Debt already paid by cheque	Where the judgment debtor has been paid by a cheque which is stopped by the third party upon being served with an interim TPDO, there will be an attachable debt (*Coyne v Hale* [1878] 3 Q.B.D. 371). However, the third party is not under any duty to stop a cheque already sent by him at the time of service of the interim TPDO and if he does not do so there will be no debt to be attached (*Elwell v Jackson* [1885] 1 T.L.R. 454).
Executors and personal representatives	Where a third party who was indebted to the judgment debtor dies, an order can be served upon his executors or personal representatives but must be directed to them as executors/administrators and not personally (*Stevens v Phelips* [1875] L.R. 10 Ch. 417).
Bill of exchange before maturity	Money which will become payable by a third party when a bill of exchange matures is attachable. The order will suspend execution until maturity and restrain the judgment debtor by injunction from dealing with the bill in the interim (*Hyam v Freeman* [1890] 35 S.J. 87).
Funds derived under international treaty	In *Philipp Brothers Ltd v Republic of Sierra Leone* [1995] 1 Lloyd's Rep. 289, the judgment debtor held monies in a bank account representing funds provided by the EC under a programme of financial aid. It was held that the transaction under which the judgment debtor received the funds was governed by international treaty and not by municipal law, and as a result obligations arising under the treaty were not justiciable in an English court and no trust or other equitable right under English law arose. The account was a debt due from the bank, and the garnishee order absolute (now a TPDO) was upheld.
Wages and persons	Wages cannot be attached by a TPDO. Instead, the alternative procedure of an Attachment of Earnings Order under the Attachment of

Wages and persons	Earnings Act 1971, CPR Sch.2, CCR Order 27 must be pursued.
Debts due from the Crown	CPR Pt 72 cannot be used against the Crown as the third party. An alternative procedure is provided by the Crown Proceedings Act 1947: Section 27 and is governed by Sch. I RSC O.77, r.16 and Sch. II CCR O.42, r.14.
Assigned Debts	Where a judgment debtor has assigned the debt to a fourth party before the interim order is served there is no debt due to the judgment debtor which can then be attached by a TPDO, even though the order was served before the third party had notice of the assignment (*Holt v Heatherfield Trust Ltd* [1942] 2 K.B. 1).
Debts recoverable outside the jurisdiction	In *Kuwait Oil Tanker Co SAK v Qabazard* [2003] UKHL 31 the judgment creditor sought to attach debts due to the judgment debtor from a Swiss Bank with a London branch. However, the judgment debtor had an account in Switzerland, not London, and the House of Lords held that as the third party proceedings were enforcement against a debt due in Switzerland, and under Art.16(5) of the Lugano Convention, the Swiss courts had exclusive jurisdiction and the TPDO order could not be made (see also *Societe Eram Shipping Co Limited v Compagnie Internationale de Navigation* [2003] UKHL 30; [2003] 3 W.L.R. 21).
Debt due to judgment debtor and another	In *Hirshcorn v Evans* [1938] 2 K.B. 801, it was held that it was not possible to obtain a garnishee order (now a TPDO) against a bank account in the joint names of the judgment debtor and his wife. Although this authority was looked at in the Government's review of enforcement, the White Paper "Effective Enforcement" suggests that the position will remain the same and it will not be possible to attach joint bank accounts.

What types of debt have been held to be "unattachable"?

8–06

A claim for unliquidated damages	*Johnson v Diamond* (1855) 11 Exch. 73; *Jones v Thompson* (1858) E.B. & E.63
A legacy in the hands of an executor	A legacy will not be attachable unless there has been an account stated which would constitute the legacy as a legal debt in the hands of a legal debtor (*McDowall v Hollister* (1855) 25 L.T.O.S. 185)
Money in court under a judgment	*Dolphin v Layton* (1879) 4 Q.P.D. 130, approved in *Spence v Coleman* [1901] 2 K.B. 199, CA (but see para. CPR 72.10)
A dividend distributable amongst creditors in the hands of an official receiver	*Prout v Gregory* (1889) 24 Q.B.D. 281
A debt due to a judgment debtor and another who is not a party to the judgment	*Macdonald v Tacquah Gold Mines Co* (1884) 13 Q.B.D. 535
Money which the judgment debtor and his wife have in a joint bank account, even though either has authority to draw on the account	*Hirschhorn v Evans* [1938] 2 K.B. 801, [1938] 3 All E.R. 491, CA
The future income of the tenant for life of a trust fund	*Webb v Stenton* (1883) L.R. 11 Q.B.D. 518, CA
Salary accruing, but not actually due	*Hall v Pritchett* (1877) 3 Q.B.D. 215
The pay of an officer	*Apthorpe v Apthorpe* (1886) 35 W.R. 728, CA and as to the pay or allowances due to a member of HM Forces, see s.203 of the Army Act 1955
The pension of an officer, though given solely in respect of past services	*Lucas v Harris* (1886) 18 Q.B.D. 127
Fees due from a solicitor to counsel	*Wells v Wells* [1914] P. 157, CA
Money in the London banking account of a foreign state	Such monies cannot be the subject of a TPDO unless the judgment creditor of the state can show that the money is solely intended to meet liabilities incurred in commercial transactions *Alcom Ltd v Republic of Colombia* [1984] A.C. 580, [1984] 2 All E.R. 6, HL

Seamen's wages	By s.34 of the Merchant Shipping Act 1995, seamen's wages cannot be attached
Salary or compensation of customs officers	By s.7(1) of the Customs and Excise Management Act 1979 the salary or compensation of customs officers cannot be attached and see Vol. 12(2) *Halsbury's Statutes* (1994, 4th Edn—Reissue "Customs and Excise)

Does the third party have to be within the jurisdiction of the court?

8–07 CPR 72.1 provides for the judgment creditor to obtain an order for the payment of money which a third party, who is within the jurisdiction of the courts of England and Wales, owes to the judgment debtor.

There is no provision to make an order under this rule if the third party is not within the jurisdiction. For a definition of the jurisdiction, see CPR 2.3. However, even the temporary physical presence of the third party within the jurisdiction at the time of the making of the interim order will be sufficient to enable a TPDO to be made. Alternatively, a third party may agree to submit to the jurisdiction of the court for the purpose of the application, and that agreement will be sufficient to enable an interim order to be made, even if the third party then leaves the jurisdiction before the final order is made (see *SCF Finance Co Ltd v Masri (No. 3)* [1987] Q.B. 1028; [1987] 2 W.L.R. 81 CA (Civ Div).

8–08 There is no requirement that the third party debt must be properly recoverable within the jurisdiction. As a matter of discretion, though, the Court will not make a TPDO where, although the third party is within the jurisdiction, the debt itself is recoverable outside the jurisdiction, in order to expose the third party to the risk of having to pay the debt twice over (*Martin v Nadel* [1906] 2 K.B. 26; *SCF Finance Co Ltd v Masri (No. 3)* [1987] QB 1028; *Interpool Ltd v Galani* [1988] Q.B. 738). To resist an order being made against it, the third party must show that the risk of paying twice is "real" or "substantial" (*Swiss Bank Corp v Boehmische Industrial Bank* [1923] 1 K.B. 673, although in this case, the court found that the perceived risk was too vague to establish the possibility of a double payment).

It is an integral feature of third party debt proceedings that on compliance the third party discharges the judgment creditor's debt from the extent of the liability owed to the judgment debtor. In the case of *Societe Eram Shipping Co Ltd v Compagnie Internationale de Navigation* [2003] UKHL 30; [2003] 3 W.L.R. 21, the House of Lords overruled the Court of Appeal by finding that a Hong Kong Bank with a branch in London was held to be "within the jurisdiction" and could therefore make the payment as required under the TPDO.

It is interesting to note that much of the case law developing around TPDOs involves an international flavour, and although the method of enforcement remains unpopular in the bulk debt collection industry it clearly has a place where international proceedings involve bank accounts.

What is the effect of the Limitation Act on the TPDO procedure?

8–09 Under s.24(1) of the Limitation Act 1980 there was a provision that an action cannot be brought on any judgment after the expiration of six years from the date on which that judgment became enforceable. The exception to this is where an extension is granted, allowing the judgment creditor's application.

In *Westacre Investments Inc v Jugoimport SPDR Holding Co Ltd* [2008] EWCA 801 (comm.) the commercial court considered the longevity of third party debt orders.

The facts of the case concerned an award against defendants in Switzerland, who had an English judgment registered against them in March 1998. The judgment creditor sought to enforce this award in Singapore in October 2004. This, of course, would be outside the usual six-year period, so the judgment debtors sought to set the judgment aside. The Singapore Court directed that a declaration should be sought from the English Court as follows:

> "On the assumption that there was a third party within the jurisdiction of the English Court who owed or held money to the credit of the judgment debtors, whether an English court in the exercise of its discretion would have given leave to enforce the English Judgment dated 13th March 1998, if the judgment creditors had applied for a third party debt order on 5th October 2004".

8–10 In the English jurisdiction, Mr Justice Tomlinson held that third party debt orders are subject to no limitations in relation to time. The civil procedure rule which governs them being CPR Pt 72 makes absolutely no reference to the time elapsed since the date of judgment. This is in contrast to the rules relating to writs of execution still governed by CPR Sch.1, RSC Order 46, which limits the issue of execution without the need for an application to the court after six years has elapsed. The learned judge observed that differences in longevity have existed for well over 100 years between the two types of enforcement procedure. Thus, the lapse of six years since judgment enjoyed no special significance as far as third party debt orders were concerned. It was just one fact to be taken in to account in the overall exercise of the court's discretion. As such, there has never been any practice of declining an interim order on that basis alone.

How do the rules define a "bank or building society"?

8–11 Rule 72.1(2) defines a "bank or building society" to include any person carrying on a business in the course of which he lawfully accepts deposits in the United Kingdom. "Deposit" is defined within s.5 of the Banking Act 1987. Section 6 of the Banking Act 1987 describes a "deposit-taking business" as one where:

- in the course of the business money received by way of deposit is lent to others or;
- any other activity of the business is financed, wholly or to any material extent, out of the capital of all the interest on money received by way of deposit.

Section 3 of the Banking Act 1987 imposes a restriction on the acceptance of deposits in the course of carrying on a "deposit-taking business", unless either the person accepting the deposit is an institution authorised by the Bank of England or by s.4 is exempt from the provisions of s.3. Schedule II to the Act lists the institutions which are exempt and therefore may be regarded as "deposit-taking institutions" and so able to be joined in TPDO proceedings. The National Savings Bank is listed in Sch. II and can therefore be regarded as a "deposit-taking institution". However, it retains its anomalous status as being under the control of the Crown. Therefore, a TPDO cannot be obtained against the National Savings Bank, although an analogous procedure does exist under CPR Sch.1, RSC Order 77, r.16 and CPR Sch.2, CCR Order 42, r.14. Incidentally, s.139(2) of the Supreme Court Act 1981 enables the Lord Chancellor to order that s.27 of the Crown Proceedings Act 1947 shall not apply to the National Savings Bank, but no such order has yet been made.

How is the application for a TPDO started?

8–12 The application for a TPDO may be made without notice and must be issued in the court where the judgment or order was issued. If proceedings have been transferred to a different court, the application must be issued in that court.

The application is simplified by the introduction of Form N349 in the 2002 reforms and it must contain all the relevant information as required by the Practice Direction which accompanies the rule to CPR Pt 72. The form must be verified by a statement of truth and, as with applications for charging orders and orders to obtain information, it is important that practitioners and court users ensure that a procedure for signing the statement of truth in accordance with CPR Pt 22 is developed and followed. An affidavit in support of the application is no longer necessary.

Applications for TPDOs are treated as urgent business by the courts and are placed before the district judge or Master on the same day they are received for the interim order to be considered and, where possible, granted.

As made clear by para. 1.3 of the Practice Direction to Pt 72, applications must be informative and supported by evidence—the court will not grant speculative applications. That said, in respect of this type of enforcement an amount of speculation may be necessary until the Government's reforms on the information available on the balance in a bank account can be made the subject of a Data Disclosure Order (this reform was discussed in the White Paper "Effective Enforcement" and is discussed elsewhere in this chapter). The amount of speculation can, of course, be reduced or eliminated by using the procedure under CPR Pt 71 to gain information about a debtor's assets.

8–13 The problem with any information that a judgment creditor may have about a judgment debtor's assets is that it can go out of date very quickly. Although an application for an order to obtain information may disclose a bank account and a possible balance, by the time an application to issue the TPDO has been made the situation may have changed. It may therefore be necessary at the hearing for an order to obtain information, to go to court with an application for a TPDO already completed so that this is issued immediately after the hearing, thus minimising any delay in the freezing of the account.

What are the next steps after the interim order has been made?

8–14 Provided the judge is satisfied that the application is in order, an interim order may be made without any notice being served on the judgment debtor in the following terms:

- an order will be made fixing a hearing date to consider whether to make the interim order into a final TPDO; and
- directing that until that hearing the third party must not make any payment which reduces the amount he owes to the judgment debtor to less than the amount specified in the interim order.

The interim TPDO will also specify the amount of money the third party must retain, which will be a total of:

- the amount of money remaining due to the judgment creditor under the judgment or order; and
- an amount for the judgment creditor's fixed costs of the application for a TPDO, as specified in the Practice Direction to CPR Pt 72.

The interim TPDO becomes binding on the third party when it is served on him. The date of the hearing to consider the application should be not less than 28 days after the interim TPDO has been made.

The form of the interim TPDO will be in Form N84. In addition to complying with requirements of CPR 72.4, the interim TPDO also gives the judgment debtor information on "hardship payment orders", which are set out in CPR 72.7. Hardship payment orders are discussed later in this chapter and are a new initiative introduced in 2002.

How is the interim TPDO served?

8–15 Service of the interim TPDO is perhaps the most important area to consider strategically when using this method of enforcement.

Copies of the interim TPDO, the application notice and any documents filed in support must be served on:

- the third party, not less than 21 days before the date fixed for the hearing; and
- on the judgment debtor not less than seven days after a copy has been served on the third party; and
- seven days before the date fixed for the hearing.

To assist with ensuring that the requirements for service are met, the diagram below can be helpful:

Application for TPDO is made	Interim TPDO is made by the Court	Final hearing date is set not less than 28 days ahead	Third Party is served not less than 21 days before the final hearing date	Judgment Debtor is then served not less than 7 days AFTER a copy of the interim TPDO has been served on the Third Party and 7 days before the final hearing	Final hearing takes place with all service requirements having been met
1st June	4th June	4th July	Service on Third Party To Be Completed By 14th June	Service on Judgment Debtor To Be Completed Not Earlier Than 21st June and before 28th June	Final Hearing Takes Place On 4th July

If the judgment creditor arranges service of the interim TPDO, he must:

- file a certificate of service not less than two days before the hearing or;
- produce the certificate of service at the final hearing.

Service is, of course, governed by CPR Pt 6, with the rules for service on a company set out in CPR 6.5.

8–16 The rules on service are designed clearly to ensure that any monies due to the judgment debtor by the judgment creditor are bound by the interim TPDO, which then prevents the judgment debtor from dissipating the funds. For example, by serving the judgment debtor's bank, the bank account of the judgment debtor is bound by the interim TPDO well before the interim TPDO is served on the judgment debtor, consequently ensuring that the bank account is not emptied before the bank becomes bound by service of the order. CPR 72.5 therefore expressly requires service on the third party of the interim TPDO at least 21 days before the hearing and on the judgment debtor at least seven days before the hearing and seven days after the third party has been served. In addition, there is always the risk of a third party innocently paying the debt, or in the case of the bank account allowing the judgment debtor to withdraw the funds, therefore preventing the funds from being attached. Accordingly, service on the third party must be regarded as urgent.

How is an interim TPDO served on a bank?

8–17 As the bank or other deposit-taking institution (referred to as the "bank") will invariably be an incorporated business, the following steps should be taken to ensure that service is effected in accordance with the Rules:

- The bank should be served at the principal office of the company or "any place of business of the company within the jurisdiction which has a real connection with the claim".
- Under the old garnishee proceedings rules, the bank had to be formally served at its registered office with a copy of the garnishee order nisi being served on the local branch where it was known or suspected that the judgment debtor had an account—and it is recommended that this practice is carried on under CPR Pt 72, even though it is not expressly prescribed either in that Rule or under the Rules for service set out in CPR Pt 6.

What are a third party's obligations when served with an interim TPDO?

8–18 A bank's obligations are now codified in CPR 72.6, which expressly sets out the action to be taken when served with an interim TPDO. Banks and building societies are subject to CPR 72.6(1), (2) and (3), whereas all other third parties served with an interim TPDO are subject to CPR 72.6(4).

Obviously, it is expected that a third party bank will comply with its obligations under the Rules, and which are set out on Form 84 as it is the interim TPDO, but inevitably there will be occasions when the third party does not comply for a number of reasons.

8–19 In the case of a third party which is not a bank or building society, the answer is straightforward. If the third party does not comply with CPR 72.6(4), the court is entitled to assume that the debt is not disputed and to make a final TPDO. CPR 72.6(4) provides that a third party (being neither a bank nor building society) must notify the court and the judgment creditor in writing within seven days of being served with the interim TPDO, if he claims not to owe any money to the judgment debtor or to owe less than the amount specified in the interim TPDO. If he does not notify the court and the judgment creditor of these issues, then, certainly, the Court will assume that the money is owed and will make the final TPDO.

Under the terms of CPR 72.6, once served with an interim TPDO a bank or building society must carry out a search to identify all the accounts held with it by the judgment debtor. Unless ordered otherwise, the bank or building society is required to do the following:

- to retain money in accounts held solely for the judgment debtor (or if there are joint judgment debtors, accounts held jointly by them or solely by either of them);
- to search for and disclose information about such accounts.

The bank or building society is not required, for example, to retain money in, or disclose information about, accounts in the joint names of the judgment debtor and another person who is not a party to the proceedings or, if the interim TPDO has been made against a firm, then accounts in the names of individual members of that firm.

8–20 The bank or building society must disclose to the court and the judgment creditor within seven days of being served with the interim TPDO the details of each account held by the judgment debtor including:

- the bank account number;
- whether the bank account is in credit and, if in credit:
  - whether the balance of the account is sufficient to cover the amount specified in the interim TPDO;
  - if the balance in the account is less than the amount specified in the interim TPDO, then the information given should pertain to the amount in the account on the day the bank was served;
  - whether the bank or building society has served notice on the judgment debtor of its right to the money in the account, for example pursuant to a right of set-off or some other reason—details of the bank's claim must be given.

What are the bank's obligations if it does not have an account for the judgment debtor?

After making its searches, the bank confirms: **8–21**

- the judgment debtor does not hold an account within the bank; or
- the bank or building society is unable to comply with the order for any other reason, for example because it has more than one account holder whose details match the information contained in the order and cannot identify to which account the order relates.

then the bank or building society must inform the court and the judgment creditor of that fact within seven days of being served with the interim TPDO.

Obviously, the automation of accounting information and databases within banks and building societies should enable their computer systems to process the interim TPDO quickly to enable compliance with the obligations set out in this Rule.

If the bank cannot comply with the requirements of the TPDO for any reason, and in the absence of any response from the bank, the court will use its discretion whether or not to make a TPDO based on the facts before it, including other evidence before the court.

If the bank did not comply or attend, no doubt the court could make "use of technology" pursuant to its duty to manage cases in accordance with CPR 1.4 by telephoning the bank to ascertain the position. However, in practice, despite the short time limit, banks do comply with the requirements of the Rule to supply information to the court.

The form of the interim TPDO (Form 84) does expressly contain the provision that "A bank or building society may deduct an amount from any money held for the judgment debtor for its expenses in complying with this order".

What happens if a third party makes an unauthorised payment?

8–22 If the third party makes an unauthorised payment out of funds after service of the interim TPDO, the third party runs the risk of having to pay the amount twice, in the event that the interim TPDO is then made into a final order (see *Crantrave Ltd (In Liquidation) v Lloyds Bank Plc* [2000] Q.B. 917; [2000] 3 W.L.R. 877).

To prevent this happening, the third party should not pay the judgment creditor when served with an interim TPDO, but should instead wait for the court's decision on whether or not the order is to be made final.

Service of the interim TPDO does not operate to transfer the property in the debt, but is an equitable charge on the debt. The third party cannot pay the debt to anybody without incurring the risk of having to pay it over again (*Galbraith v Grimshaw* [1910] A.C. 508).

What happens if the account of the judgment debtor is a joint account?

8–23 Despite significant consultation on the vexed question of whether joint accounts could be subject to a TPDO, the Government concluded in its review of enforcement that there were "compelling" reasons why not to make joint accounts open to this type of enforcement. In Ch. 4 of the White Paper "Effective Enforcement" in paras 409–430, the discussion was rehearsed and concluded that the difficulties in defining "joint accounts", combined with the problem of allocating ownership of funds in joint accounts and addressing the rights of "innocent" third parties, meant that joint accounts could not be the subject of TPDOs. This is, of course, unless the joint account holders are also joint debtors, who are to be subject to the TPDO application.

The legal position regarding joint accounts stems from the case of *Beasley v Roney* in 1891, which established that,

> "the debt owing by a garnishee [*now a third party*] to a judgment debtor which can be attached to answer the judgment debt must be a debt due to the judgment debtor alone, and that where it is only due to him jointly with another it cannot be attached."

The current legal position confirming this approach was stated in the case of *Hirschon v Evans* [1938] 2 K.B. 801; [1938] 3 ALL E.R. 491 by the Court of Appeal.

8–24 However, despite the Government's obvious concerns in allowing TPDOs to be used in connection with joint accounts, it is envisaged that when the White Paper is enacted, the court will have greater powers to access information about possible accounts belonging to a judgment debtor through the introduction of Data Disclosure Orders, outlined in Ch.3, where a TPDO has been unsuccessful.

The upshot of the conclusions to the White Paper and the reforms to enforcement carried out in 2002 maintains the current position in law that to successfully attach a bank account, all account holders must be judgment debtors (see CPR 72.2.15). We wait to see if, by allowing greater information about a judgment debtor's finances, TPDO will increase in popularity as a method of enforcement.

How does a hardship payment order affect the operation of a TPDO?

8–25 A bank is under no obligation to disclose or freeze an account in the name of the judgment debtor and another person such as a spouse. Hardship payment orders were introduced as part of the changes to the enforcement regime in March 2002 (see Civil Procedure (Amendment No 4) Rules 2001 (SI 2001/2792)).

The service of an interim TPDO on a bank or building society has the effect of freezing the account of the judgment debtor. The third party bank cannot pay out on any of the judgment debtor's cheques or allow him to withdraw cash without the authority of the court. Clearly, the effect of this is that a judgment debtor may then be unable to pay his mortgage or rent, or buy food for himself and his family while access to his account remains frozen. There will also inevitably be some time delay prior to the service of the interim TPDO and the decision as to whether the interim order should be made final. In addition, the third party is entitled to at least 21 days notice of the hearing, but in practice may receive much more.

The new provision for a hardship payment order ("HPO") seeks to strike a balance between the rights of the judgment creditor and the rights of the judgment debtor. It enables the judgment debtor to apply to the court for specified payments to be made to him, notwithstanding that the account is frozen by the interim TPDO.

If the judgment debtor is an individual, and is prevented from withdrawing money from his account at the bank as a result of the interim TPDO *and* he or his family are suffering hardship in meeting ordinary living expenses as a result of the interim position, then the Court may on the application by the judgment debtor make an order permitting the bank to make a payment(s) out of the frozen account using the mechanism of an HPO.

How does a judgment debtor make an application for an HPO?

8–26 The application for a hardship payment order may be made in the High Court at the Royal Courts of Justice or to any District Registry and in the county courts, but the judgment debtor can only apply to one court for an HPO.

The application notice seeking the hardship payment order must include detailed evidence explaining why the judgment debtor needs a payment of the amount requested, and be verified by a statement of truth.

Unless the court orders to the contrary, the application in support of the HPO needs to be served on the judgment creditor at least two days before the hearing of the application. However, it does not need to be served on the third party.

If made, an HPO may permit the third party to make one or more payments out of the account and specify to whom the payments may be made.

As the judgment debtor does not have to make the application to the court which made the interim TPDO, and as the application for the HPO will not be transferred (see para. 5.2, of the Practice Direction to CPR Pt 72), if the application for the HPO is made to a different court from the one dealing with the TPDO itself, then, to ensure both courts work in tandem, the Practice Direction makes the following stipulations:

- the application for the TPDO will not be transferred to the court hearing the HPO; but
- the court dealing with the TPDO will send copies of the application notice for the TPDO and the interim TPDO to the court hearing the application for the HPO.

8–27 Under the same paragraph of the Practice Direction (para. 5.4), if the application for the HPO is one of a matter of "exceptional urgency", the court can deal with the application without notice being served on the judgment creditor and allow representations by the judgment creditor to be made by telephone/fax or other "appropriate methods of communication".

The judgment debtor's evidence in support of the application for an HPO must be documented, and para. 5.6 of the Practice Direction to CPR Pt 72 outlines examples of the documentation required including bank statements, wage slips and mortgage statements (as appropriate), in order to prove the judgment debtor's financial position and the need for the payment to be made from the frozen account.

If the judgment debtor wishes to oppose the judgment creditor's application for a TPDO, he can apply under para. 4 of the Practice Direction to CPR Pt 72 to the court hearing the TPDO proceedings, to transfer those proceedings to the court for the district where the judgment debtor resides or carries on business, or to another court.

Where the application for the TPDO and the application for the HPO are both proceeding in the same court, it is generally preferable to expedite the hearing date for further consideration (as required by CPR 72.8) to be heard simultaneously with the judgment debtor's application. Judgment creditors are encouraged to seek combined hearings of both applications if the court administration fails to list both hearings together (see the note to CPR Pt 72 at 72.7.5 of the White Book Service 2006). If combined, costs can be saved and all the issues of the applications resolved in one hearing. Of course, where the applications are made in different courts, it is not possible to combine the hearings, which is perhaps unfortunate.

What orders can the court make at the final hearing of a TPDO?

8–28 If the judgment debtor or third party objects to the court making a final TPDO, he must file and serve written evidence stating the grounds for this objection (see CPR 72.8(1)). If the judgment debtor or the third party believes that a person other than the judgment debtor has a claim to the money specified in the interim TPDO, that person must file and serve written evidence stating his knowledge of that matter (see CPR 72.8(2)).

If the third party gives notice under CPR 72.6 that he does not owe the money to the judgment debtor, or that the amount which he owes is less than the amount specified in the interim TPDO and this is disputed by the judgment creditor, then the judgment creditor must file and serve written evidence setting out the grounds on which he disputes the third party's position.

In any event, written evidence under paras 1, 2 or 3 of CPR 72.8 must be filed and served on whichever party as soon as possible—and in any event not less than three days before the final hearing.

If the court is notified that some person other than the judgment debtor may have a claim to the money specified in the interim TPDO, the court will serve that further person with notice of the application for the TPDO and the hearing.

Often, it will not be worthwhile for the judgment creditor to contest an issue, and so he may prefer to cut his losses and abandon the application either prior to or at the hearing, in which case he may be liable for costs (*Wintle v Williams* [1858] 3 H&N 288).

8–29 As the interim TPDO was made on a without notice basis, the next hearing is where the court decides whether to make the interim order a "final" order or some other order depending on the evidence and submissions made.

In the White Book Service 2006 it is stated that "most cases are straightforward". The third party is not prejudiced by the making of an order (see CPR 72.9), as the third party owes the money anyway to the judgment debtor and is merely directed to pay out to the judgment creditor instead of the judgment debtor. To that extent, the third party receives discharge of his obligations to the judgment debtor.

At the hearing of the final TPDO the court may make any of the following orders:

- a final TPDO;
- an order discharging the interim TPDO and dismissing the application;
- an order to decide any issues and disputes between the parties or between any of the parties and any other person who claims the money specified in the interim order; or
- an order directing a trial of any such issues with necessary directions being given, although CPR 72.8 (6) makes it clear that the district judge or Master can decide the issues raised by the parties, but only exceptionally will it be necessary to give directions or order a trial pursuant to CPR 72.8(6)(d).

8–30 In considering whether or not to exercise his discretion to make a final order, the judge must bear in mind not only the position of the judgment creditor but also the judgment debtor and the third party, together with the position of other creditors. Previous cases where a final TPDO (or garnishee order absolute as they were then) was not granted include:

Where the court considers the making of a final order would be inequitable	*Roberts Petroleum Ltd v Bernard Kenny Ltd* [1983] A.C. 192
	Prichard v Westminster Bank Ltd [1969] 1 W.L.R. 547
If there are proceedings underway for the distribution of available assets to the	*D Wilson (Birmingham) Ltd v Metropolitan Property Developments Ltd* [1975] 2 All E.R. 814

judgment debtor amongst his creditors on a percentage basis	
	Rainbow v Moorgate Properties Ltd [1975] 1 W.L.R. 788; [1975] 2 All E.R. 821
If there is any doubt whether the estate of a deceased is insolvent, in which case the money in the hands of a third party can be ordered to be paid in to court pending any enquiry to assess whether or not the estate is insolvent	*George Lee & Sons (Builders) Ltd v Olink* [1972] 1 W.L.R. 214; [1972] 1 All E.R. 359
If money is due to the judgment debtor as a trustee for another	*Roberts v Death* [1881] 8 Q.B.D. 319
If the third party can prove that he would still be liable in a foreign court	*Martin v Nadel* [1906] 2 K.B. 26

What is the effect of a final TPDO?

8–31 The final TPDO is enforceable as an order to pay money, as provided under CPR Pt 72.9. If the third party pays the money to the judgment creditor in compliance with the TPDO, or the order is enforced against him, then the third party is discharged from his debt to the judgment debtor. Enforcement of the TPDO against the third party is sometimes required if the third party refuses to obey the order, which is unlikely where the third party is a bank. However, a third party who owes a debt to the judgment debtor, perhaps in respect of an unpaid invoice, can then be subject to enforcement action, perhaps by executing against goods or charging property. Indeed, by virtue of para. 2 of CPR 72.9, this will remain the position even if the TPDO or the original judgment or order is later set aside.

It would be extremely unusual for a third party to refuse or fail to comply with the final order to pay the money over. If the third party considered that the TPD should not have been made, and was present at the final hearing, then his remedy is to appeal that final order.

If he was not present at that hearing, or if new information comes to light, he should promptly apply for the final TPDO to be set aside.

Can money in court be subject to a final TPDO?

8–32 Money paid in to court as either security for costs in another claim or as part of a Pt 36 offer under the CPR is not "money standing to the credit of the judgment creditor", but instead is money to the credit of the claim in which that payment was made, and remains in court to await the court's direction or order in relation to those proceedings.

As a result, under CPR 72.10(1) if money is standing to the credit of the judgment debtor in court, then this money is not available to be used by the judgment creditor to satisfy his judgment using the TPDO procedure. Instead, the judgment creditor may apply for an order that the money in court, or as much of it as is sufficient to satisfy the judgment or order and the costs of the application, be paid to him.

An application notice seeking an order under this rule must be served on the judgment debtor and the Accountant General of the Courts Funds Office (*cfoenquiries@hmcourts-service.gsi.gov.uk*).

If the application notice has been issued under this rule, the money in court must not be paid out until the application had been disposed of. It is obviously not appropriate for the court itself to be the subject of court proceedings, and therefore it is not and never has been possible to obtain a TPDO in respect of money in court. However, where there is money in court standing to the credit of the judgment debtor, CPR 72.10 provides a simple and alternative procedure that a judgment creditor can use.

It has been held (in an unreported case) that the money paid in to court in other pending proceedings is not "money standing to the credit of the judgment debtor in court", as it remains subject to the direction of the court in those proceedings.

Who pays the costs of the TPDO application?

8–33 Under CPR 72.11, if the judgment creditor is awarded costs on the application for an order under either CPR 72.2 for an interim TPDO, or a final TPDO under CPR 72.10, or money held in court, he must retain those costs out of the money recovered by him under the order. The costs should be deemed to be paid as a priority to the judgment debt, unless the court orders the contrary.

CPR 72.11 deals only with the costs of the judgment creditor who has made a successful application for a TPDO.

If the application is unsuccessful, the judgment creditor may be ordered to pay costs, especially if the third party has been put to any expense. Judgment creditors must tread carefully and recognise this potential risk on costs. The effect of the rule is to reduce the judgment debt by the net amount received after deducting costs of the third party debt proceedings.

In relation to the bank's expenses or other deposit-taking institutions, in addition to any ordinary costs they are entitled to deduct a sum for administrative expenses from the balance held when complying with a final TPDO. The sum is prescribed under the Attachment of Debts (Expenses) Order 1996 (SI 1996/3098) and is currently £55.00. Reference can also be made to s.40A of the Supreme Court Act 1981 and s.108 of the County Courts Act 1984. The final TPDO should be for the amount which the bank actually has to pay after deducting its expenses. Where there are insufficient funds for the bank to pay the full sum due under the order, it will deduct expenses from the judgment debtor's account.

In relation to final orders relating to building society accounts, it is important to note that Practice Direction deals with the pre-March 2002 regime by stating that a final third party debt order will not require a payment which would reduce to less than £1 the amount in the judgment creditor's account with the building society or credit union.

What happens if there are insufficient funds in the judgment debtor's account?

8–34 A bank account is an obvious target for third party debt proceedings, but the order will only bite if the credit balance in the account *at the time of service* of the interim TPDO is sufficient to meet the amount of the interim order. This point is crucial to the success or otherwise of the application and is probably the single most important reason for the unpopular nature of this method of enforcement. At present, there is no procedure or machinery to confirm or verify when the application is issued that funds thought to be in the account are still held, and, of course, for some judgment creditors they just do not want to embark on proceedings with any risk of costs attached. Ways to improve the likelihood of funds being in the bank account include:

- obtaining further information from the judgment debtor under CPR Pt 71;
- identifying dates of salary payments and other credits which may be paid to the judgment debtor on regular dates and ensuring that on the day the interim TPDO is served the funds have cleared and are available in the bank account;
- using information from third parties that they are about to make a payment to a judgment debtor—such as payment of a large invoice owed to the judgment debtor;
- checking if assets have or are about to be sold by the judgment debtor, such as the judgment debtor's home, with funds being available in the judgment debtor's solicitor's bank account—the interim TPDO is served on the bank holding the client's funds. If the money is wholly client's money, it is subject to a

trust and a final TPDO cannot be made (*Plunkett v Barclays Bank* [1936] 2 K.B. 107)

If the funds are not available and in the account on the day the order is served, then a further order is needed to attach to any money paid in subsequently (see *Heppenstall v Jackson* [1939] 1 K.B. 585).

What is the effect of the judgment debtor's insolvency on a TPDO application?

8–35 Under s.346 of the Insolvency Act 1986, the judgment creditor is not entitled to retain the benefit of the attachment against the judgment debtor's trustee in bankruptcy, unless he has completed the attachment by the receipt of the debt before the commencement of the bankruptcy. The definition of what constitutes a "receipt" was set out in the case of *George v Tompson's Trustee* [1949] Ch. 322; [1949] 1 All E.R. 554. The court may, however, set aside the trustee's rights. Similar provisions apply where the judgment debtor is a company under s.183 of the Insolvency Act 1986. Again, as with other methods of enforcement to ensure the judgment creditor recovers his judgment debt, costs and interest, without sharing this with any other creditors, it is important there is no delay in the proceedings.

Tribunal, courts and enforcement act 2007

8–36 Third party debt orders are the only enforcement method not to be directly amended or updated as a consequence of the above Act.

Indirectly, it is possible that judgment creditors will choose to use departmental information requests and information orders to try and obtain financial information from government departments and third parties, to assist them in making TPDO applications.

The final process for the method of application for these requests and orders is yet to be finalised by statutory instruments.

Chapter 9

CPR Part 73–Charging Orders

Introductory comments

9–01 In recent years, and no doubt due to the increase in UK house prices, charging orders in England and Wales have become an extremely popular method of enforcement. Judgment creditors are securing their judgment debts against the increased value in the home or property of the judgment debtor to protect their position. Since the recession, though, their popularity has declined in correlation with the decline in property prices and a dip in the housing market.

CPR Pt 73 provides the mechanism for enforcement against the real property of the judgment debtor, as well as the less popular approach to enforce against the judgment debtor's share portfolio or partnership interests.

The new rule consolidated the previous regime in the High Court and county court by coming in to force on March 25, 2002 and replacing RSC Order 50 and CCR Order 51. The changes give the necessary procedural efficacy to the Charging Orders Act 1979.

Section 1 of the Charging Orders Act 1979 provides that, where a judgment debtor is required to pay a sum of money to a judgment creditor, for the purpose of enforcing the judgment or order the "appropriate" court may make a "charging order", which imposes on any available property of the judgment debtor specified in the order a charge for securing the payment of any money due under the judgment or order. The charging order must be in accordance with the provisions of the 1979 Act.

What are the different types of charging order?

9–02 Broadly speaking, there are three types of charging order, the most popular of which is definitely the charging order over land. Judicial statistics for the last period in which they were recorded and published shows that charging orders had increased to a total number of applications of 65,696 compared to 10 years ago when the number was 21,584.

CPR Pt 73 is therefore divided into three sections, each dealing with the three types of charging order available:

- Section I deals with charging orders over land;
- Section II deals with stock orders;
- Section III deals with stock notices.

The Charging Orders Act 1979 is the guiding statute. However, CPR 73.1 also refers to the Council Tax (Administration and Enforcement) Regulations 1992, (SI 1992/613), which are important in relation to charging orders, as they provide the machinery for local authorities to enforce payment of council tax by charging order where the amount outstanding is over £1,000. The Regulations were made under powers conferred by Sch.4 to the Local Government Finance Act 1992. The text for Regs 50 and 51 can be found set out at paras CPR 73.7 and CPR 73.8.

Funds in Court include securities held in court. Securities means any kinds of securities specified in s.2 (2) (b) of the 1979 Charging Orders Act.

9–03 It is also possible to have a charging order on securities by virtue of s.2(b) of the Charging Orders Act 1979, and a charge over the judgment debtor's interest in partnership property, s.23 of the Partnership Act 1890.

A charging order will not be made in relation to an order for assessed costs (see *A and M Records v Darakdjian* [1975] 1 W.L.R. 1610; [1975] 3 All E.R. 983. However, in contrast, it may be possible to obtain in exceptional cases an order for the payment of a sum of money in the future (see *Bagnall v Carlton* (1877) L.R. 6 Ch. D. 130 and *Robinson v Bailey* [1942] Ch. 268.

What is the effect of a charging order?

9–04 A charging order made under CPR Pt 73 is, in essence, equivalent to an "equitable mortgage under hand" (for a description of an equitable mortgage under hand, please see Vol. 32 "Mortgage" of *Halsbury's Laws* (4th Edn—Reissue). A charging order over land therefore provides the judgment creditor with security equivalent to a mortgage over the land specified in the order. It is, of course, subject to any prior mortgages and charges.

A charging order is an indirect method of enforcement, since it secures the judgment debt, but it does not result in the sum being paid. To ensure payment of the debt is made, a judgment creditor must apply for an order for sale of the charged asset—see CPR 73.10. Many judgment creditors do not take this additional step because of the complexities involved in satisfying the court that an order for sale should be made. However, if the necessary criteria can be satisfied, the ultimate sanction of a charging order application is that the judgment debtor can lose the charged asset, which can be the judgment debtor's home.

Which courts have jurisdiction?

9–05 The jurisdiction of the High Court and county court to make charging orders is set out in s.1 (2) of the 1979 Act.

Depending on the value of the judgment debt, the following principles apply:

- The jurisdiction of the county court to make a charging order over land is unlimited—see CPR 73.3(2)—and therefore most charging orders are made in the county court.
- The High Court only has jurisdiction to make a charging order—even in respect of one of its own judgments or orders—where the amount of the original judgment is more than £5,000 (and this sum does not take into account any subsequent interest which may be charged or any payments on account being made (see Charging Orders Act 1979, s.1). This means that where a judgment creditor wishes to pursue a charging order in respect of a High Court judgment less than £5,000, he must transfer the judgment to the county court for the application for the charging order to be issued.

However, it should be borne in mind that, although these jurisdictional limits apply to the application for a charging order, different rules apply when it comes to the application for an order for sale of the property which is charged. These rules are set out below. In essence, where an order for the sale of property involves a sum in excess of £30,000, the application for the order to sell must be transferred to the Chancery Division of the High Court.

What consideration needs to be given by the court to other creditors?

9–06 The interests of other creditors need to be considered by the court under s.1(5) of the Charging Orders Act 1979 in its decision to grant a final charging order.

For this reason, it is important that other creditors of the judgment debtor known to the judgment creditor are disclosed (see CPR PD73 para. 1.2(5)).

The existence and identity of other creditors may have been discovered at an order to obtain information hearing under CPR Pt 71. However, it should be remembered that the burden of establishing why a charging order should *not* be made is on the judgment debtor and on any other creditors.

What happens if the judgment is in a foreign currency?

9–07 Under CPR 73.10.8, where the judgment debt is expressed in a foreign currency the court may order the amount to be expressed in the sterling equivalent, which was recommended in a Practice Direction dating back to 1976 (see *Practice Direction (QBD: Judgment: Foreign Currency) (No. 1)* [1976] 1 W.L.R. 83. If converted, the date for conversion should be as close as practicable to the date of payment, having regard to the reality of enforcement procedures (see *Miliangos v George Frank (Textiles) Ltd (No. 1)* [1976] A.C. 433). Nevertheless, as a result of the case of *Carnegie v Giessen* [2005] EWCA Civ 191; [2005] C.P. Rep. 24, the court has discretion as to whether or not to order the judgment debt to be converted. As a result of this case, the enforcement of a foreign currency judgment by means of a charging order did not require the judgment debt to be converted into sterling before enforcement was completed. Any judgment not so converted will not therefore offend the rules derived from the *Miliangos* case and the 1976 Practice Direction.

What is the effect of the Limitation Act on the Charging Order procedure?

9–08 We mentioned in the third party debt order chapter of this book that under s.24(1) of the Limitation Act 1980 there is a provision that an action cannot be brought on any judgment after the expiration of six years from the date of that judgment after an extension is granted on application by the judgment creditor.

As with third party debt orders, charging orders themselves have been found to be immune from this position. In fact, not only are charging orders immune from the provisions of s.24(1) of the 1980 Act, but also from s.20(1) of the Limitation Act, which places a 12-year limitation on enforcement in relation to a charge on land running from the date on which the right to receive the money under the charged accrued.

In the case of *Yorkshire Bank Finance Ltd v Mulhall* [2008] EWCA Civ 1156; [2009] 2 All E.R. (Comm) 164, the judgment having been obtained against the defendants in April 1991, the claimant then obtained the charging order absolute against the property owned by Mrs. Mulhall on June 25, 1991. In January 2007, Mrs. Mulhall sought to set the judgment aside because, amongst other things, the bank had taken no steps to enforce it since 1991 and she believed that they meant enforcement was no longer possible. Her application failed. The leading case on this topic is *Ezekiel v Orakpo* [1997] 1 W.L.R. 340, which underlines that in seeking to enforce a charging order the judgment creditor was not seeking to enforce the judgment; he had already done that when he got his charging order. Therefore, the enforcement of the charging order was not affected by s.20(1) or s.24(1) of the Limitation Act. The distinction between Ezekiel and Mulhall was that more than 12 years had passed since the entry of the judgment and the making of the charging order. That made no difference to s.24(1) or s.20(1). There were therefore no provisions in the Limitation Act 1980 that affected the enforcement of the charging order on the part of the bank, despite the lapse of time.

Is there a minimum judgment debt for applying for a charging order?

9–09 At the present time, there is no financial minimum judgment debt to be able to apply for a charging order.

Under the new Act, the Lord Chancellor does have the power to set financial limits below which both a charging order and an Order for Sale cannot be obtained. A new s.3(A) Charging Orders Act 1979 is created.

At the present time, the statutory instruments required to introduce these financial limits have not been finalised, and it is therefore not known what the thresholds will be. It is, however, anticipated that the financial limit for applying for charging orders will be higher than the current £1000 limit in relation to charging orders for non-payment of council tax.

It should also be noted that the Office of Fair Trading states in its guidance *Irresponsible Lending—OFT guidance for creditors* (March 2010) that creditors should not use the *threat* of charging orders or orders for sale to try to induce their debtors into paying, regardless of the amount of the debt.

What is the procedure in applying for a charging order?

9–10 A charging order application is made up of a two-stage process similar to the procedure under the former regime of charging order nisi and order absolute. These terms have been replaced by an interim charging order (see CPR 73.4), which is then followed by a final charging order (see CPR 73.8). The interim charging order is obtained without notice being given to the judgment debtor.

Information on land owned by the judgment debtor, if not already known by the judgment creditor, can be obtained using an application to obtain information under CPR Pt 71. Since December 3, 1990 (when the Land Registration Act 1988 came in to force), leave to inspect the land register is not necessary, and anyone can search against any property which is registered at HM Land Registry. A set of "office copy entries" is frequently used as evidence of the judgment debtor's ownership of the land, which is subject to a charging order application. Online access to HM Land Registry is now available (see *http://www.landregisteronline.gov.uk* [Accessed October 14, 2010). Copies provided to the court with the application should be official and bear the Land Registry watermark in order to ensure that the application is not rejected by the court.

However, where the title to the land in question is not registered, then the application under CPR Pt 71 would enable a judgment creditor to inspect the title deeds to the property to establish ownership.

For a flow diagram of the procedure, see the Charging Orders Flowchart set out in the Appendix.

Which parties need to be notified about the application for a charging order?

9–11 The court will generally order that joint proprietors and other interested parties (revealed on a Land Registry Certificate in respect of registered land) should be served with notice of the hearing at which the judgment debtor must "show cause" why the interim order should not be made final.

The court will also order notice needs to be given to other judgment creditors whose position may be unduly prejudiced by the final charging order, particularly where the amount of the judgment debt is substantial—although the burden of finding such creditors is not that of the judgment creditor's (see s.1(5) of the Charging Orders Act 1979).

What happens if there is a dispute as to who owns the asset to be charged?

9–12 Where there is a dispute as to the beneficial ownership of any property subject to an interim order, the court has power to direct that the issue be tried and to adjourn the application until the issue has been decided. The burden of showing cause why an interim order should not be made final is on either:

- the judgment debtor or any third party claimant; or
- any other creditor.

(See *Rosseel NV v Oriental Commercial and Shipping (UK) Ltd* [1990] 1 W.L.R. 1387; [1990] 3 All E.R. 545 CA).

What is the court's discretion in making a charging order?

9–13 The court has discretion whether to make a final charging order or not. Section 1(5) of the Charging Orders Act 1979 requires the court to consider all the circumstances of the case and, in particular, the evidence before it as to:

- the personal circumstances of the debtor; and
- whether any other creditors of the judgment debtor would be unduly prejudiced by the making of the order.

The principles under which the court will exercise its discretion were outlined in *Roberts Petroleum Ltd v Bernard Kenny Ltd* [1982] 1 W.L.R. 301 CA, which was subsequently reversed by the decision of the House of Lords (see its reported decision at [1983] 1 All E.R. 564, HL (the House of Lords reversed the decision of the Court of Appeal on the narrow point that as the judgment debtor had been made bankrupt after the making of the interim order, that event was "sufficient cause" to not make the charging order final).

From experience, the writer has seen many practitioners vex over whether a court would be prepared to make a final charging order or not. Local practice and the use of judicial discretion naturally mean that there will be differences in the way that the rules are applied by members of the judiciary. What practitioners can do is to use the rules in a consistent way to ensure that, whatever court they are before, they make out a case for the grant of a final charging order on the basis that this is the right thing to do in the enforcement of their judgment.

9–14 Following the Court of Appeal's decision in *Roberts Petroleum* mentioned above, the principles in exercising discretion in the making of a charging order can be summarised as follows:

- Whether an interim order should be made final is a decision which requires the exercise of the court's discretion.
- The burden of showing cause why an interim order should *not* be made final is on the judgment debtor, and it is for the judgment debtor to make the necessary submissions at the final hearing on that point.
- In determining the exercise of discretion, there is to be no material difference between applications for third party debt orders and charging orders.

- In exercising its discretion, the court must take in to account all the relevant circumstances, regardless of whether they arose before or after the interim order.
- The court should exercise its discretion equitably, having regard to the interests of all the parties involved including other secure creditors as well as those of the judgment creditor and the judgment debtor.
- The liquidation of the judgment debtor's company, whether by voluntary or compulsory means, brings into operation the statutory scheme for dealing with the company's assets; therefore, if the winding up occurs before the final order is made, the court will decline to make a final order (see *Roberts Petroleum Limited v Bernard Kenny* [1983] 2 A.C. 192 HL—the same principle would apply if an individual were to be made bankrupt after the interim order but before the final order).
- It would not normally be a proper exercise of discretion to make a charging order on an asset of a substantial value in respect of a small debt (per Simmonds J. in *Robinson v Bailey* [1942] Ch. 268 at 271. However, see the comments made below in preparing the application for a charging order over land, and in particular preparing evidence of the judgment debtor's "won't pay" attitude.
- The court has a discretion which cannot be interfered with on appeal, unless it exercises a wrong principle (*Wicks v Shanks* [1893] 67 L.T. 109).
- Where execution by writ of fi fa has been stayed on terms that the judgment debtor pays by instalments (or, similarly, where the court has ordered payment by instalments pursuant to CPR r.40.11) and where the judgment debtor is complying with the court's order and is not in arrears, the court may exercise its discretion not to make a charging order (see *Mercantile Credit Co Limited v Ellis, The Times*, April 1, 1987, CA). The county court s.86(1) of the County Courts Act 1984 prevents the making of a charging order, where the county court has ordered payment by instalments, until there is a default.

In a charging order over land, what is the effect of a charging order?

9–15 To answer this question, the judgment creditor needs to examine the actual interest in the land owned by the judgment debtor, after which the following points can be made:

- If the judgment debtor is the sole owner of the land intended as the subject of the charging order, then the charging order will create a charge over the legal and beneficial interest in that land.
- If the land to be charged is held by joint judgment debtors who hold the whole beneficial interest in the land as well as the legal estate, which they hold as trustees, again the legal and beneficial estates will be charged (see s.2 of the Charging Orders Act 1979, and *Clark v Chief Land Registrar* [1994] Ch. 370; [1994] 3 W.L.R. 593).
- If the judgment debtor is a co-owner of the property to be charged, with another person who is *not* jointly liable for the debt but is just the joint owner of the property, only the judgment debtor's beneficial interest may be charged (see *National Westminster Bank Limited v Stockman* [1981] 1 W.L.R. 67; [1981] 1 All E.R. 800).

As a result of this reasoning, the complexities in relation to charging orders over the judgment debtor's property arise when the property is jointly owned by another person (usually with a spouse) who is not liable for the debt of the judgment debtor, but whose interest in the land becomes the subject of enforcement action.

What happens when the property to be charged is jointly owned?

9–16 A judgment creditor who has a charging order in respect of the beneficial interest of one of two joint owners of land may apply under CPR 73.10 and under s.14 of the Trusts of Land and Appointment of Trustees Act 1996 for the land to be sold (see *Midland Bank Plc v Pike* [1988] 2 All E.R. 434). However, the judgment creditor has no such remedy where the beneficial interest under the trust is discretionary, and therefore a defeasible interest (see *Skyparks Group Plc v Marks* [2001] EWCA Civ 319).

What is the position of the judgment debtor's spouse?

9–17 As a general rule, in any contest between a judgment creditor and a joint owner of the judgment debtor's, the interest of the judgment creditor will sooner or later prevail. If the property is in the sole name of the judgment debtor, or owned jointly by spouses who are both judgment debtors, then the charge will be against the land itself (as set out above).

However, where the property is in respect of land which the judgment debtor owns jointly with his or her spouse, where the spouse is not a judgment debtor (see *National Westminster Bank Limited v Stockman* [1981] 1 W.L.R. 67), the charging order ranks as a charge on only the judgment debtor's beneficial interest rather than on the land itself.

As a result the spouse of a judgment debtor may, in effect, be an "innocent bystander" in the proceedings for the enforcement of the judgment, and yet his or her home may be at risk. The position of the spouse of a judgment debtor in relation to the making and enforcement of charging orders involving the matrimonial home has therefore been the subject of case law over the years, and the principles set by these cases have endured to become part of the fabric of the CPR (see *Harman v Glencross* [1986] Fam. 81; [1986] 2 W.L.R. 637; *Austin-Fell v Austin-Fell* [1990] Fam. 172; [1990] 3 W.L.R. 33; *Re Citro (Domenico) (A Bankrupt)* [1991] Ch. 142; *Lloyds Bank Plc v Byrne* [1991] 23 H.L.R. 472).

Where an interim order has been made under a petition for divorce, the court will usually order that the application for a final order is heard alongside the ancillary relief proceedings in the divorce and, if necessary, transfer the application to the divorce court for that purpose (*Harman v Glencross* [1986] Fam. 81).

9–18 A judgment creditor is justified in expecting that an interim order over one spouse's beneficial interest will be made final. The court must consider if there is any point in denying the judgment creditor his charge if in any event the spouse's right of occupation can be defeated by the judgment creditor making the judgment debtor bankrupt (see *First National Securities Limited v Hegerty* [1985] Q.B. 85O; [1984] 3 W.L.R. 769).

Nonetheless, there are competing interests to balance, which involve the spouse and minor children of the judgment debtor. In these situations, the court will need to consider whether the value of the equity in the matrimonial home is sufficient to enable the charging order to be made final and realised immediately. If there is sufficient equity, then any resulting order may result in the spouse and children "downsizing" to a property of a lower standard than they might reasonably have expected, had only the husband's interests been taken in to account.

If the equity in the property is not sufficient, the court should only make an order to protect the wife's right to occupy the matrimonial home. The normal course would be to postpone the sale of the house for a period only to protect the spouse's rights of occupation, whilst maintaining a balance between the rights of the spouse and those of the judgment creditor (see *Austin-Fell v Austin-Fell* [1990] Fam. 172; [1990] 3 W.L.R. 33).

It is possible for a judgment creditor to ask for a "Mesher"-type order (*Mesher v Mesher* [1980] 1 All E.R. 126, CA), which in effect "postpones" sale until a point in time, perhaps when minor children reach 18 or finish full-time education.

9–19 From the decided cases, it would require exceptional circumstances before the court would order the outright transfer of the husband's share in the house to the wife, which would leave the judgment creditor's charging order with nothing on which it could "bite".

The position of a spouse of the judgment debtor therefore requires special consideration, highlighted by the following points:

- Where the spouse is a joint proprietor, he or she is therefore a joint trustee of the property and should be named in the judgment creditor's application. The court will order that copies of the interim order and witness statement should be served on the spouse (CPR 73.5(1)(c) (also see *Harman v Glencross* [1986] Fam. 81; [1986] 2 W.L.R. 637 CA).
- A spouse in occupation of the matrimonial home is entitled to make representations under s.1(5) of the Charging Orders Act 1979 as to "all the circumstances of the case", whatever the position as to the title to the matrimonial home.
- The principles that the court should adopt when considering the "representations" mentioned above were set out by Balcombe L.J. in *Harman v Glencross* [1986] Fam. 81, CA and include:

	Timing of Charging Order	**Outcome**
(a)	Interim charging order obtained on the judgment debtor's share in the matrimonial home and the hearing to have that interim order made into a final order is heard *before any divorce proceedings are commenced*	The court should make the charging order final—the spouse's right of occupation should be adequately protected under s.14 of the Trusts of Land and Appointment of Trustees Act 1996.
(b)	Where the interim charging order is made *after a petition for divorce has been issued*	The court should consider whether it is proper to make a final charging order before the spouse's application for ancillary relief has been heard by the divorce court. The court can take into account whether or not any resulting net proceeds from a sale of the charged property will be enough to provide alternative accommodation for the spouse and any children of the family.

	Timing of Charging Order	Outcome
(c)	The court considers that the circumstances are so clear that it is proper to make a final charging order immediately	The usual practice will be to transfer the charging order proceedings to the divorce court so that they can be heard with the ancillary relief application, and the divorce court is then in a position to consider all the circumstances of the case—in *Austin-Fell v Austin-Fell* [1990] Fam. 172, it was held that a proposal by the judgment creditor to postpone operation of the charging order for ten years until the children were of age should be accepted, even though at the end of ten years the wife might not be able to re-house herself with the net proceeds of sale after discharge of the charging order.
(d)	Once the final charging order has been made	It will normally require exceptional circumstances (e.g. where the spouse has had no proper opportunity to put his or her case) for the court to set aside the charging order under s.3(5) of the Charging Orders Act 1979, thereby depriving the judgment creditor of his right to enforcement.

Finally, the court should consider whether there is any point in denying the judgment creditor his charging order if the wife's rights of occupation could, in any event, be defeated by the judgment creditor making the husband bankrupt.

Does a spouse have to be served with the application for a charging order?

9–20 No rule specifically requires service of the application for a charging order or interim order on a spouse. However, invariably a spouse will be served under one of the following provisions:

- as a "creditor" under CPR 73.5(1)(b) if there are pending proceedings, e.g. under the Matrimonial Causes Act 1973;
- as a "trustee" under CPR 73.5(1)(c);

- as a person "in possession" under para. 4.3(6) of the Practice Direction to CPR PD73;
- as a person who has registered a class F land charge, or notice under s.31(10) Family Law Act 1996 and;
- as a person specifically directed to be served by the court—in practice, virtually all courts direct that the spouse should be served to enable the court to give due consideration to "all the circumstances of the case", as required by s.1(5) of the Charging Orders Act 1979.

What interest is payable on a charging order over land?

9–21 A charging order does not affect the accrual of judgment interest on High Court or county court judgments as per their respective guiding legislation for interest, being the Judgments Act 1838 in the High Court, and the County Court (Interest on Judgment Debts) Order 1991 (SI 1991/1184)) for county court judgments.

How is the application made to the court for a charging order over land?

9–22 Since the reforms of 2002, the application for a charging order has become more straightforward; there is now no need to prepare a separate affidavit in support of the application. All the points which need to be dealt with as part of the application are set out on Form N379, which is completed and issued by the judgment creditor, and there is no requirement to give any notice to the judgment debtor of the intention to apply for a charging order. Usually, the application will be made at the court where the judgment or order was issued, unless one of the following points applies:

- the proceedings have been transferred to a different court, in which case the application for the charging order must be issued in that court;
- the application is made under the 1992 Council Tax Regulations (see above), in which case the application must be issued in the county court for the district in which the relevant dwelling (as defined in Regulation 50(3)(b) of the 1992 Regulations) is situated;
- the application is for a charging order over an interest in a fund in court, in which case it must be issued in the court in which the claim relating to that fund is or was proceeding; or

- the application is to enforce a judgment or order of the High Court and it is required by s.(1)(ii) of the Charging Orders Act 1979 to be made to a county court.

What information is required to complete form N379?

9–23 The application notice on form N379 must contain information as required by the Practice Direction to CPR Pt 73 as follows:

- the name and address of the judgment debtor must be set out;
- full details of the judgment or order to be enforced must be included;
- the amount of money outstanding under the judgment or order needs to be calculated;
- if the judgment debt is payable by instalments, the amount of any instalments which have fallen due and remain unpaid will need to be set out;
- if the judgment creditor knows of the existence of any other creditors of the judgment debtor, then their names (if known) and their addresses must be included;
- the property(s) which is the subject of the application needs to be identified;
- the names and addresses of the persons to be served must be set out as required under CPR 73.5(1).

What if the judgment debtor has more than one property?

9–24 Under the Practice Direction accompanying CPR Pt 73 it is acceptable for a judgment creditor to make a single application notice for more than one charging order over several assets. Usually, the asset to be the subject of the charging order is the judgment debtor's home. If separate orders are however made, perhaps where the judgment debtor has a number of properties which can be charged, then the court will draw up an interim charging order for service against each property.

What happens if the judgment debtor opposes the application for a charging order?

9–25 If the judgment debtor wishes to oppose the issue of the charging order in a particular court, the judgment debtor can apply to the court on an application and seek to transfer the charging order proceedings to the court for the district in which he/she/it resides or carries on business.

Is a statement of truth required on a charging order application?

9–26 The answer is yes. Since the reforms to enforcement procedures in 2002, applications for charging orders, along with orders to obtain information under CPR Pt 71, and third party debt order applications under CPR Pt 72, all need to be verified by a statement of truth signed in accordance with the requirements of CPR Pt 22. However, an affidavit in support of the application (as provided under the pre-2002) regime is no longer required.

What happens at the interim charging order stage?

9–27 The term "order nisi" has been replaced by the new term of "interim order", and the application for a charging order remains a two-stage process.

At the interim stage the application for the charging order will be dealt with by a judge without a hearing. The judge may make an order in the one of the following terms:

- he may impose a charge over the judgment debtor's interest in the asset to which the application relates and fix a hearing to consider whether to make a final charging order, as provided by CPR 73.8(2)(a);
- he may refuse to make the interim order—in the exercise of his discretion, the judge may feel that the application for a charging order is, in effect, a "sledgehammer to crack a nut" and that the amount outstanding is too small to justify the ultimate sanction of the judgment debtor losing his home if the final charging order becomes an order for sale.

9–28 A judgment creditor should as a matter of good practice anticipate that the court may exercise its discretion against making a charging order, by anticipating this decision and taking the following steps:

- If it is a case of the judgment debtor not paying the judgment debt as a "won't pay" type of debtor rather than a "can't pay" debtor, then the judgment creditor should provide evidence of the judgment debtor's wilful refusal to pay in para. 7 of the application for a charging order.

- In addition, the judgment creditor should set out any relevant information as to other abortive methods of enforcement which have been employed to try to recover payment which might include an abortive report from an HCEO, or an application for an attachment of earnings order, which has failed due to the judgment debtor's refusal to complete his statement of means.

It is for the judgment creditor to make out his case in support of the application for a charging order, particularly where the judgment debtor is evading payment and refusing to do so when it is quite clear he/she/it has sufficient assets.

What is the importance of registering the interim order?

9–29 To be effective, it is vital that the interim charging order is registered, in order to prevent it being defeated by a sale to a bona fide purchaser for value without notice. The interim charging order is registerable under s.3 of the Charging Orders Act 1979.

The steps to take in relation to registration depend on the nature of the judgment debtor's interest in the property, be it legal and/or beneficial, and whether the title relates to registered or unregistered land.

In the case of registered land, a notice or restriction will be entered pursuant to the Land Registration Act 2002. In relation to unregistered land, the necessary land charge needs to be registered at the Land Charges Registry in Plymouth under the Land Charges Act 1972.

In the past it has always been a vexed question as to whether there should be two registrations, i.e. initially, when the interim charging order is made and then to register the final charging order. However, the position is now simplified by virtue of guidance given by HM Land Registry in its various fact sheets, available at *http://www.landreg.gov.uk* [Accessed October 15, 2020], in that only one registration is required, which should be made immediately after the interim order is made.

9–30 The table below sets out the different situations that may arise in relation to the registration of an interim order, depending on the nature of the title. This table is designed to assist court users to make an immediate application for registration following the making of the interim order:

Judgment Debtor Situation	Nature of Title To The Property	Interim Order Application	Resulting Registration	Withdrawal of Charge Application
Judgment debtor is sole owner	Registered Land	Complete Form UN1	Notice	Form CN1
	Unregistered Land	Form CT1 and Form K4	Caution	Judgment creditor can use WCT, or judgment debtor can use CCT. Also need to do Form K11
Judgment debtors who are jointly liable for the judgment debt	Registered Land	Form UN1	Notice	CN1
	Unregistered Land	Form CT1 and Form K4	Caution	Judgment creditor can use WCT, or judgment debtor can use CCT. Also need to do Form K11.
Judgment debtor is the co-owner of property where the other co-owner(s) is/are not liable for the judgment debt, e.g. a spouse, co-habitee	Registered Land	Form RX1 (restriction in Form K)	Restriction	Judgment creditor can use form RX4, or judgment debtor can use RX3
	Unregistered Land	Form CT1 and Form K4	Caution	Judgment creditor can use WCT, or judgment debtor can use CCT. Also need to do form K11
Judgment debtor is a company	Registered Land	Form UN1	Notice	Form CN1
	Unregistered Land	Form CT1 and Form K4	Caution	Judgment creditor can use WCT, or judgment debtor can use CCT. Also need to do form K11

An example of how straightforward the registration of an interim charging order can be (in relation to a registered title) is as follows:

> Tom and Barbara Good own the franchise to a do-it-yourself superstore in Braintree. One of their customers, Mr. Ledbetter, has failed to pay for goods supplied to him. To protect their interest, Tom and Barbara have obtained a charging order against Mr. Ledbetter's beneficial interest in 55 Cuckoo Way, Braintree, which Mr. Ledbetter owns jointly with his wife, Margot. Tom and Barbara have applied on form RX1 to H M

Land Registry for the following form K restriction to be entered on the title to Mr. and Mrs. Ledbetter's property:

> *"RESTRICTION: No disposition of the registered estate is to be registered without a certificate signed by the applicant for registration or his conveyancer that written notice of the disposition was given to John Smith and William Smith at Unit 24 Century Drive, Braintree, Gloucester CM77 7YG, being the person with the benefit of an interim charging order on the beneficial interest of Gerald Ledbetter made by Chelmsford County Court on 15 November 2006 (Court reference CM/123)."*

9–31 This restriction means that no disposition of 55 Cuckoo Way can be registered without notice first being served on Tom and Barbara Good, which will give them the opportunity to recover their judgment debt owed by Mr. Ledbetter from the proceeds of any sale of 55 Cuckoo Way. Once the judgment debt has been paid, Mr. and Mrs. Ledbetter can apply in form RX3 for the restriction to be cancelled. Notice of the application will be sent by the Land Registry to Tom and Barbara Good. Alternatively, Tom and Barbara Good (as restrictioners) can apply on form RX4 to withdraw the restriction.

After the interim order has been made, a date will be set for the hearing of the final order which the court may make, and which will confirm that the charge imposed by the interim charging order should continue (see CPR 73.8).

If the interim charging order has been properly registered, as suggested above, there will be no need to effect another registration when the final order is made, as the final order simply continues on from the interim order. If at the hearing the interim charging order is discharged, any registration must certainly be promptly removed using form RX4 where the land in question is registered. If the nature of the title to the land relates to unregistered land, then contact the Central Land Charges Registry in Plymouth on 01752 635 600 for details.

Using the table above, where there are joint debtors who are also joint proprietors, the usual route for registration of the interim charging order would be a UN1 to register a notice. However, if one of the debtors/proprietors has already had a charging order registered against them by way of a restriction, then the "joint" charging order will have to be registered as two separate restrictions against each of the proprietors separately.

How is an interim charging order served?

9–32 Under CPR 73.5, copies of the interim charging order, the application notice and any documents filed in support of it must, not less than 21 days before the hearing of the final order, be served on the following persons:

- the judgment debtor(s);
- any other creditors which the court directs need to be served;
- where the interim order relates to an interest under a trust, then on such of the trustees as the court directs (usually, this will mean the judgment debtor's spouse as a co-trustee).

Service is carried out in accordance with the normal rules for service in CPR Pt 6. This includes the rules for service out of the jurisdiction (see CPR 6.20), which can be used if, for example, the judgment debtor no longer has an address for service in the jurisdiction but has a known address abroad. The usual course of action is for the court to serve the judgment debtor, as provided in CPR 6.3.

9–33 Surprisingly, there is no express rule requiring service of the interim charging order on the judgment debtor's spouse, although if the spouse is a co-trustee of the matrimonial home, it is likely he or she will be one of the persons upon whom the court directs service under CPR 73.5.

If the judgment creditor decides to make arrangements for service, perhaps by engaging the services of a process server, then the judgment creditor must arrange to file either a certificate of service, not less than two days before the date set for the final hearing, or produce a certificate of service at that hearing to satisfy the court that the rules on service have been met.

If the court orders service on other creditors (as it usually does pursuant to CPR 73.5(1)(b)) it can also direct that the applicant judgment creditor carries out service, and again the judgment creditor will usually do this by engaging the services of a process server.

What is the court's approach to dealing with other creditors?

9–34 Under CPR 73.8(2) the court has discretion whether or not to make a charging order. It may direct for the service of the interim order to be made on such other creditors as it directs. The judgment debtor's spouse will be regarded as a creditor where an application for ancillary relief has been registered against the property (see generally *Harman v Glencross* [1986] 1 All E.R. 545).

Naturally, it may not be equitable to make a charging order where there are other creditors and the judgment debtor is insolvent and there is or is about to be an arrangement to distribute available assets among the creditors on a pro rata basis (*Wilson (D)*

(Birmingham) v Metropolitan Property Developments [1975] 2 All E.R. 814; *Rainbow v Moorgate Properties* [1975] 1 W.L.R. 788; [1975] 2 All E.R. 821).

The judgment creditor is therefore required to state in the application for a charging order his knowledge of other creditors of the judgment debtor. The court may then direct that such creditors should be served with the interim order.

Can a charging order be made if the judgment debtor is paying by instalments

9–35 Section 1 (1) of the Charging Orders Act 1979 empowers the court to order a charge "for securing the payment of any money due or to become due" under a judgment or order. Therefore, when a judgment debt is payable by instalments, the court has power to make a charging order to secure the whole debt and not merely the arrears of any instalments.

In the High Court, the fact that the judgment debtor is up to date in complying with an order for payment of instalments is likely to be a relevant factor in the exercise of the court's discretion to make or refuse the charging order (see *Mercantile Credit Co Limited v Ellis, The Times* April 1, 1987, CA). Moreover, the effect of s.86(1) of the County Courts Act 1984 is to prevent the making of a charging order where a county court has made an order for payment of any sum by instalments, until after default in payment of one or more instalments.

Where, however, the interim charging order is obtained prior to the instalment order being made, then the court can, and usually does, confirm the charging order (see *Ropaigealach v Allied Irish Bank* [2001] EWCA Civ 1790).

The Tribunal, Courts and Enforcement Act 2007 has introduced changes to the approach to charging orders for judgments payable by instalments, although the relevant sections of the new Act have yet to be implemented and there is no date set for commencement.

Section 93 of the Act creates new s.1(6), (7) and (8) of the Charging Orders Act 1979 and provides that judgment creditors will be able to obtain a charging order where the judgment is payable by instalments and where those instalments are not in default. The judgment creditor will not, however, be able to pursue enforcement of the charging order by way of an order for sale, unless the judgment debtor defaults on the instalments.

What happens if the judgment debtor becomes insolvent?

9–36 By virtue of ss. 346 and 183 of the Insolvency Act 1986 a judgment creditor may retain the benefit of a charging order against other creditors, provided the final order is made before the commencement of the bankruptcy or winding up (see CPR 73.4.5). As will be appreciated throughout this book, the need for the judgment creditor to act quickly to complete the enforcement procedure is paramount to protect the judgment creditor's individual interest, as opposed to sharing the proceeds of any insolvency with other creditors. In the case of a charging order, provided the judgment creditor can fulfil the criteria in making the application, the process to achieve a final order can be straightforward, after which the judgment debt is secured, regardless of any possible insolvency of the judgment debtor in the future.

Can interest and costs be recovered under a charging order?

9–37 It has been held that although a charging order does not expressly provide for the payment of interest and costs, it does extend to both (see *Ezekiel v Orakpo* [1997] 1 W.L.R. 340).

It was also held in *Holder v Supperstone* [2000] 1 All E.R. 473 that interest falling due more than six years before the commencement of the proceedings is recoverable under the charge. The principle is that costs incurred after judgment can be recouped under the charge—as they would have been recouped under an equitable mortgage.

What are the possible outcomes at the final order hearing?

9–38 Under CPR 73.8, if any person objects to the court making a final charging order, he must file and serve on the applicant written evidence stating the grounds, along with his objections, not less than seven days before the date set for the final hearing.

At the hearing the court may make the following orders:

- a final charging order—confirming that the charge imposed by the interim charging order must continue with or without modification;
- to discharge the interim charging order and dismiss the application;
- decide any issues and disputes between the parties or between any of the parties and any other person who objects to the court making a final charging order (perhaps the spouse); or
- direct a trial of any such issues and, if necessary, give directions.

The final order must be served on all the parties on whom the interim charging order is required to be served.

Under CPR Pt 73.8(1) the judgment debtor can no longer just turn up at the hearing to oppose the interim charging order being confirmed into a final order. Instead, the judgment debtor must comply with the rule setting out written evidence, stating the grounds of his objections. This practice differs to the previous Rules before 2002 whereby judgment debtors could make last-minute appearances.

9–39 The district judge or Master has the power to determine the issues of the application at the final hearing (see CPR 73.8(2)(c)), and it will only be in exceptional circumstances that a trial will be directed to determine any issues (see 73.8(2)(d)).

If an issue is directed it is likely to involve the title to stocks or shares where there is a dispute. Practice will be to adjourn the application and not make the charging order final until after the decision of the issue. This approach was expressly approved by the Court of Appeal in *Rosseel NV v Oriental Commercial & Shipping (UK) Ltd* [1991] E.G. 94 C.S CA.

What is the effect of insolvency at a final order hearing?

9–40 If bankruptcy proceedings are pending, the court is unlikely to make a final order, as this would prefer one creditor over another. If the judgment debtor has obtained an interim order under the Insolvency Act 1986, the permission of the court under s.252 of that Act is required before a final charging order can be made. As you will know, the purpose of the interim order is to provide a moratorium on proceedings whilst the debtor seeks to agree an arrangement with his creditors.

Does the court have discretion to set aside the debtor's petition for bankruptcy?

9–41 In the case of *Tagore Investments SA v Official Receiver* [2008] EWHC 3495 (Ch)—November 11, the court was prepared to find that the debtor had manipulated the circumstances of his bankruptcy petition, to defeat the judgment creditor. In this case, the judgment creditor knew nothing of a particular judgment debtor's petition for bankruptcy, but the judgment debtor was aware of the creditor's application for a charging order. The judgment debtor applied for his own bankruptcy.

In such a case the judgment creditor is entitled to apply to the court under s.346 of the Insolvency Act 1986 and also s.184 (where the judgment debtor is a company) to ask for the court to exercise its discretion to set aside the petition so that the judgment creditor's enforcement can continue. In both these sections, where the judgment debtor is either made bankrupt under s.346 or wound up under s.184, any dissipation of assets, or enforcement proceedings completed after the date of the presentation of the petition, are liable to be set aside, in order to ensure that the assets of the judgment debtor are available for all creditors.

9–42 In the case of *Tagore*, the judgment creditor relied upon the judgment debtor's conduct both before and during the litigation, along with the judge's findings as to the judgment debtor's dishonest behaviour. There was an important point in the case in that the judgment debtor had not given notice of his intention to present his petition. It was found that he had no creditors apart from the judgment creditor, and hardly any unsecured creditors. The court concluded that the judgment debtor's conduct throughout was that his petition had not been issued for the benefit of all creditors or, indeed, to relieve the debtor of a debt burden, but simply to manipulate the situation and frustrate the judgment creditor's attempt at a charging order. The court was therefore able to find in exercising its discretion an appropriate degree of unfairness by the judgment debtor. As a result, the final charging order was allowed to stand and the claimant became a secured creditor in the debtor's bankruptcy.

It should be noted that this discretion would only be exercised in exceptional circumstances. The judgment creditor has to be able to show sufficient unfairness to justify the exception, but it is still a useful case for many judgment creditors to use when faced with similar situations.

What costs are allowed at a final hearing?

9–43 The costs allowed between the parties are fixed by CPR 45.6, which, of course, changes from time to time together with reasonable disbursements in respect of search fees and the registration of the order. It should be noted that in view of the comments above regarding the simple registration of the interim order, only one registration fee is permissible.

Can a charging order be discharged or varied by the judgment debtor?

9–44 An application to discharge or vary may be made by the debtor or "any person interested in any property to which the order relates", as under either s.3(5) of the Charging Orders Act or Regulation

51(4) of the 1992 Regulations in relation to council tax liabilities. An application to vary or discharge may therefore be made by the wife of a judgment debtor, who has either rights of occupation or in her capacity as a joint owner (see *Harman v Glencross* [1986] Fam. 81, [1986] 1 All E.R. 545, CA).

The application is made to the court which made the charging order on Form N244. The court may direct who is to be joined or served with notice of the application. If an order is made discharging or varying the original charging order, then this must be served on all the persons on whom the original application for the charging order was served.

At the hearing, the court should be asked to make it clear in the order to vary or discharge which party is then responsible for making any necessary application to either the Land Registry or the Land Charges Registry, to ensure the registered interest complies with the new order.

How is a final charging order enforced?

9–45 Obtaining the final charging order secures the debt; it does not enforce payment of the debt. To actually seek to enforce payment, the judgment creditor must take the next step of seeking an order for the sale of the judgment debtor's property.

CPR 73.10 states expressly that the person who has the benefit of the charging order may enforce that charging order by making a claim for an order for sale to the court where the charging order was made, unless that court does not have the necessary jurisdiction. Section 23 of the County Courts Act 1984 provides the extent of the county courts jurisdiction to hear and determine such proceedings. The section limits the equity jurisdiction of the county court to a sum of £30,000, which applies to "proceedings for enforcing any charge where the amount owing in respect of . . . charge . . . does not exceed the county court limit". Thus, where the charged judgment debt exceeds £30,000, proceedings for an order of a sale must be commenced in the High Court. In either court, the claim must be made under Pt 8 of the CPR.

Enforcement of a charging order by sale is not an action on a judgment but a *fresh action* taken by the judgment creditor, and is accordingly not subject to a six-year limitation period (*Ezekiel v Orakpo* [1997] 1 W.L.R. 340, CA).

9–46 The rule on jurisdiction means a claim seeking an order for sale involving a sum in excess of £30,000 must be started in the High Court, Chancery Division. In London, the claim would be initiated at the Chancery Division of the Royal Courts of Justice. Outside of London, the claim would be started in a court with a Chancery

District Registry, which are located in Birmingham, Bristol, Cardiff, Leeds, Liverpool, Manchester, Newcastle-upon-Tyne and Preston.

In using the CPR Pt 8 procedure, a copy of the charging order must be filed with the claim form, and the claimant's written evidence must include the information required by the accompanying Practice Direction at PD73.

9–47 The Practice Direction sets out the written evidence that must be included in the Pt 8 claim under 73.10 as follows:

- The written evidence must identify the charging order and property that is the subject of the application and needs to be sold. An example of the form of witness statement in support of this application can be found in the Appendix.
- The evidence must state the amount in respect of which the charge was imposed, and the amount due at the date of issue of the claim.
- Evidence must verify, so far as it is known, the judgment debtor's title to the property charged, which could be as simple as annexing office copy entries to the written evidence.
- The written evidence must also state, so far as the claimant is able to identify, the names and addresses of any other creditors who have a prior charge or other security over the property, and the amount owed to each such creditor.
- The evidence must give an estimate of the price which would be obtained on the sale of the property (a valuation can be obtained by a "drive past valuation" by local estate agents or enquiry agents. Websites also provide details of property values, as indeed does the land registry at *http://www.landregistry.gov.uk* [Accessed October 15, 2010).
- If the claim relates to land, the claimant's evidence must give details of every person who (to the best of the claimant's knowledge) was in possession of the property.
- If the property relates to residential property, then the written evidence must deal with the following:
    - it must state whether the land is subject to a Land Charge of Class F or a notice under s.31(10) of the Family Law Act 1996, or under any provision of an Act which preceded that section, that has been registered; and
    - if so, it must state on whose behalf the land charge or notice has been registered and that the claimant will serve notice of the claim on that person.

The claimant must then take all reasonable steps to obtain the information required by the Practice Direction in relation to claims by competing creditors, before issuing a claim for an order for sale of the judgment debtor's property.

Sample forms of order for sale are set out in the Appendix to the Practice Direction and in the Appendix to this book. These forms are not prescribed forms of order and they may be adapted or varied by the court to meet the requirement of individual cases.

9–48 In its current format, CPR 73.10 applies both where a judgment creditor seeks an order for sale of property owned by a sole proprietor and where the property is owned by more than one person (note the rules outlined above about the different procedures for registration of the interim order where the property is solely or jointly owned). An application to enforce a charging order over the interest of one of a number of co-owners will still be an application to enforce a charge. As such, the county court will be deprived of jurisdiction if the amount secured by the charging order exceeds £30,000.

What are the criteria for ordering a sale in the case of joint owners?

9–49 Where the application involves property owned by more than one person, the criteria set out in s.15 of the Trusts of Land and Appointment of Trustees Act 1996 will be applied to the facts of the application. Section 15 sets out the matters to which the court should have regard in determining an application for an order for sale under s.14 of the same Act, and include:

- the intentions of the person or persons(if any) who created the trust;
- the purposes for which the property subject to the trust is held;
- the welfare of any minor who occupies or might reasonably be expected to occupy any land subject to the trust as his home; and
- the interests of any secured creditor of any beneficiary,

Cases involving the interpretation of s.15 include:

Mortgage Corp Ltd v Shaire [2001] Ch. 743, where it was held the interests of secured creditors (in this case the mortgagee) were just one factor to be considered, and such interests were not distinguished as priority interests within the criteria set by s.15. Following on from that decision, though, in the case of *Bank of Ireland Home Mortgages*

Ltd v Bell [2001] 2 All E.R. (Comm) 920, the court held that in considering whether or not to order the sale of a property under the provisions of s.14 of the Trusts of Land and Appointment of Trustees Act 1996, the issue of whether a creditor was being recompensed for being kept out of its money was a powerful factor for consideration and would steer the court towards making the order for sale.

How does the court balance the competing interests of the family and creditor?

9–50 The decision whether or not to make an order for sale involves the court balancing the interests of the judgment creditor(s) with the interests of the judgment debtor's family.

The court will have regard to the legitimate expectation of the judgment creditor(s) that they will be able to enforce the charging order by sale. Depending on the ownership position of the property that is the subject of the application for sale, the following trends emerge:

- where the property is solely owned by the judgment debtor, the court will be likely to order a sale;
- however, if the judgment debt could be paid by other means within a reasonable time, or any hardship caused by selling the property is disproportionate to the size of the judgment debt and the circumstances of the judgment debtor, the court may decide not to make the order for sale, or alternatively postpone it on terms;
- the sale may be suspended until the judgment debtor's children are of age (see *Austin-Fell v Austin-Fell* [1990] Fam. 172; [1990] 3 W.L.R. 33, where the order was suspended for ten years);
- a sale may be ordered on the application of the solvent husband's creditors (see *Barclays Bank Plc v Hendricks* [1996] 1 F.L.R. 258; [1996] 1 F.C.R. 710 where the wife, who was the second defendant to the proceedings, failed to stop the operation of a charging order absolute (as it then was) because the court found she was in the comparatively favourable position of owning another house which could re-house herself and the children, without the need for the children to change schools).

What are the implications on human rights involving orders for sale?

9–51 In the case of *Wells v Pickering* (2002) 2 F.L.R. 798; *The Times*, June 4, 2002, the competing interests of the judgment debtor and the judgment debtor's children were examined alongside the application of Art. 8 of the European Convention on Human Rights. The judgment of David Oliver Q.C. reiterated the policy that a creditor was entitled to be paid—and to be paid in due time—and he did not believe that the introduction of Art.8 of the ECHR providing, firstly, that everyone has the right to respect for his private and family life, his home and his correspondence, and, secondly, that there should be no interference by a public authority with the exercise of this right, except such as is in accordance with the law and is necessary in a democratic society, in the interests of national security, public safety or the economic well-being of the country, for the prevention of disorder or crime, for the protection of health or morals or for the protection of the rights and freedoms of others. The judge found that his interpretation of the law was in accordance "with the law", and therefore the judgment creditor's right to be paid what was due to her was to be protected.

Is there a financial limit for applying for an order for sale?

9–52 At the present time, there is no financial limit. It is expected that the Tribunal, Courts and Enforcement Act 2007, and the statutory instruments yet to be written to implement the relevant sections, will introduce a financial minimum limit below which an order for sale cannot be obtained.

In February 2010, the Government issued a Consultation Paper on the question of orders for sale and whether a minimum threshold should be imposed on applications in relation to Consumer Credit Act debts only.

The consultation ended on April 30, 2010. It was anticipated that the response to the Paper would be published on July 2, 2010. At the time of writing, the response has yet to be published on the Government website at *http://www.justice.gov.uk* [Accessed October 15, 2010].

The Citizens Advice Bureau also published their response to the consultation paper in April 2010, providing case studies of examples of individuals struggling under debt and threatened with charging orders and orders for sale.

What is the position if the judgment debtor is legally aided?

9–53 Where the property involves the recovery of costs from a legally assisted/publicly funded person, then a charging order will not be made (see ss.17(3)(a) and 17(3)(b) of the Legal Aid Act 1988 and

Gokholl v Budaly [1983] C.L.Y. 2200 and *Buckley v JJ O'Leary* [1993] C.L.Y. 2557).

Under s.11 of the Access to Justice Act 1999 and notes at para. 4 of the Community Legal Service (Costs Protection) Regulations 2000, a charging order can now be made against an assisted person's dwelling house. It will only operate, however, to the extent that the assisted person's share of the equity exceeds £100,000, and it will not be enforceable by an order for sale.

What is the procedure to enforce an order for sale?

9–54 Under CPR 73.10, where the judgment debtor is the sole owner or where the judgment debtors are joint owners of a property, the application for an order to sell the property of the judgment debtor(s) is made under this section. It should be noted that the CPR 73.10 *does not apply* where the order for sale is sought to enforce a charging order over the interest of one or some (but not all) co-owners. In such a case, the application must be made under s.14 of the Trusts of Land and Appointment of Trustees Act 1996. A specimen order for such a sale, if an application under s.14 is made successfully, is also set out in Appendix A to Practice Direction at r.73.

If the court that made the order has jurisdiction to determine an application for an order for sale, the application should be made there, but if the sum involved is over £30,000 the application must be made in the Chancery Division of the High Court.

The judgment creditor, who becomes the claimant for the purpose of these separate proceedings, must use the CPR *Pt 8 procedure*. A copy of the charging order must be filed with the claim form. A hearing date will be given on issue of the Pt 8 claim.

9–55 In support of the claimant's application, *written evidence* must be filed which must:

- Identify the final charging order and the property that is to be the subject of the application for sale.
- State the amount of the final charging order and the outstanding amount due at the date of the issue of the claim for an order for sale.
- Verify, so far as known, the debtor's title to the property charged—no doubt by reference to the Proprietorship Register where the title is registered—and by reference to the last conveyance where the title is unregistered.

- State, so far as possible, the names and addresses of any other creditors who have a prior charge or other security over the property (no doubt by reference to the Charges Register where the title is registered—and by reference to the Land Charges Register and any other sources of information where the title is unregistered) and the amount owed to each creditor.
- Give an estimate of the price that could be obtained on any eventual sale of the property.
- Give details of every person who, to the best of the judgment creditor's knowledge, is in possession, and if the claim relates to residential property state whether a Class F land charge of Class F, or a notice under s.31(10) of the Family Law Act 1996 (or its preceding provisions) has been registered, and if either a Class F land charge or a notice has been registered, state on whose behalf it has been registered, and confirm that the judgment creditor (as claimant in these proceedings) will serve notice of the claim on that person.

The claimant must then take "all reasonable steps" to obtain the names and addresses of any creditors who may have a prior charge or security over the property, and include the amount owing in each case.

9–56 In accordance with normal procedure, the claim form (and any particulars of claim) must be verified by a statement of truth. Precedents for claims and evidence in support where the judgment debtor is a sole owner or a joint owner are set out in the Appendix.

A sample order for sale, for use when the property is solely owned by the judgment debtor, is set out in Appendix A to the Practice Direction to CPR Pt 73.

What is the nature of a charging order over securities?

9–57 If the application for a charging order relates to securities, it must be made on Form N380. The application is made and served in accordance with the usual rules for charging orders, to achieve an interim order in relation to the securities that are the subject of the order.

Under CPR 73.6, if a judgment debtor disposes of his interest and any securities while they are subject to an interim charging order which has been served on him, that disposition will be invalid against a judgment creditor, as long as the interim charging order remains in force.

A person served under CPR 73.5(1)(d) with an interim charging order relating to securities must not (unless the court gives permission) allow the subject matter of the interim charging order to be transferred, or pay any dividend out on the security, including any interest or redemption payments relating to the securities. If a person acts in breach of this rule, he will be liable to pay the judgment creditor the value of the securities transferred or the amount of the payment made, as the case may be.

Under CPR 73.6, the rules on serving the interim charging order in relation to securities are the same as in respect of a charging order over land, except that in respect of securities the following points must be followed:

9–58 If the interest to be charged is securities, other than securities held in court, then the requirements for service are as follows:

- In the case of stock to which the Bank of England keeps the register, the Bank of England must be served.
- In the case of Government stock to which the Bank of England is not the keeper of the register, the keeper of the register—wherever that may be located—must be served.
- In the case of stock of any company within England & Wales, that company's registrars must be served.
- In the case of any company incorporated outside England & Wales, or of any state or territory outside the UK which is registered in a register kept in England & Wales, the keeper of that register must be served.
- In the case of units of any unit trust in respect of which a register of the bilt holders is kept in England & Wales, the keeper of that register must be served.

Furthermore, if the interest to be charged relates to funds in court, the Accountant General at the Courts Fund Office must be served. Information about the Courts Funds Office can be found at *http://www.courtfunds.gov.uk/cfo/cfo.htm* [Accessed October 19, 2010]

What is the effect of an interim order in relation to funds in court?

9–59 If a judgment debtor disposes of his interest in funds in court while they are subject to an interim charging order which has been served on him and on the Accountant General in accordance with CPR 73.5(1), then that disposition will not be valid against a judgment creditor, as long as the interim charging order remains in force.

What are the possible outcomes at the final order hearing?

9–60 As with charging orders over land, under CPR 73.8, if any person objects to the court making a final charging order, this objection must be submitted in the form of written evidence to the court, which is then filed at least seven days before the date set for the final hearing.

At the hearing, the court may make the same type of orders, i.e.:

- a final charging order—confirming that the charge imposed by the interim charging order must continue with or without modification;
- to discharge the interim charging order and dismiss the application;
- decide any issues and dispute between the parties or between any of the parties and any other person who objects to the court making a final charging order (perhaps the spouse); or
- direct a trial of any such issues and, if necessary, give directions.

If the court makes the final charging order, which then charges securities other than those held in court, the order will include a stock notice, unless the court directs otherwise. Details of stock notices are set out in s.III of CPR Pt 73.

Any order made at the hearing must be served on all the parties on whom the interim charging order was required to be served.

What is a "stop order" in Section II of CPR Part 73?

9–61 A "stop order" is defined in s.II of CPR Pt 73 as an order of the High Court not to take any "steps" listed in s.5(5) of the 1979 Act relating to funds in– court or securities specified in the order. The "steps" mentioned in s.5(5) include:

- the registration of any transfer of the securities;
- in the case of funds in court, the transfer, sale, delivery out, payment or other dealing with the funds, or of the income thereon;

- the making of any payment by way of dividend, interest or otherwise in respect of the securities;
- in the case of a unit trust, any acquisition of or other dealing with the units by any person or body exercising functions under the trust.

What is the procedure for applying for a stop order?

9–62 The procedure for applying for a stop order is set out in CPR 73.12. The effect of a stop order is to prevent any steps being taken in relation to the various securities over which a charging order has been obtained, including funds in court (see CPR 73.7), until the court makes a further order. The purpose of the stop order is to give the applicant an opportunity to make whatever further application he considers appropriate to secure his judgment (usually a charging order on the securities—see s.2(2) of the Charging Orders Act 1979).

The High Court may make a stop order relating to funds in court or to other securities. The applicant must show an interest in the funds or securities in accordance with the requirements of the rule.

The application for a stop order must be made either by an application notice in any existing proceedings or by a CPR Pt 8 claim form if there are no existing proceedings in the High Court.

The application notice or claim form must be served on every person whose interest may be affected by the order applied for, and either:

- the Accountant General at the Court Funds Office, if the application relates to funds in court; or
- the person specified in rule 73.5(1)(d), if the application relates to securities other than securities held in court.

What is the effect of a stop order relating to funds in court?

9–63 A stop order relating to funds in court prohibits the transfer, sale, delivery out, payment or other dealing with the funds or any part of them, or any income on the funds.

What is the effect of a stop order relating to securities?

9–64 A stop order relating to securities other than securities held in court may prohibit all or any of the following steps:

- the registration of any transfer of the securities;
- the making of any payment by way of dividend, interest or otherwise in respect of the securities; and
- in the case of units of a unit trust, any acquisition of, or other dealing with, the units by any person or body exercising functions under the trust.

The order must specify:

- the securities which are the subject of the order;
- the name in which the securities stand;
- the steps which are prohibited; and
- Whether the prohibition applies to the securities only or to the dividends or interest as well.

The court may, on the application of any person claiming to have a beneficial interest in the funds or securities to which a stop order relates, make an order discharging or varying the order. An application notice seeking the variation or discharge of a stop order must be served on the person who obtained the order.

How does a stop notice operate?

9–65 Under s.III of CPR Pt 73, a "stop notice" operates to require a person or body not to take any steps listed in s.5(5) of the 1979 Act (as set out above), in relation to the securities specified in the notice, without first giving notice to the person who obtained the notice. A sample form of stop notice is set out in Appendix B to the Practice Direction supplementing CPR Pt 73.

The request for a stop notice is made to the High Court. It may be issued by someone who is beneficially entitled to an interest in the securities. The stop notice may also be included in a final charging order made by either the High Court or the county court.

The request for a stop notice to be issued is made by filing a draft notice, together with written evidence which identifies the securities and describes the applicant's interest in them. It also gives an address for service for the applicant.

If the court officer considers that the request includes all the necessary evidence, he will issue a stop notice. The applicant must then serve copies of the stop notice, along with the written evidence on anyone to whom the stop notice is addressed.

Once served, the stop notice takes effect in accordance with CPR 73.18 and remains in force until it is withdrawn or discharged.

Whilst the stop notice is in force, the person on whom it is served must not register a transfer of the securities described in the notice, or take any other step restrained by the notice, without first giving 14 days' notice to the person who obtained the stop notice. However, that person must not, by reason only of the notice, refuse to register a transfer or to take any other step after he has given 14 days' notice under para. (2)(a) and that period has expired.

What happens if the interest to be charged belongs to a partner?

9–66 Applications for orders charging a partner's interest in partnership property etc. are retained in the CPR by virtue of Sch.1, RSC Order 81, r.8. Applications to "charge" a partnership share are made by an application under CPR Pt 23 for an order under s.23 of the Partnership Act 1890. This section authorises the High Court to make certain orders on the application of a judgment creditor of a partner, including an order charging the partner's interest in the partnership property. Every application to the court by a partner of the judgment debtor made in consequence of the first mentioned application must be made in accordance with CPR Pt 23. The rules forbid execution against partnership property itself, except where the judgment is against the firm (as distinct from one against an individual partner).

RSC Order 81 permits a Master, the Admiralty Registrar or a district judge to exercise the powers conferred on a judge to deal with the application. Every application notice issued by a judgment creditor under RSC Order 81, r.8, and every order made on such an application, must be served on the judgment debtor and on such of his partners as are within the jurisdiction or, if the partnership is a cost book company, on the judgment debtor and the purser of the company.

The application notice issued by the partner of a judgment debtor under this rule, and every order made on such an application, must be served on the judgment creditor and on the judgment debtor, along with such of the other partners of the judgment debtor as do not join in the application and are within the jurisdiction or, if the partnership is a cost book company, on the purser of the company. This is because the other partners are affected by any such order, and have a statutory right to redeem the interest charged or, if a sale of any of the partnership property is ordered, to purchase it.

An application notice or order served in accordance with this rule on the purser of a cost book company or, in the case of a partnership not being such a company, on only some of the partners thereof, shall be deemed to have been served on that company or on all the partners of that partnership, as the case may be.

Chapter 10

Enforcement of Foreign Judgments—CPR Part 74

Introduction

10–01 CPR Pt 74 continues to mature as a very necessary Rule for those enforcing judgments to understand and embrace. The days of finding a judgment debtor conveniently situated within the jurisdiction of the courts of England and Wales are long gone. Today, those that possess the benefit of a judgment or order in their favour may well have to look outside the comfort of the Civil Procedure Rules to be able to enforce that judgment in another part of the United Kingdom, Europe or beyond that to countries where a reciprocal treaty is in place for enforcement purposes. Of course, beyond that there are countries where no such treaty exists, and yet a judgment has been obtained and needs to be enforced.

All these situations are accommodated for within CPR Pt 74.

The "jurisdiction" of the United Kingdom is defined in CPR 2.3 to include England and Wales and any part of the territorial waters of the United Kingdom adjoining England and Wales. "Other parts" of the United Kingdom in practical terms means Scotland and Northern Ireland but excludes the Isle and Man and the Channel Isles, which are dealt with under separate "scenarios" set out in this chapter (see also note at CPR 74.0.5 of the White Book Service 2010).

10–02 In this book we do advocate anyone who needs to be able to enforce a judgment or order to consider carefully the economics of doing so. When enforcement moves across borders, the need to assess the likely assets of the judgment debtor and the cost of the enforcement process become ever more acute. There is still plenty of work to be done to make the cost of enforcement outside England and Wales easy and transparent to follow. In many cases a person with the benefit of a judgment will have to factor in the cost of engaging a local lawyer to act as an agent, which only increases the cost of the enforcement process.

Universally, although different business rules operate, the way that judgments are enforced in England and Wales is essentially the same across the globe when the focus becomes the available assets. Houses, goods, salaries and business assets usually will have a complementary enforcement process in another part of the world.

Judgment creditors need to consider whether they are:

- Enforcing a judgment coming into England and Wales (which we shall refer to as an "incoming" judgment)—in this type of situation the judgment creditor needs to ensure that the foreign incoming judgment is capable of being recognised by the English and Welsh courts and follows the Rules so that it can be enforced.
- Enforcing a judgment outside England and Wales (which we shall refer to as an "outgoing" judgment)—in this type of situation the judgment creditor will need to follow the Rules to ensure the judgment is certified as outstanding, and will then be recognised as a judgment which is capable of being enforced in the country where enforcement is to take place.

10–03 Fortunately, the Civil Procedure Rules help practitioners by streamlining CPR Pt 74 into five separate sections relevant to the type of judgment to be enforced. With that in mind, the table below sets out the five sections of CPR Pt 74 as follows:

Section I—Enforcement in England and Wales of Judgments of Foreign Courts	For the enforcement of "incoming judgments" into England and Wales, this section of the CPR Pt 74 contains provisions for the registration and enforcement of judgments from the courts of the member states of the European Union, the European Free Trade Area (EFTA), certain Commonwealth countries and certain states with which the United Kingdom has reciprocal treaties and conventions for the enforcement of judgments in the High Court.
Section II—Enforcement in Foreign Countries of Judgments of the High Court and County Courts	For the enforcement of judgments outside the European Economic Area, this section deals with "outgoing judgments" from the English and Welsh High Court and county courts to a court in a foreign jurisdiction, under the provisions of the various Acts dating back to 1920, 1933 and 1982. The application to transfer a judgment out of the jurisdiction is usually made without notice to the court where the judgment

	was given. The application is in effect a request for a certified copy of the English or Welsh judgment. In the case of judgments for registration in member states of the EU, such a certificate will be in the form of Annex V to the new Judgment Regulation, which is set out in the Appendix (see also CPR PD74). Care should be taken to ensure that evidence in support of the application complies fully with CPR 74.13. There is some debate as to whether a judgment obtained in a county court and transferred to the High Court for enforcement can be enforced through a court abroad. It has been queried as to whether such a judgment would meet the criteria of the 1920 and/or 1933 Acts in that it should be a judgment "given" or "obtained" in a superior court. If there is doubt about whether such a difficulty can be overcome, then the better course is to issue the proceedings in the High Court. If that is not permitted (for instance under the High Court and County Courts Jurisdiction Order 1991 (SI 1991/1724), where the claim involves a Consumer Credit Act matter), then the claim should still be issued in the county court and, before any further step is taken, application made to transfer the claim to the High Court (see CPR 30.3)
Section III—Enforcement of United Kingdom Judgments in other parts of the United Kingdom	This section provides for the registration of "incoming" judgments of courts from other parts of the United Kingdom, by a certificate for the enforcement of either "money" and "non-money" provisions, as well as for obtaining a certificate for enforcing "outgoing" judgments from England and Wales to other parts of the United Kingdom. The largest traffic crossing borders in this regard will be Scottish decrees.
Section IV—Enforcement in England and Wales of European Community Judgments	The European Communities (Enforcement of Community Judgments) Order 1972, (SI 1972/1590) "The 1972" Order was made as part of the United Kingdom's accession to the Treaty of Rome. It provides for the enforcement of certain judgments of the

	European Community/Union and some of its institutions, provided that the Secretary of State has appended an order for enforcement to the judgment (see arts 2(1) and 3(1) of the Order). It is important to note that the 1972 Order and this section of Part 74 do not apply to the judgments of European Union member states' domestic courts, which are subject to The Judgment Regulation and s.I of CPR Pt 74. The 1972 Order and this section apply to judgments and orders against persons (other than member states) made by Community institutions, such as the Council of the Commission. They arise often in the nature of a penalty for breach of regulatory requirements (e.g. in respect of anti-competitive activities) and the European Court. They also include Euratom inspection orders (see para. 9 of CPR PD74).
Section V—European Enforcement Orders	This section was introduced by the Civil Procedure (Amendment No. 3) Rules 2005 (SI 2005/2292). It makes provision for the certification of judgments of the courts of England and Wales as European Enforcement Orders, and for the recognition and enforcement in England and Wales of judgments of other contracting states that have been certified as European Enforcement Orders, under Council Regulation (EC) No. 805/2004. This statutory instrument created a "European Enforcement Order for Uncontested Claims" (O.J. [2004] 143 0015–0039). EEOs have been available since October 21, 2005 for all judgments dated after January 20, 2005.

http://europa.eu.int/eur-lex/pri/en/oj/dat/2004/l_143/l_14320040430en00150039.pdf [Accessed October 15, 2010]

(To use this link the full reference needs to be typed into an internet browser such as Explorer on a PC).

10–04 Although CPR Pt 74 has streamlined the position, it does not follow a particularly logical path, and so navigating the Rules can still be confusing. To help make the subject easier, this text approaches the problem of how to enforce a judgment with a foreign element by dividing the rules into eight types of scenario in which litigators are likely to find themselves and gives the forms applicable to each type of situation.

Scenario 1—Is the judgment to be enforced an *incoming* judgment into England and Wales from another part of the United Kingdom?	SECTION III
Scenario 2—Is the judgment to be enforced an *incoming* judgment into England and Wales from another part of the EU?	SECTION V
Scenario 3—Is the judgment to be enforced an *incoming* judgment into England and Wales from another country with which England and Wales has a reciprocal treaty?	SECTION I
Scenario 4—Is the judgment to be enforced an *incoming* judgment into England and Wales from another country with which England and Wales has **NO** reciprocal treaty?	See the notes below
Scenario 5—Is the judgment to be enforced an *outgoing* judgment from England and Wales to another part of the United Kingdom?	SECTION III
Scenario 6—Is the judgment to be enforced an *outgoing* judgment from England and Wales to another country within the EU?	SECTION V
Scenario 7—Is the judgment to be enforced an *outgoing* judgment from England and Wales to another country with which England and Wales has a reciprocal treaty?	SECTION I
Scenario 8—Is the judgment to be enforced an *outgoing* judgment from England and Wales to another country where there is no reciprocal treaty in place?	See the notes below

Scenario 1—Is the judgment to be enforced an incoming judgment into England and Wales from another part of the United Kingdom?

CPR Part 74—SECTION III

10–05 If a judgment creditor wants to enforce a judgment debt in another part of the United Kingdom, the starting point in the Rules is CPR 74.14. Helpfully, United Kingdom "jurisdiction" is defined in CPR 2.3 to include England and Wales and any part of the territorial waters of the United Kingdom adjoining England and Wales. "Other parts" of the United Kingdom in practical terms means Scotland and Northern Ireland but excludes the Isle and Man and the Channel Isles, which are dealt with under separate "scenarios" set out in this chapter (see also note at CPR 74.0.7 of the White Book Service 2010).

In enforcing an incoming judgment from another part of the United Kingdom, the judgment creditor should appreciate the distinction between a "money provision" and a "non-money provision" judgment as set out in the Rules, which define each as follows:

- a "money provision" judgment is one in which the court has ordered the payment of one or more sums of money in a judgment, the enforcement of which is governed by s.18, Sch.6 the 1982 Act;
- a "non-money provision" judgment is one in which the court has made provision for any relief or remedy which does not require the payment of a sum of money and where the enforcement is governed by s.8, Sch.7 the 1982 Act.

The distinction as to the nature of the judgment to be enforced becomes important in terms of the application to register the incoming judgment.

10–06 CPR 74.15 deals with the registration of incoming money provision judgments from either Scotland or Northern Ireland and is relatively straightforward. The money judgment is registered in the High Court under para. 5 of Sch.6 to the 1982 Act by way of a certificate issued by the courts in either Scotland or Northern Ireland, which must be registered in the Central Office of the High Court within six months of issue. The certificate will need to be filed together with a certified copy and written evidence to confirm it is a true copy. For example, if a Scottish judgment creditor wanted to issue a writ of fi fa to a High Court Enforcement Officer, then the Scottish certificate, a certified copy and the writ of fi fa ready to issue could be filed at the court.

The effect of registering the judgment in the High Court means the incoming judgment becomes a High Court judgment, and the enforcement of the incoming judgment is therefore subject to rules on the enforcement of High Court judgments. To be able to use the Attachment of Earnings procedure, which is only available in the county court, a judgment creditor would then need to arrange for the judgment to be transferred to the county court for enforcement.

10–07 The response of a judgment debtor to the registration of a judgment in this situation may be to apply to the court to stay the enforcement of the judgment. Under para. 9 of Sch.6 to the 1982 Act an application may be made to stay the enforcement of the certificate issued under CPR 74.15. If such an application is made, then the registering court (being the Supreme Court of England and Wales) has to be satisfied that the applicant is entitled and intends to apply to the judgment court (being the court in Scotland or Northern Ireland which made the judgment) to set aside or stay the judgment. If the High Court is satisfied that such an application is to be made, it can make an order staying the enforcement proceedings on any terms it thinks fit, including the period of the stay, which will enable the application to be dealt with.

CPR 74.16 deals specifically with the registration of non-money judgments in the High Court under para. 5 of Sch.7 to the 1982 Act for judgments coming from either Scotland or Northern Ireland.

The application for registration of a non-money judgment may be made without notice and must be accompanied by:

- a certified copy of the judgment issued under Sch.7 to the 1982 Act; and
- a certificate, issued not more than six months before the date of the application, stating that the conditions set out in para. 3 of Sch.7 are satisfied in relation to the judgment.

Scenario 2—Is the judgment to be enforced an incoming judgment into England and Wales from another part of the EU?

CPR Part 74 SECTION V

10–08 If the judgment is incoming from another country in the European Union, the procedure to enforce the judgment in England and Wales comes under the European Enforcement Order regime, or "EEO" as it is termed throughout the rest of this chapter. Section V was introduced by the Civil Procedure (Amendment No.3) Rules 2005 (SI 2005/2292) and makes provision for the certification of judgments of the courts of England and Wales as EEOs and for the recognition and enforcement in England and Wales of judgments of other contracting states that have been certified as EEOs (see Council Regulation (EC) No 805/2004, which created the European Enforcement Order for uncontested claims (O.J. [2004] 143 0015–0039).

Indeed, barriers on moving debt around Europe have moved on in the last couple of years with the introduction of Council Regulation 1896/2006. This regulation, which came into force in 2008, is designed to simplify and reduce the costs of litigation in cross-border cases concerning "uncontested pecuniary claims". The regulation seeks to achieve this by creating a "European order for payment procedure".

The basis of the regulation is to permit the free circulation of European orders for payment throughout the member states by laying down minimum standards and compliance, which then renders it unnecessary for any intermediate proceedings in the member state of enforcement prior to recognition and enforcement.

10–09 Countries within the European Union and which therefore come within this section of the Judgments Regulation are, as from July 1, 2007:

Austria	Latvia
Belgium	Lithuania
Czech Republic	Luxembourg
Denmark	Malta
Estonia	Netherlands
Finland	Poland
France	Portugal
Germany	Republic of Ireland
Greece	Slovakia
Greek Cyprus	Slovenia
Hungary	Spain
Italy	Sweden

For completeness, and to make it clear which countries fall outside of the Judgment Regulation in the geography of Europe, the following countries are currently covered for reciprocal enforcement under the Civil Jurisdiction and Judgments Act 1982:

Denmark

Gibraltar

Iceland

Northern Ireland

Norway

Scotland

Switzerland

10–10 Under CPR 74.31 a person seeking to enforce an EEO in England and Wales must lodge the following documents at the local court in which enforcement proceedings are to issued:

- a sealed copy of the judgment;
- the sealed EEO certificate;
- a translation of the EEO certificate into the language of the country of enforcement, which must be certified by "a person qualified to do so in one of the member states"—practitioners can, of course, find online legal translators if required.

In addition, where a person applies to enforce an EEO expressed in a foreign currency in either the High Court or the county court, then the application must contain a certificate of the sterling equivalent of the judgment amount at the close of business on the date nearest to the date preceding the date of issue of the application for the EEO.

10–11 The evidential requirements of the application for an EEO are set out in CPR 74.4 at paras 1(b) and 2(e) and can be summarised as follows:

For applications to register judgments under the Judgments Regulations, CPR 74.4(6) applies, which in turn refers to CPR 74.4(1)(b) and 2(e) respectively.	Where the judgment is not in English, a translation into English must be certified by a notary public or other qualified person, or accompanied by written evidence confirming that the translation is accurate.
	Where interest is recoverable on the judgment under the law of the state of origin: ■ the amount of interest which has accrued up to the date of the application, or ■ the rate of interest, the date from which it is recoverable, and the date on which it ceases to accrue.

EEOs have their own Practice Direction in CPR PD74B, which supplements the Rules in s.V of CPR Pt 74. Paragraph 1 of the Practice Direction states that the rules relating to the certification and enforcement of EEOs are governed by Council Regulation (EC) No. 805/2004 which created EEOs for uncontested claims. The EEO Regulation is annexed to the Practice Direction and can be found at:

http://europa.eu.int/eur-lex/pri/en/oj/dat/2004/l_143/l_14320040430en00150039.pdf [Accessed October 15, 2010]

(To use this link the full reference needs to be typed in to an internet browser such as Explorer on a PC).

10–12 Provision is made in the Practice Direction to provide that if a claim does not meet the requirements of the EEO Regulation, or perhaps more importantly if a judgment creditor does not wish to enforce a judgment using the EEO Regulation, then the judgment may be enforceable using another method of enforcement.

Paragraph 5 of the Practice Direction confirms that when the EEO is lodged at a court in England or Wales where enforcement proceedings are to be commenced, then the enforcement proceedings will be assigned a case number. An official copy from the court of the member state of origin will satisfy the requirement of the regulation (see Art.20) above, for a "sealed copy of the judgment".

10–13 Rules on monetary limits for enforcement also need to be borne in mind when bringing an EEO into the courts of England and Wales for enforcement. These are:

- Section 1 of the Charging Orders Act 1979, which provides that only the High Court has jurisdiction to make a charging order where the amount of the original judgment exceeds the county court limit (currently £30,000);
- Article 8 of the High Court and County Courts Jurisdiction Order 1991 ("HCCCJO 1991"), which provides that judgments in excess of £5,000 must only be enforced by execution against goods in the High Court;
- the HCCCJO 1991, which also stipulates that judgments in excess of £600 may be enforced in the High Court and judgments for less than £600 must only be enforced in the county court.

Naturally, it is possible that the judgment creditor will run into the obstacle of the judgment debtor making an application seeking an order where the granting of the EEO is refused. Such an application is permissible under CPR 74.32 and can be made under Art.21 of the EEO Regulation in the form of a CPR Pt 23 application to the court in which the EEO is being enforced.

10–14 If the judgment debtor embarks on such a course, he or she must, as soon as possible, serve copies of any order made under Art.21(1) on all other parties to the proceedings and any other person affected by the order, along with any court in which enforcement proceedings are pending in England and Wales. Once served with such an order, all enforcement action must cease.

At para. 6 of the Practice Direction an application to refuse enforcement of the EEO in England and Wales must be accompanied by an official copy of the earlier judgment, along with any other documents relied upon and any translations required by the EEO

Regulation. In turn, this documentation must be supported by written evidence stating:

- why the earlier judgment is irreconcilable; and
- why the irreconcilability was not, and could not have been, raised as an objection in the proceedings in the court of origin.

10–15 It is also possible for the judgment debtor to apply for a stay or limitation of enforcement under CPR 74.33, which provides that where the EEO has been lodged the judgment debtor can make an application for a stay or limitation of enforcement under Art.23 of the EEO Regulation, again in accordance with the requirements of CPR Pt 23. Paragraph 7 of Practice Direction 74B deals with further evidence required in connection with an application for a stay or limitation of enforcement including strict requirements on the translation of the judgment from the country of origin.

If the application results in an order being made to stay, or limits the enforcement action, the judgment debtor must "as soon as practicable" serve a copy of the order on all the other parties to the proceedings, any other person(s) affected by the order (such as an HCEO executing a writ of fi fa) and any court in which enforcement proceedings are pending within the jurisdiction of England and Wales. The order staying or limiting enforcement will not have any effect until it has been served in accordance with CPR 74.33 and the parties to be served have received the order.

Again, at para. 5.3 of Practice Direction 74B, the judgment creditor must notify all courts in which enforcement proceedings are pending in England and Wales under the EEO if judgment is set aside in the court of origin, as soon as reasonably practicable after the order is served on the judgment creditor. Notification may be made available by any means including fax, email, post or telephone.

10–16 In relation to applications for a "certificate of lack of enforceability" the Practice Direction includes express requirements at para.3 in which the application must be supported by written evidence. Similarly, in relation to an application for the rectification or withdrawal of an EEO, the Practice Direction requires that evidence in support of that contention should be filed with the application under CPR Pt 23.

It is also possible that an EEO application may become subject to an application for security for costs. If this is the case, CPR 74.5 applies with the stipulation under CPR 74.5(2) that a judgment creditor making the application for an EEO may not be required to give security solely on the ground that he is resident outside England and Wales.

In England and Wales CPR 74.31 provides that the same documents have to be lodged as for other member states, with the additional requirement of a certificate to the sterling equivalent for a judgment in a foreign currency. The Practice Direction to CPR Pt 74.31 clarifies that in England and Wales the point of entry for the EEO is the court. As no specific court is identified, it would appear that it can be issued at any District Registry or county court subject to the usual rules on jurisdiction. The court will then give it a reference number (see CPR 74.31 and Paras 5.1 of the Practice Direction).

If the chosen method of enforcement is the High Court, the judgment creditor can choose a High Court Enforcement Officer (for a list of HCEOs, see *http://www.hceoa.org.uk* [Accessed October 15, 21010]) who has been in the position since April 1, 2004. The EEO can be issued at any District Registry and sent to the HCEO of choice. Other methods of enforcement are available in the English and Welsh courts including a warrant of execution, a charging order, an attachment of earnings, a third party debt order and an order to obtain information.

Scenario 3—Is the judgment to be enforced an incoming judgment into England and Wales from another country with which England and Wales has a reciprocal treaty?

CPR Part 74 SECTION I

Introductory comments on Scenario 3

10–17 This scenario concentrates on giving the reader a practical methodology to navigating the Rules, by looking at how an incoming judgment from a country outside of Europe will be recognised in the courts of England and Wales. The notes to s.I of CPR Pt 74 in the White Book Service 2010 are comprehensive and extend well beyond a book of this nature. From that comprehensive résumé of the law in the enforcement of foreign judgments, a practical way through the treaties and procedures has to be achieved.

Section I of CPR Pt 74 provides for applications to register judgments under a series of reciprocal Acts, which are summarised as follows:

- Section 9 of the Administration of Justice 1920 Act, in respect of judgments to which Pt II of that Act applies (referred to throughout this chapter as the "1920 Act");
- Section 2 of the Foreign Judgments (Reciprocal Enforcements) Act 1933, in respect of judgments to which Pt I of that Act applies (referred to throughout this chapter as the "1933 Act");

- Section 4 of the 1982 Act (referred to throughout this chapter as the "1982 Act").

Background to the 1920 Act

10–18 Part II of the Administration of Justice Act 1920 enabled certain judgments of the superior courts in any part of Her Majesty's dominions outside the United Kingdom to be registered in the High Court (or High Court of Northern Ireland or Court of Session in Scotland). These judgments have the same effect insofar as they relate to the execution of a judgment of the registering court.

Section 7 of the Foreign Judgments (Reciprocal Enforcement) Act 1933 provided that Pt II of AJA 1920 should cease to have effect, except in relation to the dominions to which it extended at the date of the Order in Council applying the 1933 Act to HM dominions.

The provisions of Pt II of the Administration of Justice Act 1920 have been extended by Orders in Council, although no further extensions of Pt II have been permissible since 1933. The 1920 Act no longer applies to Hong Kong and there is no provision for the registration of Hong Kong judgments in England or vice versa. Enforcement of such judgments is by action on the judgment. Gibraltar is now subject to Pt III of the Act (SI 1997/2602).

Background to the 1933 Act

10–19 Under s.1 of The Foreign Judgments (Reciprocal Enforcement) Act 1933 the Queen may, by Order in Council, direct that (subject to the terms of the Order) the provisions of the Act which relate to the registration of foreign judgments may extend to any foreign country prepared to give reciprocity of treatment to judgments given in the courts of the United Kingdom.

A "judgment" of the "court" of a foreign country—both terms are defined in the Act and the particular Order—may be registered provided the judgment is final and conclusive and the sum payable is not in respect of taxes, fines or penalties (s.1(2) and s.11(1) of the Act). Application to register may (by virtue of s.2) be made within six years of the date of the judgment, although not if the judgment has been fully satisfied or it could not be enforced by execution in the country of the original court.

Broadly speaking, a foreign judgment when registered can be treated as if it were the judgment of an English court (s.2(1)). If expressed in the currency of a foreign country, it will be registered in that currency or its sterling equivalent at the time of payment. Interest and the reasonable cost of registration may be added to the judgment when registered. This addition will depend upon the direction in the Master's order, which may be for a sum fixed or summarily assessed. Section 3 of the Act confers power to make rules for registration.

Background to the 1982 Act and the Judgments Regulation

10–20 The rules surrounding the enforcement of judgments from countries under the 1982 Act and the Judgments Regulation are complex, so the reader is referred to the leading textbooks, e.g. C.G.J. Morse, J.D. McClean, A. Briggs, *Dicey & Morris on the Conflict of Laws* 13th Edn (London: Sweet & Maxwell, 2000) and A. Briggs, P. Rees, *Civil Jurisdictions and Judgments*, 3rd Edn (Lloyds of London Press, 1993).

In practical terms, at the time of writing this book the countries subject to the 1982 Act are far more limited as a result of the introduction of the European Enforcement Order, which is dealt with in Scenario 2 of this chapter. The actual countries to which the 1982 Act applies are set out at CPR 74.6.7:

Denmark

Gibraltar

Iceland

Northern Ireland

Norway

Scotland

Switzerland

Article 26 of the Brussels Convention (being Art.33 of the Judgments Regulation) provides that a judgment given in a contracting state must be recognised in the other contracting states without any special procedure being required.

10–21 The definition of "judgment" is to be found in Art.25 of the Brussels Convention (Art.32 of the Judgments Regulation), where it is stated that,

> "for the purposes of this Convention, judgment means any judgment given by a court or tribunal of a contracting state, whatever the judgment may be called, including a decree, order, decision or writ of execution, as well as the determination of costs or expenses by an officer of the court."

That just about covers anything a reader of this text is likely to come across.

The word "judgment" refers solely to judicial decisions actually given by a court or tribunal of a contracting state, and such decisions must emanate from a judicial body of a contracting state deciding on its own authority on the issues between the parties (see *Solo Kleinmotoren GmbH v Emilio Boch* (C-414/92) [1994] E.C.R. I-2237, paras 15 and 17).

An order obtained without notice to the defendant does not qualify as a judgment for the purposes of Art.25 of the Brussels Convention, at least not until the defendant has applied unsuccessfully for it to be set aside (see *Denilauler v Couchet Frères* (C-125/79) [1980] E.C.R. 1553).

Article 27(2) of the Brussels Convention (Art.34(2) of the Judgments Regulation) prevents recognition of a judgment given in default of any appearance by the defendant if the defendant,

> "was not duly served with the document which instituted the proceedings or with an equivalent document in sufficient time to enable him to arrange for his defence".

10–22 The purpose of this Article is to ensure that a judgment is neither recognised nor enforced under the Convention or Regulation if the defendant has not had an opportunity to defend himself (see *Klomps v Michel* (C-166/80) [1981] E.C.R. 1593 para. 9, and *Sonntag v Waidmann* (C-172/91) [1993] E.C.R. I-1963 para. 38). This provision is to be strictly complied with, and if service does not comply with the "lex loci executionis", the judgment cannot be enforced (see *Minalmet GmbH v Brandeis* (C-123/91) [1992] E.C.R. I-5661).

The courts of some contracting and regulation states have been reluctant to recognise and enforce "default judgments" that have been obtained in the English courts. For this reason it has been common practice for a claim which it is ultimately intended to enforce in a Brussels/Lugano Convention contracting or regulation state to be taken to trial where the defendant is in default (see *Berliner Bank AG v Karageorgis* [1996] 1 Lloyd's Rep. 426).

If a judgment creditor finds himself in a situation where a judgment may not be recognised, as it falls under the heading of a "default judgment", then the court should be invited to make an express finding of the facts on which its jurisdiction is based under Art. 28 of the Convention (Art. 35(2) of the Judgments Regulation). It would also be advisable to rely on affidavit evidence rather than witness statements to support the veracity of the judgment that has been entered.

The position should be simplified by the arrival of the legislation that brings the European Enforcement Order to fruition (see Regulation (EC) No. 805/2004 of the European Parliament and of the Council of April 21, 2004), which came in to force on October 21, 2005. The idea is to create a simplified method of enforcement for uncontested claims throughout EU member states.

10–23 There is a considerable amount of case law regarding the requirements for due service and service in sufficient time, to be applied when dealing with the enforcement of judgments in this area of the Rules. Both issues constitute two separate and concurrent safeguards for a defendant who fails to appear, and the absence of one of those safeguards is therefore a sufficient ground for refusal to recognise a foreign judgment. Questions concerning how to cure defective service are governed by the law of the contracting state in which judgment was given, including any international agreements (see *Sabelle Lancry SA v Peters und Sickert KG* (C-305/88) [1990] E.C.R. I-2725).

In *Noirhomme v Walklate* [1992] 1 Lloyd's Rep. 427, Belgian process was served by post on a defendant in England, which of course is the normal procedure in this jurisdiction. Following on from this the defendant did not make an appearance and the claimant entered a default judgment. The judgment was subsequently registered in England and the defendant appealed on the ground that he had not been duly served. His Honour Judge Kershaw, Q.C. held that such service complied with both Art. 27 of the Brussels Convention and Art. 15 of the Hague Convention. The court further held that it had power to stay the execution of the judgment under RSC Order 47, r.1.

In the case of *Hengst Import BV v Campese* [1995] E.C.R I-2113 the Court of Justice held that an order against a defendant for payment ("the decreto ingiuntivo") obtained without notice ("procedimento d'ingiunzione") and served on the defendant, along with an application by the plaintiff, collectively constituted a "document which instituted the proceedings or an equivalent document" within the meaning of Art. 27(2) of the Brussels Convention. As the joint service of the documents started time running for the defendant to oppose the order, the plaintiff could not obtain an enforceable order before the expiry of the time limit.

10–24 To avoid interpreting the requirement of service in a restrictive and formalistic manner, in examining whether service has been effected in sufficient time, the court in which enforcement is sought may take account of exceptional circumstances which arose after service was duly effected. Such facts might include whether the claimant was aware of the defendant's new address after service was effected, or whether the defendant was responsible for the failure of the duly served document to reach the claimant (see *Debaecker v Bouwman* (C-49/84) [1985] E.C.R. 1779).

Article 37(1) of the Brussels Convention provides, insofar as relevant, that an appeal against the decision authorising enforcement shall be lodged in accordance with the rules governing procedure in contentious matters in the United Kingdom. In England and Wales, that is with the High Court of Justice or, in the case of a maintenance judgment, with the Magistrates' Court.

10–25 After the appeal has been lodged, the appellant may apply for a stay of proceedings if an ordinary appeal has been lodged against the judgment in the state of origin, or if the time for such an appeal has not yet expired (see Art. 38(1) of the Brussels Convention). However, as the Convention has established an enforcement procedure which constitutes an autonomous and complete system independent from the legal systems of the contracting states, provisions relating to the stay of proceedings pending appeal against registration must be restrictively and uniformly applied so as to avoid derogation from the Convention's object of establishing a simple and rapid machinery for the enforcement of judgments enforceable in the state of origin. Only the court seized of the appeal (the appeal under Arts 36 and 37(1) of the Convention) has the power to stay the proceedings (Jenard Report, [1979] OJ C59/52).

There is no appeal against the decision to grant or refuse a stay made in such an application (see *Van Dalfsen v Van Loon* (C-183/90) [1991] E.C.R. I-4743). Under Art. 37(2) of the Brussels Convention, the judgment given on the appeal may be contested only by a single further appeal on a point of law.

Reference should be made to the "Look Up Table" in the Appendix to this book, to check which Act applies to which country. Once that is decided, the procedure for registration becomes easier and is set out below.

Evidence in support of the application for registration

10–26 Evidence in support of the application for an incoming judgment to be recognised by the courts of England and Wales has to be filed in accordance with the requirements of each Act. Under CPR 74.4 the evidential requirements can be summarised in the table below.

Under the Acts of 1920/1933/1982 the following basic evidential requirements of points 1–6 must be met:	1. The judgment which has been verified/certified/or is an authenticated copy
	2. Where the judgment is not in English, then a translation into English, which is either certified by a notary public or similarly qualified person, or accompanied by written evidence confirming that the translation is accurate
	3. The written evidence in support of the application for registration must state the name of the judgment creditor and his address for service within the jurisdiction of England and Wales

Reciprocal Treaty	Evidence Required
	4. The written evidence must also state the name of the judgment debtor and his address or place of business, if known
	5. Where the case involves the enforcement of a money judgment, then the amount of the judgment remaining unsatisfied must be given
	6. Where interest is recoverable on the judgment under the law of the state of origin (being the country where the judgment was obtained), the amount of interest which has accrued up to the date of the application, or the rate of interest, the date from which it is recoverable and the date on which it ceases to accrue must be stated
For 1920 Act Judgments points 7–8 must also be included in the written evidence in addition to points 1–6 above	7. That the judgment is not a judgment, which under s.9 of that Act may not be ordered to be registered
	8. That the judgment is not a judgment to which s.5 of the Protection of Trading Interests Act 1980 applies
For 1933 Act Judgments the written evidence must also state in addition to points 1–6 above	9. A statement that the judgment is a money judgment
	10. Confirmation that the judgment can be enforced by execution in the state of origin
	11. Confirmation that the registration could not be set aside under s.4 of the 1933 Act
	12. Confirmation that the judgment is not a judgment to which s.5 of the Protection of Trading Interests Act 1980 applies, which prohibits the recovery of multiple damages pursuant to a foreign judgment. However, prohibition does not prevent the recovery of ordinary compensatory damages for private causes of action similar to those available under English law (see *Lewis v Eliades* [2003] EWCA Civ 1758, [2004] 1 W.L.R. 692)

Reciprocal Treaty	Evidence Required
	13. Where the judgment contains different provisions, some but not all of which can be registered for enforcement, those provisions in respect of which it is sought to register the judgment needs to be set out along with further evidence on: ■ the enforceability of the judgment in the state of origin; and ■ the law of that state under which any interest has become due under the judgment, which may be required under the relevant Order in Council extending Pt I of the 1933 Act to that state. **Note:** By virtue of s.4(5) of the 1933 Act if the judgment is in respect of different matters, and some but not all of the provisions of the judgment are such that if they had been in separate judgments they could have been registered, the judgment may be registered in respect of such provisions—see note to CPR 74.11 in the White Book Service 2006
For 1982 Act Judgments the written evidence must also exhibit in addition to points 1–6 above	14. Include documents which show that, under the law of the state of origin, the judgment is enforceable on the judgment debtor and has been served
	15. In the case of a judgment in default, a document which establishes: ■ that the party in default was served with the document instituting the proceedings or with an equivalent document; ■ if appropriate, a document showing that the judgment creditor is in receipt of legal aid in the state of origin.

Registration Procedure

10–27 Under CPR 74.3 an application can be made to register a judgment from a foreign country in the jurisdiction of England and Wales, so that it can be enforced in this jurisdiction. Applications for registration must be made to the High Court and may be made without notice being given to the judgment debtor.

The application to register a judgment either under the 1920 Act or the 1933 Act should be made without notice and supported by a witness statement or affidavit to the Master.

The application should be lodged in Room E17 (according to the White Book Service 2010), after which it will be checked in the Action Department before being submitted to a Master for him or her to consider the application. The Master may direct that instead of dealing with the application without notice being served on any other party, a claim form be filed and served. Whether this is a Pt 7 or Pt 8 claim is likely to depend upon whether there are contested issues of fact.

Particular requirements in preparing forms

10–28 Firstly, the title of the witness statement or affidavit in support of the application under this scenario should state expressly whether it is made "In the Matter of the Administration of Justice Act 1920, Part II" or "In the Matter of the Foreign Judgments (Reciprocal Enforcement) Act 1933". In either case, the title of the witness statement or affidavit should also identify the judgment by reference to the court in which it was obtained and its date.

Secondly, the rate of exchange of the foreign judgment has to be addressed. Following the decision in *Miliangos v George Frank (Textiles) Ltd* [1976] A.C. 443; [1975] 3 All E.R. 801, and the repeal of s.2(3) of the Foreign Judgments (Reciprocal Enforcement) Act 1933 by s.4 of the Administration of Justice Act 1977, the witness statement or affidavit in support of the application for the registration of a foreign judgment must not convert the amount of the foreign currency into United Kingdom currency at the rate of exchange prevailing at the date of that judgment.

Instead, the foreign judgment needs to be registered in the foreign currency in which it is expressed, or at its sterling equivalent at the time of payment; there is no power entitling the claimant to convert the currency of the foreign judgment at the rate of exchange prevailing at any earlier or other date except the date of payment. This requirement applies to judgments under both the 1920 and 1933 Acts, and so in respect of the 1920 Act negates the decision of *East India Trading Co Inc v Carmel Exporters and Importers Ltd* [1952] 2 Q.B. 439.

10–29 However, when it comes to enforcing the registered incoming foreign judgment, it is then necessary to convert the foreign currency at the date of enforcement according to the method of enforcement employed in accordance with the Queen's Bench Guide. This stipulates that a party who wishes to enforce a judgment or order expressed in a foreign currency by the issue of a writ of fieri facias must endorse the praecipe (see chapter on Execution against Goods for the requirement of a praecipe as part of the process of issuing a writ of fi fa) with the following certificate:

> "I/We certify that the rate current in London for the purchase of [*state the unit of foreign currency in which the judgment is expressed*] at the close of business on [*state the nearest preceding date to the date of issue of the writ of fieri facias*] was [*date*] to the £ sterling and at this rate the sum of [*state amount of the judgment debt in the foreign currency*] amounts to £[*amount*]"

The schedule to the writ of fieri facias should then be amended to:

- show the amount of the judgment or order in the foreign currency at para. 1;
- include a new para. 2, which states "2. Amount of the sterling equivalent as appears from the certificate endorsed on the praecipe for issue of the writ £[*amount*]";
- Renumber the remaining paragraphs of the writ of fi fa as appropriate.

Dealing with cost orders

10–30 Applications under the 1920/1933 Acts provide for the enforcement of any order for costs given or made in any country to which the Act of 1920 or the Act of 1933 applies.

Technical defects in the foreign judgment

10–31 A technical defect in a foreign judgment, e.g. the omission of certain words prescribed by foreign law, does not render that judgment a nullity but only makes it voidable, and so long as it stands it is enforceable by execution in that country and is therefore capable of being registered in this country (see *SA Consortium General Textiles v Sun and Sand Agencies* [1978] Q.B. 279; [1978] 2 W.L.R. 1; [1978] 2 All E.R. 339, CA).

Security for costs

10–32 Under CPR 74.5 the rule allows for an application for security for costs in accordance with CPR Pt 25, subject to the conditions of the Rule being met, which include:

- in relation to the 1982 Act the judgment creditor is not required to give security for costs solely on the basis that he is resident out of the jurisdiction;
- an application for security for costs will not apply to an application under a 1933 Act registration where the relevant Order in Council provides otherwise.

However, a small point in relation to French judgments prevents any application being made for security for costs on the registration of a French judgment.

Service

10–33 If an order is made allowing the foreign judgment to be registered in England and Wales, then under CPR 74.6 the order granting permission to register the judgment ("registration order") must be drawn up by the judgment creditor and served on the judgment debtor by delivering it to him personally, serving it on a judgment debtor company under the requirements of s.725 of the Companies Act 1985 or complying with any other method of service as the court may decide.

The permission of the court is not required to serve a registration order out of the jurisdiction of England and Wales, and the Rules apply to the service of the order for registration as they would to the service of a claim form outside of the jurisdiction.

The registration order must state the full particulars of the registered judgment, together with the name of the judgment creditor and his address for service within the jurisdiction. The registration order must also stipulate the rights of the judgment debtor as allowed under the various Acts, so:

- Under the 1920 and 1933 Acts the right to apply to have the registration set aside must be set out.
- Under the 1982 Act or Judgments Regulation the right to appeal against the registration order must be expressly stated to include:
  - the period within which an application or appeal may be made, and
  - that no enforcement measures will be taken before the end of the period allowed for an appeal to be made, other than measures ordered by the court to preserve the property of the judgment debtor.

Application to set aside registration

10–34 An application to set aside the registration is permissible under CPR 74.7. An application to set aside registration under the 1920 or the

1933 Act must be made within the period set out in the registration order. The court may extend that period, but an application for an extension needs to be made before the end of the period originally fixed or before any subsequent extension. The court hearing the application to set aside registration may order that any issue between the judgment creditor and the judgment debtor be tried.

There is also the right to appeal the registration order under CPR 74.8. An appeal against the granting or refusal of registration under the 1982 Act or the Judgments Regulation must be made in accordance with CPR Pt 52, subject to the provisions of that rule.

Permission is not required to appeal or to put in evidence if the judgment debtor is not domiciled within a contracting state or regulation state, as the case may be. An application to extend the time for appealing is made within two months of service of the registration order, and the court may extend the period for filing an appellant's notice against the order granting registration, but not on grounds of distance.

Where the appellant's appeal is against the granting of a registration order, notice must be served within one month of the registration order, where the party to be served is domiciled within the jurisdiction, or two months where service is to be effected on a party not domiciled within the jurisdiction.

However, where the appeal is against the refusal of registration, then the appeal notice must be served within one month of the decision on the application for registration, regardless of the issue of domicile of the person to be served.

10–35 In *Citibank NA v Rafidian Bank* [2003] EWHC 1950 (QB) it was held that the two-month time limit under CPR 74.8 was not unfair and was compliant with Art. 6 ECHR. There do not appear to be any other reported decisions in this jurisdiction in respect of appeals against the granting or refusal of registration within England and Wales, or the setting aside of registration.

The White Book Service 2010 does refer to the Singaporean case of *Liao v Burswood Nominees Limited* [2004] S.G.C.A. 45; [2005] 4 L.R.C. 8 in which the Singapore Court of Appeal refused an appeal against the setting aside of registration of an Australian judgment. In that case the court refused to accept the appellant's submissions that registration of a judgment for a gambling debt should be set aside on grounds that it was against public policy. It was held that public policy operated with less vigour in the conflict of laws than in domestic law.

Effect of registration

10–36 Once registered, a foreign judgment may become the basis of a bankruptcy notice (*Re Debtor (No.2176 of 1938)* [1939] Ch. 601;).

Enforcement steps post registration

Once the registration order is made, CPR 74.9 deals with the issue of when enforcement action may begin. To start with, under CPR 74.9(1) no steps can be taken to enforce a judgment before the end of the period specified in accordance with rule 74.6(3)(d), being the period allowed for any appeal, as set out in CPR 74.8, or any further period extended by the court.

To begin enforcement the judgment creditor must file evidence of the service on the judgment debtor of the registration order, and any other order relating to the enforcement of the judgment, and allows the court to make further orders to preserve property pending the final determination of any issue relating to the enforcement of the judgment.

Fraud

10–37 In an application to set aside a judgment on the ground that it was obtained by fraud, it is immaterial that the facts on which the defendants rely to establish fraud were known to them and could have been raised in the original proceedings. Regardless of this situation, the defendants are entitled to have the issue of fraud tried (*Syal v Heyward* [1948] 2 K.B. 443; (1948) 64 T.L.R. 476). No order for a payment into court can be made as a condition of trial.

The jurisdiction to set aside a foreign judgment obtained by fraud under s.9(2) of the 1920 Act and s.4(1)(a) of the 1933 Act has been considered by the House of Lords. The House ruled in favour of the long established common law principle that there was a special defence on a foreign judgment, namely that it had been obtained by fraud (see *Abouloff v Oppenheimer* (1882–83) L.R. 10 Q.B.D. 295 and *Vadala v Lawes* (1890) L.R. 25 Q.B.D. 310). The rule of law that a domestic judgment could only be set aside for fraud on fresh evidence that was not available at the trial did not apply to a foreign judgment and the position had not been changed by the 1920 and 1933 Acts. International comity might require that foreign judgments should be given the same degree of finality as English judgments, but that was a matter for Parliament and not the courts (*Owens Bank Ltd v Bracco* [1992] 2 A.C. 443).

Scenario 4—Is the judgment to be enforced an incoming judgment into England and Wales from another country with which England and Wales has NO reciprocal treaty?

10–38 Where a country is not a member of the EU, and has not signed a reciprocal enforcement treaty under the 1920/1933/1982 Acts or the

Judgment Regulation with the United Kingdom, then the approach to enforce an incoming judgment from such a country is to issue proceedings using the foreign judgment as the evidence for the claim and the amount due.

This approach applies to many of the world's most developed economies including the USA, China, Japan, Russia, South East Asia and most central and South American countries.

A claimant from a foreign jurisdiction, who does not have the benefit of a reciprocal treaty to rely upon, needs to issue a claim under CPR Pt 7, endorsed with a statement of case. The judgment of the foreign court becomes the basis of the claim. It is entirely within the discretion of the court as to whether the judgment of the foreign court will be followed. Whilst this method appears more time-consuming and costly than a simple registration process, this need not necessarily be the case.

10–39 Under CPR Pt 24, an application may be made for summary judgment on the basis that the defendant has no real prospect of successfully defending the claim because judgment has already been entered in a foreign jurisdiction. The foreign judgment is evidence in support of this contention. The application for summary judgment can be made at any time after the defendant has stated an intention to defend the claim. In effect, therefore, CPR Pt 24 allows the usual process of pleadings to be expedited, and the court is asked to make a final judgment on the basis of evidence exhibiting the foreign judgment.

If judgment is given, then the practicalities of enforcement involve the location of the judgment debtor's assets.

For example, a US company is the judgment creditor and has supplied Florida T-shirts to an English tour operator to promote holidays in Florida. The English company fails to pay for the T-shirts and the Floridian company issues proceedings in the Florida courts for the sum due under the contract. It serves its proceedings in accordance with local law and obtains a judgment for the sum due under the contract. It must then enforce that judgment, but as there is no reciprocal treaty with the United Kingdom (and in particular England) it commences a further set of proceedings in the English courts using the Florida judgment as evidence that the contract has been performed and the sum due for the T-shirts is due. An application is made for summary judgment, and the English court decides on whether it agrees with the finding of the Florida court. Provided it is satisfied with the basis of that judgment in that it is valid and binding, and is for an identifiable sum of money given by a court of competent jurisdiction, then judgment in the English court will be given in favour of the US company. Once given, the judgment becomes enforceable using the normal court-based methods of enforcement.

Scenario 5—Is the judgment to be enforced an outgoing judgment from England and Wales to another part of the United Kingdom? CPR Part 74—SECTION III

10–40 To be able to enforce a judgment from the courts of England and Wales in either Scotland or Northern Ireland (see Scenario 1 above for the definition of what constitutes the United Kingdom), the judgment creditor must first apply to the court where judgment was entered for a certified copy of the judgment.

CPR 74.17 provides the mechanism for this application in both the High Court and county courts in relation to money provision judgments (again, the reader is referred to the definition of "money provision" and "non-money provision" in Scenario 1 above). An application for a certificate of judgment is made under para. 2 of Sch.6 to the 1982 Act to enable the money provisions of a judgment of the High Court or of a county court of England and Wales to be enforced in either Scotland or Northern Ireland.

10–41 The judgment creditor may apply for a certificate on Form 111, which is filed at the court where the judgment was given or has been entered, together with written evidence setting out:

- the name and address of the judgment creditor and, if known, the name and address of the judgment debtor;
- the sums payable and unsatisfied under the money provisions of the judgment;
- where interest is recoverable on the judgment; either—
  - the amount of interest which has accrued up to the date of the application, or
  - the rate of interest, the date from which it is recoverable, and the date on which it ceases to accrue;
- that the judgment is not stayed;
- the date on which the time for appealing expired or will expire;
- whether an appeal notice has been filed;
- the status of any application for permission to appeal; and
- whether an appeal is pending.

If the judgment to be registered in Scotland or Northern Ireland is a non-money provision judgment, then CPR 74.18 provides the necessary mechanism for obtaining the appropriate form of certified copy judgment from either the High Court or county court under para. 2

of Sch.7 to the 1982 Act using Form 112, which appears in the Appendix together with a witness statement in support.

Scenario 6—Is the judgment to be enforced an outgoing judgment from England and Wales to another country within the EU? CPR Part 74 SECTION V

10–42 The momentum to streamline cross-border enforcement within the European Union has culminated in the creation of the "European Enforcement Order", or "EEO" as referred to throughout this chapter.

The EEO has been available to judgment creditors since October 21, 2005 for any judgment dated after January 20, 2005 for the enforcement of a judgment within the European Union.

Basically, the EEO allows:

- a judgment creditor who has an uncontested judgment from an English or Welsh court to obtain an EEO certificate from the court where judgment was entered, and then transfer that judgment to another EU country where the judgment debtor has assets as an "outgoing judgment";
- an uncontested judgment from an EU country to be enforced in the High Court or a county court in England and Wales as an "incoming judgment".

10–43 Before enforcing a judgment by way of an EEO it is important to consider the accompanying rules and regulations enshrined in new legislation, which are designed to make the procedure more straightforward. These include:

- European Council Regulation 805/2004. This is the detailed supporting Regulation to the process and needs to be examined and understood before embarking on the procedure. The Annex to the actual Regulation is in fact intended to be the "certificate" referred to in the Regulation, even though it looks more like a tick box form than a certificate (Article 9).
- Articles 1 and 5 outline the intentions of the Regulations. Article 1 states that the purposes of the Regulation is to create an EEO for uncontested claims and to allow, by laying down minimum standards, the free circulation of judgments . . . without any intermediate proceedings needing to be brought in the member state of enforcement. Article 5 states that a judgment which has been certified as an EEO in the member state of origin should be recognised and enforced in

other member states, without the need for a declaration of enforceability and without any possibility of opposing its recognition.

- Rule 74 of the Civil Procedure Rules section V and Practice Direction 74.B sets out the procedure for obtaining the EEO certificate. It also sets out the procedure for staying execution.
- Forms N219 and 219A and HM Courts Service (HMCS) Advice Sheet Ex 375 give advice on how to apply for an EEO.
- All member states recognise the EEO. The Regulation sets out the specific criteria which must be met before an application can be made for an EEO. If a case does not meet the criteria, or if a judgment creditor does not wish to use an EEO, then the judgment creditor may use the procedures set out in Scenarios 3 and 7 above, which are provided under Regulation 44/2001 and applied by Art. 27 and CPR P. 74.19–26.

How is the application started for an EEO?

10–44 The application is made on either Form N219 or N2192A and must comply with Art.16. It must contain the names and addresses of the parties, the amount of the claim, interest sought, rate of interest, the period for which interest is claimed and the basis/reason for the claim.

In the case of a judgment given in the Chancery or Queen's Bench Division of the High Court, or in a District Registry, the application is made to a Master or district judge. In the case of a county court judgment, the application is made to a district judge.

Where the application is granted, the court will send the EEO certificate and a sealed copy of the judgment to the person making the application. Where the court refuses the application, it will give reasons for the refusal and may give further directions.

Article 17 requires that certain information must also be supplied to the judgment debtor, advising how the claim can be contested.

Once the application is prepared it needs to be served in accordance with the requirements in articles 13, 14 and 15. The regulations provide various methods of service from personal to postal with no acknowledgement of receipt where the judgment debtor resides in the member state of origin.

It is important to remember that the issue of service is potentially problematic, since in England and Wales service by post is accepted whereas in most member states in the EU personal service is standard and postal service is not accepted and viewed as potentially in contravention of the ECHR.

10–45 This procedure is only available where the claim is "uncontested". Article 3 sets out what constitutes "an uncontested claim" including circumstances where:

- the judgment debtor has admitted the debt or has agreed a consent order approved by the court; or
- the judgment debtor has not filed a defence; or
- the judgment debtor has failed to attend a court hearing after he has filed a defence, "provided such conduct amounts to a tacit admission of the claim or fax"; or
- the judgment debtor has expressly agreed to it as an authentic instrument, which is defined in Art. 4.

An EEO does not appear to be available if a contested claim culminating in a hearing results in judgment for the claimant (which presumably includes judgment for the defendant on a counterclaim). However, if the claim (and presumably counterclaim) is settled "by consent" it is available.

Article 18 sets out the circumstances under which perceived defects in the procedure may be cured if appropriate evidence is put before the court at the time of applying for the EEO. If service of the summons is by post and there has been no response from the judgment debtor, it may be wise to use Art. 18 to strengthen the claimant's position by serving the judgment together with information as to what to do if disputed. The court may then be persuaded to issue the EEO.

Article 7 confirms an EEO may include both the judgment debt and costs, provided no dispute has been raised as to the liability to pay costs. Therefore, if the judgment debtor has admitted the debt but disputed entitlement to costs, notwithstanding that a cost order has been made against him, the EEO cannot include the costs because that part has been contested.

Article 8 provides for the issue of a partial EEO for a judgment where only part of the order meets the regulations. It should be noted that if the judgment debtor has accepted the liability for costs in principal, but has disputed the amount of the costs, the claim remains "uncontested" for EEO purposes.

10–46 In summary, the requirements are that the judgment is enforceable in the member state of origin and does not conflict with s.3 and s.6 of Regulation 444/2001. Section 3 deals with jurisdiction on cases involving insurance, while s.6 gives exclusive jurisdiction to certain courts in matters relating to land, property, company constitutions/solutions, patents and trademarks.

To make the application, a judgment creditor will need to submit the following to the court:

- an application fee;
- a completed form N219 or N219A;
- three completed copies of the EEO certificate for sealing (the draft certificate is annexed to the regulations);
- the court's judgment or any costs certificate;
- a duly certified translation of any documentation not in English—legal translation specialists can be found on the internet.

Proof of service may also be required for the reasons set out above.

How is an EEO enforced?

10–47 The law of the member state to which the EEO has been sent governs the enforcement procedures. Article 20 sets out what is to be sent to the member state of enforcement. The requirements include:

- a sealed copy of the judgment;
- the sealed EEO certificate;
- a translation of the EEO certificate into the language of the country of enforcement—the translation must be certified by a "person qualified to do so in one of the member states".

Interestingly, although CPR 74.31 requires that a judgment in a foreign currency has to have a certificate with the sterling equivalent, there does not seem to be a similar requirement in the regulations when sending an EEO to Europe.

Therefore, before issuing an EEO of execution in Europe, it would be advisable to obtain the rules from the country of enforcement. Article 29 obliges member states to provide information as to procedures via the European Judicial Network, which can be found at *http://ec.europa.eu/civiljustice/index_en.htm* [Accessed October 15, 2010]. Information is given in all the European languages, and the enforcement procedures for each country are set out accordingly.

10–48 Note that under Article 20(3) no security, bond or deposit can be required from the judgment creditor before enforcement, on the grounds that he is a foreign national or "... not domiciled or resident in the member state of Enforcement". Presumably, security can be given if that is the standard practice of that country, even for its own nationals.

Article 20(2) states that the "creditor shall be required to provide the competent enforcement authorities of the member state of enforcement with the documents", which raises an interesting question as to what constitutes the "competent enforcement authority". It may mean a court in the country of enforcement, but it may also mean that it should be sent directly to the enforcement agent in countries where enforcement is by independent agents, for example France and Holland. Advice from HMCS suggests that the judgment creditor contacts the relevant court of the member state and ascertains the procedure for using the EEO in that country.

Further information is also available at: *http://ec.europa.eu* [Accessed October 15, 2010] where full information about enforcement procedures and enforcement agents is given.

10–49 It is recommended that before embarking on an EEO procedure, the judgment creditor should contact the representative body of the enforcement officers in the destination member state to ascertain what type of enforcement system operates in that country and what fees will be incurred. The international association of enforcement officers originating from Europe can be contacted via their website at *http://www.uihj.com* [Accessed October 15, 2010]. It is possible that the cost of enforcement in Europe is more expensive than enforcement costs in England and Wales.

What happens if the judgment debt becomes disputed?

10–50 The procedural requirements of the Regulations are designed to limit the circumstances in which an EEO can be the subject of dispute. Regulation 17 specifies that the sums must contain details of how the defendant can contest the proceedings.

Article 19 provides that an EEO certificate can only be issued if the court of origin has a procedure to dispute the judgment in cases where the proceedings have been served in accordance with Art.14 (in other words, without proof of receipt) and as a result the judgment debtor has had insufficient time to defend or through no default of his own has not been able to defend, provided such application is made promptly (namely CPR 13).

If there are any doubts as to whether a summons came to the defendant's attention as a result of service pursuant to Art.14, Art.18 provides a procedure to cure any perceived or arguable defects.

10–51 Article 21(2) states that under no circumstances may the member state of enforcement review the judgment as to its substance (this can only be done by the member state of origin). However, there is an exception to this rule in Art.21(1) in that a member state of enforcement can refuse to enforce the judgment if it is irreconcilable with an earlier judgment given by any member state or a third party country, provided the same parties and cause of action were involved (there are several other provisos—see CPR 74.32 and para.6.1 of the Practice Direction).

Article 10 allows an application to the state of origin to rectify errors, namely mistakes in the EEO certificate, or withdraw the EEO where it has been wrongly granted, for example where the judgment fails to meet the minimum standards set out in Art.19. Annexe VI of the regulation addresses the application to rectify/withdraw. If applying in England and Wales, CPR 74.30 requires a Pt 23 application supported by written evidence.

Article 6(2) provides that where an EEO is no longer enforceable, because and/or the judgment has been set aside, and the appropriate certificate (see Annexe IV) to the Regulations has to be issued, it would seem appropriate to combine the application under CPR 74.30 with the application under CPR 74.29 (being an application under Art.6(2) of the Regulation for a certificate indicating the lack or limitation of enforceability of an EEO certificate made to the court of origin by application in accordance with CPR Pt 23).

Article 23 provides that on application of the judgment debtor, a court in the member state of enforcement can limit enforcement to protect the situation pending the outcome of an Art.10 application in the state of origin. CPR 74.33 requires a CPR Pt 23 application exhibiting evidence of the application to the court of origin (see CPR 74.33 para 7.1 of the PD). If the application is successful, the judgment debtor must serve all the parties and the court with copies of the order.

Scenario 7—Is the judgment to be enforced an outgoing judgment from England and Wales to another country with which England and Wales has a reciprocal treaty? CPR 74—Section II

10–52 Under Section II of CPR Pt 74 the enforcement of English and Welsh judgments in foreign countries where there is a reciprocal enforcement treaty, is started by the application of a certified copy of the judgment. This certified copy is then sent to the country where there is a reciprocal treaty for enforcement to begin.

Section II provides the procedure for "outgoing" judgments to be enforced in foreign jurisdictions as follows:

- For a High Court judgment under s.10 of the Administration of Justice Act 1920.
- For a High Court or county court judgment under s.10 of the Foreign Judgments (Reciprocal Enforcement) Act 1933.

- For a High Court or county court judgment under s.12 of the Civil Jurisdiction and Judgments Act 1982.
- For a High Court or county court judgment under art.54 of the Judgments Regulation.

Which Acts apply to which countries?

10–53 You will find in the Appendix the most up to date listing of countries and the respective reciprocal treaty governing the enforcement position. However, this list is subject to change, and therefore reference should always be made to the latest version of the White Book Service and the accompanying commentary.

How is the application started?

10–54 The application for a certified copy of the English or Welsh judgment is made without notice and supported by written evidence, which must include:

- copies of the claim form in the proceedings in which the judgment was given;
- evidence of service of the claim form on the defendant;
- the statements of case made in the claim;
- and, where relevant, a document stating whether the applicant was an assisted person or an LSC-funded client.

The written evidence must also deal with:

- the grounds on which the judgment was obtained;
- whether the defendant has objected to the jurisdiction and the grounds of its objection;
- confirmation that the judgment has been served in accordance with CPR Pt 6 and CPR 40.4 (regarding the service of order where it has been drawn by a party);
- confirmation that the judgment is not subject to a stay of execution;
- the date on which the time for appealing the judgment expired or will expire; or whether an appeal notice has been filed and the status of any application for permission to appeal, and whether an appeal is pending.

Of course, the statement about the "time for appealing has expired" does not apply to a judgment entered in default of any acknowledgment of service or defence under CPR Pt 12. Instead, where judgment has been entered in default, the application must show that no application has been made to set aside the judgment. The formal certificate issued by the court will then state that the defendant may apply to set the judgment aside, although he has not yet done so (Practice Direction, July 17, 1962 seems to be authority for this practice, followed by the Judgment and Orders Section of the Central Office of the Royal Courts of Justice).

10–55 For default judgments intended to be enforced in European member states, the approach should be to follow the procedure set out in Scenario 6 above and to apply for an EEO:

- whether the judgment provides for the payment of a sum of money and, if so, the outstanding and unsatisfied amount;
- the interest position—stating whether interest is recoverable on the judgment and, if so, either the amount of interest which has accrued up to the date of the application or the rate of interest the date of which is recoverable, and the date on which it ceases to accrue.

Are there any pitfalls in using Scenario 7?

10–56 As noted in the White Book Service 2010 at 74.13.1 there are a couple of pitfalls that the judgment creditor needs to be aware of when seeking to enforce the judgment under s.II of the CPR Pt 74.

Firstly, under s.10 of the 1933 Act, a certificate of judgment cannot be issued where the sum payable is "... in respect of taxes and other charges of a like nature or in respect of a fine or other penalty".

Secondly, there is some debate as to whether a judgment obtained in a county court and transferred to the High Court for enforcement can be enforced through a court abroad, as it has been queried as to whether such a judgment meets the criteria of the 1920 and/or 1933 Acts in that it should be a judgment "given" or "obtained" in a "Superior Court". The question is "will the foreign court recognise the county court judgment as judgment given or obtained in a Superior Court?"

As the 1920 and 1933 Acts are based on reciprocity, it cannot be assumed that the countries in which these reciprocal arrangements exist will enforce judgments other than those of the "High Court" or "Superior Court", as defined in the Acts.

10–57 In respect of countries not party to the various conventions, it can be stated with reasonable certainty that the Isle of Man will enforce an English or Welsh County Court judgment under the 1933 Act which has been transferred to the High Court for enforcement and certified under this rule by the High Court (see *Stapleford Flying Club v Kreisky* unreported April 18, 1991, High Court of the Isle of Man, Deemster Corrin).

However, it should be noted that The Royal Court of Jersey rejected registration of an English county court judgment transferred to the High Court for enforcement under the 1933 Act. The basis of this rejection was the absence of reciprocity in that a judgment of the Jersey Petty Debts Court would not be amenable to registration in England. Bailiff Bailhache commented that although the English Courts might be bound to regard the judgment of the county court as a judgment of the High Court for all purposes, it was not a judgment "given in a Superior Court" for the purposes of the Jersey legislation (see *Re Hardwick* [1995] the Jersey Law Reports 245).

Under the Administration of Justice Act 1920 the position remains unchanged, so a certificate can only be issued in respect of judgments "obtained in the High Court", which leaves open the question of whether the receiving court will consider a county court judgment which has been transferred to the High Court in England and Wales for enforcement.

In respect of either the 1920 or the 1930 Acts, if there is doubt about whether the receiving country will accept a transferred up county court judgment, the safest approach will be to issue the original claim in the High Court. If that is not permissible, for instance under The High Court and County Court Jurisdiction Order 1991 (SI 1991/1724), then the claim should be issued in a county court and, if before any further step is taken, application made to transfer the claim to the High Court (see CPR 30.3 relating to the criteria for an order to be transferred).

What is the procedure for applying for a certificate where judgment has been entered at a District Registry?

10–58 Applications of certified copies of judgments entered in District Registries should be sent to the District Registry where the judgment was obtained, following which the District Judge can then exercise his or her powers of a Master under this rule (see CPR 2.4 relating to the interchangeability of powers of District Judges and Masters). This brings the procedure under the 1933 Act in line with the procedure under the Brussels Convention and Judgments Regulation regime.

Scenario 8—Is the judgment to be enforced an outgoing judgment from England and Wales to another country where there is no reciprocal treaty in place?

10–59 If judgment has been obtained against a judgment debtor with assets in the jurisdiction, it is worth considering how to enforce the judgment and then use the usual methods of enforcement under the CPR. It is definitely worth considering the possibility of using a freezing injunction under CPR Pt 25 to restrain the judgment debtor from taking assets out of the jurisdiction before judgment. Such an application may be considered prudent to prevent assets being removed during the period between the judgment debtor being served with notice of registration and the expiry of the period within which he can bring an application to have the registration set aside, or the determination of such an application, during which period, as has been seen, execution may not issue.

There is no reported case in which this has been done in England in relation to a foreign judgment, but the court was prepared to grant such an injunction in the case of the enforcement in England of a foreign arbitral award, where precisely similar considerations applied (*see Deutsche Schachtbau und Tiefbohrgesellschaft mbH v Ras Al Khaimah National Oil Co* [1987] 3 W.L.R. 1023; [1987] 2 All E.R. 769) and the matter appeared to be beyond doubt. If additional support is needed, such an injunction was granted in similar circumstances in New Zealand (*see Hunt v BP Exploration Co (Libya) Ltd* [1980] 1 N.Z.L.R. 104).

10–60 If the judgment debtor only has assets abroad, consideration has to be given to whether enforcement is possible in the foreign jurisdiction. If a treaty of reciprocity exists, so much the better, but one cannot underestimate the overall cost of the exercise which reads well in a textbook but can be fraught with complications and expense in real life.

If the country is not listed in the "Look Up Table" in the Appendix to this book, then it may still be possible to enforce a judgment abroad, even if there is no reciprocal enforcement treaty.
Options include:

- starting proceedings on the English/Welsh judgment and obtaining summary judgment in that action;
- starting proceedings on the English judgment in the foreign jurisdiction where the judgment debtor has assets but does not reside, serving the proceedings out of the jurisdiction under the local equivalent of CPR Pt 6. As in England, the mere presence of assets in the jurisdiction may not of itself confer on the courts the power to hear an action, but there may be a provision allowing the grant of leave to issue a claim for service out of the jurisdiction to enforce a judgment or arbitral award.

10–61 It follows, therefore, that the first essential requirement when considering enforcing any judgment abroad is to take advice from a local agent in the foreign country concerned, in order to establish whether enforcement:

- is possible at all;
- and, if so, what the procedure will be;
- how long it will take;
- how much it will cost;
- what assistance the foreign lawyer will need.

Indeed, it will usually have been prudent to discuss these matters with a local agent before commencing any proceedings in England and Wales. A good question to ask is whether anyone has tried to use collection agents to collect the outstanding sum over the telephone or by personal visit, rather than by resorting to further legal proceedings in the uncertain enforcement arena.

It may also be worth finding out what rate of interest will run on the judgment once it has become enforceable abroad, and whether any accrued Judgments Act interest will be recoverable. It may then be possible to assess whether further pursuit of the debt is economically worthwhile. Indeed, in some cases, it will be worth doing this exercise before starting proceedings at all, especially if the debtor has no assets in England.

10–62 Usually, the foreign lawyer will be able to proceed without a visit from his English instructing solicitor, since all he will probably require is an affidavit exhibiting the judgment or a copy thereof, and setting out the facts which an English court would require in similar circumstances. However, where the sum at stake justifies it, a visit to the foreign lawyer should be undertaken, which will have the effect of clarifying for the English solicitor the procedures and timescales involved, and enable him to assess the calibre of the person he has instructed. Further, it will bring home to the foreign lawyer the importance of the matter and the need to proceed with enthusiasm.

Transforming enforcement in Europe—CPR Part 78

Introductory comments

10–63 At the beginning of this chapter it was mentioned that the global enforcement of a judgment was knowledge that a judgment creditor would have to embrace. In England and Wales the nearest examples of cross-border enforcement start with Scotland, Northern Ireland and then the rest of the EU.

Outside of the British Isles enforcement can become problematic, with areas of difficulty including the different systems of law and procedures, the obvious language barriers, the ability to locate the assets of the judgment debtor and myriad costs regimes. For many judgment creditors this is enough to put them off trying to enforce their judgment debt; nevertheless, help is at hand in the form of the "European Order for Payment Procedure" or "European Payment Order", which was created under regulation 1896/2006 and is now a part of s.1 of the Rules. The actual procedure came in to force on December 12, 2008.

This new process seeks to provide a straightforward and quick debt recovery procedure for uncontested claims across the European Union. It can be used for a small claim as well as a large outstanding commercial debt. As is common with new procedures in England and Wales, it is based on a system of standard forms. The theory behind this is that the standard format will allow the dispute to be dealt with by written procedures and, where possible, through automatic electronic data processing. The cost of the procedure is determined by national law in each member state and is equivalent to domestic court fees.

10–64 In practice, this means that a claimant in England and Wales should be able to use the European Payment Order to enforce payment of his debt in any EU country—see the countries of the EU mentioned earlier in this chapter. When the successful claimant receives the court's order for an uncontested debt in his favour, it becomes automatically enforceable in every EU country and no further steps are necessary to prove recognition of the judgment in one of the European courts.

If a defence is raised to the European Payment Order, the claim moves out of the realms of the procedure and into domestic civil procedure rules, to be handled in the normal way.

All this makes the European Payment Order an option for those wanting to enforce an uncontested debt. However, the new rule does not make it mandatory to use this procedure in a cross-border case, as a judgment creditor can still use the EEO which was set up through regulation 805/2004 of April 21, 2004.

Making an application

10–65 The European Payment Order procedure applies to all countries within the EU, except Denmark. The defendant needs to be domiciled or habitually reside in a member state other than the member state of the court in which the claim for payment has been made.

The claim is made using the recently introduced standard form application. It is important that practitioners review the rule and the practice direction carefully when making or responding to an application. Even at this stage, the Supreme Court Practice 2010 states in its editorial introduction that the guidance and checklist on procedures are currently being prepared to assist court staff with checking whether applications comply with the regulations. Judgment creditors are advised to view this application as one still very much in its infancy as a process.

If the application complies with the Rules and the forms are properly completed, the European Payment Order must be issued and served on a defendant with proof of receipt being obtained, which can be done electronically.

Unless a statement of opposition is sent to the court by the defendant within 30 days of the application, with a small amount of time allowed for the statement to arrive at court, the Court will then declare the order enforceable.

If the defendant opposes the claim, then, unless the claimant brings the case to a halt, the claim will be transferred into the normal system of court business and allocated to the court where the defendant is resident. The claim will then proceed in accordance with the CPR.

10–66 In exceptional cases the defendant can apply for a review, refusal, stay or limitation of enforcement, but the regulations do not provide a right of appeal. The procedure is designed to be dealt with on paper rather than by oral hearing, although a hearing may be allowed in certain circumstances.

Even in the commentary to the White Book 2010, concerns are raised about the successful implementation of this new directive, which is something that judgment creditors need to be aware of. As is often the case with EU directives, the language of the directive and the regulations does not translate well and may be difficult to follow; definitions used may not be the same when translated into English, which means that the process becomes open to judicial interpretation—the very thing the procedure was designed to avoid.

Another point to note is that when it comes to serving the European Payment Order, postal services across Europe can take seven to ten days to deliver a claim. This is likely to mean that despite the fact that the time limits given for service are not generous, applications for review (which means in the English context "default judgments") seem very likely.

There is a requirement to conduct the case in English, which is helpful to those of us where English is our first language, and to provide translations.

Applications to set aside the order, for example where there are disputes about the validity of service, or to seek a review or a stay, will invariably be referred to the court, which of course can lead to delay and differing interpretations of the regulations.

Applications made to a court in England and Wales

10–67 To make the application, a claimant in England and Wales must file the documents set out in Art.21 of the regulations at the court in which the enforcement proceedings are being heard.

These documents include:

- A copy of the European Order for Payment.
- A translation of the European Order for Payment.

What is the procedure for applying for a European Order for Payment?

10–68 As always, judgment creditors wishing to use this procedure must read the main Rule in CPR 78, alongside the accompanying Practice Direction.

The terms of CPR Pt. 78 are governed primarily by the regulation that created the European Payment Order process and which is set out in Annex 1 of the Practice Direction. Where the regulation is silent on any particular matter, the Civil Procedure Rules will apply with necessary modifications.

The application must be completed in English or accompanied by a certified translation, which is then filed at court. An application made to the High Court will be automatically assigned to the Queen's Bench Division, which will not prevent the application being transferred to another court, where appropriate.

The Rules provide for the filing of additional documents, such as a statement of opposition, to be faxed or emailed to the court handling the application.

The application is served using the Civil Procedure Rules for service under CPR Pt. 6.

10–69 Article 9 of the regulation makes provision for the completion or rectification of the application form within 30 days of the request by the court for completion or rectification.

Where an application is made under CPR Pt. 78, r.1, this will not normally be an oral hearing, but if an oral hearing is to be held it will normally take place by telephone or video conference.

Depending on where the application is filed, the Court in England and Wales will assign the case a court number. If the judgment is set aside in the original court, the judgment creditor will need to notify all the courts in which any enforcement proceedings are pending in England and Wales as soon as possible after the order is served on the judgment creditor. Notification of this may be by fax, email, post or telephone.

Rules 78.10 and 78.11 deal with applications being made by the judgment debtor to either refuse enforcement or to stay or limit the enforcement of the order.

Disappointingly, these rules do not deal with the actual enforcement of the order. For enforcement measures, judgment creditors will need to apply the normal enforcement rules in the country where the assets of the judgment debtor are located.

What happens if the judgment debtor makes a counter-application?

10–70 An application may be made under art.22 of the originating regulation to seek an order that the court should refuse to enforce the order. An application on this basis must be made by the judgment debtor under CPR Pt 23 in the court in which the European Payment Order is being enforced (see CPR 78.10).

If an order is made, the judgment debtor must serve copies of it on all the other parties to the proceedings, as well as any person affected by the terms of the order. This needs to be done as soon as possible. Once served, then all enforcement proceedings relating to the order will cease.

What is the procedure if the judgment debtor applies for a stay?

10–71 In the language of the regulation, the phrase "seeks a review" can be compared with the more usual term in the CPR of "applying for a stay". This may occur when the defendant has sought a review, and also applies for a stay or limitation to the enforcement action in accordance with art.23.

Again, the application for a stay must be made in accordance with CPR Pt 23 in the court in which the order is being enforced.

The defendant will again need to serve a copy of any order made on all the other parties to the proceedings and on any other persons affected by the order. The order will also need to be served on the court in which the enforcement proceedings are pending in England and Wales.

The order granting a stay or limitation on enforcement action will have no effect on anyone until it has been served in accordance with the rule and they have received it (see CPR 78.11).

How is domicile determined under the regulation?

10–72 Domicile is determined using arts.56 and 60 of Regulation 44/2001, going back as far as December 22, 2000. This determines the question of domicile in relation to the jurisdiction and recognition of the enforcement of judgments in civil and commercial matters.

The regulation states that the relevant moment for determining whether there is a cross-border matter in which the issue of domicile must be addressed is the time when the application for the European Order for Payment is submitted in accordance with the regulations.

Article 60 of the 44/2001 Regulation states that a company, other legal person or association of natural legal persons is domiciled at the place where it has a statutory seat. In the United Kingdom and Ireland this means a registered office. Where there is no registered office this applies to the place of incorporation, or where there is no place of incorporation, the place where the law of the company's formation took place. It may also mean the central administration or the principal place of business.

If the claim relates to a contract concluded by a consumer (the definition of which is given as someone who has concluded a contract outside of his trade or profession), then only the courts in the member state in which the defendant is domiciled can have jurisdiction (see CPR 78 PD.26 and art.16 of regulation 1896/2006).

How is a European Payment Order enforced?

10–73 If the time limit laid down in article 16(2) of the regulation expires, and there is no opposition to the application for an order, the court of origin (meaning the court which issued the European Order for Payment (see CPR 78PD.25)) must without delay declare the European Order for Payment enforceable using standard Form G set out at Annex VII.

The court must verify the date of service, after which it will send the enforceable European Payment Order to the judgment creditor. There is no further need for a declaration of enforceability or any need to recognise the European Payment Order as being enforceable.

Under CPR 78PD.41 the enforcement procedures are then governed by the law of the member state for enforcement; a member state is defined as the member state in which the enforcement of a European Order for Payment is sought (see CPR 78PD.25 and art.5—definitions of the regulations).

Where enforcement needs to take place in another member state, the judgment creditor must provide competent enforcement authorities of the member state with:

- a copy of the European Order for enforcement, as declared enforceable by the court of origin, which satisfies the necessary conditions to establish its authenticity; and

- where required, a translation of the European Order for Payment into the official language of the member state where enforcement is going to take place. The translation must be certified by a person qualified to do so in one of the member states.

It is not permissible for a security, bond, deposit or any other similar security to be imposed on a foreign national as part of this process.

The European small claims procedure

10–74 To complete the discussion on how enforcement law is changing in Europe, the development of cross-border dispute resolution measures continues. Under EC Regulation 861/2007 the European Small Claims Procedure ("ESCP") was implemented by all member states of the EU on January 1, 2009.

The aim of this procedure is to improve access to justice by introducing a universal procedure for cross-border claims for less than 2000 (excluding interest, costs and disbursements). The procedure can be followed where at least one of the parties is domiciled or habitually resides in the state where the action is brought and the other party is located in another member state.

The regulation provides a mechanism for a judgment to be obtained and then for that judgment to be recognised so it is capable of enforcement in other member states, without the need for a declaration of enforceability. In essence, the procedure is the equivalent of a small claims track for European money claims.

10–75 The procedure to issue the claim itself is set out at CPR 78.12.1. Naturally, in this book we look at the enforcement process of any judgment resulting from a process. Certainly, the commentary to the Supreme Court Practice 2010 anticipates a number of problems in obtaining an enforceable order under the process. It comments:

> "The claimant will have to be prepared to follow through in the defendant's member state [any enforcement] which will not be easy, and may incur more costs".

It even goes on to say that, given the difficulties,

> "the procedure will not be well used except perhaps by those returning from holidays or business trips in Europe having bought goods that proved to be faulty".

Time will tell as to how this procedure is implemented and utilised by the citizens of the EU in dealing with their small claims across the EU area.

Chapter 11

Traffic Enforcement—CPR Part 75

Introductory comments

11–01 As a result of enforcement law continuing to evolve, we need to identify new and specific areas of practice and procedure relating to particular types of enforcement on a constant basis. The area of traffic enforcement is dealt with exclusively under Pt 75 of the Civil Procedure Rules.

Under the Road Traffic Act 1991 a new regime was established for the enforcement of parking charges, which in turn decriminalised these as traffic offences and removed them from the ambit of the Magistrates' courts' enforcement regime. The 1991 Act was then replaced by the Traffic Management Act 2004.

The actual role of the court in enforcing traffic penalties is limited, and yet Pt 75 of the Civil Procedure Rules is devoted to the enforcement of these types of judgment. The penalties themselves are levied by local authorities through their own traffic enforcement schemes.

11–02 In some ways, therefore, this is a very narrow area of enforcement, and yet it is probably one of the busiest. The actual work of enforcing this type of judgment is probably handled by only a few of the major enforcement businesses. The fact that it does command an entire section of the Rules means it is an area of growing importance, particularly as local authorities are seen to continue to use parking offences as a means of generating revenue. Many more people are going to be caught by parking and speeding penalties as well as congestion charges than, say, the enforcement of an ordinary judgment debt.

Background to the rules

11–03 CPR Pt 75 through its accompanying Practice Direction lists the types of penalties that can be recovered at para.1.2. These include parking penalties, bus lane penalties, vehicle emission penalties and penalty charges under road user charging schemes.

Penalties become enforceable as if they were a county court judgment, once the local authority has gone through the CPR Pt 75 procedure, which in turn creates an enforceable order through the county court system.

The warrants of execution generated by the procedure are executed by a bailiff certified in accordance with the enforcement of Road Traffic Debts (Certificated Bailiffs) Regulations 1993 (SI 1993/2073). Under Art.4 of that statutory instrument, relevant sections of the County Courts Act 1984 apply to certificated bailiffs as if they were County Court Bailiffs.

Before an order becomes enforceable through the county court procedure, local authorities themselves are responsible for issuing the various types of penalties. Disputes are resolved by Parking and Traffic Adjudicators, who are judges dealing exclusively with the review of cases under the Traffic Management Act 2004 and its supporting regulations. A very useful website with information about the adjudication process for each type of penalty can be found at *http://www.parkingandtrafficappeals.gov.uk/index.htm* [Accessed, October 15, 2010]

11–04 The county court has no role to play in this adjudication process. The process provided for in CPR Pt 75 enables penalties incurred to be converted into enforceable judgments. The only input from the judge is a possible hearing to decide the sole issue of whether permission should be given to file a statutory declaration "out of time".

Unpaid parking penalties are therefore registered as county court judgments through the Traffic Enforcement Centre (TEC) at Northampton, which is part of the County Court Bulk Centre. According to statistics appearing on Her Majesty's Court Service website, the TEC processed some 1.2 million registrations during 2006/07, and a further one million from April 2007 to December 2007.

11–05 It is important to appreciate that CPR Pt 75 is not an appeal procedure to the court. Instead, the application is about whether permission can be granted to file a witness statement "out of time". To avoid enforcement action being taken, a respondent must pay the total sum due or file a witness statement. There are only four grounds for making a statement, namely:

1. that the penalty has been paid;
2. that no penalty charge notice was received;
3. that representation was made to the local authority but no reply was received;

4. an appeal was made to the parking and traffic appeal service, but no response was received.

If an application is made to extend the time for filing a witness statement, this will be considered by a court officer at the TEC. If the request is refused, the respondent can request a review of that decision by a district judge. A new procedure introduced from April 2009 entitles a respondent to a paper review by a district judge (which will be done at Northampton County Court) or a hearing before a district judge, in which case the application will be transferred to the respondent's local county court. **11–06**

As one can imagine, bearing in mind the numbers of parking offences which occur in England and Wales on an annual basis, there is a constant need to review and evolve this particular part of the Rules.

By virtue of the Civil Procedure (Amendment No. 3) Rules 2008 (SI 2008/3327), r.75.5 was updated to include a new r.75.5A. This enabled any review by a district judge of a court officer's decision to be determined without an oral hearing, unless the respondent asked for a hearing or the court ordered a hearing. This amendment came in to place on April 6, 2009. The accompanying Practice Direction was also updated by making amendments to para.6 of PD75.

What happens when a road traffic act penalty is incurred?

The following stages occur *before* the charge is registered with the TEC: **11–07**

- A penalty charge notice would have been issued. This should have been paid or appealed against as per instructions given on the notice.
- A Notice to Owner or Enforcement Notice would have been sent to the registered keeper of the vehicle (not necessarily the driver at the time of the offence). This amount should have been paid or disputed. Representations should have been made in writing to the local authority and, if appropriate, an appeal made to the Parking and Traffic Adjudicators (see the website above for more information).
- A Charge Certificate would have been issued, which will have increased the unpaid penalty charge by 50 per cent. This should have been paid to the local authority.

So, in effect the judgment debtor has on the face of it had plenty of opportunity to pay the amount of the penalty charge.

Set out below are a series of questions that a judgment debtor may want answered when dealing with a penalty charge.

What are the formalities for swearing a statutory declaration?

11–08

How is the penalty charge contested?	If a person wishes to contest the charge, he must file a valid Statutory Declaration with the TEC, within 36 days of the date of the penalty charge being registered. Guidance notes and a form of Statutory Declaration can be downloaded from *http://www.hmcourts-service.gov.uk/cms/files/OOTApplicationPack.pdf* [Accessed October 15, 2010]
What are the grounds for contesting a penalty charge?	There are only three grounds upon which the declaration can be based. These highlight the procedures the local authority may have failed to carry out prior to registering the penalty charge. They are: ■ the registered keeper did not receive the Notice to Owner or Enforcement Notice; ■ representations were made to the local authority, but a rejection notice was not received; and ■ an appeal was made to the Parking and Traffic Adjudicator (following the rejection, by the local authority, of the above representation) and no response was received.
What are the swearing requirements of a valid statutory declaration?	A Statutory Declaration must be sworn before any of one of the following persons, to ensure it is accepted by the TEC, which in turn prevents enforcement action being taken: ■ a court officer appointed by a judge to take the oath or affirmation on affidavits—court officers duly appointed can be found at a local county court and do not charge a fee; ■ a Justice of the Peace at any Magistrates' Court—a fee may be payable; ■ a solicitor or Commissioner for Oaths—a fee may be payable.
What is the effect of filing a valid statutory declaration?	The TEC will revoke the Order for Recovery. This does not, however, mean that the penalty charge has been cancelled. The local authority may continue to pursue the charge and will contact the judgment debtor if it intends to take further action.

What happens if a valid statutory declaration is not filed?	Failure to file a valid statutory declaration with the TEC within 21 days of the date of the Order for Recovery may result in the local authority enforcing the penalty charge by requesting a warrant of execution be issued. Once the warrant of execution has been authorised by the TEC, the local authority will appoint private bailiffs for its execution.
How can a judgment debtor request more time to complete a statutory declaration?	A judgment debtor, who perhaps is going away on holiday or will be out of the jurisdiction on business, can apply for an extension of time in writing from the TEC, which can grant up to one month's extension.
To whom does the judgment debtor pay the penalty charge?	Payment of the penalty charge must be made direct to the local authority and not to the TEC.
How does a judgment debtor know if a warrant of execution has been issued?	The judgment debtor may contact either the local authority that issued the penalty charge or the TEC to find out if a warrant has been issued.
What should a judgment debtor do if he or she has paid the penalty charge?	To prevent enforcement action escalating, a judgment debtor who has paid the penalty charge must contact the local authority with proof of payment—be that a bank statement showing a cheque being paid out of an account, or a receipt for cash paid over the counter at the town hall.

What is the procedure under Part 75 once time for payment and/or a valid statutory declaration have not been complied with?

11–09 If a judgment debtor fails to respond to the penalty charge, by using the opportunities afforded to him or her and as set out in the above table, then the penalty charge will be escalated into a warrant of execution under CPR Pt 75.

As with other Parts of the CPR there is a Rule and an accompanying Practice Direction which determines how private bailiffs will enforce the warrant.

CPR 75.1 deals with the scope and interpretation of this Part. It recognises the TEC as being established under the direction of the Lord Chancellor and defines "no relevant return to the warrant" as meaning:

- the bailiff has been unable to seize goods because he has been denied access to premises occupied by the defendant, or because the goods have been removed from those premises;
- any goods seized under a warrant of execution are insufficient to satisfy the debt and the cost of execution; or
- the goods are insufficient to cover the cost of their removal and sale.

Rule 75.2 refers to the TEC and states that proceedings under Pt 75 must be started in the TEC. Any officer exercising functions with the process of TEC business is deemed to act as an officer of that court.

11–10 As for other types of enforcement action, r.75.3 requires a request to be filed for the amount due, and the request must certify:

- that 14 days have elapsed since service of the notice of the amount due;
- the date of such service;
- the number of the notice of the amount due;
- that the amount due remains unpaid.

The request must also specify the grounds on which the local authority claims to be entitled to the penalty charge, and must state:

- the name, title and address of the respondent;
- the registration number of the vehicle concerned;
- the authority's address for service;
- the court fee; and
- such other matters as required by the Practice Direction.

Once the request is received and meets all the requirements of the Rule, the court officer—being a TEC member of staff—will seal a request and return it to the issuing local authority.

11–11 The local authority, on receipt of the sealed request from the TEC, can draw up the necessary order and attach to it a form of statutory declaration for the judgment debtor's use (the Rule refers to the judgment debtor in this scenario as the respondent, but for consistency the term "judgment debtor" has been adopted as part of this book).

Within 14 days of receipt of the sealed request from the TEC, the local authority must serve the order (and the form of statutory declaration) on the judgment debtor in accordance with CPR Pt 6. Where an order is served by first class post (or an alternative service which provides for delivery on the next working day), r.6.7 is modified so that the date of service is deemed to be the seventh day after the date on which the order was sent to the judgment debtor.

Rule 75.4 recognises that local authorities will want to deliver electronic files of information to the TEC, and so this Rule permits electronic delivery of documents in computer-readable form. Disclosure from the computer file is expressly permitted only under this Rule.

The functions of the TEC court officer permit him or her to act as both court officer and district judge in CPR 75.5, although if a decision is made by the court officer, a party may request any such decision to be reviewed by a district judge. Such a request must be made within 14 days of service of the court officer's decision.

11–12 Orders made under this Part of the Rules (CPR 75.6) can be enforced by cross reference to other parts of the enforcement rules within the CPR, as follows:

- CPR Parts 70 to 73—being the new Rules for General Enforcement, Orders To Obtain Information, Third Party Debt Orders and Charging Orders, respectively;
- CCR Order 25, rr.1 (general provisions under the CCR) and 9 (enforcement against a firm);
- CCR Order 26, r.5 (permission to issue certain warrants); and
- CCR Order 27, rr.1 to 7, 7A, 7B, 9 to 16 and 18 to 22—Attachment of Orders
- (Rule 30.2 provides for the transfer between courts in order to enforce a judgment).

How is a warrant of execution issued?

11–13 To issue a warrant of execution under r.75.7 the local authority must file the necessary request, which:

- certifies the amount remaining due under the order;
- specifies the date of service of the order on the judgment debtor (respondent); and
- certifies that the relevant period has elapsed.

The court will then seal the request and return it to the local authority, which in turn must within 7 days prepare the warrant of execution which will remain valid for 12 months starting from the date of its issue. A local authority may not renew a warrant issued under Pt 75.

Can the warrant of execution be revoked?

11–14 If an order has to be revoked under r.75.8 because the judgment debtor has filed an acceptable form of statutory declaration, then the TEC needs to serve a copy of this on the local authority, and any execution issued on the order will cease to have effect. In practical terms this means informing any bailiffs as soon as possible of the need to withdraw from executing the warrant.

What other avenues of enforcement can be pursued?

11–15 Rule 75.9 allows for the transfer of a warrant to another county court for enforcement, perhaps to attempt another court-based form of enforcement such as a charging order or attachment of earnings, as these are expressly permitted by CPR Pt 75 to be used. However, if that request is made, the local authority must give reasons as to why it has not attempted to enforce by way of execution, certify there has been no "relevant return" as set out above to the warrant, specify the date of service of the order on the judgment debtor and certify that the relevant period has elapsed.

Rule 75.10 specifies that where another form of enforcement is utilised, then in addition to the usual information for either an attachment of earnings order, an order to obtain information from a debtor, a third party debt order or a charging order, and the requirements of Pts 71, 72 or 73 or CCR Order 27, respectively, the application for the new form of enforcement must state (where applicable):

- the reasons why the local authority has not attempted to enforce by execution;
- certify that there has been no "relevant return" to the warrant of execution;

as well as specifying the date of service of the order on the judgment debtor (respondent) and certifying that the relevant period has elapsed.

Practically, r.75.11 allows a local authority with the permission of the court officer to combine information relating to different orders against the same judgment debtor in any request or application under the Rules.

Under which legislation can Part 75 be used?

11–16 The all-important Practice Direction accompanying Pt 75 sets out in para. 1 the breadth of legislation where penalty charges have been decriminalised and are now enforceable under this part of the Rules. They include:

- increased penalty charges provided for in parking charge certificates issued under para.6 of Sch.6 to The Road Traffic Act 1991 and amounts payable by a person other than an authority under an adjudication of a parking adjudicator pursuant to s.73 of the same Act.
- increased penalty charges provided for in a charge certificate issued under para.8 of Sch.1 to the London Local Authorities Act 1996 (relating to a contravention or failure to comply with an order made under a provision referred to in s.4(2) of that Act, reserving all or part of a carriageway of a road as a bus lane).
- Amounts payable by a person other than an authority under an adjudication of an adjudicator pursuant to the Sch. to the Road User Charging (Enforcement and Adjudication) (London) Regulations 2001.
- Increased fixed penalties to which regulation 17(6) of the Road Traffic (Vehicle Emissions) (Fixed Penalty) (England) Regulations 2002 and similarly for Wales.

How should a judgment debtor respond to a penalty charge?

11–17 A judgment debtor in responding to a penalty charge must send to the TEC a completed application notice (Form PE 2 may be used) and a completed statutory declaration in Form PE 3 (Forms PE 2 and PE 3 can be obtained from the Centre at Northampton County Court, Bulk Centre, 21/27 St. Katharine's Street, Northampton NN1 2LH (Telephone number: 084 5704 5007)).

If the judgment debtor responds to a penalty charge by completing a statutory declaration, the TEC will serve a copy of the application notice, and a copy of the statutory declaration on the local authority that obtained the court order, and seek representations on the application.

A court officer will deal with the application without a hearing, provided the statutory declaration is in a valid format. The matter will not be dealt with until at least 14 days after the date on which the application notice and statutory declaration have been served on the local authority. If the proceedings have been transferred to another court, the TEC will transfer the application to the new court.

Where the matter is decided by the TEC's court officer, the order will contain a statement allowing either party to request a review of that decision by a district judge at a hearing.

What happens if a hearing becomes necessary?

11–18 Should a hearing be necessary, the proceedings will be transferred to the county court for the district in which the respondent's address for service is situated. This transfer is only for the purposes of holding the hearing and serving any orders made as a result of the hearing.

The judgment debtor's address for service will be the address for service shown on the last of the following documents filed at court by the judgment debtor, being either:

- the application notice or, if more than one, the latest application notice; and
- the appellant's notice.

The court where the hearing is held will serve any orders made as a result of the hearing, before returning the papers to the TEC. If proceedings have been transferred, then the papers will be served on the court where the proceedings have been transferred.

Evidence at any hearing may be given orally or by witness statement.

Is it possible to suspend a warrant?

11–19 An application to suspend a warrant of execution under Pt 75 is permissible where the judgment debtor makes an application for a longer period in which to file a statutory declaration, or if before that application is determined a warrant of execution is issued by the local authority, which must be suspended until the application for the extension has been determined. If the outcome of that hearing is that the court order is revoked, then any execution issued on that order will cease to be effective.

What are the practical effects of a warrant of execution under CPR Part 75?

11–20

What should a judgment debtor do if the bailiff has been instructed and he or she wishes to appeal the penalty charge?	Provided a statutory declaration can be filed under one or more of the three grounds, and there was a good reason why the statutory declaration was not filed earlier (within the 21 day time limit), the judgment debtor should contact the TEC on 084 5704 5007 to request a Late Statutory Declaration. This should be sent to the TEC and not the local authority. The TEC can be emailed at *customerservice.tec@hmcourts-service.gsi.gov.uk* [Accessed October 15, 2010] and the TEC website has more useful information at *http://www.hmcourts-service.gov.uk/cms/1039.htm* [Accessed October 15, 2010]
Who should a judgment debtor contact regarding bailiff action?	As the local authority employs the bailiffs, any bailiff queries must be addressed to the bailiff's company or the local authority. The TEC cannot suspend or cancel any bailiff action. Any complaints about the conduct of a bailiff must be made to the county court that issued the certificate to the bailiff. Bailiff companies can be found on the internet, or try one of the professional associations such as *http://www.ensas.org.uk/* [Accessed October 15, 2010] or *http://www.acea.org.uk/* [Accessed October 15, 2010]
What happens if a judgment debtor serves the statutory declaration, after the necessary time period?	A copy of the judgment debtor's form is faxed to the local authority concerned. Upon receipt, the local authority will suspend any enforcement action. If the local authority accepts the judgment debtor's application within 14 days, the Order for Recovery will be revoked (cancelled). If the local authority rejects the judgment debtor's application, the appeal will be referred to the Officer of the Court, who will make an impartial judicial decision. The judgment debtor will then be notified of the results. This decision can be reviewed by a district judge in accordance with Pt 75
How does a judgment debtor appeal against the Court Officer's decision?	A judgment debtor may appeal by completing a standard Application Notice on Form N244 stating that he wishes to set aside the Court Officer's order. Upon

How does a judgment debtor appeal against the Court Officer's decision? – *Cont*	receipt of the judgment debtor's form, the TEC will transfer the matter to the judgment debtor's local county court and the appeal will be listed for a hearing
Will the penalty charge be registered as a judgment?	A penalty charge registration is not registered on a collective register such as the Register of County Court Judgments and Fines

What fees are payable in relation to this type of enforcement?

11–21 The table below details the fees and charges as set out in Sch.1 of the Enforcement of Road Traffic Debts (Certificated Bailiffs) Regulations 1993 (as amended by the Enforcement of Road Traffic Debts (Certificated Bailiffs) (Amendment) Regulations 2003).

Fee Type	**Fee Payable**
1. Fee for preparing and sending a letter advising the debtor that a warrant is with the bailiff and requesting the total sum due (fee recoverable only if the letter is sent before a first visit is made to the debtor's premises)	£11.20
2. For levying distress i. Where the sum demanded and due does not exceed £100 ii. Where the sum demanded and due exceeds £100	 £28 28% on first £200; 5.5% on any additional sum over £200
3. Reasonable costs and charges for attending to levy distress, but where levy is not made	The costs and charges are not to exceed the fees and charges which would have been due under 2 above if the distress had been levied
4. For taking possession— i. Where a man is left in physical possession (close possession) ii. Where walking possession is agreed	 £5.60 each day; 55p each day for the first 14 days; 5p each day thereafter
5. Valuation	Reasonable fees, charges and expenses of the broker

6. Removing goods or attending to remove goods where no goods are removed	Reasonable costs and charges
7. Sale of goods	15% of the proceeds of sale if the sale is held on an auctioneer's premises, to cover the auctioneer's commission and out-of-pocket expenses plus the reasonable cost of advertising, removal and storage OR 7.5% of the proceeds of the sale where the sale is held on the debtor's premises, to cover the auctioneer's commission plus out-of-pocket expenses actually and reasonable incurred

Chapter 12

Taking Control of Goods

Introductory comments

12–01 Execution against goods remains the most popular method of enforcement in both the county courts and High Court. Its popularity as a method of enforcement no doubt stems from its simplicity.

The judgment creditor needs only to issue a warrant of execution in the county court to enable a county court bailiff to be instructed to take possession of goods. The High Court process is slightly more complex, but as this is the process on which the county court warrant of execution process is built, it is fundamentally the same. Many of the rules are mirrored by the county court in its Rules.

The procedural differences that exist between the lower and higher court stem from the approach taken by the county courts' own bailiffs, employed by Her Majesty's Court Service ("HMCS"), and High Court Enforcement Officers (formerly known as Sheriffs), who are referred to in this chapter as "HCEOs".

These procedural differences are set out in this chapter by distinguishing between county court and High Court business as it is today, and how it may change once the Tribunals Courts and Enforcement Act 2007 is enabled through supporting regulations and changes to the CPR.

12–02 For judgment creditors and judgment debtors caught up in the current system, the overlap between when a county court warrant of execution is used and when a High Court writ of fieri facias (fi fa) can be issued leads to confusion and uncertainty, which hopefully future reforms will overcome.

It is perhaps for this reason that Pt 3 of the Tribunals Courts and Enforcement Act 2007, which looks at a streamlined process for taking control of goods as a means of enforcement, is to be welcomed. Under s.62 of the Act, the powers that will be used to take control of goods and sell them to recover a sum of money are set out in Sch.12. Current legislation affected by Pt 3 of the Act is then set out in Sch.13.

At the time of writing this book, the Act has been on the statute books for three years, but the relevant sections have not been commented on and the underlying regulations that will support the Act have yet to be published.

12–03 In this chapter, therefore, we will use the structure of Sch.12 to Pt 3 of the 2007 Act as a framework against which we shall determine how the law of execution will evolve in relation to "enforcement by taking control of goods".

Schedule 12 is a very good starting point for understanding both how the current system of execution against goods operates now and how it will work in the future. Schedule 12 will, however, require supporting regulations to be enacted before the new approach under the Act becomes a working set of rules.

Nonetheless, as we prepare for the new Act to come into place, which could be as early as April 2012, we can start to use the structure of Sch.12 to look at the present work of enforcement agents in the civil courts and how this will change forwarding the future. Schedule 12 creates an outline around the enforcement of a judgment or order in a very logical way—from the time goods are first seized (or taken into control), through to the payment out of proceeds from a sale of such goods.

Using this approach we can see how the enforcement of a warrant or Writ will progress from start to finish. In addition, we will look at the new Act structure in conjunction with the present High Court and county court position. In this way, future editions of this book can continue to develop the content of this chapter in a structured way.

Introductory changes—paragraph 1, Schedule 12

Current High Court position

12–04 A Writ of execution against goods is the most commonly used method of enforcement in the High Court. The term "Writ" survived the "Access to Justice" reforms introduced in April 1999 on the introduction of the Civil Procedure Rules.

The system of High Court enforcement through the Office of Sheriff was the first part of a series of such planned reforms by Government. Section 99, Sch.7 of the Courts Act 2003 removed the responsibility for the enforcement of a High Court Writ of execution from the High Sheriff of the county and moved this to HCEOs. In March 2004, delegated legislation in the form of The High Court Enforcement Officers Regulations 2004 was brought into force to regulate the business of the officers authorised by the Lord Chancellor under the Act.

HCEOs are responsible for the enforcement of High Court Writs of execution, the most popular being the "Writ of Fieri Facias", or "Writ of Fi Fa", which provides for the seizure and sale of the judgment debtor's goods. The writ of fi fa is the High Court equivalent of the more widely known county court "warrant of execution".

12–05 The High Court route provides for the seizure and sale of the judgment debtor's goods and chattels (or in common parlance "belongings"), which are sufficient to satisfy the judgment debt, costs, interest and charges of the HCEO. "Fieri Facias" comes from the Latin meaning "that you cause to be done." This will change when Pt 3 of the Tribunals Courts and Enforcement Act 2007 is implemented through supporting Regulations, when the writ of fi fa will become the "Writ of control". However the objective remains the same, which is to instruct an HCEO to seize and sell the judgment debtor's goods in order to satisfy a money judgment.

Current county court position

12–06 The rules on enforcement of county court warrants echo their High Court counterparts, and much of the established case authority surrounding the use of execution comes from the development of the writ of fi fa over the centuries in the development of the common law.

Execution in the county court is based on issuing a warrant of execution, which is the most popular method of court-based enforcement in England and Wales. It is relatively easy to produce a warrant of execution, and the fee payable is fixed.

12–07 As the most popular and, dare it be said, easiest form of enforcement, there are a few points that judgment creditors should be aware of in relation to how to use warrants for better results:

- For court users who issue in their local court, the machinery of "home" court and "foreign" court has to be appreciated. Where a warrant of execution is issued in the court where judgment was obtained, this becomes the "home court". If a warrant of execution is issued in that court, but has to be sent to another court for enforcement, being the court responsible for the area in which the judgment debtor's goods are located, this court then becomes the "foreign court" for enforcement purposes.
- If the warrant of execution has not been executed within one month from the date of its issue, the court officer of the court responsible for its execution must send a monthly report to the

judgment creditor for every month during which the warrant remains outstanding, outlining the reason for non-execution.

- The county court bailiff will usually attempt execution three times before submitting a final return under the warrant. These three attempts could all be made in the first three months of the warrant. If a judgment creditor requires the bailiff to take further action under the warrant for the rest of the life of the warrant, which is a nine-month period, then Form N445 will need to be completed. It may not be necessary to go through the exercise of completing this form if the judgment creditor can show that the court and/or bailiff have erred in some way in the execution of the warrant and that the final return should therefore not have been given in the form that it was. In this instance, a letter requesting further action be taken by the bailiff will usually suffice.
- The County Court Bulk Centre (CCBC), based in Northampton, now allows for warrants to be issued using email facilities as well as other standard electronic media. CCBC users request their judgments and warrants to be issued in computer-readable form. Court users are given guaranteed levels of service—judgment requests are processed on the date of receipt, dated in the same way and then printed and posted to the defendant within 48 hours. The CCBC offers a personalised judgment order, which also contains a payment slip, should users wish to take advantage of this service. Warrant requests are processed automatically the same day and the details are sent electronically to the defendant's local court overnight. As well as a saving of £5 on each warrant issued, there is no warrant reissue fee for CCBC warrants. Where the claimant wishes to enforce through the High Court, the CCBC will deal with the request within a maximum of two days. More information about the CCBC can be found at *http://www.hmcourts-service.gov.uk/cms/1054.htm* [Accessed October 20, 2010].
- Judgment creditors are well advised to give as much information as possible to the bailiff in the form of warrant of execution, including details of the availability of the judgment debtor, any known assets and other issues to be aware of.

New Act position

12–08 The new Act changes the terminology of a writ of fieri facias to a "Writ of Control", and a warrant of execution to a "warrant of control", both of which are defined in s.62(4)(a)(b), respectively.

Under s.67 the responsibility for county court enforcement is likely to be taken away from district judges (which no doubt will be a relief for them) and transferred to "any person authorised by or on behalf of the Lord Chancellor". At present, under s.85(2) of the County Courts Act 1984 the district judge has power to execute judgments or orders for the payment of money.

Supporting regulations as to who will have the responsibility of that power in future have yet to be determined.

Changes to enforcement agents—paragraph 2, Schedule 12

Current High Court position

12–09 High Court Enforcement Officers are the successors to the Sheriff system of enforcement and have personal liability for any writ of fi fa issued in their name. They have inherited all the traditional duties, powers, rights, privileges and liabilities of their predecessors—the High Sheriffs—by virtue of s.99 of the Courts Act 2003, Sch.7.

The starting point in establishing the HCEO's position between the parties in executing the writ is that the HCEO must have regard to the interests and instructions of the judgment creditor, as far as compatible with his or her own duty (see *Re Crook* (1894) 63 L.J.Q.B. 756).

Some judgment creditors like to view the HCEO as their agent, and although in some ways an HCEO might be perceived as such, the HCEO is in fact a "public functionary" who has duties to perform to both parties to the writ. The case law in this regard is well established (see per Lord Cranworth LC in *Hooper v Lane* (1857) 6 H.L. Cas. 443, 549–550, which was cited in *Re A Debtor (No. 2 of 1977)*, [1979] 1 W.L.R. 956; [1979] 1 All E.R. 870).

Current County Court position

12–10 Each county court has its own officers "commonly called county court bailiffs", who are appointed and employed as part of their duties to carry out the enforcement of warrants under s.2 of the Courts Act 2003.

New Act position

12–11 Part 3, Ch. 1 of the Act sets out the regime for how enforcement agents will be appointed in future. The Act streamlines the creation and regulation of enforcement agents in different parts of the enforcement industry, which includes the appointment and certification of High Court Enforcement Officers, certificated bailiffs and private bailiffs. The Act stops short of regulating:

- an Officer of Her Majesty's Revenue and Customs; or
- a person appointed under s.2(1) of the Courts Act 2003 (which includes court officers and staff)

Introducing new terms—paragraph 3, Schedule 12

Current High Court position

12–12 The preamble to the 2007 Act states that, amongst other things, the purpose of Pt 3 is to amend the law relating to the enforcement of judgments and debts and to make further provision about the management of relief of debts.

This in turn requires a change from current terminology, and so whereas we are used to seeing writ of fieri facias within the Civil Procedure Rules, s.62 introduces new terms including a Writ of Control. This new form of writ is defined as taking control of goods and selling them to recover a sum of money, which is a much easier definition than its predecessor!

Current county court position

12–13 As with the change of term in relation to a High Court writ, the county court warrant becomes a warrant of control.

New Act position

12–14 Under Pt 3 of Sch.12 to the Tribunals, Courts and Enforcement Act 2007, the general interpretation clause sets out a number of new definitions, which then appear throughout the rest of Sch.12 and will no doubt appear in supporting regulations.

Binding property in the debtor's goods—paragraph 4, Schedule 12

Current High Court position

12–15 In the High Court, as the law stands at the time of writing this book, the issue of a writ of fi fa "binds" the property in the goods of the judgment debtor from the time when the writ is received by the person who is under a duty to enforce it (see Courts Act 2003, Sch.7, para.8).

The timing of the writ on delivery to an HCEO is an important management procedure for the smooth running of any HCEO office. On delivery of the writ to the HCEO, the HCEO must endorse the writ with the date and time of its receipt. The time endorsed is then used to establish the priority of the writ with competing judgment creditors, either in the High Court or county court, and so far as other proceedings are concerned, particularly where moves are afoot to make the judgment debtor insolvent.

The term "binding the property in the goods of the . . . debtor" has been defined as meaning that on delivery of the writ of fi fa, the enforcement agent acquires a legal right to seize enough of the judgment debtor's goods to satisfy the amount specified in the writ. As stated in the case of *Samuel v Sir J. Duke* (1838) 3 M.&W. 622, it is as if,

> ". . . from such delivery the goods become, as it were, impressed with a superimposed right of the enforcement agent to deal with the goods".

12–16 Once seized, the judgment debtor cannot deal with his goods except by sale to a bona fide purchaser for value who has no notice of the delivery of the writ to the HCEO. How frequent is that? In practice, very infrequent, but the law does anticipate such a situation and very occasionally it does happen that an innocent purchaser acquires goods which have been seized by an HCEO, without appreciating that the goods have in fact been seized. In these rare circumstances, the existence of the writ of fi fa will not prejudice the title to goods acquired by:

- a person in good faith, and
- who for valuable consideration,
- had at the time when he acquired his title notice that the writ or any other writ, by virtue of which the goods of the judgment debtor might be seized or attached,
- which had been delivered to and remained unexecuted in the hands of the enforcement agent.

12–17 Occasionally, a judgment debtor does manage to sell the goods to a purchaser in good faith, at a market value, without telling the purchaser that a writ of fi fa is in existence, either because the judgment debtor is not aware that a writ has been issued or because the judgment debtor conceals that information from the purchaser.

Although the debtor may pass a good title to a purchaser who buys these goods in good faith, for both valuable consideration and without notice of the writ or seizure, under Courts Act 2003, Sch.7, para.8(2) the goods remain subject to the HCEO's rights. Therefore, any sale to such a purchaser, though it may pass a good title, will be in breach of the implied warranties as to quiet possession and freedom from encumbrances for which the purchaser will be liable in damages (see *Lloyds and Scottish Finance Ltd v Modern Cars and Caravans (Kingston) Ltd* [1966] 1 Q.B. 764; [1964] 3 W.L.R. 859).

Current county court position

12–18 A warrant of execution in the county court binds the property in the goods of the judgment debtor from the time the warrant is applied for (see s.99(1) County Courts Act 1984).

The county court procedure does differ from the High Court, as priority is calculated from the time the application for the warrant of execution is made, and not the time it is delivered to the county court bailiff for execution (see *Murgatroyd v Wright* [1907] 2 K.B. 333).

New Act position

12–19 Under the TCEA 2007 the binding of the property in the goods of the judgment debtor takes place at an early stage in the enforcement process.

In relation to a High Court writ, the goods will be bound from the time the writ is received by the High Court Enforcement Officer (see para.4(3) of Sch.12), which in effect replaces para.8 to Sch.7 of the Courts Act 2003, as mentioned above.

Where the enforcement is commenced in the county court by a warrant of control, or in the magistrates' court, the goods will again be bound from the time the warrant is received by the county court or magistrates' court's enforcement agent. This ensures that the timing for purposes of priority in either the county court or the High Court is treated in the same way.

So far as other types of warrant of control are concerned, for example where commercial rent arrears recovery procedures are being used by a landlord, the goods will be bound from the time the landlord gives notice of enforcement under a para.7 notice.

12–20 The new Act repeats the position as at present, so that where a person acquires goods in good faith for valuable consideration and without notice of the commencement of the enforcement action, the innocent purchaser is able to acquire good title to the debtor's goods, free from the enforcement agent's interest.

Goods will be bound under para. 6 of Sch.12 until:

- the goods are sold—in which case they will no longer be bound (although remaining goods may continue to be bound);
- where the goods seized include money and any amount is used to pay the amount outstanding (again, the debtor's remaining goods will be bound);
- if the entire amount outstanding under the judgment debt or penalty is paid, the goods will stop being bound and all the debtor's goods can be released;
- the writ or warrant expires or is set aside.

Effect of property being bound—paragraph 5, Schedule 12

Current High Court position

12–21 The effect of the writ is to bind the property in the goods of the judgment debtor from the time it is delivered to the enforcement officer for execution (see para.8(1) Sch.7 of the Courts Act 2003).

On receipt of the writ the enforcement officer must (without charging any fee) endorse on the back of the writ the date and time it was received (see para.7 Sch.7 of the Courts Act 2003).

If the writ has been directed to more than one officer, the endorsement is made by the individual responsible for allocating it to the officers. It is slightly different to say such an individual exists in practice, but all HCEOs are very good at timing the priority of any writ they receive and also using their central database to calculate if another HCEO is in priority to them.

Not all goods can be seized; those that are exempt from seizure are set out in para.9 of Sch.7. That is not to say the goods will not be seized, though. In fact, the procedure is often for the HCEO to seize much of what is found with the possible exception of bedding, clothing and other necessary items, and then wait for the judgment debtor to make an application that any goods seized are exempt under RSC Order 17, r.2(A). This rule puts the onus on proving whether goods are exempt on the person making the claim.

Current county court position

12–22 The county court position is similar to the High Court position. A person's title to goods belonging to a judgment debtor will not be prejudiced if acquired by a person in good faith and for valuable consideration, unless he had notice that an application for the issue of a warrant had been made to the district judge and that the warrant remained unexecuted.

New Act position

12–23 Under the new Act the effect of property being bound is set out in para.5 to Sch.12, but the provisions go further than the current law. Where there has been an assignment or transfer of any interest in the judgment debtor's goods, which are bound for the purpose of an enforcement power (see Sch.12, Pt 1, para.1(2)), then any transfer or assignment is subject to that power. The application of Sch.12 in relation to those goods will not be affected, except where there is an assignment or transfer that is dealt with expressly in the Act.

Where a person acquires title to any of the judgment debtor's goods in good faith for valuable consideration and without notice, the position is as it is today. Schedule 12 does go further by saying that,

> "a thing is to be treated as done in good faith if it is in fact done honestly (whether it is done negligently or not)",

something which the current law does not attempt to define.

In practical terms, how often are HCEOs met by a purchaser of goods in good faith, paying consideration for those goods, who does not already appreciate that the judgment debtor is in some difficulty financially and that therefore the goods are in fact bound? The answer to that is very rare in practice.

Time when property ceases to be bound—paragraph 6, Schedule 12

Current High Court position

12–24 What is clear under the current Rules is that property will cease to be bound when the following outcomes are achieved:

- goods are sold;
- money is paid to avoid sale;
- the Officer is withdrawn for some reason.

Current county court position

12–25 It is the duty of the district judge responsible for executing a warrant to give information to the judgment creditor as to progress (see CCR Order 25, r.7(3)).

If the warrant has not been executed within one month from the date of issue of its receipt, a notice must be sent to the judgment creditor to this effect by the court. That notice must also be sent at the end of every subsequent month while the warrant remains outstanding (see CCR Order 25, r.7(2)).

The district judge may go further and send a communication outlining particular difficulties that are being experienced in relation to the execution. The district judge may then ask for further instructions or inform the judgment debtor of what future action he intends to take.

New Act position

12–26 Again, for the purposes of exercising any enforcement power, the property in the goods of the judgment debtor will cease to be bound under the writ or warrant of control in accordance with the terms of this new section (see para.6 of Sch.12).

As one might expect, the property which was bound in any goods will cease to be so when those goods are either sold or, in the case of money used to pay the amount outstanding, when that money is so used.

The goods will also cease to be bound where the amount outstanding is paid out of the proceeds or by some other means, or where the instrument under which the power is exercisable ceases to have an effect, i.e. the writ of control or warrant of control expires by effluxion of time or the power to take goods into control is no longer exercisable.

Notice of enforcement—paragraph 7, Schedule 12

12–27 Under the present legislation there is only a limited requirement to give notice before taking control of a judgment debtor's goods. At common law there is no requirement at all, but under some of the statutory regimes the enforcement agent is required to give a form of notice.

Current High Court position

12–28 High Court Enforcement Officers are under no duty to give notice of their intention to attend an address appearing on a High Court writ of fi fa.

Current county court position

12–29 County court judgments carry a notification that the claimant has the right to make an application for a warrant, while County Court

Rules 1981, Order 26, r.7 requires notice to be given when levying execution. There is no statutory requirement to give such a preliminary warning notice, but the practice in the county court is for the court to send a warning letter.

New Act position

12–30 Under the TCEA 2007 there will be a uniform requirement for notice to be given of impending enforcement action by either a writ of control or warrant of control. Consequently, the enforcement agent will not be able to take control of goods unless the Debtor has been given this statutory notice. The regulations to support the requirements of the TCEA will no doubt include requirements that a minimum notice period is given and the form of any notice prescribed, which will in turn detail the contents of the notice and stipulate how the notice must be given and who must give it.

We wait to see whether the regulations allow for shorter notice periods to be provided for, with perhaps no notice being given in cases of emergency. The enforcement agent will be required to keep a record of the time the notice was given, which will be seen as crucial evidence if the Debtor claims that he received no notice at all. Clearly, for enforcement agents going forward they will need to be able to demonstrate to the court that notice was properly given in full compliance with any regulations, and no doubt enforcement agents will invest in their computer systems to ensure that the giving and receipt of notice can be recorded, as far as possible, in an uncontroversial manner.

Under the TCEA 2007 enforcement agents will not be able to take control of goods after a period prescribed by the regulations (see para.8(1) of Sch.12). It is anticipated at this stage that the prescribed period will be six years, which follows the current High Court and County Court position.

Time limit for taking control—paragraph 8, Schedule 12

Current High Court position

12–31 By virtue of RSC Order 46, r.8, a writ of fi fa or any other writ of execution is valid in the first instance for 12 months, beginning from the date it is issued by the court.

This is important. Practitioners should note computer systems and diaries with the date of the issue of the writ (referred to as the "teste" date). As a matter of good practice, judgment creditors or their advisors should diarise forward 10 months, at which point they should check if the writ needs to be renewed by an application, before it expires. This is to ensure that the judgment creditor maintains priority over any other judgment creditor. The issue of priority becomes important if the execution exceeds the 12 month period or if monies are paid to avoid sale by way of a long instalment plan.

If it appears that a further 12 months is required to complete the execution of the writ, or to allow a payment plan to continue, then an application should be made to the court in which the writ was issued, to extend the writ for a further period of 12 months. The application is made without notice and supported by a witness statement or an affidavit stating the reason why the writ has not been fully executed. In a case where the writ was issued in a District Registry, the application to extend the validity of a writ of execution needs to be made in that forum to the district judge.

If the application is successful, the 12 month period begins on the day of the court's order. Again, judgment creditors should diarise forward for 10 months from this new date and make a note to check if they need to apply again for a further extension.

12–32 When the court allows the writ to be extended, a new writ must be prepared. This new writ must again be sealed by the court out of which it was issued, showing the date on which the order extending its validity was made. Alternatively, the applicant for the order to extend the writ must serve a notice on the High Court Enforcement Officer. The notice must inform the HCEO that the writ has been extended and give the date the order was made.

If, during any 12 month period when the writ of fi fa is valid, an Interpleader application is issued in relation to a third party claim to goods seized by the enforcement agent, the writ is automatically extended for a further 12 month period from the date of the final order in the Interpleader proceedings. The purpose behind this rule is to allow the third party claim to be dealt with by the court, and then depending on the outcome of the Interpleader proceedings for any further enforcement of the writ to be within the time frame of a valid writ, instead of the writ expiring at some point during the Interpleader proceedings.

Alternatively, it is possible to avoid making an application to renew the writ of fi fa by allowing the 12 month period to expire and then simply completing a certificate confirming that nothing has been levied under the first writ, which will allow a fresh writ to be issued. The risk in this approach is that another judgment will have been obtained against the judgment debtor in the meantime, and another judgment creditor will have issued a writ of fi fa, thereby gaining priority.

Current county court position

As in the High Court, the question of renewing a warrant is not a mere formality, particularly if it raises questions of priority between judgment creditors. A warrant of execution is valid for 12 months initially from the date of its issue, and can be renewed for a period of 12 months at any one time from either: **12–33**

- the day after its expiry if it is renewed pursuant to an application made before that day; or
- the day it expires or such later day (if any) as the court shall allow if not made until after expiry.

The county court may accept a letter as sufficient application for renewal, although this differs from county court to county court. Normally, in practice, application to renew will need to be made on Form N445.

New Act position

An enforcement agent may not take control of goods after the prescribed period. This period will be prescribed by reference to the date of notice of enforcement or to any writ of warrant which includes an enforcement power or any other date. We await the publication of regulations to see how these new provisions will impact on the work of enforcement officers in the future. **12–34**

Goods which may be taken—paragraphs 9–11, Schedule 12

Current High Court position

As part of the Government's review of enforcement, the subject of what can and cannot be seized is a recurring theme. **12–35**

In common law, only the goods and chattels of the judgment debtor can be taken in execution under a writ of fi fa. However, under para.9 to sch.7 of the Courts Act 2003, an HCEO may seize:

- "... any goods of the judgment debtor that are not exempt goods"; and
- "... any money, banknotes, bills of exchange, promissory notes, bonds, specialties or securities for money belonging to the judgment debtor".

"Goods" can cover a wide spectrum of items. At one end it can be the mundane, such as the contents of an office, the stock in a shop or the judgment debtor's motor car. These are goods which, if asked, a judgment creditor might try to visualise for the purposes of deciding whether to issue a writ or warrant of execution in the first place. On another level, goods can include a train, boats and ships or even a commercial aircraft.

12–36 So, in the analysis of how to use this method of execution to best effect, judgment creditors should be encouraged to "visualise" the goods or belongings of their judgment debtor. If this exercise is carried out, *even before a claim is launched*, then when the time comes to enforce the judgment, the judgment creditor can be far more realistic about the likely outcome of issuing a writ.

"Exempt goods" are also defined by The Courts Act 2003, Sch.7, para. 9 to include:

- "such tools, books, vehicles and other items of equipment as are necessary to the judgment debtor for use personally by him in his employment, business or vocation"; and
- "such clothing, bedding, furniture, household equipment and provisions as are necessary for satisfying the basic domestic needs of the judgment debtor and his family".

It should be noted that limited companies are not entitled to claim that their goods are "tools of the trade"—this exemption is only available to individuals, sole traders and partners sued in their individual capacity.

Of course, this leaves open to interpretation what constitutes a "tool of the trade", so to assist the HCEO, a mechanism was tagged on to the rule for interpleader applications in RSC Order 17, r.2A (which appears in Sch.1 to the CPR). This provides that a judgment debtor will need to make a claim within five days of the date of seizure, identifying the goods that are said to be exempt.

12–37 A number of decisions show the court's thought process in determining whether an item constitutes a tool of trade, although decisions on what constitutes an item to satisfy a basic domestic need are scarce.

In *Toseland Building Supplies Limited v Bishop (t/a Bishop Groundworks)*, October 28, 1993, CA Lord Justice Steyn stated,

> "The general principle is that prima facie all the judgment debtor's goods are liable to seizure under a writ of Fieri Facias. If a judgment debtor claims the benefit of a statutory exemption, the

burden of showing that the exemption applies rests squarely on him".

In that case, a JCB digger was claimed as a "tool of the trade" but the court found that as the JCB was on lease, it could not be claimed as the judgment debtor's tool of the trade within the meaning of s.15 of the Courts and Legal Services Act 1990 (being the forerunner to para.9, Sch.7 of the Courts Act 2003) because the judgment debtor had the opportunity to go and lease another JCB.

12–38 In the reported case of *Brookes v Harris* [1995] 1 W.L.R. 918, the judgment debtor's record collection was found to be a "tool of the trade", as he was a disc jockey. Ironically, in that case, he had used legal aid to defend the claim against him, and the issue arose as to whether having successfully defended his case the Legal Aid Board might be entitled to the benefit of the record collection being "property recovered or preserved for the legally aided party" in the proceedings for which the judgment debtor had obtained legal aid, as allowed under s.16(6) of the Legal Aid Act 1988. The court allowed the judgment debtor's appeal against this decision by finding that the initial execution had been illegal, and therefore that the Legal Aid Board's statutory charge could not attach to that property.

Current county court position

12–39 The county court position mirrors that of the High Court above.

New Act position

12–40 An enforcement agent will only be able to take control of goods if they are either on the premises where they have power to enter or on a highway.

In practice, this means that an enforcement agent will only be able to take control of goods at an address he is directed to under the writ or warrant of control or where the goods are situated on the highway, such as a vehicle or caravan. If goods are located in another place where the enforcement agent has no right of entry under Sch.12, then those goods cannot be taken into control unless they are situated on a highway. This changes the current position in which High Court Enforcement Officers have been prepared on the written instructions of judgment creditors or their solicitors to go to another address not on the face of the writ of fi fa to take control of goods based on business efficacy.

A landlord will also have the right to apply to a county court for a warrant of entry to specific property. This alters the current position in that if this relates to premises other than the demised premises, this will give landlords greater flexibility on where they can exercise their enforcement choice under the new CRAR procedure.

12–41 The new Act also enables commercial landlords to take control of goods on the highway, again extending the current position in law. In practical terms this means that an enforcement agent acting on behalf of a commercial landlord could exercise the CRAR procedure on the highway outside the tenant's domestic premises or wherever the tenant's goods can be found provided they are on the highway. Certainly, with the majority of goods taking the form of a vehicle, the ability to seize goods on the highway gives landlords more opportunities to enforce via their enforcement agents.

Value of goods which may be taken—paragraph 12, Schedule 12

Current High Court position

12–42 Again, at the present time the law is relatively "grey" in terms of how a valuation must be obtained and communicated to either a judgment creditor or judgment debtor. What is clear is that when the time comes for any judicial scrutiny of the work of an HCEO, one can expect a Master or district judge to ask the question as to how the valuation was arrived at and how it has been relied upon.

For this reason, in the High Court, HCEOs have systems for the valuation of goods which link to the way in which their fees are charged. One of the fees an HCEO can charge is a percentage fee on the value of goods seized in execution of a writ.

Current county court position

12–43 In the county court, the bailiffs will have their own system to appraise and value seized goods.

In the future, what we can expect is that the supporting Regs to Sch.12 will codify how enforcement agents value goods, and how that valuation is then communicated to the parties.

New Act position

12–44 Again, under Sch.12, para.12, the new law is far more prescriptive than the current legislation. An enforcement agent in the future will not be able to take control of goods where the aggregate value is more than either:

- the amount outstanding; and
- an amount in respect of future costs calculated in accordance with the regulations as to the enforcement agent's fees.

If an enforcement agent has to take control of goods of a higher value at the premises or on a highway, this will only be permitted where there are not enough goods of a lower value within a reasonable distance of either the highway or the premises. This addresses the problem where enforcement officers in the past have taken goods that are way beyond the value of the judgment debt, and yet they have seized on something more valuable even though lower value goods were present. The new Act addresses this unfair practice and prevents it from happening in future.

Ways of taking control—paragraph 13, Schedule 12

Current High Court position

12–45 In High Court proceedings, goods can be either subject to "walking possession" or "close possession". In the case of walking possession, goods are not actually taken into custody ("close possession") but are left with the judgment debtor or a person who is seen to be in control of the goods. An agreement is signed in which the person signing the form undertakes both to keep the goods safe and also to notify the HCEO if another enforcement agent attempts to seize those goods under another writ or other form of enforcement.

12–46 Where goods are actually removed from the premises and taken into safekeeping, the status of possession changes to one of "close possession", which literally means that the goods are kept in a safe and secure facility pending either payment or sale. This is not a common occurrence because of the expense of storing goods, which may ultimately have to be borne by the judgment creditor.

On occasion, goods do have to be taken into custody to ensure they are protected from any threat of unauthorised removal, which in turn could disadvantage the judgment creditor and possibly leave the HCEO open to an action for negligence for failing in his duty to execute the writ.

Current county court position

12–47 The county court position mirrors that of the High Court.

New Act position

12–48 We can expect the provisions of the TCEA 2007 and Sch.12 to go considerably further and to clarify the working practices we will eventually see in the CPR, for example regulations being made about the care and control of goods and removing goods to storage to comply with para.35 of Sch.12.

Under the new Act the term "walking possession agreement" is removed and is replaced by the term "controlled goods agreement".

12–49 Under such an agreement, and subject to para.13(4) of Sch.12, the enforcement agent and judgment debtor can enter into an agreement whereby the judgment debtor acknowledges that the enforcement agent has taken control of the goods and is then permitted to retain custody of the goods, and agrees not to remove or dispose of the goods or to permit anyone else to do so before the debt is paid.

Once more, we can expect regulations supporting Sch.12 to be extremely prescriptive as to how a controlled goods agreement will look in the future.

Entry without a warrant—paragraph 14, Schedule 12

High Court position

12–50 A High Court Enforcement Officer is not entitled to break open the outer door of a dwelling house in order to levy execution. From this comes the maxim "An Englishman's home is his castle", which is based on the decision in *Semayne's Case* (1604) 5 Co. 91. From this simple position in law the following points should be noted:

- An enforcement officer is not entitled to force his way into a dwelling house for the purpose of gaining entry (*Vaughan v McKenzie* [1969] 1 Q.B. 557; [1968] 1 All E.R. 1154, DC).
- An enforcement agent may, however, break open the outer door of the judgment debtor's workshop or other building which is not the judgment debtor's home and is not connected to the dwelling house (*Hodder v Williams* [1895] 2 Q.B. 663).
- An enforcement agent who has already entered the judgment debtor's home may lawfully break the lock to regain access to seize the goods inside (*McLeod v Butterwick*, *The Times*, March 12, 1996), although this decision remains open to criticism, particularly where vulnerable people are found to be inside the property.

County court position

12–51 Broadly, the powers of a county court bailiff executing a warrant are the same as those of a HCEO.

The statutory authority for seizure is the County Courts Act 1984, s.89, which does not give express power to force entry. However, if the county court bailiff has a "walking possession" agreement and is deliberately excluded, he can force entry (*Khazanchi v Faircharm Investments* [1998] 1 W.L.R. 1603).

Although there is some authority for a bailiff forcing entry back into the debtor's home after entry has been made lawfully, in practice this rarely, if ever, happens. The cases of *McLeod* and *Khazanchi* have highlighted a number of concerns by the court as to the actions taken by enforcement agents. In today's climate, the court would no doubt go further than in the previous decisions by disapproving of any such action.

New Act position

12–52 Again, we can expect the supporting regulations to reinforce the current voluntary national standards into a prescriptive code as to when entry without a warrant will be permissible, if at all.

Entry under a warrant—paragraph 15, Schedule 12

12–53 The TCEA 2007 started life on the statute book with a very clear position on allowing forced entry, so that no debt could be considered "unenforceable" simply because the judgment debtor continuously refused to allow a regulated enforcement agent access to a property. Not surprisingly, this change in the law, which would overturn the decision in *Semayne's* case, has attracted adverse publicity in the media. As a result, ministers have given assurances in the House of Commons that this part of the new Act will in fact not make its way into the accompanying regulations to support Sch.12.

It is likely that the supporting regulations will instead be framed to prevent enforcement taking place in a private house. For other types of premises and for goods on the highway, we can expect that the regulations will make provision that an enforcement agent will be able to use reasonable force under paras. 20(2) or 31(1) of Sch.12 where all other methods of entry have failed. We will have to wait to see whether the use of force in such circumstances needs to be sanctioned by an order from the court.

What is expected is that the new law will sweep away the old case law about whether an enforcement agent can gain access to premises by climbing through a window or turning the handle on a door which is not locked. The regulations may well prescribe how entry is to be made to a variety of structures and vehicles.

Re-entry to premises—paragraph 16, Schedule 12

Current High Court position

12–54 An enforcement officer who already has walking possession of goods may lawfully break the lock to gain access to a house to seize the goods (see *McLeod v Butterwick*, *The Times,* March, 1996). Again, the likelihood of a similar situation happening in today's climate is extremely rare, and certainly it would be a prudent step by an HCEO to seek a court order, perhaps using a general application under CPR Pt 23, to sanction any such action before attempting to re-enter a private house.

Current county court position

12–55 The statutory provision that authorises county court bailiffs to seize goods under a warrant of execution does not authorise forcible entry, and there is no other authority under statute or rule which permits bailiffs to force entry into any premises.

County court bailiffs cannot break doors, locks or windows to gain entry to premises where they believe the goods of the judgment debtor are stored. They may open and unlock the door to gain entry (see generally County Courts Act 1984 s.89, as amended by the Courts and Legal Services Act 1990 s.15(2)), but again in reality this is not something a judgment creditor should expect when enforcing a judgment debt using a warrant of execution.

New Act position

12–56 We can expect regulations in supporting para.16 of Sch.12 to clarify when enforcement agents may enter, re-enter or remain on premises, particularly where the occupants inside the property may be either minors or people who can be classified as having a form of vulnerability.

Although the case of *Butterwick* is relatively recent, dating back to only 1996, it did raise concerns at the time. We can expect the new regulations in support of Sch.12 to remedy this situation so there is as little scope as possible for misinterpretation of the law as to when enforcement officers can and cannot force entry to any type of property.

General powers to use reasonable force—paragraphs 17–19, Schedule 12

Current High Court position

12–57 The new Act states that an enforcement agent may, if necessary, use reasonable force to enter premises or to do anything for which entry is authorised. In so doing, certain conditions must be met, in which case the Act gives the enforcement agent a power to enter. In the High Court rules today, RSC Order 46 provides that *Semayne's* case (dating back to 1604) is still the leading authority under which a High Court Enforcement Officer is not entitled to break open the outer door of a dwelling house in order to levy execution. In relation to non-residential property such as offices, warehouses, public houses, shops and other types of commercial property, an HCEO may break open the outer door to seize the goods of the judgment debtor found inside. The 19th century case of *Hodder v Williams* [1895] 2 Q.B. 663 is the authority for this proposition, and today judgment creditors can rely on HCEOs to use this power to force entry to commercial property to seize the goods inside.

Current county court position

12–58 The case of *Vaughan v McKenzie* applies equally in the county court so that county court bailiffs can open and unlock doors to gain entry. However, the statutory provision that authorises a seizure by county court bailiffs to goods under a warrant of execution does not authorise forcible entry, and there is no authority under statute or rule which permits county court bailiffs to force entry into any premises, as per s.89 of the County Courts Act 1984 (as amended).

New Act position

12–59 The new Act gives general powers to use reasonable force, and is designed to clarify the existing law. Under para.17 to Sch.12 an enforcement agent may use reasonable force to enter premises or to do anything for which entry is authorised, subject to conditions being met. This will put on a proper statutory footing the circumstances in which enforcement officers will be able to use "reasonable force", which may be no more than simply turning a key in a lock or pushing a door open to gain entry. Note that the mere acts of turning the key or pushing the door both involve an element of force.

However, what is envisaged is that the regulations supporting paras. 17 to 19 of Sch.12 will provide for applications to be made to the court by enforcement agents to sanction the use of reasonable force to gain entry in certain situations. The nature of this application is likely to mean that the enforcement officer will have to satisfy the court that all attempts to gain entry without using force have been exhausted and that the premises themselves are commercial in nature. Going further than that we can expect the regulations to be supported by changes to the Civil Procedure Rules to outline the format of such applications to the court.

Application for power to use reasonable force—paragraphs 20–22, Schedule 12

Current High Court position

12–60 Currently, HCEOs do not need to apply to the court for permission to use reasonable force before going into a property. At present, the nature of this type of issue coming before the court is likely to be after entry has been forced, when the court is asked to rule on the enforcement officer's conduct, perhaps when an application for interpleader relief is made to the court and the officer seeks an order for "no action" as part of the final interpleader order.

A recent example of where the court made a ruling on the officer's conduct was in the case of *Huntress Search Limited v Canapeum* [2010] EWHC 1270 (QB). In this case, Eady J. supported the Master's decision that the officer's conduct in pragmatically attending a neighbouring address to the one mentioned in the writ of fi fa, which in turn led to execution being carried out at the wrong address, was "heavy handed" because the officer had relied on the pre-2004 position where Sheriffs would attend any address within their bailiwick to seek out goods belonging to the judgment debtor.

Current county court position

12–61 Again, at present it is highly unlikely there would be any application made to the court for power to use reasonable force to gain entry, but there is no doubt that informal discussions do take place between county court bailiff managers and district judges as to the approach to be taken by the court in executing any warrant of execution.

New Act position

12–62 Once more, we can expect the supporting regulations to Sch.12 to outline the circumstances and conditions that must be present to enable the court to make an order allowing reasonable force to be used.

Other provisions about powers of entry—paragraphs 23–30, Schedule 12

Current High Court position

12–63 How HCEOs carry out their functions and discharge their duties is prescribed to a certain extent by the High Court Enforcement Officers Regulations 2004 and the Rules of the Supreme Court. Alongside these formal sources of guidance are the National Standards for Enforcement Agents, which were introduced by the then Lord Chancellor's Department in 2002. The National Standards set out a number of matters relating to conduct, to which all HCEOs subscribe as part of their appointment. The standards deal with matters such as the hours that HCEOs may attend a judgment debtor's address, the days on which enforcement can be carried out and generally give guidance as to the conduct of enforcement agents (which includes HCEOs) when going about their business (see *http://www.dca.gov.uk/enforcement/agents02.htm* [Accessed October 20, 2010]).

Current county court position

12–64 Generally speaking, county court bailiffs will mirror the approach taken by their High Court counterparts, and of course will receive guidance from the district judge on how to execute any warrant sent to them for enforcement.

New Act position

12–65 The new Act goes considerably further by consolidating the existing rules and guidance into statutory provisions under Sch.12. We can expect supporting regulations to go even further. In effect, the regulations may well codify the areas currently outlined in the National Standards, which in turn move the voluntary code of good conduct into an area of statutory compliance. For example, we could expect to see the regulations dealing with the times of the day when an enforcement officer can enter and remain on premises, as well as making it a requirement for enforcement officers to carry and show identity cards.

Goods on a highway—paragraphs 31–33, Schedule 12

Current High Court position

12–66 Whilst the TCEA and Sch.12 refer to "goods on a highway", and the circumstances in which those goods can be dealt with, the current High Court rules are silent on the matter.

Current county court position

12–67 The county court position is the same as the High Court position, and any authority to seize any type of goods flows from the warrant in the hands of the bailiff. A distinction as to where those goods are situated is not made in the current Rules.

New Act position

12–68 An enforcement officer will be able to apply to the court to issue a warrant which authorises him to use reasonable force (if necessary) to take control of goods on the highway. In making this application the court will need to be satisfied that prescribed conditions, which will be set out in supporting regulations, have been met. We can expect these regulations to deal with matters such as make, model and registration number of any vehicle and issues surrounding the immobilisation of a vehicle as part of the taking control of goods process.

Inventory—paragraph 34, Schedule 12

Current High Court position

12–69 Case law dating back to 1698 states that a "levy of part is good for levy of the whole" (see *Cole v Davis* (1698) 1 Ld. Raym Cases 725). When it comes to interpleader proceedings in the High Court, having a detailed inventory available to the court becomes vital to being able to give an accurate report to the court of the goods that have been seized. However, the inventory does not have to particularise every single item as a result of the established case law in this area.

HCEOs are encouraged to prepare detailed inventories as part of assisting the court when outlining the circumstances of any particular execution, which ensures that an accurate picture is given to the court of any items seized. Nowadays, digital cameras make it far easier to photograph and include photographs in reports for both the court and the judgment creditor. Photographs also make it easier to establish claims to goods made by third parties.

When first executing a writ of fieri facias, the High Court Enforcement Officer will deliver to the debtor or leave at each place where execution is levied a notice of seizure in Form No. 55. As mentioned earlier in this chapter, this stage of the execution process is known as "walking possession". The notice explains to the debtor the situation with regard to the goods seized and what he or she then has to do.

Current county court position

12–70 In the county court, where goods are seized and removed, the court will deliver or send an inventory to the judgment debtor immediately (see CCR Order 26, r.12(1)). The county court practice seems to follow the High Court position in that there is no requirement to produce an inventory at the time that the goods are seized.

As in the High Court, when first attending the address on the warrant, the county court bailiff must leave a form similar to the notice of seizure, but which is actually called a "warrant of execution". This notice is on county court form No. 42 and again explains to the judgment debtor the situation with regard to the goods seized and what he or she then has to do (see CCR Order 26, r.7).

New Act position

12–71 Under the new Act an inventory must be provided to the judgment debtor for any goods that are taken into control under the writ or warrant. There is a clear requirement coming under para.34 of Sch.12 that an inventory must be provided "as soon as reasonably practicable".

At present, enforcement agents prepare their own form of inventory list, but under the new regulations to accompany Sch.12 we can expect this to be far more prescriptive.

Certainly, proper descriptions of goods to enable the judgment debtor or any co-owner to identify goods correctly, including manufacture details, model details and serial numbers, as well as in the case of a vehicle the manufacture, model, colour and registration mark of the vehicle, are all likely to be prescribed.

Care of goods removed—paragraph 35, Schedule 12

Current High Court position

12–72 Under the National Standards for Enforcement Agents, which, as mentioned above, is currently only voluntary in terms of compliance, enforcement officers must ensure that goods are handled with reasonable care so that they do not suffer any damage whilst in their possession. Enforcement officers are required to have insurance in place for goods in transit so that if damage occurs, this is covered by the terms of the policy.

Under s.8 of Pt 3 of the High Court Enforcement Officers Regulations 2004 every enforcement officer authorised by the Lord Chancellor is required under para.(c) to hold current and relevant insurance policies.

Current county court position

12–73 County court rules as to the level of insurance and care will mirror the High Court position, although the rules themselves are silent as to the extent of this responsibility.

New Act position

12–74 At present, the enforcement agent taking control of goods becomes a bailee of the goods that have been seized. In this position, he owes the judgment debtor a duty of care in relation to the handling of any goods. In para.35 of Sch.12 this duty is made into a statutory provision whereby the enforcement officer will be required to take reasonable care of controlled goods. Again, we can expect supporting regulations to require the enforcement officer to keep the goods to the same standard in which he found them and when they are removed, to ensure that storage facilities are secure and appropriate.

Valuation—paragraph 36, Schedule 12

Current High Court position

12–75 Under the High Court Enforcement Officer's Regulations 2004 provision is made at para. (6)2 of Sch. 3 for fees to be charged where a detailed inventory of goods seized has been prepared.

It is vitally important that the HCEO concerned takes a full and detailed inventory of all such goods, firstly because the judgment debtor is entitled to have that as a matter of good practice, and secondly because without it he will not be able to charge the fee that is provided for under the current regulations.

Current county court position

12–76 County Court Form N332 is a form of inventory and notice to a judgment debtor who fails to pay the county court bailiff. As a result, the bailiff leaves a notice with the judgment debtor of the goods that are being removed for sale.

New Act position

12–77 The TCEA takes this further, as enforcement officers will be required to obtain a valuation of the goods under their control, which must be in place before any sale takes place. Para.36(1) of

Sch.12 will no doubt be supported by prescriptive regulations, and we can expect to see enforcement officers having to make valuations that are in writing, signed and dated with a separate value given for each item taken into control. We can also expect enforcement agents to provide copies of that written valuation to the judgment debtor and any co-owner, and to see the regulations requiring qualified independent valuers to be instructed.

Best price—paragraph 37, Schedule 12

Current High Court position

12–78 The overriding position is that goods must be sold at public auction unless ordered to the contrary by the court (see Courts Act 2003, para.10, Sch.7, which replaced the old provision under the Supreme Court Act 1981, s.138A(1)).

If it is thought that an application for permission to sell the debtor's goods by private contract will achieve more in terms of net proceeds than an auction sale, then the necessary form of application (prescribed by RSC Order 47, r.6) can be issued. Usually, this is done by the HCEO, although under RSC Order 47, r.1 there is provision for the application to be made by either the judgment creditor or judgment debtor.

If the HCEO has had notice of another execution against the judgment debtor, the court cannot consider an application for permission to sell privately until notice has been given to the other judgment creditor(s).

The application should be made in accordance with CPR Pt 23, and the application notice should contain a short statement of the grounds on which it is made. This is usually in the form that permission is sought to sell the goods seized on the basis that a better price will be obtained by private treaty, rather than by selling the goods at public auction.

The application works best where the goods are unique, antique or valuable. Although it is not a routine application, it can make all the difference in the eventual proceeds that are achieved for the judgment creditor and may result in a refund of surplus cash being paid to the judgment debtor.

12–79 Where the applicant for the order for private sale is not the HCEO, then on the demand of the applicant the HCEO must send the applicant a list stating whether he has notice of the issue of another writ(s) of execution against the goods of the judgment debtor, and so far as is known to him, the name and address of every creditor who has issued a writ of execution. If the HCEO is the applicant, then he or she must prepare such a list and have it available to show the court at the hearing of the application.

The application for permission to sell by private treaty needs to be served by the applicant at least four clear days before the date of the hearing on each person named in the list.

Each person served with the application may attend and be heard on the hearing of the application.

County court position

12–80 There is also provision in CCR Order 26, r.15 that a sale under the warrant of execution may be made "otherwise than by public auction" on the application of the judgment creditor, judgment debtor or the district judge responsible for the execution of the warrant.

Unlike in the High Court, the most common reason for ordering a private sale in the county court is said to be that the "goods are of a perishable nature".

New Act position

12–81 The new Act goes further, as under para.37 of Sch.12 enforcement officers will be required to sell or dispose of goods "for the best price that can be reasonably obtained in accordance with the Schedule".

We can expect supporting regulations to prescribe the timetable for the sale of controlled goods including a minimum period before any sale takes place, as well as the minimum period for the notice of any sale.

We can also expect to see that the form and contents of the notice for sale are heavily prescribed and that the method for giving notice is made clear under supporting regulations.

The methods of sale may also be prescribed, perhaps providing for both private contract, sealed bids and advertising to take place. Accompanying regulations will no doubt also prescribe the place where the sale is to be held in an effort to promote transparency and fairness to the judgment debtor and ensure that the conduct of any sale is conducted by either a qualified auctioneer or, where the auction takes place on an internet auction site, by a reputable provider.

Sale—paragraphs 38–42, Schedule 12

Current High Court position

12–82 Perhaps one of the distinct differences between the High Court procedure and that of the county court is that High Court Enforcement Officers have an infrastructure across England and Wales to be able to remove goods and to proceed to sale, in accordance with their common law duties and without delay.

Unlike the mandatory county court position there is no requirement to delay sale for a period of five days. Judgment creditors will find that High Court Enforcement Officers have the skills to be able to sell goods at general auction or to identify goods which should be sold by more specialist auctioneers, particularly in relation to antiques, cars, jewellery, stock, medicines, firearms, aircraft, vessels, livestock and unusual items.

It is perhaps an art of the High Court Enforcement Officer to be able to sell something with value in a number of different ways, in order to not only achieve the best price for the judgment creditor, but also to ensure the best price is obtained for the judgment debtor.

Current county court position

12–83 The county court procedure for the sale of goods is dealt with under CCR Order 26, r.12. Where goods are removed for sale, the court will send to the judgment debtor a "sufficient" inventory of the goods removed, and not less than four days before the auction sale will give the judgment debtor the details of the date, time and location of the auction.

The form of notice is in Form N332, while the sale is governed by s.97 of the County Courts Act 1984. Where goods are sold under an execution, the court must furnish the judgment debtor with a detailed account in writing of the sale and the application of the proceeds.

New Act position

12–84 The new Act looks to regularise current procedures in the county court, High Court and elsewhere. Certainly, insofar as High Court practice is concerned, the sale of any goods must not be before the end of the minimum period, except with the agreement of the judgment debtor and any co-owner. The regulations will specify what this minimum period will be. As with the current practice in the High Court and county court, regulations to support paras. 38 to 42 of Sch.12 will set out in detail how the sale of any goods is to be conducted in future, and all methods of sale will effectively be the same.

Place of sale—paragraphs 43 to 46, Schedule 12

Current high court position

12–85 A High Court Enforcement Officer is obliged to ensure that a realistic price is received for the goods offered. Case law going back many decades allows the court to set aside a sale if it considers that it has been badly advertised or where it decides that goods have been undervalued (see *Edge v Kavanagh* (1884) 24 L.R. Ir.1).

The sale must be by public auction unless the items offered are being sold under an execution for less than £20. The sale must be publicly advertised "on, and during three days, preceding the date of sale".

Although there is no statutory requirement to do so, the enforcement officer should ensure that catalogues of the sale are sent to the judgment debtor and to the judgment creditor in sufficient time to allow either party to attend the sale.

Current county court position

12–86 S.97 of the County Courts Act 1984 provides that the sale of goods under a warrant of execution for more than £20 must be by public auction unless the court makes an order to the contrary.

A sale that does not conform to the statutory requirements becomes irregular and may be set aside by the court. Only a court which has issued a warrant of execution has the power to order a sale by private treaty under CCR Order 16, r.15. This rule corresponds with RSC Order 47, r.6, which then enables the district judge responsible for the execution of the warrant to take the initiative and order a sale by private treaty.

New Act position

12–87 Schedule 12 moves the position forward considerably as to how sales are to be conducted in future by enforcement officers. Supporting regulations will provide for where sales of controlled goods are to take place, as well as the circumstances in which those sales may be held on premises where goods are found.

Holding and disposal of securities—paragraphs 47–49, Schedule 12

Current High Court position

12–88 The seizure of securities of shares by HCEOs is extremely rare, although the case of *Robinson v Jenkins* (1890) L.R 24 Q.B.D. 275 does provide the authority for shares in a company to be viewed as "chattels", which in turn allows them to be available for seizure.

Under the current CPR, provision is made under Pt 73 for charging orders as the method of enforcement; the rule provides a complete process for the enforcement of a judgment involving a share portfolio. Again, the instances of this happening in practice are very rare.

Current county court position

12–89 The county court position mirrors the High Court and CPR positions.

New Act position

12–90 The new statutory provision authorising the seizure of money, bank notes, bills of exchange, promissory notes etc. now extends to all forms of enforcement. The suggestion is that an enforcement agent will only be given permission to seize securities if they are qualified and experienced in that kind of enforcement.

Application of proceeds—paragraph 50, Schedule 12

Current High Court position

12–91 A judgment creditor can expect a HCEO to apply fees as a first charge on monies recovered, unless a different commercial agreement can be achieved.

The date of the receipt of the monies is taken as being the date of the sale, and the auctioneer acts for the HCEO. If the sale produces sufficient money to satisfy the writ, then any surplus should be refunded to the judgment debtor. All funds will be held for the 14 days required by the provisions of the Insolvency Act 1986.

Current county court position

12–92 Under CCR Order 26, r.13, where goods are sold under a warrant, the court must furnish the judgment debtor with a detailed account in writing of any sale and the application of the proceeds.

New Act position

12–93 However, under the accompanying regulations to para.50 of Sch.12 the application of proceeds from any sale will be stipulated, and in the event there is a dispute as to the share of proceeds payable to a co-owner, we should be able to expect that regulations will provide for a person to be able to apply to court to determine the amount of the co-owner's share.

Passing of title—paragraph 51, Schedule 12

Current High Court position

12–94 Statutory protection is offered to a person who acquires title to the judgment debtor's goods in good faith and for valuable consideration, without having had notice that a writ has been delivered to the enforcement officer for execution and is unexecuted (see para.8(2) to Sch.7 to the Courts Act 2003). Under para.8(3) and 8(4) provisos are made under which this protection is lost if notice has been received by the purchaser.

Current county court position

12–95 The county court position follows the High Court position.

New Act position

12–96 An enforcement officer will be able to give good title to a purchaser of controlled goods except where:

- a claimant has lawfully made a claim to the title of the goods in court;
- a purchaser, creditor or enforcement officer has notice that the goods are not the judgment debtor's at the time of sale.

A lawful claimant to the goods is defined in para.51(5) of Sch.12 as a person who has an interest in those goods which at the time of sale were goods other than those assigned or transferred to him while the property or the goods were bound for the purposes of the enforcement action.

Abandonment of goods other than securities—paragraphs 52–54, Schedule 12

Current High Court position

12–97 Where an enforcement officer, who has seized goods under a writ of fi fa, fails in his duty to maintain "walking possession" of those goods, then a question may be raised as to whether he has "abandoned possession" of the goods he has seized. Enforcement officers are trained to ensure walking possession is actually evidenced, by securing a signed "walking possession agreement" from either:

- the judgment debtor; or
- a responsible person over the age of 18, who is at the premises at the time of the enforcement agent's visit.

The form of the agreement is set out in Reg. 15 of The High Court Enforcement Officers Regulations 2004, while a form of agreement is set out in Sch.4.

If the judgment debtor refuses to sign a walking possession agreement or a signed walking possession agreement cannot be obtained—for whatever reason—then the enforcement officer is under a duty to remove the goods as soon as practicable or at the very least to inspect the goods at frequent intervals. If this is not done, then on examination of the facts the court may well hold that possession of the goods has been abandoned and the judgment debtor will be under no penalty if he disposes of them, regardless of the initial seizure by the enforcement agent.

This in turns raises issues of liability by the enforcement officer to the judgment creditor, whose ability to recover the amount due under the writ has been prejudiced by the enforcement officer's failure to remove and sell as soon as practicable in the absence of a signed walking possession agreement.

A series of decisions for particular cases is set out in *Bagshawes Ltd v Deacon* [1898] 2 Q.B. 173; *National Commercial Bank of Scotland v Arcam Demolition, and Construction* [1966] 2 Q.B. 593; [1966] 3 All E.R. 113, CA); and *Lloyds and Scottish Finance Ltd v Modern Cars and Caravans (Kingston)* [1966] 1 Q.B. 764; [1964] 2 All E.R. 732.

Current county court position

12–98 In the absence of any expressed provision in the rules, the county court position will follow the High Court position.

New Act position

12–99 The new Act deals expressly with the position where goods are "abandoned" by the enforcement agent. Pursuant to para. 54(1)(b) of Sch.12 we can expect supporting regulations to make provision as to what happens to goods in these circumstances and how they are made available for collection by the judgment debtor.

At the moment, procedure in this arena is somewhat haphazard. Circumstances in which goods may be abandoned occur when they are found to have little or no resale value at auction or by any other method of sale, and yet the judgment debtor wants the goods returned. This is particularly relevant in relation to vehicles of a certain age and type. Whilst on the one hand they may have a very low auction value, they may on the other hand be the judgment debtor's only means of transport.

Where abandonment takes place, the enforcement officer will be in a position of being a bailee of the goods until the judgment debtor collects them. The enforcement officer still owes a duty of care for the safe custody of the goods in that position, but can fall back on the protection of the Torts (Interference with Goods) Act 1977. Under s.12 of that Act an enforcement officer in this situation becomes an involuntary bailee and can discharge his duty of care by serving a notice on the owner of the goods. This notice will invite the owner to collect the goods within a reasonable time, after which the bailee has the right to sell or dispose of the goods pursuant to the Act.

Abandonment of securities—pararaphs 55–57, Schedule 12

Current High Court position

12–100 There is no current similarity between the existing High Court rules and the provisions made under Sch.12 for the abandonment of securities.

Current county court position

12–101 Similarly, there is no express provision in the county court rules at present in relation to the county court bailiff dealing with the abandonment of securities.

New Act position

12–102 Under this paragraph, securities are abandoned if an enforcement officer does not give the judgment debtor or any co-owner notice under para.49 of a notice of disposal of those goods within a permitted period. We can expect accompanying regulations to Sch.12 to provide a process for the disposal of securities to supplement the wording of the relevant paragraph within the Schedule.

Where securities are "controlled goods" under the terms of the new Act, these will become abandoned if the enforcement officer does not give the judgment debtor or any co-owner of the securities a proper notice under para.49 of the Act dealing with disposal. This notice must be given within the permitted period. Supporting regulations may also deal with other circumstances in which securities are abandoned, in which case the enforcement power itself ceases to be exercisable, and as soon as reasonably practicable the enforcement officer will need to make the securities available for collection by the judgment debtor if they have been removed from where he found them. Practically speaking, this will take the form of returning a share certificate to the judgment debtor.

Payment of amount outstanding—paragraphs 58–59, Schedule 12

Current High Court position

12–103 It was held under previous law that if a sheriff failed to pay the proceeds of execution to the judgment creditor, it was then open to the judgment creditor to apply for the money to be paid to him by a form of motion (see *Delmar v Fremantle* [1878] 3 Ex. D. 237). In today's law we can expect that the court would entertain an application by a judgment creditor against an enforcement officer, if brought under CPR Pt 23, in making a general application to the court to compel the enforcement officer to pay over what was due under the writ.

At present, the High Court position is left to convention rather than any rule or statutory provision. The new Act envisages, however, that where the judgment debtor pays the amount outstanding in full, either after the enforcement officer has taken control of goods or before they are sold or abandoned, the enforcement officer must as soon as reasonably practicable make those goods available for collection by the judgment debtor. Once this is done, no further enforcement step may be taken.

Monies received from the judgment debtor are due to be paid over to the judgment creditor without delay. However, HCEOs will retain sums in excess of £500 for a period of 14 days before making a payment to a judgment creditor, so that those monies are outside of any insolvency that should then occur.

Current county court position

12–104 We can expect the county court position to mirror that of the High Court.

New Act position

12–105 The new Act and supporting regulations are far more prescriptive than the current rules. The rationale for the new Act's approach appears to come from the independent review of enforcement law, which was given by Professor J. Beatson Q.C. as long ago as June 2000. His recommendation was that the legislation should provide that any form of enforcement should cease if the judgment debtor tenders the amount owed, together with the costs, either:

- before the enforcement officer takes legal control of the goods; or
- at any time before sale, except during the process of taking legal control or removing the goods from the premises.

Paragraph 58 of Sch.12 now provides that if the judgment debtor pays:

- the amount outstanding in full;
- after the enforcement officer has taken control of the goods;
- and before they are sold or abandoned;

no further steps may be taken under the enforcement power concerned.

The amount that the judgment debtor must pay is calculated in accordance with the definition in para.50(3), which provides that the amount outstanding to be paid is both the amount of the debt together with any outstanding costs.

Provision under the new Act does not give the judgment debtor a right to make payment at any time. What it does do, though, is give the judgment debtor the right to pay the amount outstanding and bring the process to an end. If the judgment debtor pays during the period of the warning notice served pursuant to para.7 of Sch.12, the judgment debtor will have to pay the full amount outstanding (a figure which includes costs). Again, the new law codifies what actually happens in practice.

12–106 Once a tender of payment is made pursuant to para.58, then no further steps can be taken under the enforcement power concerned, and the controlled goods must be made available for collection by the judgment debtor (see para.58(2) of Sch.12). Where in certain cases the enforcement officer has seized money as the form of "controlled goods", the judgment debtor is to be given credit for this in relation to the amount outstanding, which is then reduced accordingly (see para.58(4) of Sch.12).

If a payment is made direct by the judgment debtor to the judgment creditor, and no notice is given to the enforcement officer, the enforcement officer will not be liable for any further steps taken in relation to the enforcement action, even if the amount has been paid in full (see para.59(2) of Sch.12).

Enforcement officers frequently have to remind judgment creditors of the need to keep them informed as to payments made under either a writ or a warrant.

If an enforcement officer sells the goods without notice that the judgment debtor has paid the judgment creditor, the judgment debtor may have a claim against the judgment creditor.

Where the judgment creditor has been paid the amount outstanding in full, he may be liable if he fails to notify the enforcement officer of the position, with further steps taken against the judgment debtor. This is an improvement on the current system, as it clarifies the position in law of the judgment debtor and his remedy when faced with this situation (see para.58(6) of Sch.12).

Third party claims to goods—paragraph 60, Schedule 12

Current High Court position

12–107 Where the HCEO has seized goods in execution of a writ of fi fa, and a person other than the judgment debtor makes a claim to ownership of the goods seized, the third party must give notice of his claim to the HCEO, including in his notice a statement of his address, which will act as his address for service.

This is the start of what are known as "interpleader" proceedings under CPR Sch.1, RSC Order 17. Third party claims to goods seized are common, and although not fatal to the execution of the writ of fi fa have to be given careful consideration. This is because even if a third party claim is received, the judgment debt, costs and interest remain outstanding, and often a third party claim can be used to deflect the execution of the writ without any proper basis in law.

Consequently, when a third party claim is received, the HCEO has to go through the process of giving notice (in Form PF 23) of the claim to the judgment creditor on whose behalf the goods were seized. This notice requires the claimant to state whether he "admits or disputes" the claim. If admitted, the HCEO withdraws from possessing the goods that were the subject of the claim—and which may involve all or some of the goods seized or intended to be seized.

If disputed, the HCEO will apply to the court for interpleader relief.

12–108 The judgment creditor must respond to the notice of the third party's claim within 7 days of receipt of the HCEO's notice and may use form PF 24 to do so, although usually the response from the third party is in the form of a simple letter admitting or disputing the claim.

Where the judgment creditor admits the claim, the HCEO will withdraw from possession of the goods and may apply under RSC Order 17, r.2(4) for an order to restrain a claim being brought against him for having taken possession of the goods.

Where the judgment creditor disputes the claim, the HCEO may apply for interpleader relief. An application for interpleader relief—if made in existing proceedings—is made by an application in accordance with Pt 23; otherwise, it is made by the issue of a Pt 8 claim form. Usually, it is made within the existing proceedings.

12–109 The Master may deal with the third party claim summarily, direct an issue to be tried between the parties in dispute (see RSC Order 17, r.5) or make any other order which he or she considers appropriate. Masters of the Queen's Bench Division have lists of appointments for interpleader relief at the High Court in London, and the listing of the case is carried out in conjunction with Central Office staff and local HCEOs.

There are a number of practical issues to consider if faced with a third party claim. The judgment creditor should ask him or herself:

- What are the goods that have been claimed? Are they valuable and worth selling at auction to recover the full amount due under the Writ?
- Can other goods be seized outside of the third party claim?
- What will be the likely costs of the application?
- What are the chances of enforcing any costs order against an interpleader claimant?
- What will be the costs of the HCEO and their legal team?
- What evidence is available to dispute the third party claim?

County court position

12–110 In the county court, the approach taken to a claim made by a third party to ownership of goods seized by a county court bailiff should be subject to the same thought process. If a third party claim is disputed, then under CPR Sch.2, CCR Order 33 the county court has similar procedural rules to adjudicate on that claim through the use of interpleader proceedings.

New Act position

12–111 If, at an address appearing on the writ of fi fa, an enforcement officer inadvertently seizes goods belonging to a third party, the interpleader procedure should protect the enforcement officer from any action, provided he has acted lawfully and within the rules of the court.

This regime, however, will be updated by implementation of para.60 of Sch.12, which will replace the rules on interpleaders in the High Court and county courts. Under the new Act, enforcement officers will only be able to take control of goods that belong to the judgment debtor. Accordingly, where a third party claims that goods which in fact belong to him and not the judgment debtor were taken by an enforcement officer, the third party will be able to make an application under the relevant regulations, which will no doubt become an updated part of the Civil Procedure Rules in relation to High Court and county court judgment debts.

It is likely that regulations supporting the Sch.12 provisions will pick up on the change in emphasis in interpleader proceedings, but beyond those regulations amendments may need to be made to CPR Sch.1 RSC Order 17 and CCR Order 33.

Application to an assignee or transferee—paragraph 61, Schedule 12

Current High Court position

The new Act looks at the positions of assignees and transferees in ways in which the current law and rules do not.

Current county court position

12–112 County court rules do not deal with this topic in a direct fashion either.

New Act position

12–113 The new Act provides that where there has been an assignment or transfer in good faith for valuable consideration and without notice, the assignee/transferee under the new legislation has all the benefits of the provisions in relation to co-owners.

An assignee will be entitled to receive an inventory, take part in the valuation process, receive all the information relating to the sale and benefit from the remedies that co-owners enjoy under para.59(6) of Sch.12.

Where the assignee or transferee does not acquire their interest in good faith for valuable consideration and without notice, their only true right is to receive any surplus payable once a sale has taken place pursuant to para.50(5) of Sch.12.

Costs—paragraph 62, Schedule 12

Current High Court position

12–114 Currently, High Court Enforcement Officers charge fees which are prescribed by the High Court Enforcement Officers Regulations 2004 (SI 2004/400), Reg. 13 and Sch.3. Under Reg. 13 (4), an enforcement officer or a party liable to pay any fees under Sch.3 of these Regs may apply to a costs judge or District Judge of the High Court for an assessment of the amount payable, through the detailed assessment procedure in accordance with the Civil Procedure Rules 1998. In the case of *Loynes v Beswicks Solicitors* Unreported May 20, 2010, the court agreed that it was also open for a HCEO to apply to the court under CPR Pt 23 for the fees to be reviewed by summary assessment.

The provision entitling the judgment creditor to "levy the poundage, fees and expenses of execution over and above the sum recovered" is contained in the prescribed forms of writs of fi fa. In the execution of the writ, where money is recovered by the High Court Enforcement Officer as a result of seizure of the judgment debtor's goods, the enforcement officer has a right to his poundage (see *Mortimore v Cragg* (1878) 3 C.P.D. 216), even if there has been no sale. However, it is settled procedure that there must be an actual seizure (see *Bissicks v Bath Colliery Co* (1878) 3 Ex.D. 174), without which only an agreed nominal charge can be made.

12–115 The enforcement officer is entitled to a percentage of monies recovered, where he has actually obtained the money by compulsion from the judgment debtor and has it ready to hand over to the judgment creditor (per Cave J. in see *Re Ludmore* (1884) 13 Q.B.D. 415 at 417).

If after seizure the judgment creditor becomes disentitled to recover the judgment debt, perhaps because the judgment is set aside by the court, then the enforcement officer cannot sell the judgment debtor's goods for the purpose of realising his possession money, fees and expenses (see *Sneary v Abdy* (1876) 1 Ex.D. 299). However, the judgment debtor's bankruptcy and an injunction restraining a sale do not actually affect the enforcement officer's right to payment of his fees by the judgment debtor's trustee in bankruptcy (see *Re Craycraft* (1878) 8 Ch.D. 596).

Therefore, where two seizures are made under different writs in different counties, poundage is disallowed under one of the writs because the whole debt is realised under the other writ (*Lee v Dangar* [1892] 1 Q.B. 231 2).

12–116 The new post April 1, 2004 regime for High Court enforcement means that where two seizures are made under writs directed to different enforcement officers, it is the first enforcement officer to seize goods and receive monies due for the whole debt who will be entitled to charge full fees. The National Information Centre for Enforcement is a database which manages the priorities of writs between High Court Enforcement Officers.

A High Court Enforcement Officer is not entitled to a percentage of monies recovered where, after seizure, a bankruptcy order is made against the judgment debtor and the goods are delivered to the Official Receiver under s.346 of the Insolvency Act 1986 (see *Re Thomas Ex p. Sheriff of Middlesex*, [1899] 1 Q.B. 460).

If the execution is stayed before the sale of the judgment debtor's goods, the judgment creditor is liable to pay the enforcement officer his fees, unless the order staying the execution provides otherwise or the sale is stopped at the insistance of the trustee in bankruptcy or the Official Receiver of the judgment debtor, who are in such cases liable for the fees.

Where, by a bona fide accident, the enforcement officer levies too much for poundage, he cannot be held liable for the penalty under s.29 of the Sheriffs Act 1887 (see *Shoppee v Nathan* [1892] 1 Q.B. 245).

12–117 The right of the enforcement officer to charge poundage (now referred to as a percentage of monies recovered) where no sale took place was recognised in *Re Thomas, Ex p. Sheriff of Middlesex* [1899] 1 Q.B. 460, per Lindley M.R. at page 462, where it was stated,

> "the Sheriff has seized no doubt but he has not sold. It has been by law settled for years that he is not entitled to poundage. I am aware there has been a qualification on that where the Sheriff has seized but has not sold in consequence of a compromise between the parties; there the law regards him as having secured the money for the creditor and gives him poundage".

Current county court position

12–118 The costs of enforcing a warrant of execution are dealt with under CPR 45.6 Table 5. Such costs are added to the warrant executed. There is provision within the rules for costs to be assessed.

New Act position

12–119 The issue of costs is probably one of the most controversial areas in which enforcement agents need clarity, particularly under the new regulations. The introduction of standard charges will be welcomed across the enforcement industry.

The approach of the Act is to ensure that the amount recoverable will be calculated on the same basis, regardless of whether the process is pursued through the High Court, county court, Magistrates' Court or CRAR.

Regulations are being developed by the Ministry of Justice at the time of preparing this book, but have yet to go out to public consultation. What is clear is that the regulations will make provision for the assessment of costs, fee scales and the amounts that can be recovered from the proceeds of sale. These regulations will govern costs in relation to all enforcement-related services.

Limitation of liability for sale or payment proceeds—paragraphs 63–65, Schedule 12

Current High Court position

12–120 Where a HCEO sells goods in the possession of the judgment debtor, which turn out to belong to a third party, and that party fails to make a valid claim under RSC Order 17, r.2, the HCEO is protected from any liability by virtue of Sch.7 of s.99 to the Courts 2003 Act, which replaced the Supreme Court Act 1981, s.138B(1).

To ensure that protection is secured, it is incumbent on the HCEO to make reasonable inquiries as to whether the goods seized were, or were not, the property of the judgment debtor at the time of seizure. In the case of *Observer Ltd v Gordon* [1983] 1 W.L.R. 1008; [1983] 2 All E.R. 945, Sheriff's Officers seized and sold a number of grand pianos that were in the piano repair shop of Reeva Gordon, without making inquiries as to the ownership of each piano. The Sheriff was able to argue successfully that sufficient inquiries had been made, which in turn protected him from any liability.

Where the third party has a "substantial grievance" against an enforcement officer on the grounds that his goods have been wrongfully, yet without misconduct, seized, and then sold at auction at a far lower price than their apparent value, the onus is on the third party to show that there was a substantial difference between the value of the goods at the date of the sale and the price in fact realised. In the absence of such proof, the enforcement officer is entitled to an order protecting him from proceedings by the third party (see *Neumann v Bakeaway Ltd* [1983] 1 W.L.R. 1016, CA).

Current county court position

12–121 Case law for the above cases in *Neumann* and *Observer* is relevant within the jurisdiction of the county courts.

District Judges are protected in relation to any claims made in respect of a seizure, but this will only be granted where it is just to do so. Indeed, a District Judge may see any relief being refused if a claimant has suffered a substantial grievance as a result of the seizure of goods (see *Cave v Capel* [1954] 1 Q.B. 367); it is the quality of a District Judge's act which becomes relevant. For example, where goods have been sold at a grossly undervalued price, a District Judge may see himself as being liable for the loss to the judgment creditor (see *Neumann v Bakeaway Ltd* [1983] 2 All E.R. 935).

The test in this situation is to determine whether the claimant would be allowed to bring a claim against the District Judge, and whether it is fairly arguable that his claim overrides the District Judge's defences under s.98 of the County Courts Act 1984 or at common law (see *Observer v Gordon* [1983] 2 All E.R. 945).

New Act position

Under the new Act the liability of an enforcement officer for the sale of any controlled goods will be excluded except where: **12–122**

- at the time of the sale the enforcement officer had notice that the goods were not the judgment debtor's or not his alone; or
- before the sale, claimants had lawfully made an application to the court claiming an interest in the goods.

Such situations are common occurrences in relation to the High Court enforcement business, and they have now been included and codified in the new legislation.

A lawful claimant will be a person who has an interest in the goods at the time of sale, although this will not include a person whose interest was assigned or transferred to him after the goods were bound in the control of the enforcement officer. **12–123**

The protection for enforcement officers is extended by para.64 of Sch.12, which excludes liability for officers who pay over proceeds, except where:

- the enforcement officer had notice that the goods were the judgment debtor's and not his alone;
- before making a payment to a claimant, the enforcement officer had received an application to the court claiming an interest in the goods.

In relation to para.64 a lawful claimant is simply one who has an interest in the goods at the time of sale.

Enforcement officers in the future will be expected to make reasonable enquiries before being entitled to the protection of the Act under paras.63 and 64.

The protection enforcement officers will enjoy under the new legislation will also extend to related parties such as auctioneers, removal agents and locksmiths.

Remedies available to the creditor—paragraph 67, Schedule 12

Current High Court position

12–124 One of the frustrations for judgment creditors is that the law is sometimes unhelpful as far as what can be done to pursue goods that have been removed from an address by a judgment debtor in order to avoid the enforcement of the writ. In the High Court, the remedy for a judgment creditor may well be to issue an application endorsed with a penal notice seeking the return of any goods that have been removed out of reach of the HCEO, particularly where a walking possession agreement has been signed.

Current county court position

12–125 The county court position follows the High Court position.

New Act position

12–126 Where a judgment debtor wrongfully interferes with controlled goods, and the judgment creditor suffers loss as a result, the new Act creates a general remedy for all creditors to claim against the debtor in respect of that loss.

The remedy applies only to those goods subject to a controlled goods agreement and does not apply to goods bound pursuant to para.4 of Sch.12, prior to the goods being taken into control. This in some ways mirrors the current position, whereby goods have got to be levied on to be subject to any further action.

Offences—paragraph 68, Schedule 12

Current High Court position

12–127 Under s.189 of the Courts Act 2003 a person is guilty of an offence if he resists or intentionally obstructs any person who is an enforcement officer or who is acting under the authority of any enforcement officer and is engaged in executing a High Court writ.

Current county court position

12–128 The County Court position follows that of the High Court.

New Act position

12–129 Under para.68 of Sch.12, where a person intentionally obstructs an enforcement officer, under the new Act he will be guilty of an offence. A further offence can also be committed where a person intentionally interferes with controlled goods without lawful excuse.

Both offences on successful prosecution and conviction will lead to a sentence of either imprisonment for a term not exceeding 51 weeks or a fine not exceeding level 4 on the standard scale, or indeed both (see para.68(3) of Sch.12).

Relationship with insolvency procedures—paragraph 69, Schedule 12

Current High Court position

12–130 The impact of insolvency on any enforcement method generally puts creditors on a pari passu footing and defeats a judgment creditor's sole right to enjoy the proceeds of the enforcement.

The general rule is that an insolvency procedure may well defeat the position of a judgment creditor, unless the execution has been "completed" by the sale and holding of net proceeds for a 14-day statutory period after the receipt of monies. If money has been paid "to avoid sale" by a judgment debtor in some form of payment plan or instalment arrangement, then each payment attracts its own 14-day window from the date of receipt by the High Court Enforcement Officer.

Of course, due to changes in insolvency legislation there are now a number of insolvency measures that can affect the execution of a writ of fi fa, and therefore the table below seeks to offer the reader an encapsulated guide on the impact of each on the execution of a writ of fi fa (or indeed warrant of execution)

Corporate Insolvency Table

12–131

Type of Insolvency/ Charge	Reference	Impact on the writ of fi fa
Compulsory Liquidation of a Judgment Debtor Company	See s.183 of the IA 1986 and s.129(2) IA 1986	Under this section, where execution has been issued against a company and the company is subsequently wound up, the creditor cannot retain the benefit of the execution against the liquidator *unless* he has "completed" the execution *before* the commencement of the winding up (as to the definition of "commencement", see s.129(2) IA 1986, which in the case of compulsory liquidation means the date of commencement of the winding up is taken back to the date of the presentation of the petition on which the winding up order is subsequently made). The section does give the court discretion to defeat the rights conferred on the liquidator, either wholly or partially, according to what is right and fair in the circumstances of the case (*Re Governor Metal Co Ltd* [1950] Ch. 63). "Completed" means there has been either a sale of the goods (see *Re Standard Manufacturing Co* [1891] 1 Ch. 627 or monies have been paid to avoid sale. In these instances, the HCEO is bound to retain the money less the costs of execution for 14 days, with time running from the time of payment (see *Re Walkden Sheet Metal Co Ltd* at page 178). If no notice is served within the 14 days, the HCEO is at liberty to pay the money to the judgment creditor.
Appointment of a Provisional Liquidator	Companies Act 1985, s.622	Where any goods of a company are taken in execution, and before the sale or completion of the execution, notice is served on the HCEO that a provisional liquidator has been appointed or a winding-up order made, etc., the HCEO on being required is to deliver to the liquidator the goods or money seized, but the

Type of Insolvency/ Charge	Reference	Impact on the writ of fi fa
Appointment of a Provisional Liquidator—*cont.*	Companies Act 1985, s.622—*cont.*	costs of the execution are a first charge on the goods or money so delivered, and the liquidator may sell the goods or a sufficient part of them to satisfy that charge. The "costs" referred to in this section only include costs incurred by the HCEO himself and do not include any costs of the judgment creditor (*Re Woods (Bristol) Ltd* (1931) 75 S.J. 458).
Voluntary Liquidation	See s.183 of the IA 1986 and s.129(1) IA 1986	Similar considerations and timings apply to the voluntary liquidation of a judgment debtor company *except* where the company resolves to wind itself up and the date of commencement begins on the date of the resolution.
Administration		Where a company is facing financial difficulties it can be placed into "administration", which is a procedure created under the Enterprise Act 2002 with streamlined objectives. The procedure places a company under the control of an insolvency practitioner and the protection of the court, with the objective of viewing the company as a going concern or achieving a better result for creditors as a group and realising property in order to make a distribution to creditors. While a company is in administration, creditors are prevented from taking any actions against it except with the permission of the court. A widely drafted moratorium expressly prevents execution being continued or commenced without the consent of the administrator or leave of the court.
Administration Receiver		Administrative receivers are normally appointed by a bank or a lender when a company breaches the terms of its borrowing from a creditor. This type of receivership (there are others) is an enforcement remedy available to a creditor holding a security which includes a floating charge over all (or substantially all) of the assets of a company. An administrative receiver is appointed by the holder of the security, but normally acts as an agent

Type of Insolvency/ Charge	**Reference**	**Impact on the writ of fi fa**
Administration Receiver—*cont.*		of the company over whose assets he is appointed. His principal function is to recover the monies owed to the creditor by whom he is appointed. It is common for an administrative receiver to continue to operate the business or try to sell it as a going concern. However, an administrative receiver is simply a third party and does not enjoy any particular privilege as against the HCEO to surrender any goods which have been seized.
Company Voluntary Arrangement (CVA)		On January 1, 2003, CVAs were brought into line with IVAs, giving the courts power to order a moratorium of 28 days' duration whilst the proposals for a CVA are formulated. The impact of such a moratorium is that "no other proceedings and no execution or other legal process may be commenced or continued, and no distress may be levied against the company or its property except with the leave of the court and subject to such terms as the court may impose".
Debenture		Where a charge under a debenture agreement crystallises after the valid appointment of a receiver, and before the completion of the execution (i.e. by seizure and sale of goods), the rights of the debenture holder will take priority over those from the creditor (see re *Standard Manufacturing Co* [1891] 1 Ch. 627, CA). If the debenture holder decides to make a third party claim to the goods seized (or intended to be seized), then that claim will be treated as notice of a claim within the terms of RSC Order 17, r.2, which may occur for example if the validity of the receiver's appointment is disputed. An HCEO managing the execution of the writ will seek a copy of the debenture holder's agreement, which will then besubmitted to the judgment creditor for a decision on whether the claim should be admitted or disputed.

Personal Insolvency Table

12–132

Type of Insolvency	Reference	Impact on the writ of fi fa
Bankruptcy	See s.346 of the IA 1986	In order for a judgment creditor to retain the benefit of his execution against the trustee in bankruptcy of the judgment debtor, then, as for liquidation, the judgment creditor must have *completed* the execution of his writ of fi fa, by seizure *and* sale before the commencement of the bankruptcy order. To ensure the monies recovered under the writ are secure from any competing claim by the judgment debtor's trustee in bankruptcy, the following points should be noted: ■ The execution of the writ of fi fa will be *completed* by the seizure and sale or receipt of the full amount of the levy (*Figg v Moore* [1894] 2 Q.B. 690); ■ The execution of the writ of fi fa will also be completed by a return of no goods (or, as the form of return is commonly known, a return of "nulla bona") as in *Re Fairley, Ex p. Low and Bonar Ltd* [1922] 2 Ch. 791; ■ The *completion* must have taken place before the commencement of the bankruptcy (*Burns-Burns, Trustees v Brown* [1895] 1 Q.B. 324); ■ The execution is not "completed" under s.346 of the Insolvency Act 1986, unless payment has been made direct to the HCEO—it is important to note that payment of monies directly to the judgment creditor or their solicitor does not amount to *completion* (*Re Godding* [1914] 2 K.B. 70 and *Re Pollock* (1902) 87 L.T. 238); ■ If a judgment debtor pays money to the HCEO in order to avoid a sale of goods taken in execution by the HCEO, then that money will be treated as "money in order to avoid sale" under s.346 of the Insolvency

Type of Insolvency	Reference	Impact on the writ of fi fa
Bankruptcy—*cont.*	See s.346 of the IA 1986 —*cont.*	Act 1986, and not for "money received in part satisfaction of the execution" under the same section. The effect of this is that money paid to the HCEO in order to avoid a sale of the judgment debtor's goods becomes vested in the judgment creditor and can only be nullified if within 14 days of its receipt the HCEO receives notice of the debtor's bankruptcy (*Marley Tile Co Ltd v Burrows* [1978] 1 All E.R. 657, CA); ■ A payment made by the judgment debtor to the enforcement officer, even before a bankruptcy order is made against him, operates in satisfaction of a judgment creditor's debt only when the judgment creditor is in a position to maintain an action against the enforcement officer for money "had and received" (*Re A Debtor (No. 2 of 1977),* [1979] 1 All E.R. 870). In practical terms, this means the payment must have been made to the enforcement officer, banked by the enforcement officer, and then held for the statutory period of 14 days. The date for clearance of a cheque or credit/debit card payment is computed from the date the enforcement officer's bank account is actually credited with the funds that the enforcement officer could use to pay the judgment creditor, and not the date the payment (in the case in question it was a cheque) was received (*Parkside Leasing v Smith (Inspector of Taxes) The Times*, November 19, 1984).
Individual Voluntary Arrangement		The making of an interim order prevents all execution being continued or commenced without the leave of the court (IA 1986, s.252). However, the mere application for an interim order under that section is not a stay of execution, but the court may stay any action, execution or legal process

Type of Insolvency	Reference	Impact on the writ of fi fa
Individual Voluntary Arrangement —*cont.*		pending the granting of the interim order. It should be noted that judgment creditors who have not been served with the proposal or agreed to the proposal are not therefore bound by the terms of the IVA. This becomes important if the HCEO has levied execution. In the following little known case of *Peck v Craighead* [1955] 1 B.C.L.C 337, the seizure of goods by the Sheriff was held to secure the goods for the benefit of the writ of fi fa, and so the Sheriff could continue with the execution of the writ by the sale and relief of net proceeds of the sale.
Administration Order		Under s.114 of the County Courts Act 1984, no creditor will have any remedy against the property of the judgment debtor in respect of those debts notified to the court before an administration order is made, or in respect of those debts which subsequently become scheduled to the order by additions to the list of debts. The objective of an administration order is to secure equal division of the judgment debtor's property amongst all the creditors, and therefore leave is not given because to do so would in effect amount to setting aside the order (see *Re Frank* [1984] 1 Q.B. 9). On learning that an administration order has come into effect, a HCEO should confirm with the judgment creditor to the Writ of Fi Fa whether the judgment creditor's debt is or is not a "scheduled debt", and therefore may or may not be bound by the administration order. Debts that have not been scheduled can be added at a later date, which means any hint of an administration order could thwart the successful execution of the Writ by the HCEO.

12–133 Whilst all monies received from the judgment debtor must be applied to the writ of fi fa in order of priority, payments made by third parties on behalf of the judgment debtor may be allocated to specific writs (*Bower v Hett* [1895] 2 Q.B. 51; (1895) 73 L.T. 176).

A third party payment is not subject to the provisions of s.346 of the Insolvency Act 1986, as it does not deplete the assets of the judgment debtor and is therefore outside the judgment debtor's estate for the purposes of bankruptcy.

Current county court position

12–134 Reference can be made to CPR Sch.2, CCR Order 26, r.8(1), but in essence the position is the same as for High Court business. In this case, the reader is referred to the table above showing the various insolvency procedures involving corporate and personal insolvency, as well as the effect of these on execution against goods.

New Act position

12–135 Schedule 12 to the TCEA reflects the provisions of ss.183, 184 and 346 of the Insolvency Act 1986.

Other areas outside the Act

Current High Court and county court enforcement thresholds

12–136 Earlier in this book the rules relating to the value and type of judgment debts that could be enforced in the county court and High Court were set out.

The table below is a quick reminder on these rules, because today as the law stands there are clear differences between the levels of debt enforceable in either the lower or higher courts.

Judgment Debt Amount to be Enforced (including costs and interest where applicable)	High Court	County Court
Below £600	No	Yes
Consumer Credit Act Judgments*	No	Yes
Between £600–£5,000	Yes	Yes
Above £5,000	Yes	No

* If a Consumer Credit Act judgment can be said to be exempt from the provisions of the prevailing legislation, it should be possible to transfer the judgment to the High Court for enforcement.

New Act position

12–137 The new Act is silent as to any changes in threshold that would enable judgment creditors to choose their forum between the county court and the High Court in the enforcement of their judgment debts.

We know that by virtue of s.62(4) of the Tribunals, Courts and Enforcement Act, writs of fieri facias will be renamed writs of control, and warrants of execution will become warrants of control. However, what the new writs will look like and whether they will follow the existing form of writs in some shape or form has yet to be disclosed, but we can expect significant changes in the Civil Procedure Rules to reflect the new approach.

Paperwork

Current High Court position

12–138 The following Queen's Bench Masters' Practice Forms are relevant to the preparation and issue of a writ of fi fa. Under CPR Sch.1, RSC Order 47, the forms used in the High Court include:

- An N.293A, the Combined Certificate of Judgment and Request for writ of fieri facias, which is believed to be the only dual forum form in the CPR. It relates to county court business on one side, and when turned over becomes a High Court form of praecipe.
- PF86 is the praecipe for a writ of fi fa, which is issued on a High Court judgment when the judgment is not transferred from the county court.
- Form No. 53 is the standard form of writ of fi fa.
- PF97 provides for an order for sale by an HCEO using a private treaty between parties, rather than a forced public auction sale, on the ground that a better price may be obtained (see comments throughout this chapter in relation to sales by private treaty).

In accordance with RSC Order 46, r.6, the writ of fi fa needs to be prepared along with its accompanying form of praecipe, which is the form containing the particulars of the writ of fi fa and lodged in the court office out of which the writ is to be issued. Both forms are taken to the court and a fee is payable on sealing the Writ.

12–139 In the High Court in London, the practice is to attend the Fees Room in E01, pay the fee and then walk round to the Action

Department, which will issue the writ once the formalities have been checked.

In checking the paperwork, the court staff will review the praecipe and evidence of the judgment or order. The writ is then sealed. The court's seal includes the date on which it was issued along with details of the court out of which it was issued. This date is known as the "teste date". It is from this date that the 12-month time period of the life of the writ is calculated.

The praecipe is filed at the court, having been signed by, or on behalf of, the solicitor entitled to execute the writ.

The form of writ was updated as a result of changes to High Court enforcement in 2004, but in essence the document remains the same (a table explaining the structure of a writ of fi fa is set out below). The many forms of writ of fi fa are set out in Practice Direction (Forms) Table 2 at para. 4PD 4. The varieties of writ reflect different circumstances relating to the judgment, but the standard version is in Form No. 53.

As the forms of writ are prescribed, they must be used wherever applicable, with variations drafted into the writ as the case requires. For example, in the case of a judgment expressed in a foreign currency this must include the sterling equivalent.

12–140 The writ itself then follows the form of a royal command to a named High Court Enforcement Officer or the enforcement officers for the district in which it is required that the writ is executed. The structure of the writ is set out in the table below:

Heading	This should follow the heading in the proceedings. If the judgment was obtained in the county court, the heading needs to be completed to reflect that the judgment has been transferred.
Greeting	The real innovation in implementing the Courts Act 2003 is that judgment creditors and their advisors can choose the HCEO of their choice or send their writ to the National Information Centre for Enforcement for allocation of a HCEO on a rota basis. It is no longer necessary to consider the address of the judgment debtor in terms of the old bailiwick structure, which existed prior to April 1, 2004. The Directory of High Court Enforcement Officers contains the names of all authorised HCEOs, which can be found at *http://www.hceoa.org.uk* [Accessed October 20, 2010]. Alternatively, the judgment creditor can address the writ to the High Court Enforcement Officers of England and Wales and allow it to be allocated through the cab rank system of the National Information Centre for Enforcement.

	As changes to High Court enforcement have removed the bailiwick system, HCEOs can now operate across the jurisdiction of the High Court or limit their area of operation to designated postcodes, of which there are 105 within the jurisdiction of the courts of England and Wales. The directory of High Court Enforcement Officers shows the postcodes in which they are authorised to operate.
Recital of judgment	The detail of the judgment is summarised: where there has been a change of parties, the order giving leave should be recited.
Command to the HCEO	The wording must carefully follow that of the judgment. If there is no judgment (e.g. on an order for costs on discontinuance of an action: see *Bolton v Bolton* (1876) L.R. 3 Ch.D. 276), the circumstances must be set out. The writ of fi fa will direct the HCEO to pay the judgment creditor the amount levied.
The sum of money to be levied [this section only applies to the execution of money judgments i.e. in a writ of fi fa]	The court has power to give judgment for a sum of money expressed in a foreign currency (*Miliangos v George Frank (Textiles) Ltd* [1976] A.C. 443) and see paragraph 11(a) of the *Practice Direction (QBD Judgment: Foreign Currency)* (No.1) [1976] 1 W.L.R. 83; [1976] 1 All E.R. 669). Where the judgment creditor has obtained a judgment or order expressed in foreign currency, before enforcement through execution either by warrant or by writ he must first certify the sterling equivalent. The reason for the issue of the writ must be indorsed, signed and dated by or on behalf of the claimant: *I/We certify that the rate current in London for the purpose of [state the unit of the foreign currency in which the judgment is expressed] at the close of business on the day of 20 [being the date nearest or most nearly preceding the date of the issue of the Writ of Fi Fa] was to the sterling and at this rate the sum of [state the amount of the judgment debt in foreign currency] amounts to £.'* Of course, this avoids the necessity for the agency enforcing the writ, be it the county court bailiff or the HCEO, from having to undertake complicated currency conversions which may vary daily throughout the period that the warrant or writ is held. It also allows the claimant to take account of movements in the money markets.
Fixed costs of execution	At the time of publication, these are £101.75. Under RSC Order 47, r.4, where a judgment or order other than an order for costs is for less than £600 (SI 1981/1734) and does not entitle the judgment creditor to cost against the person against whom the writ is

Fixed costs of execution —*cont.*	issued, the writ may not authorise the High Court Enforcement Officer to levy any fees or other costs of execution. After the introduction of the Civil Procedure Rules in 1999, it is suggested that this rule is virtually redundant, as a High Court claim must be at least £15,000 and a county court judgment can only be transferred to the High Court for a sum in excess of £600.
Interest	A writ of execution for the payment of money may be indorsed to levy interest on the debt at the appropriate rate from the date of the judgment or order. The rate of interest is governed by statutory instrument made under ss.17 and 18 of the Judgments Act 1838. The current statutory instrument is the Judgment Debts (Rate of Interest Order) 1993 (SI 1993/564), which specifies a rate of 8 per cent from April 1, 1993. For a table of previous rates of interest, see the notes in the 2010 White Book Service. Interest is also payable on an order for costs, which is chargeable from the date of the judgment or order for payment (see *Hunt v R M Douglas (Roofing) Ltd* [1988] 3 All E.R. 823, HL, overruling *K v K* [1977] 2 W.L.R. 55). Statutory interest is not recoverable on a judgment by consent payable by instalments that have been regularly paid (see *Caudery v Finnerty* (1892) 66 L.T. 684). A higher rate of interest can only be enforced if there is an express agreement which provides that the higher rate should run under a judgment and then the judgment itself should provide for it (see *Re European Central Railway Ltd* (1876) 4 Ch.D. 33). It is helpful to send a copy of the order to the HCEO instructed to enforce the order, to show any variation in the interest rate applicable for the period after judgment until payment. Where the county court judgment or order has been transferred for enforcement in the High Court by a High Court Enforcement Officer, interest at the statutory rate only runs from the date of the certificate of judgment issued by the county court for the amount due.
Command for indorsement	This requires the HCEO to give a report on the outcome of the execution of the writ, which is commonly referred to as a "Return".
The witness	The name of the witness must appear at the foot of the writ. In Queen's Bench and Chancery cases, the name of the Lord Chancellor must be recited. As the position of Lord Chancellor is a political post and subject to change, the name of the current incumbent can be found at *http://en.wikipedia.org/wiki/Lord_Chancellor* [Accessed October 20, 2010].

The witness *—cont.*	In family cases, the name to be indorsed as a witness is the President of the Family Division, which again is subject to change and can be checked at *http://en.wikipedia.org/wiki/High_Court_of_Justice#Family_Division* [Accessed October 20, 2010].
Issue	Note that the date of issue and the teste date must coincide—the term "teste date" comes from the Latin for the witnessing of a document, and is in practical terms the date of the seal given to the writ by the High Court.
Indorsement of the name and address of the issuing solicitor (if any)	The party's name and address must be given in all cases, regardless of whether or not he acts in person. This information may be vital to check facts urgently where, for example, the debtor maintains that he has just paid the amount due direct to the judgment creditor. It must also be indorsed with the name and address of the solicitor actually issuing it, and if he is acting as agent for another solicitor, the name and address of the other solicitor for whom he acts as agent must be set out in the writ of fi fa. Where there has been a change of solicitor, the new solicitor must place his name on the record before he can issue a writ of fi fa (see CPR Pt 42 for the necessary formalities).
Indorsement of the residence or place of business of the debtor	The old rules on addressing writs of fi fa to the bailiwick of the Sheriff of the county were reformed under the provisions of s.99, Sch.7 to the Courts Act 2003. Whilst it is still possible to send a writ of fi fa to the High Sheriff of the bailiwick, in practice this is virtually unheard of; instead, a judgment creditor will send the writ to the High Court Enforcement Officer either by choice or by using the cab rank system of selection provided by the National Information Centre for Enforcement. It is always in the creditor's interest to inform the High Court Enforcement Officer about the financial situation of the judgment debtor and whether there are likely to be any goods which will satisfy the judgment debt. Useful information includes: ■ trading address(es) for the judgment debtor; ■ the debtor's home address; ■ the debtor's working hours or work pattern; ■ at what time the debtor is likely to be at home; ■ whether any credit reference checks have been carried out against the debtor and the result of these searches; and ■ vehicle information including details of where the debtor keeps his vehicle.

Indorsement of the residence or place of business of the debtor —*cont.*	Particular care should be taken to ensure the accuracy of any information. Indeed, if the address given to the Sheriff is incorrect and leads to the seizure of the wrong goods, both creditor (*Morris v Salberg* [1889] L.R. 22 Q.B.D. 614) and solicitor (see *Rowles v Senior* [1846] 8 Q.B. 677) may be liable for trespass.

Current county court position

12–141 Under CCR Order 26, r.1 the judgment creditor must file a request for a warrant of execution on Form N323, certifying:

- the amount remaining due under the judgment or order;
- where the order made is for payment of a sum of money by instalments, that the whole or part of any instalment due remains unpaid—although it should be noted that the amount cannot be for less than £50 or the amount of one monthly instalment or four weekly instalments (whichever is the greater);
- the amount for which the warrant is to be issued.

An up to date fee payable on the issue of the request for the warrant is available from the Court Service website at *http://www.hmcs.gov.uk* [Accessed October 20, 2010].

If the judgment to be enforced is a High Court judgment or order, the judgment creditor must also file:

- an office copy of the judgment or order;
- a certificate verifying the amount due;
- if a writ of execution has been issued, a copy of the relevant HCEO's return;
- a copy of the order for transfer.

12–142 The court officer will issue the warrant and give it a reference number. Under s.85(3) of the County Courts Act 1984 the court staff must enter into their records the precise time of the making of the application to issue the warrant and/or under s.103(1) of the same Act, the time they send a warrant of execution to another county court.

The court staff must then give notice to the judgment debtor that a warrant of execution has been issued, which will be forwarded to the county court bailiff section for the court in which the debtor resides or trades. The notice given to the judgment debtor is a requirement under CCR Order 26, r.7 and will be in Form N326. There is no equivalent of a notice in Form N326 in the High Court.

A further seven days must elapse before a county court bailiff can attempt to levy on the judgment debtor's goods.

The notice gives the judgment debtor an opportunity to pay without a levy, but equally provides an unscrupulous judgment debtor with an opportunity to hide goods. If it is thought that the judgment debtor might do this, then consideration should seriously be given to transferring the enforcement activity to the High Court, where HCEOs will take responsibility for the enforcement of the judgment.

Applying for permission to issue

High Court position

12–143 Under CPR Sch.1, RSC Order 46, r.4, the application is made in accordance with CPR Pt 23, but the application notice does not need to be served on the judgment debtor unless the court makes a specific direction to that effect.

The application for permission to issue the writ must be supported by a witness statement or affidavit which identifies the judgment or order where permission is required. For money judgments the evidence must include details of the original amount due and the amount due on the date the evidence is filed. The evidence must also set out the reasons for the application, i.e. the reason for the delay, and details of any change in the parties, as outlined in the Rule, so that the court can be satisfied that the application for permission should be granted and execution can ensue.

County court position

12–144 CCR Order 26, r.5(1) outlines the situations where the permission of the court is required to issue a warrant of execution. The application for permission is made on Form N244. The most frequent case where permission is required is where six years have elapsed since the date of the judgment or order (see *Duer v Fraser* [2001] 1 All E.R. 249).

County court rules on what permission is needed to issue a warrant of execution are based largely on RSC Order 46, r.2. The county court rule dealing with the application for permission is set out in CCR Order 26, r.5. The county court application must be supported by either a witness statement or affidavit establishing the applicant's right to relief and may be made without notice being served on any other party in the first instance, although the court may direct the application notice to be served on such persons as it thinks fit.

The requirement to obtain permission if Order 26, r.5 applies is mandatory, and it is an abuse of process to issue without it (see *Hackney LBC v White* (1996) 28 H.L.R. 219 involving a warrant of possession).

As in the High Court, the application for permission to issue a warrant of execution after six years have elapsed since judgment is "no mere formality". Although CCR Order 26.5(2) enables the application to be made without notice, it also gives power to direct that notice be given. In all cases the rule requires the application to be supported by evidence.

Venue for taking legal control of goods

Current High Court position

12–145 The rules on which court to issue your writ are dictated by where the proceedings for the main action were commenced, so for example:

If the action was issued and heard in the District Registry	Then the writ of fi fa will be issued in that District Registry
If the action was issued and heard in Admiralty or Commercial Courts that are not in a District Registry	Then the writ of fi fa will be issued in the Admiralty Court or Commercial Court in London
If proceedings have been dealt with in the Chancery Division, Chancery Chambers	Then proceedings will be issued in the Chancery Division
For all other cases not included as above	The writ of fi fa will be issued in the Central Office of the Supreme Court in London

A county court judgment may be transferred to the High Court for enforcement purposes using Form N293A. Many of the larger HCEO offices offer a transfer up service to assist judgment creditors to turn a county court judgment into a writ for enforcement in the High Court. Usually, there is no fee for arranging the preparation and sealing of the High Court writ. Judgment creditors who do not wish to draft the form of writ can use a transfer up service to speed things up by getting the certificate of judgment stamped by the appropriate county court on Pt 2 of the N293A, before sending it to the transfer up service provider.

Current county court position

12–146 The County Court position follows that of the High Court.

New Act

12–147 Under the terms of the new Act the place where enforcement agents can take control of goods has been unified so that landlords are brought under the same regime.

The place where an enforcement agent can take control of goods is defined by the right of entry or where goods are situated on a highway.

The court enforcement agents have the right to enter premises where the debtor lives or carries on business.

Wrongful seizure

High Court position

12–148 Where an HCEO is misled by an indorsement made by the judgment creditor's solicitor on the writ of fi fa sent to him for enforcement, which then results in the HCEO seizing goods belonging to a person who has no connection to the judgment debt, it has been held that the judgment creditor is liable to an action of trespass (see *Morris v Salberg* (1889) L.R. 22 Q.B.D. 614). Care must therefore be taken to direct the HCEO to an address where the judgment creditor or his solicitor *believes* the goods of the judgment debtor are located. A HCEO will be exempt from penalties for an innocent mistake (see *Lee v Dangar* [1892] 2 Q.B. 337).

If there is nothing in the indorsement to mislead the enforcement agent, then an action for trespass cannot be maintained against the judgment creditor (see *Condy v Blaiberg* (1891) 7 T.L.R. 424, in which the enforcement officer seized the goods of a third person and not the judgment debtor).

12–149 The fear of seizing goods that do not belong to the judgment debtor is an occupational hazard for HCEOs, and indeed all types of bailiff. However, relief from continual actions for trespass is found in the interpleader procedure—which for High Court business is set out in CPR Sch.1, RSC Order 17. Where neither the premises where the goods are seized nor the goods seized belong to the judgment debtor, the HCEO can apply to the court for an order to be protected against an action for trespass that may be taken against him by the owner of the address or the true owner of the goods. This relief is available to the HCEO provided:

- no substantial grievance has been done to the person whose premises are wrongfully entered (see *Smith v Critchfield* (1885) L.R. 14 QBD 873); and

- the evidence shows that the HCEO has made all the necessary and proper inquiries as to the ownership of the goods (see *Salberg v Morris* (1888) 4 T.L.R. 47).

However, in the past, enforcement agents have been found not to be entitled to the protection of an order for "no action" to prevent an action of trespass where a substantial grievance has been done to the third party (see *De Coppett v Barnett* (1901) 17 T.L.R. 273 and more recently *Huntress Search Ltd v Canapeum Ltd*).

County court position

12–150 The District Judge remains liable for any Act taken under the warrant in his name, but we can expect this to be changed under the new Act.

New Act position

12–151 The strict procedure and compliance anticipated by the new Act should mean that wrongful seizure will be highly unlikely.

Concluding the enforcement

High Court position

12–152 A "Return" by an HCEO is a form of report summarising the action taken by the HCEO in the execution of the writ. Either the judgment creditor or the judgment debtor may require the appointed enforcement agent, within a stipulated time period, to prepare a "Return" that sets out this form of report, which in turn determines the manner in which the writ has been executed. The "Return" must be sent by the HCEO to the party making the request. The rules are set out in RSC Order 46, r.9.

If a HCEO fails to produce the necessary form of "Return", the party making the request can apply to the court for an order compelling the enforcement officer to comply.

A judgment creditor has no right to a return whilst an interpleader is pending (*Angell v Baddeley* (1877) L.R. 3 Ex.D. 49, CA).

County court position

12–153 The county court position is similar to the High Court position insofar as the county court bailiff will issue a final return to the judgment creditor confirming that all attempts to enforce the warrant have been exhausted.

Instalment arrangements

High Court position

12–154 CPR Sch.1, RSC Order 47 does not contain an express provision to allow for payment by instalments, which contrasts with the position in the county court, where the Rules do provide for an order to be stayed pending payment by instalments. The mechanism to achieve payments by instalments in the High Court involves the judgment debtor applying to the court for a stay under this order and seeking a stay of execution on terms.

However, by virtue of CPR Pt 40.11, both the High Court and county court have power to order payment by instalments at the time when judgment is given. Unless an order is therefore made, allowing for payment by instalments, a party must comply with a judgment or order for the payment of money, which must be made within 14 days of the date of the judgment or order.

County court position

12–155 A warrant of execution cannot be issued in a county court where there is an instalment order in existence *which is not in arrears* (see the County Courts Act 1984 s.86).

If the payments are in arrears, a warrant can be issued for all or part of the unpaid debt (subject to a minimum of £50 or one month's or four weeks' instalments), as stipulated in CCR Order 26, r.1(3).

New Act position

12–156 We wait to see what the rules will say in relation to instalment arrangements for writs and warrants of control.

Power to stay execution

Current High Court position

12–157 Referring to the express rule on writs of fi fa, under RSC Order 47, r.1 the High Court has the power to stay the execution of a writ of fi fa either absolutely or for such period and subject to such conditions as the court thinks fit, provided that the applicant can satisfy the court that either:

- there are special circumstances which render it inexpedient to enforce the judgment or order; or
- the applicant is unable, for any reason, to pay the money.

Previously, applications were very common, as the High Court, unlike the county court, had no power to order payment by instalments. Now, as a result of CPR r.40.11 the time for complying with a judgment or order means a party must comply with a judgment or order for the payment of an amount of money (including costs) within 14 days of the date of the judgment or order, unless under paragraph (a) the judgment or order specifies a different date for compliance (including specifying payment by instalments) or under para.(c) the court has stayed the proceedings or judgment.

12–158 Commentary in the White Book Service 2010 suggests that where execution has been issued, a judgment debtor may need to apply for a stay of execution pursuant to RSC Order 47, r.1, whereas if execution has not been issued it may have been preferable to apply to vary the judgment to provide for payment by instalments (or lower instalments).

The usual form of order granting a stay of execution under RSC Order 47, r.1 is as follows:

> "... stay of execution (under Order 47, r.1) so long as the defendant pays the judgment debt and costs by instalments at the rate of £——per month on the——day of each month, the first instalment to commence on the——day of——, 20—, provided that if he should make default in the payment of the said instalments or any part thereof on the due date, the stay be forthwith removed in respect of the whole outstanding balance at the time of such default and the judgment creditor do have permission forthwith to issue execution by Writ of Fi Fa on the said judgment and costs" (see Form 1124 from *Chitty and Jacob's Queen's Bench Forms,* 21st edn with 8th Supp, (London: Sweet & Maxwell, 1996)).

Paragraph (2) of RSC Order 47, r.1 makes it clear that the judgment debtor is entitled to apply for a stay of execution by fi fa, even if the judgment debtor has not acknowledged the service of the claim form or taken part in the proceedings.

12–159 It should perhaps be emphasised that the court has power to order a stay of execution by writ of fi fa either absolutely or for such period and subject to such conditions as the court thinks fit. If the debtor is the owner of premises, the court has power there and then to impose a final charging order on the premises, provided the judgment debtor agrees, so that the judgment creditor need not go through the machinery of obtaining a final charging order under CPR Pt 73. In the absence of such agreement, the court should endeavour as far as possible to maintain a fair and proper balance between the needs of the judgment debtor to be granted a stay of execution and the needs of the judgment creditor to obtain due and prompt satisfaction of his judgment debt.

In any application for a stay of execution, the starting point is that there has to be a good reason to deny the judgment creditor the immediate "fruits" of his judgment (see *Winchester Cigarette Machinery Ltd v Payne (No. 2), The Times*, December 15, 1993).

12–160 The power to stay execution under this rule is separate and distinct from the power to stay execution pending an appeal under CPR Pt 52 (see *Ellis v Scott (Practice Note)* [1964] 1 W.L.R. 976; [1964] 2 All E.R. 987). This distinction is important, as the lodging of papers or the issue of a notice to appeal a judgment will not be sufficient to prevent the HCEO from continuing with the execution of a writ of fi fa.

If execution has been improperly issued it may be set aside, even after execution has been levied. If the court sets aside a default judgment pursuant to CPR Pt 13, it will be necessary for the order to deal with payment of the costs of execution. These will have to be paid by the judgment debtor if the judgment was regular.

It is the duty of the judgment debtor to find the creditor if the latter is within the jurisdiction, but if neither the creditor nor anyone authorised to receive payment is within the jurisdiction, a stay of execution may also be obtained (see *Re A Debtor (1838 of 1911)* [1912] 1 K.B. 53 at 62, CA).

Current county court position

12–161 The warrant of execution may be suspended by the court at the judgment creditor's request, normally as a result of an arrangement made with the judgment debtor. If, however, the judgment debtor then defaults, the judgment creditor can request the reissue of the warrant upon payment of a fee. When reissued, the warrant will, however, have lost its priority against other warrants issued during the period of suspension.

Stays of execution are more common in the county court, with the power of the court to suspend or stay a warrant of execution exercisable by a District Judge and in accordance with the rules by a court officer (see CCR Order 25, r.8).

If the judgment debtor makes the application, it should be on form N245, with any reply by the judgment creditor being on Form N246A. If the judgment or order is suspended, the order is on Form N41.

New Act position

12–162 We wait to see what the new Act says in relation to applications for stays of execution in relation to writs and warrants of control.

Two or more judgments to enforce

Current High Court position

12–163 The general rule of practice is summed up in the maxim "One judgment, one execution", i.e. a judgment creditor cannot issue a series of small executions upon his judgment, making up the value of the judgment debt. For each one a judgment creditor can therefore only issue one execution (see *Forster v Baker* [1910] 2 K.B. 636, CA, per Vaughan Williams L.J. at 641; *Rothschild v Fisher* [1920] 2 K.B. 243, CA). It is for this reason that assignees of part of a judgment debt cannot issue execution.

The position in the county court is dealt with in CPR Sch.2, CCR Order 26.

If, however, the judgment or order is for the recovery or payment of money, as well as some other property, then appropriate writs for the enforcement of the two parts of the judgment or order may be issued simultaneously or successively.

Current county court position

12–164 It is possible for two or more warrants of execution to be issued concurrently for execution in different districts under CCR Order 26, r.4. However, the value to be levied under all the warrants cannot exceed the total value of the judgment debt and costs. In addition, the costs of more than one such warrant cannot be allowed against the judgment debtor except by order of the court.

New Act position

12–165 We wait to see what the new Act says in relation to the concurrent enforcement of warrants and/or writs of control.

Permission to issue

Current High Court position

12–166 A writ of fi fa can be issued immediately after the court's judgment or order is made to enforce a judgment or order for either the payment or recovery of money and/or costs by the successful party—subject to the points made below. So, unless any stipulations are attached to the judgment or order, there is no need to seek the court's permission to issue the writ and no need to give prior notice to the judgment debtor that a writ of fi fa has been issued (see *Land Credit Company of Ireland v Fermoy* (1870) L.R. 5 Ch. 323 and other related cases).

For clarity, CPR 40.7(1) now states expressly that a judgment or order takes effect from the day when it is given or made, or any later date which the court may specify.

Occasions when immediate enforcement cannot be initiated may include:

- where the judgment contains directions allowing payment within a specified time, so that the writ of fi fa cannot be issued within that specified time;
- where the judgment contains directions regarding service on the judgment debtor, so that the writ of fi fa cannot be issued until service of the writ has been effected and proof of service lodged with the court;
- where the judgment or order is conditional, so that a writ can only be issued once the judgment debtor has defaulted in complying with any conditions.

Care needs to be taken not to issue a writ in the following circumstances:

- after payment has been made (see *Clissold v Cratchley* [1910] 2 K.B. 244); or
- after a valid tender of payment tender (see *Cubitt v Gamble* (1919) 35 T.L.R. 23);
- where the sum claimed in the writ is greater than the amount actually due at the time of issue.

12–167 A person (including the judgment creditor's solicitor) who issues a writ of fi fa in these circumstances is liable in trespass to any action taken to enforce the writ. Ignorance that any payment has been made or tendered is no excuse.

Permission to issue a writ of fi fa will be required in accordance with CPR Sch.1, RSC Order 46, r.2 in the following situations:

- where six years or more have elapsed since the date of the judgment or order;
- where any change has taken place in the parties entitled or liable to execution under the judgment or order, such as a death of one of the parties;

- where the judgment or order is against the assets of a deceased person coming into the hands of his executors or administrators after the date of the judgment or order, and it is proposed to issue a writ against these assets;
- where a condition attached to any remedy has been fulfilled;
- where any goods sought to be seized under a writ of execution are in the hands of either a receiver appointed by the court or a sequestrator.

If the court grants permission, whether under this rule or for any other reason, the writ has to be issued within one year of the order granting permission; otherwise, a further application will need to be made.

Generally speaking, a High Court Enforcement Officer cannot execute a writ of fi fa on a Sunday, Good Friday or Christmas Day.

Nevertheless, the claimant/judgment creditor/High Court Enforcement Officer can apply to the court for permission to execute a writ on these days by outlining why this permission is required.

12–168 If a warrant is set aside but restored on appeal, it resumes its original priority (*Bankers Trust Co v Abdul Latif E Galadari* [1987] Q.B. 222). Priority is governed not merely by date but by the *precise* time of issue in the county court (see County Courts Act 1984 s.85) or the precise time of receipt by the HCEO in the High Court (see Courts Act 2003, para.7, Sch.7).

The first writ or warrant in time has priority, regardless of whether it is in the High Court or a county court. Where there are multiple warrants and/or writs against a judgment debtor, these times become crucial in establishing the priority of judgment creditors so that each one is paid in accordance with the date and time of the "queue" of warrants or writs.

12–169 To enforce a judgment which is more than six years old, the application needs to be made without notice and supported by the necessary evidence in the form of a witness statement by the applicant or his solicitor. The evidence in support of the application should state

- the date of the judgment;
- the amount of the original judgment debt;
- the amount remaining due;
- the causes of delay;
- that the applicant is entitled to execution, i.e. that there has been no change of parties or devolution of interest (or, if there has been, the precise nature thereof).

The Master or District Judge naturally reserves the right to require the application to be made on notice, and for the judgment debtor to be served with the application and evidence in support.

12–170 In the case of *National Westminster Bank Plc v Powney* [1991] Ch. 339; [1990] 2 All E.R. 416, CA, the application to issue or to extend the time for execution under a judgment was held not to be an "action" within the meaning of s.38(1) of the Limitation Act 1980. The effect of this decision meant that the application did not come within the provision of s.24(1) of the Limitation Act 1980, which prohibits the bringing of an action on a judgment after the expiration of six years.

If an application is dismissed under this rule, it does not negate the possibility of a second application, but the second one should not be granted unless it is founded on new evidence that has not previously been before the court (see *W T Lamb & Sons v Rider* [1948] 2 K.B. 331).

12–171 Supreme Court Practice makes it clear that ". . . obtaining permission to enforce by execution a judgment over six years old is no mere formality". The court may refuse permission, as in the case of *Patel v Singh* [2002], where the court made it plain that the starting point for the court was that there had been a six-year delay. In that case the judgment creditor was shown to have absolutely nothing to seek to enforce the judgment.

That case can be contrasted with the case of *Society of Lloyd's v Longtin* [2005] EWHC 2491 (Comm), in which the delay of more than six years by Lloyds in pursuing a judgment debt against a former Lloyd's name was seen as no more than "simply a hurdle which could be jumped more than once, as Order 46, Rule 2.3 made clear". The court also found that there had been no deliberate delay on Lloyd's part and that it had acted "appropriately and promptly" in seeking to enforce its judgment against the judgment debtor.

The burden on the judgment creditor is to show the court that it is demonstrably just to grant permission to enforce after six years, by perhaps repeated attempts to enforce, deviousness on the part of the judgment debtor or steps to locate the judgment debtor's assets (*Duer v Frazer* [2001] 1 W.L.R. 919).

Current county court position

12–172 County court rules on what permission is needed to issue warrants of execution are based largely on RSC Order 46, r.2. The county court rule dealing with the application for permission is set out in CCR Order 26, r.5. The county court application must be supported by either a witness statement or affidavit establishing the applicant's right to relief and may be made without notice being served on any other party in the first instance, although the court may direct the application notice to be served on such persons as it thinks fit.

As in the High Court, the application for permission to issue a warrant of execution after six years have elapsed since judgment is "no mere formality". Although CCR Order 26.5(2) enables the application to be made without notice, it also gives power to direct that notice be given. In all cases, the rule requires the application to be supported by evidence.

New Act position

12–173 We wait to see what the new Act says in relation to permission to issue a writ of control or a warrant of control, but we can expect the regulations and court rules to give clear guidance on this particular issue.

Withdrawing or suspending enforcement

Current High Court position

12–174 Where the writ of fi fa is withdrawn on instructions from the judgment creditor or his solicitor, then the HCEO cannot re-enter the premises without further instructions. If a second judgment creditor subsequently issues a writ against the same debtor, the enforcement officer is justified in executing it without notice to the former judgment creditor (see *Shaw v Kirby* (1888) 52 J.P. 182).

Although a judgment creditor or his solicitor, after delivery of the writ to the HCEO, may withdraw the execution or postpone the sale of chattels seized under it, there is no implied power in the managing clerk of the solicitor to do so (*Whyte v Nutting* [1897] 2 Ir.R.241). As can be seen from the cases referred to in this chapter, many are from the 19th century and their application in today's litigation environment should be treated with care.

Current county court position

12–175 The judgment creditor can request under CCR Order 26, r.10 that a warrant be either withdrawn or suspended. If a judgment creditor makes such a request, he is treated as having abandoned the execution, in which case the court must mark the warrant as withdrawn by request of the judgment creditor.

If the request to withdraw is made as a result of a third party claim to goods taken into legal control by the county court bailiff under CCR Order 33, r.1, then the execution of the warrant will be treated as being abandoned in respect of the goods claimed. Usually, that will mean all the goods at the address of the judgment debtor, although occasionally it will mean that some of the goods at the address fall outside the third party claim, and will therefore be subject to interpleader proceedings.

Where the parties come to an agreement to suspend the execution of a warrant of execution, the court will mark the warrant as suspended at the request of the judgment creditor, who may subsequently apply to the District Judge holding the warrant for it to be reissued. An application for a suspended warrant to be reissued will be treated under s.85(3) of the County Courts Act 1984 as an application to issue the warrant.

By suspending a warrant, a creditor loses priority to any other warrant issued during the suspension (*Hunt v Hooper* (1844) 12 M. & W. 664). If it were just to do so, the court could suspend the later warrant until the first has been paid, but there is no right to this. A judgment creditor should therefore think carefully about suspending a warrant with the court, where the judgment debtor may have a number of judgments recorded against him/her/it. A check with a credit reference agency or Registry Trust Limited, through their website *http://www.trustonline.org.uk* [Accessed October 20, 2010], may well prove to be a prudent move before relenting on priority.

12–176 The power to suspend or stay a judgment, and the power to stay execution, are given by ss.71 and 88 of the County Courts Act 1984, respectively. Under CCR Order 25, r.8, the county court District Judge has power to suspend or stay a judgment or order. The power to stay a warrant of execution lays with both the District Judge and, under the provisions of this rule, a court officer.

To apply for a stay the judgment debtor must make an application in the appropriate form, setting out the grounds of the application along with supplying a signed statement as to the judgment debtor's means.

The judgment creditor will then be notified of the judgment debtor's application and statement of means. The judgment creditor then has 14 days in which to object to all or part of the application.

If the judgment creditor does not object to the granting of a stay of execution, then the court officer may make an order suspending the warrant, subject to terms on payment.

12–177 However, if the judgment creditor does object, the outcome of the order will be influenced by whether the judgment creditor objects just to the terms offered (in which case the court officer may determine the date and rate of payment and make an order suspending the warrant on those terms). Furthermore, if the judgment creditor states he wants the court to continue with the execution of the warrant, the court must fix a day for a hearing before the District Judge of the debtor's application.

In *Islington LBC v Harridge, The Times*, June 30, 1993, a tenant attending at court to issue an application to suspend a warrant was wrongly turned away by court staff. In these circumstances, the court treated the application as having been issued at that time. Accordingly, there was jurisdiction to suspend the warrant, notwithstanding that by the actual hearing the warrant had been executed.

New Act position

12–178 We wait to see what the new rules will say in relation to withdrawing or suspending enforcement action in relation to writs and warrants of control

Taking control of goods belonging to a farmer

Current high court position

12–179 The rules on the enforcement of a High Court writ of fi fa involving a farmer are far less regimented than the county court rules (see below).

However, where the HCEO or judgment creditor becomes aware that the address where goods are said to be located is on farmland and involves any of the activities listed below, as well as the more traditional methods of farming such as keeping a herd or arable farming, then the steps outlined below should be taken to ensure that any goods seized are free from registered charges at HM Land Registry.

Current County Court Position

12–180 Under CCR Order 26, r.3 if after the issue of a warrant of execution the District Judge for the district in which the warrant is to be executed has reason to believe that the judgment debtor is a farmer, the judgment creditor must provide an official certificate, dated not more than three days beforehand, or the result of a search at the Land Registry confirming the existence of any charge registered against the judgment debtor under the Agricultural Credits Act 1928.

The 1928 Act defines a farmer as,

> "any person (not being an incorporated company or society) who, as tenant or owner of an agricultural holding, cultivates the holding for profit". This then includes:

- poultry farming;
- beekeeping;
- fruit and vegetable growing.

Searches against farmers can be carried out by completing Land Registry Form AC6 and sending this to:

The Agricultural Credits Department
Plumer House
Tailyour Road
Crownhill
Plymouth
PL6 5HY

A fee is payable, which is currently £0.50. A Land Registry telephone search on 084 5308 4545, quoting any Land Registry credit account number, can also be used.

12–181 Alternatively commercial resellers of search information such as Jordans will carry out the search for you. Information is given on their website at *http://www.jordansproperty.co.uk* [Accessed October 20, 2010]. As at the time of publication the fee for the search on the website is £22.91 including VAT, plus an additional £1.00 per variation of a name to be checked. A request can be faxed to Jordans on 011 7925 5927 and a response will either be emailed or faxed back within 2/3 working days. Alternatively you can e-mail them at *http://helpline@jordansproperty.co.uk* [Accessed October 20, 2010] with details of the names and property to be searched.

Either way, a certificate on Land Registry Form AC6 will be issued, which should be attached to Form N323. The request for the warrant of execution must be made to the court within three days of the date of the certificate.

Taking control of goods that are jointly owned

Current High Court position

12–182 Where the enforcement officer seizes goods which appear to be co-owned, he is able to seize and sell those goods, and then seek interpleader relief from the court as to the division of the proceeds of sale (see *Farrar v Beswick* (1836) 1 M. & W. 682; *Mayhew v Herrick* (1849) 7 C.B. 229). This is on the basis that where two or more people own chattels as co-owners, whether as:

- "joint tenants", which means if one owner dies, the survivor automatically inherits the deceased's owner's share, or
- "tenants in common", which means if one owner dies, the other does not automatically take the entire estate of the deceased owner,

each co-owner is entitled to possession of those chattels or "goods" and can sell them without the consent of the other co-owner(s).

Accordingly, the enforcement officer acting under a writ of fi fa on a judgment against one co-owner (named as the judgment debtor) is in no worse position than that of a "co-owner", and so can seize and sell the whole of the property.

If this happens, the enforcement officer can then apply to the court under RSC Order 17, as referred to earlier in this chapter, where he asks the court for a decision on how to divide the proceeds of sale based on the competing claims of the co-owners (*The James W Elwell* [1921] p. 351).

12–183 When two people have separate and different interests in a chattel(s), for example one person is an owner subject to another's charge or lien, i.e. goods stored in a warehouse, then the enforcement officer may seize the goods subject to that charge or lien, which will then have to be discharged before the goods are available for sale.

The position under writs of fi fa for dealing with jointly owned goods can be contrasted with the attachment of debts and joint bank accounts where Third Party Debt Orders under CPR Pt 72 are involved. Almost confusingly, CPR Pt 72 prevents debts owed to co-owners (which includes joint bank accounts) from being the subject of a third party debt order application.

Current county court position

12–184 The county court position mirrors the High Court position in the route to deciding the ownership of the goods which have been seized is through the application for interpleader relief under CCR Order 33.

New Act position

12–185 The new Act expressly provides for dealing with the issue of third party claims in Sch.12, and supporting regulations will enable the necessary application to be formulated within the Civil Procedure Rules.

Taking control of goods belonging to a company

Current High Court position

As a legal person in his or her own right, a HCEO can seize goods belonging to a company without any problem. The complications arise when the solvency of the company is in doubt or an insolvency procedure has commenced against the company. The effect of an insolvency procedure is, of course, for all the creditors to be paid, not just one judgment creditor who has been efficient in enforcing a judgment debt. **12–186**

In seizing the goods of a company, the HCEO should be directed by the judgment creditor to an address where the company has goods. This will usually be the trading address of the company, which is not always the same as the registered office. Occasionally, the two addresses are the same, but often the registered office is no more than the address of the company's accountant or solicitor, and as such the goods at the address belong to a third party. If a HCEO is directed to such an address, it will usually be evident from enquiries that a valid third party claim exists, which will be reported to the judgment creditor for further instructions.

The situation also arises where the HCEO is directed to an address of one company, only to find that another company, perhaps connected, perhaps not, is at the address. In these situations, the HCEO must make proper enquiries, by asking for the company registration number of the company at the address and comparing it to the company registration number of the company named in the writ of fi fa. If there is a difference, then the new company must be asked to make a third party claim as required by RSC Order 17, r.2, which the judgment creditor must consider and then decide whether the third party claim is to be disputed. If that is the case, then an application for interpleader relief will be initiated by the HCEO to resolve the question of ownership. **12–187**

Current county court position

The county court position largely reflects the High Court position in relation to taking control of goods belonging to a company. **12–188**

New Act position

We wait to see what the new Act says in relation to any particular rules in relation to taking control of goods belonging to a company under a writ or warrant of control. **12–189**

Taking control of a ship

Current High Court position

12–190 Under CPR Pt 61 the Admiralty Court deals with shipping matters. The two most common matters dealt with are damage to cargo and the collision of ships. Most cases are dealt with at the Royal Courts of Justice in London, but some are disposed of in District Registries with appropriate jurisdiction.

One Admiralty Judge hears all Admiralty cases and a number of interlocutory matters. The Judge is supported by the Admiralty Registrar, who hears interlocutory matters and post-judgment applications. The Admiralty Marshal is responsible for the detention and sale of ships subject to proceedings in the Admiralty Court.

Although the execution of a writ of fi fa in relation to a ship is rare in terms of the usual goods that are the subject of writs of fi fa, HCEOs are trained to follow a standard procedure in executing a writ of fi fa should the judgment debtor's goods consist of a ship and the proceedings for enforcement are not within the jurisdiction of the Admiralty Court.

If this occurs, background checks should be made by the judgment creditor as to the port of registry of the ship. The judgment creditor can make those checks as part of the litigation process, whilst the HCEO will check the port of registry by looking at the stern of the ship (see Merchant Shipping Act 1894, s.7, as amended). If the ship is a fishing vessel, different requirements apply under the Merchant Shipping Act s.4 (as amended), as such vessels do not need to display their port of registry on the stern.

12–191 The property in a registered vessel is divided into 64 shares. The ownership of those shares is recorded at the Custom House of the vessel's port of registry, which the HCEO may establish by simple inquiry.

The shares in a ship may only be sold by a properly registered Bill of Sale. Where the judgment debtor owns some or all of the shares in a foreign ship, the enforcement officer is entitled to seize the ship as a whole and sell the shares (*The James W Ewell* [1921] p. 351).

The seizure of the ship is effected by the HCEO going aboard and affixing a copy of the writ of fi fa to the mast. Historically, this was carried out to inform the crew that the ship was the subject of a seizure. Nowadays, HCEOs are trained to attach a further copy of the writ of fi fa to the bridge, which puts the Master or pilot on notice that they sail the ship at their peril.

The maritime lien of the Master of the ship for wages—even after seizure—has priority to the claims of the judgment creditor. The Master's lien also has priority over the claim of the enforcement officer in respect of his costs of execution (*The Ile de Ceylan* [1922] p. 256).

Current county court position

12–192 There is no corresponding position in the county court, as the taking control of a ship is within the jurisdiction of the High Court.

New Act position

12–193 Neither the new Act nor its enabling Sch.12 expressly deals with the taking control of a ship.

Taking control of the goods of a patient in control of the Court of Protection

Current High Court position

12–194 When the property of a patient becomes subject to the control of the Court of Protection by the appointment of a receiver, the patient's property cannot be seized under a writ of fi fa by the patient's judgment creditor (see *Re Winkle* [1894] 2 Ch. 519).

If, however, before the appointment of a receiver, an HCEO seizes goods belonging to a judgment debtor who is a mental patient, then that seizure takes priority over any competing claim for the sale of the judgment debtor's goods, in order to meet the costs of maintaining the judgment debtor (see *Re Clarke* [1898] 1 Ch. 336 and see now Mental Health Act 1983, s.96).

Current county court position

12–195 The county court position would likely reflect the High Court position although the instances of such a seizure would be rare.

New Act position

12–196 We wait to see what, if any, rules and regulations are made in relation to taking control of the goods of a patient in the court of protection in relation to writs or warrants of control.

Taking control of goods consisting of equitable interests

Current High Court position

Execution involving equitable interests in chattels is very rare.

12–197 The general rule is that an HCEO cannot seize chattels in which the judgment debtor only has an equitable interest. However, this rule does not extend to cases where the whole beneficial interest in the goods is vested in the judgment debtor, e.g. where furniture has been assigned to trustees upon trust to allow one of two judgment debtors to use it during the joint lives of himself and his wife (the other judgment debtor) and after the death of either upon trust for the survivor (see *Stevens v Hince* [1914] W.N. 148).

Current county court position

12–198 The county court position is likely to reflect the High Court position, where this is applicable.

New Act position

12–199 We wait to see what new rules or regulations are made in relation to writs and warrants of control in these circumstances.

Dealing with changes to the parties

Current High Court position

12–200

What happens if the judgment creditor dies?	An application should be made "without notice" (see *Mercer v Lawrence* (1878) 26 WR 506, for a form of order). Until the executors have obtained permission under this Rule, they cannot issue a statutory demand under the Insolvency Act 1986 (see *Ex p. Woodall* (1884) 13 Q.B.D. 479, a case involving a "bankruptcy notice"—now superseded by the "statutory demand"). Executors can obtain permission and issue the demand without being added as parties (see CPR 19.2 and *Re Bagley* [1911] 1 K.B. 317).
What happens if the judgment debtor dies?	Notice of the application must be served on the personal representative(s) (see *Re Shephard* (1890) 43 Ch.D. 131 at 137). Any permission given to allow execution against the executor of the deceased judgment debtor is not a judgment against the execution; it dispenses with the necessity of recovering judgment against him (*Stewart v Rhodes* [1900] 1 Ch. 386). An interim charging order against the interest of a deceased judgment debtor is not valid against his executor (see *Scott v Scott* [1952] 2 All E.R. 890).

What is the situation if the judgment debt is assigned?	An application must be made "without notice", as per *Re Bagley* [1911] 1 K.B. 317, CA. The assignment of part of a judgment does not effect a change in the parties so as to enable the assignee to issue execution. Execution can only be levied in respect of the whole judgment (*Forster v Baker* [1910] 2 K.B. 636, CA. An assignee of a judgment debt must apply for leave to issue execution under this rule, but an order adding him as a party under CPR 19.2 is not required (see *Re Bagley*, as above).
What happens if a surety seeks to enforce a judgment obtained on assignment?	Permission to issue execution must be obtained under this rule (*Kayley v Hothersall* [1925] 1 K.B. 607). The Master/District Judge will often direct an application to be made on notice under CPR Pt 23.
What happens if a partner retires?	The retirement by a partner does not amount to a change in the parties entitled to execution (*Re Frank Hill* [1921] 2 K.B. 831)
What happens to persons within the Reserve and Auxiliary Forces (Protection of Civil Interests) Act 1951?	A judgment or order for the payment or recovery of a sum of money may not be enforced against a person protected by this Act (see s.2(1) of the 1951 Act).

Current county court position

The county court position largely reflects that of the High Court. **12–201**

New Act position

We wait to see what rules and regulations are made in relation to warrants and writs of control. **12–202**

Last word—positive results from taking control of goods

In instructing either county court bailiffs or High Court Enforcement Officers, the success of this type of enforcement can be positively improved by sending all the available information about the location of assets and the whereabouts of the judgment debtor to the enforcement officer concerned. **12–203**

If a choice has been made to use this method of enforcement, then hopefully some thought will have been given to the goods that might be available. Judgment creditors should be encouraged to "visualise" the goods of the judgment debtor.

For example, if the judgment debtor lives in a modest home and drives a modest car, then the judgment creditor will want to see a report being made of an attendance at the address of the debtor, which locates and takes legal control of those items. If these goods cannot be found, or the judgment debtor will not open the door to allow the enforcement officer access, then this needs to be explained in a report to the judgment creditor.

If the judgment debtor has a factory, warehouse, office or shop, as these premises on the face of it constitute commercial premises, the enforcement officer can force entry to take legal control of any goods. Again, if the judgment creditor visualises the goods available such as stock, plant and/or machinery, it is these items that the enforcement officer will be expected to find and take legal control of.

12–204 Of course, it is not always possible to visualise what goods may be available. Sometimes, the judgment creditor is acting on no more than a "hunch" that taking control of goods is the right choice when it comes to enforcing the court's judgment; it may seem as if it is the only choice available. If that is the case, the likelihood of recovery becomes more a question of luck than judgment, and naturally a judgment creditor can be disappointed if the outcome is less than what was expected.

With that in mind, a judgment creditor can improve the chance of recovery by including in the instruction to the enforcement officer information relating to the judgment debtor's address, telephone contact number and, nowadays, even email. All these points can make a difference between taking legal control of goods or not.

Judgment creditors should be encouraged to look at their files and papers to establish as much information about available addresses and contact details as possible, and in doing so may of course consider another concurrent method of enforcement such as a charging order perhaps. CPR Pt 70 expressly provides for simultaneous enforcement, except where an application is made for an attachment of earnings order.

Enforcement of commercial rent arrears

Introduction

12–205 Currently landlords enjoy a common law right to levy on the goods of their tenant where rent is outstanding.

Distress for rent is an ancient common law remedy which gives landlords the right to recover rent as soon as it is overdue and to enter property to seize and hold goods found there until payment is made. Distress might well be seen as merely compulsion to pay rather than enforcement.

Previous editions of this book have not touched on distress for rent as this has not been seen as coming within the ambit of this book. However the Tribunal, Courts and Enforcement Act 2007 is changing the common law position and is bringing on the recovery of commercial rent arrears within the ambit of the civil courts. When the terms of the new Act are introduced there will be an order for payment that will be enforceable as one which has been produced by the civil court system. As a result of this and while we wait for regulations to be published in support of the Act we can now look at this in readiness for the next edition of this book when we would expect the commercial rent arrears recovery procedure or "CRAR" to be fully effective.

How does distress work today?

12–206 A landlord who is owed rent is able to take goods from the demised premises of his tenant and sell them. There is no need for a claim form to be issued; there is no need for a judgment to be entered. Based on his common law rights a landlord is able to do this. From the proceeds of sale of goods sold at auction, a landlord is then able to satisfy the arrears of rent together with the cost of using distress as the remedy to compel payment.

Of course in reality, distress for rent is not as simple as that and is now subject to various regulations which govern the exercise of this ancient right. There are some occasions where distress for rent is prohibited without first obtaining the court's express permission but in the majority of cases no permission is required.

When is the court's permission required?

12–207 Distress for rent involving residential premises is rare if not impossible. For properties involving a residential use the landlord will need to serve whatever notices are required under the various statutes, and issue a claim for non-payment of rent and/or possession. Once an order for possession has been granted that will need to be enforced through the county court system. There is a possibility for landlords to try and transfer orders for possession from the county court to the High Court with the express permission of the court the court's discretion given in s.42 (2) of the County Courts Act 1984. In the light of the current acute delays in county court enforcement more and more landlords are turning to this remedy to give them the opportunity to take back possession of premises as quickly as possible.

What has been the effect of the ECHR on distress for rent?

12–208 When the landlord exercises the right to distress as it is available today, he does not need to give any notice of his intention to enter the tenant's property and seize goods to the value of the rent outstanding. Distress for rent of course cuts right across some of the tenets of the ECHR including a right to a fair trial, the right to respect for home, privacy and family life and the right to quiet enjoyment of possessions. The lack of warning to the tenant and any procedure to check the validity of the claim for rent potentially puts the procedure in conflict with the European Convention on Human Rights.

In the case of *Fuller v Happy Shopper Markets Limited* (2001) 1 W.L.R. 1681 Lightman J. stated that the ancient self help remedy of distress involved a serious interference with the right of the tenant under Art.8 of the European Convention on Human Rights in relation to privacy in the home, and under Art.1 of the First Protocol of the ECHR interfered with the tenant's right to the peaceful enjoyment of his possessions.

A law commission report back in 1991 concluded that the right to distress for rent should be abolished when improvements to the court system could be made. The report anticipated that court procedures would need to offer good prospects of being able to cope sufficiently with the extra work created by landlords having to bring their claims into the civil court system. Ultimately the Tribunals Courts and Enforcement Act in Pt 3 has set out the process for creating the necessary court procedures to move distress into the civil court arena.

What does the new Act provide?

12–209 Section 71 of the TCEA 2007 abolishes the common law right to distrain for arrears of rent and requires landlords to use the procedure set out in Schedule 12 to recover outstanding rent from their tenants. The new procedure entitled "commercial rent arrears recovery" appears in s.72 of the TCEA.

What are the conditions for using the CRAR procedure?

12–210 A landlord wishing to use the CRAR procedure must satisfy the following:

(1) that the premises are let on a commercial lease and no part of the premises is used as a dwelling (see ss.71 and 72 of the TCEA 2007);

(2) the procedure is limited to the recovery of rent which is defined in the Act and which must be in excess of the minimum amount outstanding which has yet to be set by regulations. The CRAR procedure cannot be used in respect of business rates, council tax, repairs, maintenance or other services even if those sums have been provided for in the lease as rent (see s.76 TCEA 2007);

(3) the lease of the commercial premises must be in writing and must still be in existence.

How is the term "landlord" defined?

12–211 Under s.73 of the TCEA 2007 the term landlord is defined as the person "being entitled to the immediate reversion in the property comprised in the lease". That definition itself is open to broad interpretation but what it does mean is that the CRAR is not available to superior landlords (see s.73(1) of the TCEA 2007).

How is "lease" defined?

12–212 Whilst the new Act provides that in order to use the CRAR procedure there must be a lease, it goes further under s.74 of the TCEA 2007 by stating that a lease will mean a tenancy both in law and in equity and include a tenancy at will but will not include a tenancy at sufferance. A lease is the grant of a right to the exclusive possession of a property for a term less than the landlord enjoys himself. A lease may be for term of years absolute or it may run on a period by period basis determinable on notice (see Law of Property Act 1925 s.1 (1)).

The classic case of *Street v Mountford* [1985] A.C. 809 set out the definitions and differences between a lease and a licence (a license is merely the right to occupy premises). Under the new Act the CRAR procedure can only be used where the relationship of landlord and tenant exists whether in law or in equity (see s.74(1) of the new Act). For a more detailed analysis of the difference between a lease and a license the reader is referred to the standard texts of landlord and tenant law.

How is a lease to be evidenced in writing?

12–213 The TCEA 2007 requires that the lease must be evidenced in writing (see s.74(2)). That is not the same as saying that the lease must be in writing. What s.74 requires is that the lease may either be in writing or it may be implied, for example where periodical payments have been made. An application under the CRAR procedure could therefore be made where the lease was based on an old tenancy with no express written terms but the necessary evidence as to the lease being in existence comes in the form of rent payments made and any correspondence between the landlord and tenant in relation to the implied tenancy. (see *Swindon BC v Aston* [2002] EWCA Civ 1850; [2003] H.L.R. 42).

What constitutes "commercial premises"?

12–214 The TCEA 2007 expressly stipulates that premises subject to any CRAR procedure must be "purely commercial". As a result no part of the demised premises under the lease can be let as a dwelling. So for example where a public house has a residential flat on the first floor then CRAR cannot be used to take back possession of the public house. This is the case even if no one is living in the flat.

Landlords need to be very aware of this condition within the CRAR procedure because it does create the possibility for an unscrupulous tenant to claim that he is in occupation of premises as a dwelling which would therefore render the use of the procedure impossible.

Unless there is an express clause in the lease or superior lease whereby a tenant or superior tenant covenants not to use any part of the premises as dwelling then any form of residential occupation on the part of the premises will render the use of CRAR impossible for the landlord (see s.75(5) of the TCEA 2007).

How is rent defined under the new act?

12–215 Under the common law, sums other than rent can be subject to distress for rent in certain situations. The TCEA takes that away. Under s.72 the CRAR procedure is only available to recover rent payable under a lease. Rent itself is defined in s.76 as the amount payable under a lease (in advance or in arrear) for possession and use of the demised premises, together with any interest payable on that amount under the lease plus any VAT.

As a result rent does not include other sums such as non-domestic rates, council tax, maintenance charges, service charges, insurance or other types of payment. Even if these sums are reserved under the lease and called "rent" they cannot be recovered using the CRAR procedure (see s.76(2)).

What are the conditions relating to rent must be present?

12–216 The CRAR procedure can only be exercised when the rent itself has become due and payable before notice of enforcement is given and the rent must be certain or capable of being calculated with certainty (see s.77(1) of the TCEA 2007)).

In addition a minimum amount will be set by the CRAR procedure which will calculated as the amount of unpaid net rent due immediately before the notice of enforcement is given and immediately before goods are taken into control after the notice is served (see s.77 of the TCEA 2007).

The point to note here is that if a tenant pays the outstanding rent after receiving a notice of enforcement but prior to the visit of the enforcement officer to take control of goods then the CRAR procedure will not continue. A tenant will only have to pay enough to reduce the rent to below the minimum amount as stipulated by the regulations so as to take away the landlord's right to use the CRAR procedure.

Can the tenant make permitted deductions from the outstanding rent?

12–217 Under s.77(7) of the TCEA 2007 permitted deductions against the outstanding rent are permissible. These include any deduction, recoupment or set-off that the tenant would be entitled to claim (in law or equity) in an action by the landlord for that rent.

At common law a tenant can of course make deductions from rent in a number of situations including claims for breach of covenants resulting in loss or expense being incurred by the tenant, repairs where the landlord is in breach of his repairing covenants and the tenant has to carry out the repairs.

There are also many types of deductions which are permitted by statute, these include:

- Compensation to a tenant who has made improvements under the Landlord and Tenant Act 1927.
- Compensation to a tenant for an agricultural holding under the Agricultural Holdings Act 1986.
- Unpaid tax which is payable by a superior landlord but which is recouped from a tenant by HMRC under the Income and Corporation Taxes Act 1988 (s.23 (2)).

Can CRAR be used after the lease has expired?

12–218 Under the common law rent could only be recovered using distress for rent where there was a continuing landlord and tenant relationship. Under the law as it currently stands if a landlord elects to forfeit a lease for breach of a covenant then the landlord also loses the right to distress (see *Serjeant v Nash Field & Co* [1903] 2 K.B. 304). In addition once a tenancy comes to an end the right to distress is usually lost.

Under s.79 of the TCEA 2007 the CRAR procedure is no longer available once a lease comes to an end such to some exceptions.

Where a lease expires by effluxion of time but then continues under Pt II of the Landlord and Tenant Act 1954 the CRAR procedure is still available (see s.79(7)).

If the CRAR procedure is commenced before the lease comes to an end then it continues to be available after the lease has expired (see s.79(2)(a) of the TCEA 2007).

Where the parties have contracted out the provisions of the Landlord and Tenant Act 1954 and the lease comes to an end leaving the tenant in the property to negotiate the terms of a new lease then the CRAR procedure will be available and any new tenancy will not need to be evidenced in writing (see s.79(5) of the new Act).

What happens if the lease has come to an end?

12–219 In the CRAR procedure when the lease does come to an end, the procedure will still be available if the following conditions are met:

- the tenant remains in possession of part of the demised premises;
- not more than six months have passed since the day the lease ended;
- the lease did not end by forfeiture;
- the rent that is due is from a person who was considered to be the tenant at the end of the lease;
- if there was a new lease then it must be a commercial lease;
- the person who was the landlord at the end of the lease must continue to be the landlord and will be entitled to an immediate reversion in relation to the new period of possession.

Can CRAR be used for rent arrears under an old lease which has come to an end?

12–220 Under s.79(4) the CRAR procedure can be used in these circumstances so if a landlord has a defaulting tenant who has not paid rent for a lease which has come to an end and is not paying rent for any new arrangements then the landlord can exercise the CRAR procedure in relation to both periods subject to certain conditions (see s.79(4) of the TCEA 2007).

Is CRAR necessary?

12–221 There is no doubt that the law of distress is an important remedy for landlords. Based on a reported survey of 684,000 commercial tenancies in England and Wales some 121,000 or 17.7 per cent were thought to be in rent arrears at any one time. It is estimated the total value of these arrears were said to be in the region of £365 million. Out of this total amount of debt nearly 50 per cent was successfully recovered with 43 per cent of that being recovered using agents relying on either the current distress procedure or court action. Interestingly only 1 per cent of the arrears were successfully recovered using debt recovery procedures through the courts.

One can see the immediate commercial implications of changing from the current system to one in which a more traditional court based procedure is introduced. Distress is quicker and more decisive than an elongated litigation process and its teeth as an enforcement process compels tenants to pay what is due.

It is thought that the CRAR procedure will not be as immediate and decisive for landlords as the current law. We will have to wait and see when and how the CRAR approach develops to modernise the recovery of commercial rent arrears.

Chapter 13

Attachment of Earnings—CPR Schedule 2, CCR Order 27

Introductory comments

13–01 The attachment of earnings procedure remains an enforcement method confined to use in the county court. Where a judgment debt is outstanding and the judgment debtor is in Pay As You Earn (PAYE) employment, the judgment creditor can make an application to the court to order the judgment debtor's employer to make deductions from the judgment debtor's earnings. If the court makes an order, the employer has to make deductions, at weekly or monthly intervals (or whenever they are paid), until the judgment debt is satisfied. This is known as "attaching" the debtor's earnings.

The AEO is one of the most popular methods of court-based enforcement. Judicial statistics for the year ending 2005 confirmed that 91,949 applications were issued in the county court.

The county courts can make Attachment of Earnings Orders (AEOs) to secure payments under either a:

- High Court or county court maintenance order, or
- a judgment debt, or
- payments under an Administration Order.

13–02 The popularity of this enforcement method is due to the fact that where there is the possibility of employment, the AEO is a relatively straightforward remedy. Administratively, the courts operate the Centralised Attachment of earnings Payments System, or "CAPS" as it is known (see *http://www.hmcourts-service.gov.uk/cms/caps* [Accessed October 16, 2010]), to deal with the centralised collection and distribution of funds.

The procedure involves completing a request for the AEO in Form N337 and payment of the prescribed fee. The rest of the application is dealt with by the county court.

The use of attachment of earnings as an enforcement method in the High Court was terminated by the revocation of the Rule dating back to 1991. Under the Attachment of Earnings Act 1971 the High Court can only make an AEO to secure payments under a High Court maintenance order, which then has to be transferred to the county court for administration. It is possible for High Court judgments to be transferred to the county court for the purpose of enforcement using this method. For details on how to transfer a High Court judgment to the county court for an AEO to be made.

How does an AEO operate?

13–03 An attachment of earnings order (AEO) tells the employer:

- the total debt owed by the judgment debtor;
- the amount of the weekly or monthly deductions to be made by the employer ("the normal deduction rate");
- the amount below which the court considers that a judgment debtor's earnings should not be reduced, in order to allow a judgment debtor to support themselves and any dependants ("the protected earnings rate").

In fixing the protected earnings rate, the court considers the amount the judgment debtor would receive in state benefits if unemployed. If the judgment debtor has a large family and low earnings, the normal deduction rate is likely to be fairly modest.

At each payday the employer is ordered to:

- set aside the employee's *protected earnings*;
- calculate the employee's attachable earnings;
- deduct the amount specified in the order;
- pay the remainder to the employee.

The employer sends the money deducted periodically to the court (or the CAPS system) to be paid over to the judgment creditor.

How is payment under an AEO calculated?

13–04 Two "rates" are fixed by the order under s.6 (5) of 1971 Act. These are:

- The **Normal Deduction Rate (NDR)**—this is the rate at which the court thinks it is reasonable for the judgment debtor's earnings to be applied in meeting the liability under the order. In a maintenance case this is determined after taking into account any right or liability to deduct income tax, and is limited to keeping down current payments and the paying of arrears within a reasonable time (see s.6(6) of the 1971 Act).
- The **Protected Earnings Rate (PER)**—this is the rate below which, having regard to the judgment debtor's resources and needs, or income and expenditure, the court thinks it is reasonable that the earnings actually paid to him must not be reduced. The needs of those whom the judgment debtor must or reasonably may provide for are to be taken in to account by virtue of s.25(3) of the 1971 Act. In *Billington v Billington* [1974] Fam. 24; [1974] 2 W.L.R. 53. George Baker P. said that the best guide in most cases was to apply the calculation of normal requirements under the Supplementary Benefits Act. Set out below is more guidance on the calculation to determine the PER and where to find current rates for current state benefit scheme to assist court users in determining the likely payment available under an AEO.

On each payday, the employer must make the deduction, *provided the judgment debtor's earnings for the particular pay period are sufficient to enable this to be done*.

If the attachable earnings are more than the protected earnings, the employer must deduct from the attachable earnings the normal deduction (see Example A below) or the excess (see Example B below), whichever is the lesser amount.

13–05 If the attachable earnings are equal to or less than the protected earnings, the employer must not make a deduction (see Example C).

These examples show amounts payable weekly.

Example A—Where Attachable Earnings = More than Protected Earnings

The judgment debtor's attachable earnings	£200.00
Protected Earnings Rate (PER)	£108.60
Leaves	£ 91.40
Normal Deduction Rate (NDR)	£ 50.00
Leaves	£ 41.40
The employer must pay:	
To the judgment debtor £108.60 as the PER + £41.40 being the amount left after the NDR =	£150.00
Available funds to pay the judgment creditor via CAPS	£ 50.00

Example B—Where the Attachable Earnings are in Excess

The judgment debtor's attachable earnings	£150.00
Protected Earnings Rate (PER)	£108.60
Leaves	£ 41.40
Normal Deduction Rate (NDR)	£ 50.00
	£ (8.60)
The employer must pay:	
To the judgment debtor	£108.60
Available funds to pay the judgment creditor via CAPS	£ 41.40

Example C—Where Attachable Earnings are Equal/Lesser than the PER

The judgment debtor's attachable earnings	£100.00
Protected Earnings Rate (PER)	£108.60
No available funds to pay the judgment creditor via CAPS	£ (8.60)
The employer must pay:	
To the judgment debtor	£100.00

Which Earnings can and cannot be attached?

13–06

Which "earnings" can be attached?	"Attachable earnings" is PAYE income payable to the judgment debtor after deductions for PAYE, NIC and superannuation. This includes wages or salary, overtime, bonuses, commission, occupational pensions and statutory sick pay
	The earnings of a director of a limited company can be attached, provided that the judgment debt is the director's personal liability, because a director is an employee
Which "earnings" cannot be attached?	State "old age" pensions
	Disability pensions
	Benefit payments
	Tax credits
	Armed Forces pay (but arrangements can be made for deductions from a serviceman's pay)
	Merchant seamen's wages (except wages paid to a seaman of a fishing boat)
	Self-employed earnings

What happens if a judgment creditor is unsure about whether earnings can be attached?	An employer, judgment debtor or judgment creditor who is uncertain whether particular payments are "earnings", may apply to the court for a ruling. If the employer or the judgment debtor makes such an application, the court will notify you of the date and time when the application will be considered

How are protected earnings calculated?

13–07 In all cases where the judgment creditor is considering applying for an AEO, an exercise to calculate the judgment debtor's earnings can be made to anticipate the likely protected earnings of the judgment debtor. If the calculation indicates that a judgment debtor's earnings are likely to be less than the protected earnings rate, or the ratio of protected earnings to attachable earnings is high, the judgment creditor should consider whether another method of enforcement should be used.

When deciding on the protected earnings rate for a judgment debtor, the court will consider the amount that the judgment debtor would receive in state benefits if unemployed. The court will base its calculations on income-related sources, for example Income Support and Tax Credits.

13–08 A judgment creditor can estimate the weekly protected earnings rate in a similar way by carrying out the following exercise:

1. Calculate the personal allowances available to an unemployed person, which can be found at: *http://www.direct.gov.uk/en/MoneyTaxAndBenefits/BenefitsTaxCreditsAndOtherSupport/Employedorlookingforwork/DG_10018757* [Accessed October 15, 2010].
2. Then add the amount payable weekly in respect of:
    a. The judgment debtor's rent/mortgage, council tax, insurance premiums, court orders (excepting the judgment debt which is the subject of the AEO), water rates, travelling expenses to and from work, and
    b. any other essential expenses (remembering that the "applicable amount" figure(s) includes an allowance for normal living expenses such as food, clothing, heating and so on.
3. Then deduct income from sources other than the judgment debtor's employment such as state benefits (child benefit, family credit, disability pension, etc.), spouse's earnings, payments from a working son or daughter, rent received.

4. The judgment creditor must ignore the first £5 of any disability pension and of the spouse's earnings paid to the judgment debtor.
5. The judgment creditor must add the appropriate premium amount to the personal allowance amount to obtain the protected earnings figure—the premium amount is again found at: *http://www.direct.gov.uk/en/MoneyTaxAndBenefits/BenefitsTaxCreditsAndOtherSupport/Employedorlookingforwork/DG_10018757* [Accessed October 15, 2010]

How are deductions and irregular payments dealt with by the court?

13–09 The 1971 Act does not assume that all judgment debtors, if earning at all, are paid on a strict weekly basis, although an employer may find it worth ensuring that this is the case in handling any such order, to streamline administration. Help for employers in complying with an AEO in paying by BACS or CHAPS to the CAPS system is available at *http://www.hmcourts-service.gov.uk/cms/7741.htm* [Accessed October 15, 2010] and a guidance booklet for employers at *http://www.hmcourts-service.gov.uk/courtfinder/forms/aehandbook_e.pdf.* [Accessed October 15, 2010].

Where should the application for an AEO be made?

13–10 The general rule is that the application for the AEO is made to the court for the district in which the judgment debtor resides (see CPR Sch.2, CCR Order 27, r.3). If necessary, the case can be transferred pursuant to CPR 70.3 and the accompanying Practice Direction at 70.2.

If the judgment creditor does not know the whereabouts of the judgment debtor, or the judgment debtor does not reside in the jurisdiction of England and Wales, then the application for the AEO can be made to the court, or the district, where the judgment or order was obtained.

Where the judgment creditor applies for an AEO in respect of two or more judgment debtors who are jointly liable under the same judgment or order, then the application for the AEO can be made to the court for the district in which either, or any, of the judgment debtors reside.

If the judgment creditor started their claim through the County Court Bulk Centre, the case will need to be transferred to the local court where the judgment debtor resides or carries on business, before starting the application for an AEO.

What is the jurisdiction of the county court to make an AEO?

13–11 By s.1(2) of the Attachment of Earnings Act 1971, a county court can make an AEO to secure the:

- payment of a judgment debt which is more than £50 by virtue of CPR Sch.2, CCR Order 27, r.7(9)
- payment under a maintenance order of the High Court or the county court
- payments under an Administration Order (as defined under s.112 of the County Courts Act 1984, and CPR Sch.2, CCR Order 39, r.14(d)).

"Judgment Debt" is defined to include not only a sum payable under a judgment enforceable in the High Court or county court, but also money recoverable summarily as a civil debt under an order of a Magistrates' court. The "Maintenance Order" itself is given an extended definition under Sch.1 to the 1971 Act to include not only financial orders in divorce or other matrimonial matters, but also orders under other legislation aimed at extracting from a person whose dependants are supported out of the public purse.

Who may apply for an attachment of earnings order?

13–12 In relation to:

- **Maintenance Orders**—both the judgment creditor and the judgment debtor can apply to the court for an AEO—see s.3(1)(d)(II) of the Attachment of Earnings Act 1971. Under the Maintenance Enforcement Act 1991 the court may of its own motion or on application of an "interested party" make an AEO under s.1 of that Act. An interested party is defined under s.1(10) of the Maintenance Enforcement Act 1991 as either the debtor, the creditor or a person who has applied for a qualifying periodical maintenance order.
- **Other Types of Order**—in regard to the enforcement of other orders and judgments, the applicant must be the judgment creditor, whether directly or through the officer of any court (s.3) (i) (a) of the 1971 Act.

What conditions need to be satisfied for an AEO application?

13–13 A number of points need to be considered before starting an application for an AEO. These can be summarised as follows:

The judgment debtor must have failed to pay at least one of the relevant payments	By virtue of s.3(3) and s.3(3A) of the Attachment of Earnings Act 1971 it must appear to the court that the judgment debtor has failed to pay at least one of the relevant payments (unless it is the judgment debtor who is making the application where a maintenance order is concerned).
Any outstanding committal order against the judgment debtor must have been discharged	Any order or warrant for the judgment debtor's committal under the Debtor's Act 1869 needs to have been discharged before an AEO can be made in the county court. The court seized of the application for such an order may effect the discharge, for example, at the hearing, with a view to substituting an AEO in its place (See s.3(7) of the 1971 Act)
The judgment debtor needs to have an identifiable employer	In practice it is a further condition that the judgment debtor shall have an identifiable employer from whom he receives earnings. Earnings are defined to include "wages or salary" such as fees, bonus, commission, overtime pay or other emoluments payable in addition to wages or salary or payable under a contract for service. It includes pensions as well as annuities for past services and periodical payments for compensation for loss of office. A pension payable at the discretion of trustees and not as of right may be attached, but not money merely applied for the judgment debtor's benefit (*Edmonds v Edmonds* [1965] 1 W.L.R. 58). It also includes statutory sick pay (for which, see s.24 of the 1971 Act). A person who, as a principal and not as a servant or agent, pays the judgment debtor any sum defined as earnings is an employer within the 1971 Act under s.6 (2).
Special rules apply for armed service employees	The 1971 Act does not apply to judgment debtors who are members of Her Majesty's Armed Forces, but analogous remedies are available under the Armed Forces Act 1971.

The minimum amount outstanding must be at least £50	The minimum amount outstanding under the judgment must be at least £50 for the order to be applied for—CPR Sch.2, CCR Order 27, r.7(9).
Jurisdictional issues	The 1971 Act applies so as to make it possible to attach the pay of government employees and public service pensions in Great Britain, despite any pre-1970 strategy provision (see 1971 Act, s.22 (5)). The sums payable by a public department in Northern Ireland, or by a territory outside the UK, are not treated as earnings; neither is the pay of HM Forces, social security, child benefit payments, disablement pensions or allowances or certain wages of seamen under s.24 of the 1971 Act. Section 16 of the 1971 Act gives the court information as to how to determine whether particular receipts constitute "earnings" for the purposes of a particular AEO. The procedure for this is set out at CPR Sch.2, CCR Order 27.11.

What is the first procedural step in making an application for an AEO?

13–14 The first step as a matter of good practice should not be issuing the application for the AEO. Instead, court users should consider making a search of the AEO Index in the court where the AEO is to be issued to see if other AEOs are in priority.

Under the court rules relating to AEOs each county court is required to keep an index of the names of judgment debtors residing within the district of the court which have an AEO registered against them. A search will also give a judgment creditor details of any AEOs made in the magistrates' court. This is a useful way of gaining information about the judgment debtor's ability to pay. The search may reveal whether a judgment debtor has a series of county court judgments against him or her, or a maintenance order, all of which may impact on the ability to pay a larger sum, where there is more than one outstanding judgment debt.

The search of the index is carried out by using Form N336. The application for making the search is simple. The judgment creditor completes the form giving the judgment debtor's name, address, court where the judgment was obtained, and the claim number. This is handed in to the court staff.

A note to CCR Order 27.2.1 in The White Book Service 2006 suggests that, surprisingly, little use is made of the facility. No fee is payable. If the search reveals that there is an order in force, it may be possible to apply to the court for a "consolidated" AEO to be made under CPR Sch. 2 CCR Order 27, r.19.

What is the procedure for making a request for an AEO?

13–15 Strictly speaking, the judgment creditor should file a request for an AEO on form N337, with the court then completing and issuing form N55 (Notice of Application for Attachment of Earnings Order) to the judgment debtor. However, CPR r.5.2(1) permits the claimant to complete the N55 notice so that the judgment creditor can apply for an AEO on form N55, without the need for the earlier request.

If an application involves two or more judgment debtors under the same judgment at the same time, the judgment creditor should use a separate form N55 for each judgment debtor, showing the full amount of the judgment on each form, and pay the appropriate court fee for each application.

Once the N55 is completed the judgment creditor needs to take this to the court where the application is to be made (see above), together with the court fee (see *http://www.hmcourts-service.gov.uk/courtfinder/forms/ex50_web_0610.pdf* [Accessed October 15, 2010] for up to date information on the current court fee for issuing this application).

The court will allocate a number to the application and return a copy of form N55 to the judgment creditor, showing the application number. This number will need to be quoted along with the title of the action in any subsequent correspondence with the court.

Examples of N55 and N337 appear in the Appendix.

What do the court staff do on receipt of form N55?

13–16 The court will serve notice of the application on the judgment debtor by first class post and enclose form N56.

What are the judgment debtor's options on receipt of the N55?

13–17 The judgment debtor has the choice of whether to pay the judgment creditor the balance of the judgment debt and costs, plus the fee for application for the AEO, or to complete and return form N56 to the court within eight days of the service of the notice. The court should be informed of any payment received directly by the judgment creditor, in order to halt the process and service of Form N56 being sent out to the judgment debtor where a payment has been made.

What if form N55 is returned undelivered?

13–18 If the notice is returned undelivered, the court will send the judgment creditor a notice of non-service on Form N216, advising the judgment creditor that he must now attempt service of the notice himself. Form N55 may then be served at any time within 12 months of issue.

Where there are difficulties in serving a notice, for example where the judgment creditor is trying to trace a new address, the judgment creditor should consider making an application to the court to renew Form N55. Such an application needs to be made in good time so that the 12-month period does not expire.

If the judgment debtor is found to be still resident in the area of the home court (being the court where judgment was obtained), the judgment creditor can serve the N55 (amended and correctly endorsed to reflect the new address) on the judgment debtor personally or by first class post. Form N215 (being the standard Certificate of Service) should be filed with the court, attaching a copy of the amended form N55, once service has been achieved.

If the judgment debtor has moved outside the area of the home court, then the proceedings need to be transferred to the new court where the debtor resides or carries on business for service to be effected at the new address.

What are the judgment debtor's options on receipt of form N56?

13–19 The judgment debtor must either pay the judgment creditor the balance of the judgment debt and costs, plus the fee for application for the AEO, or complete and return form N56 to the court within eight days of the date of service.

If payment in full is made, there is no need for the defendant to return form N56 (CCR Order 27, r.5).

Form N56—Replying to an Attachment of Earnings Application—requires the judgment debtor to provide details of his or her employment, income, expenditure, savings, other debts and so on, together with an offer of payment to be deducted from his or her pay.

If the judgment debtor returns a completed form N56 to the court, a court officer will, if there is sufficient information to do so:

- make an attachment of earnings order without a hearing;
- send the order to the judgment debtor's employer (see CCR Order 27, r.7(1));
- send copies of the order and form N56 to both parties.

If the N56 does not give sufficient information for the court officer to make an AEO, the matter is referred to the district judge, who will either determine the application and make an order or list the case for hearing.

13–20 The judgment creditor or judgment debtor may then, within 14 days of being served with the order (and upon giving reasons), apply to the district judge to review the matter and the decision of the court staff (see CCR Order 27, r.7(2))

Form N56 also provides for the judgment debtor to ask that the AEO be suspended, on the promise that he or she will pay voluntarily without their employer being ordered to make deductions from pay. The debtor has to provide a valid reason for the application to be suspended. Again, this is why an AEO can be an effective method of enforcement, as people who have judgment debts recorded against them do not want their employers to find out, or perhaps their contract of employment provides for the termination of employment if a county court judgment were to be registered against the employee (asking to see a contract of employment in an Order To Obtain Information hearing under CPR Pt 71 would not be unreasonable).

What happens if the judgment debtor fails to complete form N56?

13–21 If the judgment debtor fails to return form N56, the court will serve him or her with form N61 (an Order for Production of Statement of Means). The judgment debtor must ensure that the statement of means reaches the court office within eight days of receipt of the order, or pay in full.

If the judgment debtor still fails to return form N56, or to pay, the court will serve him or her with form N63 (Failure to Provide Statement of Means). This orders the judgment debtor to attend court at an appointed time to give good reason why he or she should not be sent to prison for 14 days or fined up to £250 (see CCR Order 27, r.7A(2)). The N63 also advises that if the debt is paid in full or the statement of means is returned to the court immediately, the judgment debtor may not have to attend the court.

If this sanction does not prompt the judgment debtor to pay and the failure to co-operate continues, then the court will make an order for the judgment debtor to be arrested and brought before the court.

These steps are taken by the court, without any need for action by the judgment creditor. It is the threat of imprisonment which is, of course, the real sanction behind the AEO.

What are the current problems with the AEO procedure?

13–22 In many ways the AEO procedure seems simple enough, but evidence gathered in the review of enforcement from court users indicates a high level of dissatisfaction with the current rules. In a sample of applications taken between May 2001 and May 2002, the average time taken from the filing of the N337 to the making of a suspended order was found to be 7.56 weeks. The sample also found it took 11.60 weeks to make a full AEO. Other areas of concern included the fact that information about current and future stated incomes and expenditure were just not verified and there was a lack of consistency taken in the courts on what was considered a reasonable allowance, In this instance, judgment creditors could not easily estimate the likely repayment amount prior to the assessment by the court staff, making it more difficult to consider offers from the judgment debtor prior to the application being made.

What is the procedure for obtaining an AEO involving payment of maintenance?

13–23 The procedure for maintenance cases as opposed to non-maintenance cases is set out under CPR Sch.2, CCR Order 27, r.17.

The application for an AEO to secure payments under a maintenance order made by a particular county court is made to the court which made the order—CCR Order 27.17 (2).

Any application under s.32 of the Matrimonial Causes Act 1973 for permission to enforce the payment of arrears, which became due more than 12 months before the application for the AEO, must be made in that application (see CCR Order 27, r.17(3)).

13–24 Notice of the application for the AEO, together with a form of reply in the appropriate form, must be served on the judgment debtor as set out in CPR r.6.2. Service of the notice must be effected not less than 21 days before the hearing, although service may be effected at any time before the hearing of the application if the applicant satisfies the court by witness statement or affidavit that the respondent to the application is about to move from the address for service.

The application for an AEO is heard and determined by a district judge, and the application is made in private as opposed to open court (see CCR Order 27, r.5).

The AEO to enforce a maintenance order is a priority order and ranks above non-priority orders.

The effect of this is that arrears are treated differently in the case of priority orders. Any arrears are carried forward and, subject to the protected earning rate (PER), deducted from subsequent earnings (see s.6 of the Attachment of Earnings Act 1971).

What happens to a judgment debtor who fails to comply with the AEO?

13–25 If a judgment debtor fails to comply with the requirement under CCR Order 27, r.5.2 to return Form N56 or to make payment to the judgment creditor, the court officer can issue an order under s.14(1) of the Attachment of Earnings Order Act 1971, which must be endorsed with or incorporate a notice warning the judgment debtor of the consequences of disobedience to the AEO. This order must be served on the judgment debtor personally, and direct any payments made after the service of that order must be paid in to the court and not direct to the judgment creditor. The consequences of disobedience become severe where the judgment debtor fails to co-operate with the court if this order is disobeyed.

If the person served with an order outlining the disobedience fails to file a statement of his or her means, or make the necessary payment to the court, or indeed disobeys the order in any other way, then the court will issue a notice calling on the judgment debtor to show good reasons why he or she should not be imprisoned. This notice must be served on the judgment debtor personally and not less than five days before the hearing.

13–26 If the judgment debtor fails to attend the adjourned hearing of an application for AEO and a committal order is made, the district judge may direct that the committal order must be suspended, provided the judgment debtor attends at the time and place specified in the committal order.

If the committal order is suspended and the judgment debtor fails to attend at the time and place specified, then a certificate to that effect issued by a court officer will be sufficient authority for the court to issue a warrant of committal in form N118, as provided under s.23 Attachment of Earnings Act 1971.

What are the duties of an employer?

13–27 On receipt of the AEO the employer has seven days before he is bound to comply with the AEO. The employer has a further ten days in which to notify the court that the judgment debtor is not in his employment.

If an employer fails to notify the court, he may commit an offence under s.7(2) of the 1971 Act.

In addition to remitting the money to the court as directed, the employer must notify the judgment debtor in writing of each deduction made. The employer may deduct £1 for his administrative costs from the judgment debtor's earnings in relation to each deduction, but the employer cannot charge this unless the deduction is actually made. The employer is not actually entitled to charge anything simply for seeing whether a deduction ought to be made.

Where there is more than one order against the judgment debtor, the employer has to make deductions in accordance with the system of priorities set out in Pt II of Sch.3 to the 1971 Act. Where all the orders are non-priority, the deduction may have to be dealt with according to the date on which the order was made.

13–28 Although the employer is without assistance in the arithmetical calculation of priorities, either the employer, judgment creditor or judgment debtor is able to apply to the court under s.16 of the Act and under CCR O. 27 r 11. Where an AEO is in place, the employer, the judgment debtor and the judgment creditor may apply to the court for determination as to whether or not the payments of the judgment debtor (as specified in the application) are or are not earnings for the purposes of the order.

While the application or any appeal is pending, the employer is not obliged to take in to account payments which are the subject of the application. The application itself is made in writing to the district judge, who then fixes a date and gives notice to the parties requiring them to attend. The application is made to the court in which the order was made.

"Attachable earnings" are the full earnings less the deductions specified in Sch.3, para.3 to the 1971 Act, and for no other deductions. Thus, an employer cannot take account of any deductions for a private sick fund, loan payments, etc. He cannot give himself any priority. The deductions specified are Income Tax, Primary Class 1 National Insurance contributions and the amounts deductible under any statute or pursuant to a request in writing by the judgment debtor for the purposes of any superannuation scheme.

What happens if the employer fails to make the deductions to CAPS?

13–29 Employers are required to send the deductions to CAPS at regular intervals, as required by the AEO. CAPS will normally issue two reminder letters if payment is not made.

If a judgment creditor does not receive an expected payment;

- being the first payment within, say, three months of the making of the order, or
- a later payment within, say, two months of the previous payment and has received no explanation for the non-payment,

then the judgment creditor should contact CAPS to find out the reason. Obviously, earlier contact with CAPS can be made if the judgment creditor is anxious to find out what has happened to the expected payment under the AEO. It is CAPS' responsibility to investigate the reason for non-payment. It may be that the judgment debtor's attachable earnings are at the time less than the protected earnings rate. If no explanation can be given, then CAPS should be asked to investigate the reason and inform the judgment creditor of the result. If an employer has failed to make the necessary deduction, he/she/it can be required to attend court and explain the failure to comply with the AEO.

What happens if the judgment debtor becomes self-employed?

13–30 If the judgment debtor becomes self-employed at any point during the continuance of the AEO, the AEO will be discharged and the judgment creditor will be required to enforce the judgment by other means.

It is important that the judgment creditor continue to keep the progress of an AEO under review. In addition to following up any apparent failure to pay, the judgment creditor should be aware of other developments, for example the AEO may be yielding less than expected because a priority order or a consolidated order has been made since the judgment creditor's AEO was made.

How does a judgment creditor apply for a consolidated AEO?

13–31 Under s.17 of the 1971 Act it is possible to create a "consolidated attachment of earnings order", the detail for which is set out in CCR Order 27, rr.18–22.

Any of the parties involved, whether the judgment debtor, the employer or the judgment creditor, may apply for a consolidated order at any time when there are two or more non-priority orders in force. The court may also make a consolidated order of its own volition.

Procedure on application by judgment debtor	Where the judgment debtor applies for a consolidated AEO, a court officer will notify all parties of the terms of the application. Any party who objects to the application must send their reasons for any objection to the court in writing within 14 days of the date of service. If no objection is received, the court officer will make a consolidated AEO. If any party objects to the making of a consolidated AEO, the court officer will refer the matter to the district judge, who will give appropriate directions.

Procedure on application by judgment creditor	Where a judgment creditor applies for an AEO and there is already an order in force, the court may occasionally suggest that the judgment creditor applies for a consolidated order. Alternatively, a judgment creditor may consider this a better route where the judgment creditor has an existing AEO in place under another judgment or order, or another AEO exists in favour of another judgment creditor and the judgment debtor has insufficient income to sustain a separate AEO. The application for a consolidated AEO is made on form N66A under cover of a letter to the court manager showing the balance due at the date of application.

How does a consolidated AEO operate?

13–32 Under a consolidated AEO, the employer has to make just one deduction each payday. The money collected, using the CAPS system, is allocated to each creditor in proportion to the amount of each judgment debt and is paid out periodically by CAPS. Where a judgment creditor has two or more debts included in the consolidated AEO, funds must be allocated upon receipt in accordance with the court's instructions.

How is a consolidated AEO varied?

13–33 If the judgment creditor's application to vary the AEO relates to a consolidated order, the judgment creditor should check with the court office whether notice needs to be given to all the other judgment creditors covered by the consolidated order. If so, sufficient copies of the application on form N244 to vary the AEO need to be provided to the court.

A judgment creditor may need to attend the hearing to determine or vary the AEO, either as a result of the application made or on the application of the judgment debtor or as a result of any case management decision taken by the court on its own initiative.

At the hearing to determine/vary/amend an AEO, the judgment creditor needs to draw the district judge's attention to the evidence regarding the judgment debtor's means and ask the court to make or vary the order.

Usually, the hearing will result in a straightforward AEO, in which case CAPS will send a notice of the order on form N60 to the employer, the claimant and the judgment debtor.

13–34 The court has the power by virtue of the Civil Procedure Rules to make any order it sees fit, so, for example, the court could:

- make a consolidated AEO if there are no objections and a non-priority AEO is already in force;
- make an Administration Order, or order the judgment debtor to supply a list of creditors and the amounts owing to each of them on form N93;
- make an AEO but suspend it as long as the judgment debtor meets the terms for payment where the judgment debtor has offered to pay by instalments. If the judgment debtor subsequently defaults, then the judgment creditor should apply to the court for the suspended AEO to be activated using form N446;
- and, of course, the court can adjourn or dismiss the judgment creditor's application based on the evidence before it.

If a new AEO is made, the employer will be sent a copy on form N60 through the CAPS based at Northampton. From the next payday following receipt of the order, the employer must make the deductions as ordered by the court (being CAPS) and send them to CAPS. In turn, CAPS makes the payment to the judgment creditor.

Employers are entitled to deduct £1 for their costs whenever they make a deduction under a court order.

What happens if a judgment debtor leaves employment when an AEO is in force?

13–35 Where the judgment debtor changes employment (or becomes unemployed), the AEO remains in force but is ineffective until it is redirected to a new employer. This area can create problems for judgment creditors who are unaware of a judgment debtor's change in employment and/or status, and is one of the areas to be tackled in the Government's new regime for attaching earnings when the current legislation is changed to improve the current procedure.

At a point, the court will notify a judgment creditor if it has no information about the new employment and cannot redirect the order, but there may be some delay in this information being made available, by which time a judgment debtor may not be easy to find.

Enquiries of CAPS, the judgment debtor and the former employer are good places to start in establishing where the judgment debtor may now be working, but personal information about a person is heavily protected by the Data Protection Act 1998, and employers may well be reluctant or unable to release any such information as a result of enquiries.

What is the next step after a new employer is found?

13–36 If a new employer is found, the judgment creditor should ask the court to redirect the AEO to the new employer's business. If information about a new employer cannot be gleaned from either CAPS, the judgment debtor or any other source, including the former employer, then the judgment creditor would be well advised to enforce the judgment debt by another method of enforcement, leaving the AEO in the court so that it can be re-activated at a later date if information about the judgment debtor's employment comes to light.

How is an AEO varied by a judgment creditor?

13–37 Once an AEO has been made, it is open to both parties, within 14 days of the service of the order, to apply for the order to be reconsidered.

If a judgment creditor has evidence which would justify a higher rate of deductions, or a lower amount of protected earnings, an application can be made to vary the AEO using form N244.

The judgment debtor's employer is required to make deductions under the original order pending the outcome of any reconsideration hearing.

On receipt of the judgment creditor's application to vary the order, the court will set the matter down for hearing before the district judge, who will hear the evidence and make an appropriate order.

If the district judge makes an order without a hearing, the judgment creditor only has five days from the date of the order to apply for the order to be reconsidered.

As part of the file review for cases subject to an AEO, it is important that judgment creditors design a review system and a way of collating information about a judgment debtor's circumstances, perhaps by telephone contact, a status report, or an Order To Obtain Information application, so that if it is found that the judgment debtor's circumstances have materially improved, an application can be made to vary the AEO.

13–38 The application to vary is made by preparing three copies of form N244, in which the judgment creditor makes the following request:

> "...an order under the provisions of Section 9(1) of the Attachment of Earnings Act 1971 increasing the normal deduction rate specified in the attachment of earnings order made in this court on [...........] on the grounds that such an order would be reasonable having regard to the judgment debtor's improved circumstances."

The court will list the case for hearing and send one copy of the application to the judgment debtor and return one copy to the judgment creditor

How is an AEO varied or discharged by the court?

13–39 In certain circumstances the court may discharge or vary the terms of an AEO of its own motion. The court must first give notice to both the judgment debtor and the creditor to allow either party an opportunity to be heard.

If a judgment creditor receives such a notice from the court, then attendance at the court is essential, and evidence as to the judgment debtor's means, and details of the judgment debtor's current employer, should be taken to assist the court where necessary in the making of any order.

13–40 Often, the outcome of the court's decision to vary an existing AEO will not require any action, for example where the court simply redirects the AEO to a new employer, or where the court makes a consolidated order. However, in certain circumstances the following points may need to be considered:

Change in circumstances	Action to be considered
If AEO is discharged because the person to whom it was directed is not the debtor's employer	■ the judgment creditor should attempt to find out who is the debtor's new employer; ■ and an application for a fresh AEO should be made to the court; ■ it should be noted that the fee for the original application will be irrecoverable; ■ if the judgment debtor is no longer an employee (consider an alternative method of enforcement).
The court has made a subsequent priority AEO	■ consider an alternative method of enforcement
A bankruptcy order has been made against the judgment debtor	■ in these circumstances, the judgment debtor's trustee in bankruptcy will be appointed, and no further enforcement action can be taken
The court has ordered the judgment debtor to provide a list of creditors	■ the court may order the judgment debtor to supply a list of creditors and the amounts owing to each of them on form N93, and the court then decides to continue as if the judgment debtor had applied for an Administration Order and CCR Order 39, r.2(2) of the County Court Rules 1981.

How is the pay of armed forces personnel to be dealt with under an AEO?

13–41 The courts cannot make an AEO against the pay or allowances of a member of the Armed Forces. Arrangements can be made for compulsory deductions from pay through the Defence Council, whether the debtor is stationed in the United Kingdom or not, under the following legislation:

- Section 151A of The Army Act 1955;
- Section 151A of The Air Force Act 1955; or
- Section 128E of The Naval Discipline Act 1957.

Where the judgment creditor finds the judgment debtor is a member of the Armed Forces, the first step should be to write to the judgment debtor requesting payment in the terms of the judgment. If the response is that payment cannot be made, the judgment creditor should invite proposals for settlement from the judgment debtor, supported by a statement of means.

Where the judgment creditor is able to agree an instalment arrangement, the judgment debtor should be asked to send payments direct to the judgment creditor. Alternatively, the judgment creditor can approach the judgment debtor's paying officer, to arrange for voluntary deductions from service pay to be made and sent to the judgment creditor.

13–42 If the judgment debtor does not reply to the judgment creditor's request for payment, or fails to make payments, then a further letter should be sent to the judgment debtor warning that if payment is not made, the judgment creditor will approach the service authorities for compulsory deductions from pay to be made.

If the failure to pay either in full or by instalments continues, the judgment creditor should obtain a certificate of the judgment or order from the court where judgment was obtained. The judgment creditor should then send the certificate of the judgment or order with an accompanying letter to the appropriate service authority with the following details:

- the judgment debtor's rank and service number (where known);
- a chronology of the attempts made to persuade the judgment debtor to comply with the court judgment or order;
- a request that an order be made under the provisions of the appropriate Act for deductions from pay to be made;

- the name and address of the court (and the claim number) to which payment(s) should be made.

Addresses for where to send any correspondence to the service authority of the judgment debtor appear in the Appendix.

If the judgment creditor does not receive payment within, say, three months of writing to the service address, then enquiries should be made at the court office to find out if a payment has been received. If not, a further letter should be written to the appropriate service address enquiring why payment has not been made.

What costs are permitted in an AEO?

13–43 There are two points in answer to this question.

- A solicitor who has prepared a witness statement or affidavit or request for a judgment creditor under r.7 (8) is treated as having attended the hearing. The cost of the application may be fixed and allowed without detailed assessment under CPR Pt 47.
- An employer making deductions pursuant to an AEO is entitled to deduct a further sum of £1 for his own costs under the Attachment of Earnings (Employers Deduction) Order 1991 (SI 1991/356).

How does the court system manage payments?

13–44 The contents of the AEO are governed by s.6 of the 1971 Act and by the prescribed forms, namely form N60 or N64 (suspended). The AEO identifies the judgment debtor by his name and, where appropriate, the employer's reference. It directs the employer to make periodical deductions from the judgment debtor's earnings and to pay the amounts to CAPS, which was introduced in 1996. The website for CAPS is set out in the introductory comments to this chapter.

Before CAPS, each local county court would produce its own attachment of earnings orders and deal with payments made under the order. The local court was also responsible for enforcement of the order, but as this was not computer-supported, it was impractical and enforcement was only instigated following individual requests from judgment creditors. Following development of the CAPS computer system, courts converted their existing orders to become payable at CAPS' Northampton base, plus all new orders were sent to the Bulk Centre for production.

The CAPS system monitors for payment, processes payments and, where enforcement is required, will refer orders back to the local court. It provides a streamlined and effective form of enforcement to claimants, and also provides one payment point for employers. CAPS prides itself on receipting all payments on the day of receipt. Payments under a maintenance order are paid out at the earliest opportunity (the following working day). Payments under a judgment order are paid out weekly.

What is the effect of an employee moving jobs?

Employer's Position

13–45 Where an employer takes on an employee against whom there is an AEO, he must notify the court which made the order within seven days of employing the judgment debtor (or on learning that there is an order in force if he did not know of it when the employment of the judgment debtor started, which of course many employers do not). The notification to the court must state that the employer is the judgment debtor's employer, and the judgment debtor's earnings and his anticipated earnings must be notified under s.15 (c) of the 1971 Act. Failure to comply with this obligation is an offence by the employer.

There is, however, no obligation upon the employer to take positive steps to ascertain if there is an order in force against a new employee.

When a judgment debtor leaves his or her employment, the AEO order lapses from the date of termination and remains in abeyance until the court directs payment against a new employer.

13–46 However, there is an obligation on the old employer to notify the court of the termination of the employment within 10 days of that termination, and again failure to do so is an offence.

The employer must also continue to make deductions in respect of earnings paid after the cessation of employment and remit all deductions to the court (see generally s.7(2) and 9(4) of the 1971 Act).

The obligation to make deductions from earnings paid from the termination of the employment is not effected by the immediate redirection of the order to another employer. If this should happen, each employer must apply the order independently and, in effect, duplicate its operation.

If there is to be a cessation of earnings without a cessation of employment of any length at all, the employer should notify the court.

At any time while an AEO is in force, the court may use its powers under s.14(2) of the 1971 Act to call for an employer to give a statement of the judgment debtor's earnings and anticipated earnings (see CCR Order 27, r.15).

Employee's position

13–47 The judgment debtor has an obligation under s.15 of the 1971 Act to give written notification to the court within seven days from the date on which he left any employment, or became employed or re-employed. This notification must include particulars of his earnings and anticipated earnings. Failure to observe this obligation is an offence by the judgment debtor.

What are the court's powers when the employment relationship changes?

The court has various options to handle changes in employment by its own motion under CCR Order 27, r.13, as follows: **13–48**

- Where it appears that an employer does not employ the judgment debtor, the order may be discharged.
- Where an order has lapsed and it is then directed to a new employer, the appropriate variation may be made and the court can increase the normal deduction rate in an attempt to recoup some of the lost instalments.
- Where a priority order is notified to the court, any order may be varied having regard to that priority.
- Where the court makes a consolidated AEO, an existing order may be discharged.
- Where the court makes an AO, an existing order may be discharged or varied in conjunction with the AO.
- Where the judgment debtor is adjudicated bankrupt or a receiving order is made against him, the court may discharge the order.
- Where the court gives leaves for the issue of execution, the order may also be discharged.

Before varying or discharging any order the court must give the judgment debtor and the judgment creditor an opportunity to be heard appointing a date time and place for that purpose unless it thinks it unnecessary in the circumstances to do so. Both parties are at liberty at any stage to make an application for the variation or discharge of an order under the general provisions of the CCR.

Where an order is varied the court must notify the variation to the employer, who has seven days within which to give effect to the variation. Again, failure to comply by the employer is an offence under the Act. **13–49**

At the conclusion of any of the above orders the order is not automatically discharged simply because the employer has deducted and remitted the total sum specified in the order. The court must inform the employer of the completion of deductions and, pending this, the employer should continue with the deductions. Obviously, it makes sense to seek clarification from the court administering the order.

What consideration will the court give to an administration order?

13–50 Under s.4 of the 1971 Act on the application for an AEO, if it appears to the court that the judgment debtor also has other debts, the court *must* consider whether or not all of the judgment debtor's liabilities should be dealt with together under an administration order. For this purpose the court may order the judgment debtor to furnish a list of creditors and the amounts owed to them on Form N93.

Although the court has a positive duty to consider whether or not an administration order should be made, the other requirements of such an application must still be satisfied (again, see Ch.15). The judgment debtor's indebtedness must not exceed £5,000, although this limit will be removed when s.13 of the Courts and Legal Services Act 1990 is implemented.

Notice must be given to all the creditors before an AO is made. The judgment debtor's existing right to ask for an AO to be made is not affected.

An AEO may be made to support an administration order, either at the time it is made or later if it appears to the court that the judgment debtor has failed to make payment under an AO.

What sanctions, offences and penalties are in place under the Attachment of Earnings Order Act 1971 Section 23?

13–51 Section 23 (1) provides that non-attendance by a judgment debtor served with an application for an AEO, or refusal to give evidence of earnings, may result in imprisonment for not more than 14 days. This power may be exercised only by a county court judge.

A series of offences is specified in s.23(2), which are as follows:

- Failure by an employer to comply with an AEO as made or varied within seven days after service (see s.7(1) and 9(2)).
- Failure by a person served with an AEO to notify the court within ten days that the judgment debtor is not, or has ceased, to be within his employment (s.7(2)).
- Failure by an employer or judgment debtor to comply with an order or notice to provide information to the court as to

earnings and anticipated earnings under s.14 (1) and (4), CCR Order 27.5.2 and CCR Order 27.5.15.

- Failure to notify the cessation and commencement of employment under s.15.
- Giving a notice under s.7(2) or s.15 which is known to be false in a material particular or which is given recklessly and is false in a material particular, or making a similar statement in compliance with s.7(2) or s.15, an order under s.14(1), or a notice under s.14(4) and CCR Order 27, r.5 (2) and (15) which is punishable by imprisonment of not more than 14 days if committed by the judgment debtor.

What is the anticipated impact of The Tribunals, Courts and Enforcement Act 2007 (TCEA 2007) on this method of enforcement?

13–52 Under the current regime for the enforcement of judgment debts by attachment of earnings, it can be very difficult for a judgment creditor to track any changes in the judgment debtor's employment, which leads to the AEO becoming unenforceable.

The TCEA 2007 aims to address this problem by making it easier for a judgment creditor to redirect an AEO when the judgment debtor changes employment (s.15A–15D). The intention is that Her Majesty's Revenue & Customs will provide the necessary information to the court, by using its database of tax and national insurance details, to enable the AEO to be redirected to the new employer and thus for deductions to be made.

Unfortunately, as with many of the details of the new Act, necessary regulations governing the use and supply of the judgment debtor's information to the court system have yet to be drafted. Once the new regulations are in force, the new s.15A–15D will apply to all AEOs, regardless of whether they were granted before or after the commencement of the new act.

In addition, one of the complexities for employers of the AEO regime is that the deduction system is overly complicated, which was highlighted in consultation before the TCEA 2007 was enacted. Section 91 of the TCEA introduces a fixed-rate deduction scheme so that rather than deductions being made as they are at present, in accordance with Pt 1 of Sch.3 of the 1971 Act, the level and frequency of fixed deductions will be set down in accompanying regulations. Again, those regulations are currently awaited. Schedule 15 to the new Act makes the amendments to the Attachment of Earnings Act 1971 to bring this new scheme in to force.

What will the new fixed rate scheme look like?

13–53 Once the TCEA is in force with its accompanying regulations, discretion in relation to the deductions made will disappear. Section 6A is introduced into the Attachment of Earnings Act 1971, which allows the Lord Chancellor to make any scheme which specifies the rates and frequency at which deductions are to be made under the Act so as to secure the repayment of judgment debts. Commentators looking for a basis on which such a fixed rate deduction scheme might be made could look at the AEOs for Magistrates' courts and fines which specify deductions from daily, weekly and monthly earnings. Whilst it is not certain as to what the deductions are likely to be, certainly this format of deductions gives an early indication of what the scheme may entail.

How will fixed rates work in practice?

13–54 At the moment rate deductions are made through set criteria, but there is an element of discretion. In future, when new regulations under the TCEA, which amend the Attachment of Earnings Order Act, come in to force, that discretion will be removed. A judgment debtor will be faced with having to meet the deductions set out in the fixed rate tables, although there will be the ability to apply for a "suspension order" of any Fixed Rate Deduction Order made. The effect of a suspension order would be to suspend the current order for deductions whilst at the same time replacing it with a new set of payments. Again, new payments could be higher or lower than those currently being paid.

Under s.9A(1) of the Attachment of Earnings Order Act 1971 (as amended) a county court will have to make an order suspending a Fixed Rate Deduction Order if it is satisfied:

- that the Fixed Deduction Order which has been made requires deductions to be made at a rate which is no longer appropriate; and/or
- that the Fixed Deductions Order which has been made requires deductions to be made at times which are not appropriate.

13–55 Where the court is satisfied that either the rate or the time for payment is not appropriate, it will make its suspension order. As one might expect, the court can order additional terms to be incorporated into any suspension order made. When the order is served on the employer, he will be under a duty to stop making any deductions under the current Fixed Deductions Order, and instead change the deductions to fit with the terms of the suspension order. A suspension order can be revoked if any of its terms are broken by virtue of s.9A(4) of the Attachment of Earnings Act 1971 (as amended). Again, as one might expect, the county court has discretion to revoke any suspension order in any circumstances where it sees a necessity to do so.

Chapter 14

Insolvency—The Impact on Enforcement

Introductory comments

14–01 Enforcement of a judgment inevitably means that a judgment creditor may need to use the pressure of an insolvency procedure to force a debtor to pay an outstanding sum of money. Using the procedures as a debt collection exercise has been positively discouraged by the courts. However, a judgment creditor will need to have a working knowledge of these procedures if the strict requirements of the Insolvency Act 1986 are to be met. It is a commercial reality that some debtors will not recognise the obligation to pay their debts unless taken to the brink of insolvency, or as an ultimate sanction to be made insolvent.

14–02 Insolvency is a major and separate area, and the aim of this chapter is to give a guide to a judgment creditor on how to:

- wind up a company;
- bankrupt an individual; and
- deal with insolvent partnerships.

In addition, this chapter will explain the impact of other insolvency measures on any enforcement action being taken by a judgment creditor under a range of measures, some of which have been introduced under Pt 5 of the Tribunals Courts and Enforcement Act 2007. Insolvency will often defeat an enforcement procedure, and yet for many practitioners this remains a confusing and difficult area to appreciate.

Naturally, insolvency is a far larger topic in its own right than a book on the enforcement of a judgment could ever hope to cover, so for a more thorough and in-depth discussion on this topic, reference should be made to leading texts and practitioners' textbooks on the subject. Statutory references throughout this chapter are to the 1986 Insolvency Act, referred to as "IA 1986", and the Insolvency Rules 1986, referred to as IR 1986, unless otherwise stated. References to the Tribunals Courts and Enforcement Act 2007 are made as "TCEA 2007".

14–03 To begin with, the judgment creditor needs to ensure the following key issues are dealt with:

- recheck the identity and status of the judgment debtor either as an individual or as an organisation since legal proceedings were issued and judgment was entered;
- assess whether the use of an insolvency procedure is available and will result in payment;
- assess whether the judgment debtor has other creditors and therefore, in the event an insolvency order is made, what will be the benefit to the judgment creditor; and
- assess the cost of the entire exercise.

Information obtained at the commencement of legal proceedings as to the solvency of the judgment debtor should be rechecked and updated continually, as it is a mistake to assume that a judgment debtor of any shape or size has remained in a solvent position in the period since the claim was issued through to the enforcement of the court's judgment.

Company insolvency—general considerations

14–04 A creditor will normally be in the driving seat in insolvency proceedings, so the first question a judgment creditor has to decide when using insolvency is whether the judgment debtor company is insolvent within the terms of the insolvency legislation. Two circumstances in which a company can be served with a winding up petition are:

- the company fails to pay an undisputed debt in excess of £750; and
- the company's balance sheet shows that liabilities exceed assets (IA 1986, s.123(2)).

It is also possible for a petition to be presented to the court if a company has failed to respond to the terms of a statutory demand served upon it by a creditor for a minimum sum of £750. The requirements of a statutory demand are outlined in brief detail below (see "Enforcing a judgment or serving a statutory demand—does the creditor have a choice?").

How can a company's assets be protected against dissipation between the presentation of the petition and winding up order?

14–05 A provisional liquidator may be appointed by the court immediately after the presentation of any winding up petition if the company's assets are considered to be at risk (IA 1986, s.135 and IR 1986 4.25). The appointment may be taken up by the Official Receiver or by an insolvency practitioner, being a "fit person" within the meaning of the section.

What is the position if the judgment debtor disputes that a debt is owed?

14–06 If a dispute to the debt is made by the debtor, a creditor needs to be sure he can continue with the insolvency proceedings without being at risk of paying costs. The question of whether there is a genuine dispute will depend on the circumstances of the case.

If a company disputes a claim in good faith and on substantial grounds, the court will be unlikely to be persuaded to make a winding up order on the hearing of the petition.

What are the available grounds for the presentation of a winding up petition?

14–07 As stated above, a winding up petition may be presented to the court if a company is unable to pay its debts.

Certain circumstances are then outlined in IA 1986, s.123, where a company is deemed to fall within the definition:

- if a creditor of the company, who is owed in excess of £750, has served the company with a statutory demand in the prescribed form, at the debtor company's registered office, which required the company to pay the sum due within three weeks, and the company has failed to do so, or failed to secure or compound the debt, to the creditor's reasonable satisfaction (IA 1986, s.123(1)(a))
- if within England and Wales, execution or other process issued on a judgment, decree or order of any court in favour of a creditor of the debtor company has been returned unsatisfied in whole or in part (IA 1986, s.123(1)(b))

- it is proved to the court's satisfaction that the debtor company is unable to pay its debts as they fall due, that the court is satisfied that the value of the Debtor Company's assets are less than the value of its liabilities (1A 1986 s.123(2)).

Enforcing a judgment or serving a statutory demand—does the creditor have a choice?

14–08 Some creditors regularly issue statutory demands as the first step to securing payment of the debt, as an alternative to issuing a claim for the amount they are owed. Some creditors prefer to seek a judgment from the court, which can be enforced using a combination of court-based enforcement and insolvency methods. So, which approach works best?

In terms of time and cost, the statutory demand may well be preferable to the issue of court proceedings, but there are no short-cuts to producing a perfect demand because the document must be completed with precision and the rules for service strictly observed. This can be done by a creditor without the need for a solicitor, but obviously it is the creditor's choice on how to manage this aspect of their enforcement strategy.

As detailed information about the use of a statutory demand without a court judgment is outside the scope of this book, some bullet points on when to use a statutory demand without a judgment include:

- the debt should be for a minimum of £750;
- the demand should be in the prescribed form;
- it must be served by the creditor on the debtor in accordance with the strict rules on service; and
- it must be dated and signed by the creditor or person stating himself to be authorised.

14–09 When it comes to preparing a statutory demand after judgment has been entered, the need for precision is just as important, but the form of the demand reflects the fact that the debt has passed the judgment stage. The statutory demand should follow Form 6.2 provided under s.268(1)(a) of the Insolvency Act 1986.

The demand itself will state the following:

- whether it relates to a debt payable immediately or at some time in the future;
- the amount of the debt and the consideration, or a summary of how the debt arose;

- if the amount includes any charge for interest not previously notified to the debtor, or any other charge which is accrued, then the amount or rate of charge must be separately identified and the grounds on which payment is claimed set out.
- details of any judgment or order on which the demand is founded, for example:

  The creditor claims that you owe the sum of £__, full particulars of which are set out elsewhere in the demand.

  By a judgment/order of the _____ court in proceedings entitled [court case] number [insert court reference number] between [insert name of the claimant] claimant and [insert name of defendant] defendant, it was adjudged/ordered that you pay to the creditor the sum of £_____ [insert amount of judgment or order] and £_____ [insert amount of any cost of orders] for costs.

Once a demand has been prepared in the correct form it will be for the judgment creditor to serve the demand on the debtor. The creditor is required to do all that is reasonable for the purpose of bringing the demand to the judgment debtor's attention. Where possible, the demand should be served personally on the judgment debtor in accordance with the rules on service of documents.

14–10 Where the sum is due as a result of the judgment or order, and the creditor knows or reasonably believes that the debtor has absconded or is avoiding service and as a result there is no real prospect of the sum due being recovered by execution or other process, then the creditor may advertise the demand in a local newspaper (Volume 2 of the CPR s.3E Insolvency Proceedings para. 11.2).

Other methods of service which are set out in the rules:

- Making a personal call at each and every business and residential address of the debtor known to the judgment creditor.
- Sending letters by first class post to one address and copies to each of the other addresses known to the judgment creditor. These letters should refer to the calls which have been made by the judgment creditor, the purpose of the call and the failure to meet and make an appointment at a specified time and place with two business days' notice to meet the debtor.
  - The letter should also state that if the proposed time and place are inconvenient, the judgment debtor should offer an alternative convenient time and place to meet so that the demand can be served.
  - Finally, the letter should state that in the event the judgment debtor fails to keep to any appointment, the

judgment creditor will serve the demand by some other means, for example by advertising or by insertion through a letterbox, and will ask the court to accept this as good service at the hearing of any petition.

Further reference should be made to Volume 2 of the CPR s.3E Insolvency Proceedings para. 11.4(3).

14–11 A statutory demand can be served on a judgment debtor who is abroad. As the statutory demand is not a document issued by the court, leave to serve it out of the jurisdiction is not required. The method of service, though, will depend on whether there is a convention for the service of extrajudicial documents for the country concerned (Volume 2 of the CPR s.3E Insolvency Proceedings para. 10) or not.

If there is no convention, service can be effected by a private arrangement in accordance with the Insolvency Rules 1986 and the local laws of the relevant foreign jurisdiction (Volume 2 of the CPR s.3E Insolvency Proceedings para. 10.4).

Where there is a convention in place relating to how documents can be served, the procedure prescribed by CPR 6.42 and CPR 6.43 should be followed. If the assistance of the British Consul is desired, the rules must be adopted in all such cases. In case of doubt, enquiry should be made with the Queen's Bench Masters' Secretary Department, Room E216, Royal Courts of Justice, Strand, London WC2A 2LL.

Where the demand is served abroad, any reference to the period of 21 or 18 days must be amended. The time limit must state the period given in the extra jurisdictional tables in the Practice Direction supplementing s.IV of CPR Pt 6 (Volume 2 of the CPR s.3E Insolvency Proceedings para. 10.5).

14–12 In using this table the judgment creditor needs to ascertain the number of days stipulated for the "time for acknowledgment of service" in respect of the country concerned. Where the reference to the number of days to be given is, say, 18 days in the standard form of demand, then the number of days should be substituted with the number appearing in the table, with an additional four days added. Similarly, for any reference to 21 days set out in the table, the number of days set out should be substituted and seven further days added. Care should be taken to alter all references throughout the statutory demand, as the figures 18 and 21 occur in more than one place.

What is the court's jurisdiction relating to winding up proceedings?

14–13 The High Court has jurisdiction to wind up any company. In London, the business is carried out by the Companies Court, which is a specialist court of the Chancery Division. Outside London, eight district registries have chancery jurisdiction to deal with winding up proceedings. These include:

Birmingham

Bristol

Cardiff

Leeds

Liverpool

Manchester

Newcastle upon Tyne

Preston

The county court has concurrent jurisdiction with the High Court for the winding up of companies whose:

- issued and paid up share capital does not exceed £120,000; and
- registered office is in the county court district of the court designated as having winding up jurisdiction (see IA 1986, s.117 and 118).

14–14 **Not every county court has jurisdiction**, but those courts which have bankruptcy jurisdiction also have winding up jurisdiction. It is worth noting that county courts in London do not have jurisdiction to deal with winding up or bankruptcy petitions, as such proceedings are handled by the Royal Courts of Justice.

The Court of Appeal is only able to hear appeals relating to petitions for winding up orders, and it does not have the power to hear petitions in the first instance (see *Re Dunraven Adare Coal & Iron Co* (1875) 33 L.T. 371).

14–15 In relation to insolvency proceedings involving a foreign element, the following points are worth noting:

Scotland: where a company has been registered in Scotland, it must be wound up in Scotland (see s.120 IA 1986). Where a company has been registered in Northern Ireland, it may be wound up by the High Court as an unregistered company if it has a principal place of business in England and Wales (see *Re Normandy Marketing Limited*, [1993] B.C.C. 879).

Europe: Reference should be made to Art.3 of EU Regulation 1346/2000 on Insolvency Proceedings. The article provides that where the centre of a debtor's main interests is in a member state of the EU, that state will have jurisdiction to open insolvency proceedings, and the place where a company has its registered office is presumed to be the centre of the company's main interests.

Proceedings for winding up cannot be commenced in another member state unless the company has an establishment in that state's territory. In *Telia AB v Hillcourt (Docklands) Ltd* [2002] EWHC 2377; [2003] B.C.C. 856 the court took the view that winding up proceedings could not be brought in England and Wales against a Swedish company, in view of the fact that the company had no such "establishment" within the jurisdiction. It was further held that the existence of "business premises" was not sufficient to provide the company with an "establishment" within England and Wales for the purposes of Art.3.

If proceedings are started in one member state where a debtor company has a registered office, then proceedings commenced elsewhere in the EU will be regarded as secondary proceedings. The reader is advised to refer to the notes to EU Regulation 1346/2000 on Insolvency Proceedings, Art.3.

What is the procedure for obtaining a winding up order?

14–16 The paperwork for the application for a winding up order has to be extremely precise. Close attention should be paid to the Insolvency Rules in the preparation of the petition itself, while r.4.7 of IR 1986 sets out the requirements for the presentation and filing of the winding up petition.

It is worth taking the time to check office procedures in advance of making the application, to ensure that up to date information about the judgment debtor company is obtained. In particular, details of the judgment debtor's registered office should be checked, as should the fact that no petitions have been presented against the debtor company immediately before the petition is presented. The court will carry out a search to ensure that there is no existing petition against the company, but will only do this when the petition has been presented to the court and the relevant issue fee paid.

Form of petition

14–17 The form of petition is set out in Form 4.2 of the Insolvency Rules. Once again, the need for precision in the preparation of paperwork is vital, in order to ensure the hearing of the petition is not adjourned or that the petition is dismissed. Even the incorrect recital of the debtor company's name can be fatal to the application for a winding up order to be made (see *Re Vidiofusion Ltd* [1974] 1 W.L.R. 1548).

The other relevant information required includes:

- the amount of the debt;
- the consideration for the debt;
- details of the debtor company's registered office;
- the date of incorporation of the debtor company;
- the authorised and issued share capital of the debtor company;
- whether the EC Regulation on insolvency applies; and
- The principal objects of the debtor company.

What checks should be made before the winding up petition is presented?

14–18 A check should be made to ensure that there are no other outstanding petitions against the company. If this check is not made and there are other outstanding petitions, a petitioning creditor may not be able to claim his petition costs (see *Re Dramstar Ltd The Times*, October 29, 1980).

Whilst such a check is carried out by the court on the issue of the petition, further investigation can be carried out through the London Gazette or by using the telephone enquiry service on 090 6754 0043 to find out whether any petitions are pending against a company registered in England and Wales. Please note the telephone number given is a premium rate line, which is currently charged at £0.75 per minute.

What if the judgment debt in question is more than six years old?

14–19 Following the recent judgment of *Ridgeway Motors (Isleworth) Ltd v Altis Ltd* [2004] EWHC 1535 (Ch), the six-year limitation period under the Limitation Act 1980 s.24(1) was found not to apply to bankruptcy or winding up proceedings relating to judgment debts. Therefore, even if a judgment debt is more than six years old, it is now possible to issue an insolvency petition against the judgment debtor—provided, of course, they are still solvent.

What is the procedure for issuing the winding up petition?

14–20 Referring to IR 1986, Rule 4.7, the following steps need to be taken:

- three copies of the winding up petition (or sufficient copies for service) should be taken to court for sealing and issue;
- a copy of the petition and a verifying witness statement or affidavit (see below for a detailed explanation of this document) are filed at court—in the High Court attendance should be made at the Companies Court;
- a deposit of £1000.00 (as at September 2010) to the Official Receiver is payable, together with the court fee of £190.00 (as at September 2010), and a cheque should be made payable to HMCS. This deposit will be repaid if funds are available or the petition is withdrawn because the debt is paid, but it will not be repayable if the petition is struck out—for details of up to date court fees, reference should be made to the Fees Section of *http://www.hmcs.gov.uk* [Accessed October 15, 2010]
- a search fee of £5.00 is payable when issuing a petition in the High Court, following which the court will fix a hearing date and seal the petition and the copies for service.

The petition must proceed as soon as possible after it is issued and the court will not normally agree to long adjournments while the petition hangs over the company's head.

What evidence must be filed in support of the petition?

14–21 The verifying affidavit (Form 4.3) is prima facie evidence of the statements contained in the winding up petition. A copy of the petition itself must be exhibited to the affidavit. The deponent to the affidavit should be either:

- the petitioning creditor;
- or the petitioning creditor's solicitor;
- or an authorised person who can depose to the facts contained in the petition on behalf of the petitioning creditor.

If the petitioning creditor is not the deponent to the affidavit, then the affidavit should state his capacity, authority and means of knowledge (see IR 1986, r.4.12).

A petition can be verified with a witness statement rather than an affidavit, and this form of evidence in support is acceptable in all courts. The advantage of a witness statement is that it attracts no fee, unlike an affidavit which needs to be sworn and in turn requires an oath fee to be paid.

What is the procedure for serving the winding up petition?

14–22 Under IR 1986, r.4.8, the petition must then be served personally on:

- a director of the debtor company; or
- a duly authorised person of the debtor company; or
- by leaving a copy of the winding up petition at the debtor company's registered office.

If no registered office exists, service should take place at the last known principal place of business or the intended registered office.

As a practical safeguard, the services of a trusted process server should be used and a witness statement of service obtained immediately following service, to confirm the circumstances in which service of the petition took place. Once service has been effected, the witness statement of service (in Form 4.4 exhibiting a sealed copy of the petition) should be filed at the court. If service takes place following an application for substituted service, then the witness statement should follow the wording of Form 4.5.

Service of the winding up petition on an overseas company is effected under s.695 of the Companies Act 1985.

14–23 The following persons are also entitled to be furnished with a copy of the winding up petition within two days of requesting it, subject to the payment of a fee (see IR 1986, r.4.13):

- any director of the debtor company;
- contributory; and
- any creditor.

What are the requirements in advertising the petition?

14–24 Under IR 1986, r.4.11, the petition must be advertised in the *London Gazette*. It is easy to place an advert using the Gazette's online facility, for which further information on how to place an advert is given at *http://www.london-gazette.co.uk* [Accessed October 15, 2010]. Full details of fees and the information required are given on the website.

The timing of the advertisement must be as follows:

- at least seven days after service of the petition so as to allow the debtor company time to object; and
- at least seven days before the hearing of the petition.

The court will dismiss a petition if it is advertised too early (*Re Signland Ltd* [1982] 2 All E.R. 609) and will take a dim view of failure to comply with the correct procedure for advertising the petition (*Re Shusella Ltd* [1983] B.C.L.C. 505).

14–25 Once advertised, the petition is constructive notice to the world of the existence of the winding up petition. The period between service of the petition and the appearance of the advertisement will often result in negotiations by the debtor to try to pay the debt or make satisfactory proposals for payment. The advertising of the petition is, of course, designed to give other creditors an opportunity to support the petition, and after advertisement the petition must be heard in court on its return date to give all creditors an opportunity to appear and be heard.

The court has power to restrain the advertising of a winding up petition if the debt is disputed or it views the issue of the petition as an abuse of the court process.

Do petitioning creditors living outside the jurisdiction need to provide security for costs?

14–26 Petitioning creditors living outside the jurisdiction (even in Scotland or Northern Ireland) may be required to provide security for costs in relation to any petition presented to the courts in England and Wales.

How does a petitioning creditor withdraw a petition?

14–27 The petitioning creditor may wish to withdraw a petition because the judgment debt has been paid.

IR 1986 r.4.5 provides the mechanism to allow a petition to be withdrawn on a without notice application if, at least five days before the hearing of the petition, the court is satisfied that the petition has not been advertised, no notices, whether supported or opposing the petition, have been received regarding the petition and that the judgment debtor company consents to the petition being withdrawn.

If the above conditions are satisfied, the court may allow the petitioning creditor to withdraw the petition on terms as to costs which the parties agree between themselves.

The application is dealt with by the Court Manager of the Companies Court in relation to High Court business by virtue of Volume 2 of the CPR s.3E Insolvency Proceedings para. 54(3). In relation to county court business, applications should be addressed to the District Judge.

What are the requirements relating to a certificate of compliance?

14–28 A certificate of compliance must be filed by the petitioning creditor or the petitioning creditor's solicitor at least five days before the hearing. Under IR 1986 r.4.14(2), the certificate must show:

- the date of the presentation of the petition;
- the date fixed for the hearing of the petition;
- the date of service of the petition; and
- that the advertising rules have been complied with (a copy of the advertisement should be filed with this certificate).

Failure to file this certificate may result in the petition being dismissed by the court (see IR 1986, r.4.14(3) and Form 4.7).

As a footnote to IR 4.14, practitioners are allowed some leeway in filing the certificate by virtue of Volume 2 of the CPR s.3E Insolvency Proceedings para. 3.1. This allows for the certificate to be filed by no later than 4.30 pm on the Friday preceding the day on which the petition is to be heard. However, filing after this time will only be permitted where there is some good reason for the delay.

What is the position of other creditors?

14–29 As liquidation is a collective remedy (as opposed to say execution against goods, which is sought on behalf of one judgment creditor), then creditors are given the opportunity of indicating whether they support or oppose the petition.

Under IR 4.16 every person who intends to appear on the hearing of the petition must give notice to the petitioning creditor of his intention to either support or oppose the petition.

Once notice has been given, under IR 4.17 the petitioning creditor must prepare for the court a list of any persons who have given notice under IR 4.16, specifying their names and addresses and where possible their respective solicitors. Against the name of each creditor, the petitioning creditor should indicate whether there is an intention to support or oppose the petition. On the day of the hearing of the petition, this list must be handed to the court before the hearing begins.

It is also possible under IR 4.19 to substitute a creditor or contributory for the petitioning creditor. For example, if the creditor who presents the petition is paid the amount due before the hearing of the petition and then consents to withdraw the petition, but another creditor is still owed money, the other creditor can effectively step in to the shoes of the petitioning creditor in accordance with this rule.

In making any such order, the court must strike a balance between not allowing companies to trade where they are clearly insolvent, which in turn could prejudice both existing and future creditors, as against not allowing the insolvency procedure to be used for debt collection purposes or as an instrument of oppression where the debt in question is subject to a genuine dispute (see *Mann v Goldstein* [1968] 1 W.L.R. 1091, and *South East Water v Kitoria Pty Limited* (1996) 14 A.C.L.C. 1328).

14–30 To prevent unnecessary costs of advertising and service being incurred, the courts have taken a pragmatic approach to substitution and agreed to dispense with the need to re-advertise or re-serve (as occurred in *Re Commercial and Industrial Insulations Ltd* (1986) 2 B.C.C. 98901).

Successive substitutions on one petition may be allowed (see *Re Bostals Ltd* [1968] 1 Ch. 346 at 350). Even if the original winding up order was set aside on appeal, then the courts have allowed another person to apply to be substituted in relation to the original petition. In such a case the court hearing the appeal has given leave for the substitution to proceed (see *Re Goldthorpe and Lacey Ltd* (1987) 3 B.C.C. 595, CA).

In terms of who can be substituted, it seems that the courts are again willing to take a pragmatic approach by allowing a creditor who at the time of the application to substitute has the right to petition, rather than limiting the right to substitute only a creditor who had a right to petition at the time of the original petition (see *Perak Pioneer Ltd v Petroliam Nasional* Bhd [1986] A.C. 849; [1986] 3 W.L.R. 105).

What are the likely outcomes at the hearing of the winding up petition?

14–31 The decision as to whether to make a winding up order is entirely within the discretion of the court (see IA 1986, s.125(1)). At the hearing the court may:

- dismiss the petition;
- adjourn the hearing conditionally or unconditionally;
- make a compulsory winding up order; or
- make any other order it thinks fit.

Moreover, creditors may combine debts to bring the level of debt above the £750 minimum amount set by the Secretary of State (*Re Leyton & Walthamstow Cycle Co* [1901] V.V.N. 275).

As mentioned above, the petitioning creditor must prepare a list of creditors who have given an intention to appear to either support or oppose the petition.

If there has been no indication from other creditors that they intend to appear, then the list in Form 4.10 should be completed by adding the word "none" at the appropriate place and this list will then be handed to the court clerk.

A straightforward hearing will usually last one minute and be heard in open court. It is normal for counsel to attend to obtain the winding up order and then report back to the instructing solicitor, on the basis that counsel will attend on a number of hearings in one session and charge a brief fee, which would normally be less than the cost of the instructing solicitor attending court for one hearing.

What is the position on costs?

14–32 If a winding up order is made, the costs will usually be ordered to be paid out of the debtor company's assets (*Re Bostels Ltd* [1968] Ch.346). These costs will be a first charge on the company's assets and will be payable ahead of all other claims of secured creditors.

If the petition is dismissed, the petitioning creditor will be liable to meet a costs order made by the court, although this may not be the case if the debtor company was, due to its behaviour, responsible for the petition being presented in the first place. Quite often petitions are dismissed by the court because the company has paid the debt claimed in the petition, in which circumstances it is usual for the debtor company to be ordered to pay the creditor's costs.

If the debtor company wrongfully opposes a petition and a winding up order is made, then the costs of the petition may be ordered to be paid by the directors or shareholders (see *Re Company (No. 004055 of 1991), Ex p.* Record Tennis Centres [1991] 1 W.L.R. 1003).

What steps are taken after the winding up order is made?

14–33 The effect of taking this form of enforcement action (subject to the comments above about not using insolvency for debt collection purposes or as a means of oppression) is that if the winding up order is made by the court, the date of the commencement of the compulsory liquidation procedure will be fixed for the date when the petition was presented to the court which resulted in the winding up order being made.

When the winding up order is granted, it should:

- be officially notified in the *London Gazette* (see Companies Act 1985, s.42(1)(a)); and

- recorded at the Companies Registry (the registrar will place the notice in the *London Gazette* and this will constitute official notification—see Companies Act 2006, s.116).

The court must also notify the Official Receiver of its order, who will then notify the company of his appointment and deal with the notification of the winding up order under IA 1986, s.130(1)

How is the Official Receiver appointed?

14–34 Following the making of the winding up order, the court will appoint the Official Receiver to act, pending the appointment of a private insolvency practitioner by the company's creditors.

The court will send three sealed copies of the winding up order to the Official Receiver's office. The Official Receiver will then serve a copy of the winding up order on the Registrar of Companies and on the company itself.

The Official Receiver will also arrange for the winding up order to be advertised in the *London Gazette* and one local newspaper (see IA 1986, s.130 and IR 1986, rr.4.20 and 4.21).

What is the effect of a winding up order on a judgment debtor company?

14–35 The main effects can be summarised as follows:

- no actions or proceedings against the debtor company or its property can be commenced or continue, except with the leave of the court (see IA 1986, s.130(2));
- the winding up will be deemed to commence at the time of presentation of the winding up petition (see IA 1986, s.129);
- execution against goods is effectively stayed (see IA 1986, s.183) and the duties of the High Court Enforcement Officer (who has by virtue of the Courts Act 2003 taken over the responsibilities of the Sheriff) are set out in IA 1986, s.184; and
- unless the court orders otherwise, any disposition of the company's property between presentation of the petition and the order is void (see IA 1986, s.127).

Does winding up work as a post-judgment strategy and an alternative to enforcement?

14–36 At this point, the likelihood of the petitioning creditor being paid the amount of the judgment debt is remote. The reader is therefore directed to one of the main texts on insolvency law as to the ensuing procedures and rights of the creditor, if by this time the debt has not been paid.

Naturally, there is a wealth of information available on the internet about the work of insolvency practitioners. Numerous sites exist which should guide a judgment creditor as to what is possible and what can be expected as a result of the judgment debtor's insolvency.

Bankruptcy—general considerations

14–37 This section deals with the insolvency of the individual and the action to be taken by a creditor to present a bankruptcy petition. Again, the use of an insolvency procedure has been positively discouraged by the courts as a debt collection tool, as mentioned earlier in this chapter, but nevertheless, for the persistent debtor, particularly in a trading relationship with the creditor, the threat of insolvency may be the only way to seek payment. As provided under IA 1986, s.264(1)(a), a creditor is one of the class of persons who may issue a bankruptcy petition against a debtor.

Of course, the availability of bankruptcy and its impact on the ability to enforce the court's order has continued to be a problem for anyone who has the benefit of a judgment to enforce. As a result of changes introduced into insolvency law over the last decade, coupled with the severe economic challenges that we face in the United Kingdom today, it is easier for a person in debt to apply to make themselves bankrupt and shelter from their creditors. Internet sites such as The Insolvency Service website at *http://www.insolvency.gov.uk* [Accessed October 19, 2010] publish figures that show growing upward trends in all forms of insolvency procedure, so regular consultation with these sources of information is encouraged.

What conditions need to be satisfied by a judgment creditor to issue a bankruptcy petition?

14–38 Section 265 of the IA 1986 sets out the conditions that must be satisfied before a bankruptcy petition can be issued to the court. The debtor must:

- be domiciled in England and Wales;
- be personally present within the jurisdiction of England and Wales on the day the bankruptcy petition is presented to the court; or
- at any time within three years following the day on which the petition is presented to the court have been ordinarily

resident, have had a place of residence in England and Wales or have carried on business in England and Wales.

Except for the requirement in s.265(1)(c)(i), which requires the debtor to have been ordinarily resident or had a place of residence within England and Wales in the three years before the day of the presentation of the bankruptcy petition, there is no requirement that the debtor be actually resident in England and Wales. The provisions do not refer to the debtor's nationality or state of his citizenship.

However, the Court of Appeal has previously dealt with the issue of domicile, as mentioned in 265(1)(a) in the decision of *Re Bird v Inland Revenue Commissioners, Ex p. Debtor* [1962] 1 W.L.R. 686 and *Re Branch (A Debtor), Ex p. Brittanic Securities & Investments* [1978] Ch. 316.

As to the length of time a person must be in the jurisdiction to satisfy the requirement of s.265(1)(b), this in fact only requires a debtor to be personally present for a very short period (see *Re Thulin* [1995] 1 W.L.R. 165).

14–39 In the case of *Cross Construction Sussex Ltd v Tseliki* [2006] EWHC 1056 (Ch) a District Judge concluded that there was not enough evidence to establish a connection between a debtor and the jurisdiction of England and Wales based on the evidence before him. Clearly, ensuring sufficient evidence is available should it be required is something a judgment creditor must consider in preparing for a hearing, particularly if the judgment debtor is known to have connections outside England and Wales.

In the case of *Skjevesland v Geveran Trading Co* [2002] EWHC 2898 (Ch), [2003] B.C.C. 391, the issue of whether a businessman with residences in several countries including the United Kingdom would be considered "ordinarily resident" for the purposes of the s.265 was considered. The court came to the decision that it is a question of fact and degree in each case, with the need to look at the cumulative effect of the evidence. The decision also confirmed that the criteria for ascertaining the centre of main interests in the case of personal insolvency were similar to those for a company.

As to whether an individual has "carried on business" within the preceding three-year period under s.265(1)(c)(ii) has been held to "include", but is not limited to, the circumstances set out in s.265(2). Therefore, if an individual has carried on business within the jurisdiction and leaves unpaid debts behind, then even if the business ceases to trade, that individual will be deemed to have continued to carry on business so as to be susceptible to a petition being presented against him (see *Theophile v Solicitor General* [1950] A.C. 186, which was followed by *Re a Debtor (No.784 of 1991)* [1992] Ch.554, in the judgment of Hoffman J.).

What are the grounds upon which a creditor can issue a bankruptcy petition?

14–40 The debtor must owe the petitioning creditor a debt or debts (IA 1986, s.267(1)). Subject to this initial requirement the following conditions need to be present (IA 1986, s.267(2)):

- the amount of the debt or the aggregate is equal to or exceeds the bankruptcy level (at present £750);
- the debt is for a liquidated sum payable to the petitioning creditor either immediately or at some certain future time and is unsecured;
- the debt is one which the debtor appears either to be unable to pay or to have no reasonable prospect of being able to pay; and
- there is no outstanding application to set aside a statutory demand that has been served under IA 1986, s.268 in respect of the debt (however, this condition will be outside the scope of the circumstances where the petition is based on a return that execution was unsatisfied in whole or in part).

How is "unable to pay" defined in the insolvency act for the purposes of bankruptcy?

14–41 "Unable to pay" is defined as either:

- a failure by the debtor to comply with a "statutory demand" in the prescribed form (the procedure for which is outlined on the *http://www.insolvency.gov.uk* [Accessed October 19, 2010] website). The statutory demand may be served either before any court proceedings have been issued (in which case the full basis of how the debt arises will need to be set out in the form of statutory demand on Form 6.1) or after judgment has been obtained using Form 6.2;
- the result of execution against goods for a judgment or order of the court in favour of the petitioning creditor which has been returned unsatisfied in whole or in part (IA 1986, s.268 (1)(a) and (b)).

14–42 Evidence of an unsatisfied execution mentioned above is provided by the "return" of the High Court Enforcement Officer (formerly referred to as a "Sheriff's return") obtained under the provisions of RSC Order 46, r.9. The return must show that execution was levied on some goods, which, if in turn does not result in payment, shows that the execution was indeed "unsatisfied". This small point was tested in the case of *Re a Debtor* (No. 340 of 1992) [1996] 2 All E.R. 211, in which the court came to the decision that where the Sheriff had been unable to execute the writ of fi fa by entering the property under which he was directed on the writ, a return of *nulla bona* (or "no goods") would not be sufficient evidence of the debtor's inability to pay, and therefore the definition of "unable to pay" for these purposes was not shown. The logic behind the judgment was that the sheriff could not make a return in the form required where he had not been able to get into the property to see what goods (if any) were available. The remedy for a judgment creditor in this situation is to use the judgment itself as a basis for the statutory demand in Form 6.2, which may incur a short delay but will be acceptable to the court as satisfying the requirements of the definition of "unable to pay".

Which court has jurisdiction?

14–43 The High Court (IR 1986, r.6.9(1)) has jurisdiction if:

- the debtor has resided or carried on business within the London insolvency district for the greater part of the six months immediately preceding presentation of the petition, or for a longer period in those six months than in any other insolvency district;
- the debtor is not resident in England and Wales; or
- the petitioning creditor is unable to trace the residence of the debtor or his place of business.

The London insolvency district is made up of the City of London together with the districts of the county courts for:

Barnet, Bow, Brentford, Central London, Clerkenwell, Edmonton, Lambeth, Shoreditch, Wandsworth, West London and Willesden.

14–44 The county court has jurisdiction in all other cases:

- if the debtor has not carried on business or resided within the London insolvency district as set out above. The petition should be presented in the court for the insolvency district in which the debtor has resided or carried on business for the longest period of time during those six months;
- if the debtor has carried on business in one insolvency district and resided in another, the petition should be presented in the insolvency court for the district in which he has carried on business; and

- if the debtor has carried on business in more than one insolvency district, the petition must be presented to the court for the district in which he has had his principal place of business for the longest period within those six months.

It should be noted that not all county courts have jurisdiction, so reference should be made to the most up to date version of the Civil Procedure Rules, available at *http://www.justice.gov.uk/civil/procrules fin* [Accessed October 19, 2010] or in the various reference books containing the rules. If proceedings are issued in the wrong court, then the court can transfer the proceedings to the correct court or allow them to continue, provided that the court has jurisdiction, or the proceedings may be struck out.

What is the format of a bankruptcy petition?

14–45 A bankruptcy petition has to be in the prescribed form, which will usually be Form 6.2 in the case of post-judgment applications where the execution has been returned unsatisfied.

It cannot be stressed too strongly that with all insolvency documentation the need for accuracy and up to date information is paramount, as shortcomings in paperwork will result in adjourned or dismissed petitions which inevitably cause problems in explanations to clients.

What are the required contents of a bankruptcy petition?

14–46 The petition must, so far as it is within the knowledge of the petitioning creditor, state the following matters relating to the debtor (IR 1986, r.6.7):

- the debtor's name, place of residence and occupation (if any);
- the name or names in which the debtor carries on business, if other than the debtor's true name, and whether, in the case of any business of a specified nature, the debtor carries it on alone or with others;
- the nature of the debtor's business and its address;
- any name, other than the debtor's true name, in which the debtor has carried on business at or after the time the debt was incurred, and whether the debtor has done so alone or with others; and
- any address or addresses at which the debtor has resided or carried on business at or after that date, and the nature of that business.

It must also state the following details relating to the debt itself (IR 1986, r.6.8): **14–47**

- the amount of the debt, the consideration for it and the fact that it is owed to the petitioning creditor;
- the date the debt was incurred or became due;
- details of any interest charge not previously notified to the debtor, and the grounds on which it is claimed to form part of the debt;
- that the debt is for a liquidated sum payable immediately and that the debtor appears to be unable to pay it;
- or that the debt is for a liquidated sum payable at some certain time in the future (the date must be specified) and that the debtor appears to have no reasonable prospect of being able to pay it;
- that the debt is unsecured, although this is subject to the exception set out in IA 1986, s.269;
- whether the EC Regulation on Insolvency applies.

If the petition is being presented on the basis that it has been preceded by a statutory demand, then proof of service of the statutory demand must be filed at court with the petition in accordance with IR 6.11.

What is the procedure for presenting and filing a bankruptcy petition?

The petition must be verified by a witness statement or affidavit (IR 1986, r.6.10) and delivered to the court. Two extra copies will be required, one of which is for service on the debtor and the other for exhibiting to the witness statement for service of the petition. The court will fix the date and time for hearing the petition when it is filed. **14–48**

How are the contents of the bankruptcy petition verified?

- The petition must be verified by a witness statement or an affidavit that the statements made therein are true to the best of the deponent's knowledge, information and belief. The witness statement or affidavit must exhibit a sealed copy of the petition (IR 1986, r.6.12). **14–49**

- The witness statement or affidavit should be made by the petitioning creditor or some other person directly involved in the facts giving rise to the presentation of the petition, i.e. the petitioning creditor's solicitor or any other responsible person who could be authorised to make the witness statement or affidavit on the petitioning creditor's behalf and who has sufficient knowledge of the debt and the contents of the petition.
- Indeed, where the deponent to the witness statement or affidavit verifying the petition is not the petitioning creditor, the capacity of the deponent must be stated, together with the deponent's authority in which the witness statement or affidavit is made and the deponent's means of knowledge of the matters deposed to.

What deposit needs to be paid to the court?

14–50 The petitioning creditor is required to pay a deposit to cover the Official Receiver's fees when the bankruptcy petition is initially presented to the court. For many creditors this upfront charge can deter the use of bankruptcy proceedings as a method of enforcement.

Insolvency court fees recently increased, so as with all court fees it is worth checking on the HMCS website at *http://www.hmcs.gov.uk* [Accessed October 19, 2010] for the most recent listing. At the time of writing, the deposit is £600.00 plus a court fee of £190.00. In London, the fees are paid at the fee room, which is currently situated on the ground floor in the East wing of the Royal Courts of Justice. A cheque for the fees made payable to "HMCS" will be required, and you will also need to pay a £5 search fee when presenting your petition to enable the court to carry out a search to ensure that there are no other outstanding petitions.

It is also worthwhile carrying out a search using the Insolvency Services website's free search facility to see if the debtor is already bankrupt at *http://www.insolvency.gov.uk/eiir/*[Accessed October 19, 2010], which allows a search to be made by name and/or trading name.

What notice is given to HM Land Registry?

14–51 On filing the bankruptcy petition, the court automatically sends a notice to the Chief Land Registrar of the petition, together with a request that it is registered in the register of pending actions at HM Land Registry (IR 1986, r.6.13).

What are the rules on serving a bankruptcy petition?

14–52 As with any other legal procedure, the need for precision to prove that service has been carried out is vital to a successful application. Service of the petition may be effected either by the petitioning creditor, his solicitor or by some other authorised person on his behalf (e.g. a process server), who must deliver a sealed copy to the debtor (IR 1986, r.6.14). The witness statement or affidavit of service exhibiting the sealed copy petition must be delivered to the court for filing immediately after service.

In all cases it is suggested that the best form of service is by personal service on the debtor, and that the process server immediately prepares a witness statement or an affidavit of service confirming the exact circumstances in which service took place.

If a debtor attempts to avoid service, and the court is satisfied, on seeing the evidence that service of the petition is being deliberately avoided, the court may make an order for substituted service in such manner as the court thinks fit. If a debtor dies before service of the bankruptcy petition is carried out, the court may order service on the debtor's personal representatives or such other persons as it thinks fit (IR 1986, r.6.16).

What happens if the debtor opposes the bankruptcy order?

14–53 The court has discretion to make the bankruptcy order, regardless of whether or not the application is opposed by the debtor (IA 1986, s.271).

If a debtor intends to oppose the presentation of a bankruptcy petition, then IR 1986, r.6.21 provides that not later than seven days before the date fixed for the hearing the debtor must:

- file in court a notice specifying the grounds of objection to a bankruptcy order being made; and
- send a copy of the notice to the petitioning creditor or to his solicitor.

The form of affidavit or witness statement outlining the debtor's opposition is on a prescribed form in Form 6.19.

Can the bankruptcy petition be amended?

14–54 Subject to the leave of the court, the petition may be amended at any time after it has been presented. The court also has jurisdiction to amend a petition under CPR 17.1 (previously RSC Order 20, r.8) (also see *Aspinalls Club Ltd v Halabi* [1998] B.P.I.R. 322).

What happens at the hearing of the bankruptcy petition?

14–55 Firstly, at least 14 days must elapse between the service of the bankruptcy petition and the date of the hearing to ensure the Official Receiver's fees are paid.

In readiness for the hearing the petitioning creditor must prepare for the court a list of creditors (if any) who have given notice under IR 1986, r.6.23 of their intention to support or oppose the petition. This list in Form 6.21 is available *at http://www.insolvency.gov.uk/forms/englandwalesforms.htm* [Accessed October 19, 2010]. The list must be handed to the Court prior to the commencement of the hearing.

Where the petition is brought in respect of a judgment debt or a sum due under a court order, the court may stay or dismiss the petition on the grounds that an appeal is pending from the judgment or order, or that there has been a stay of execution on the judgment (IR 1986, r.6.25).

What are the possible outcomes of the hearing of the petition?

14–56 On hearing the petition the court can:

- make the bankruptcy order;
- adjourn the hearing;
- dismiss the petition.

If the court is satisfied that the statements in the petition are true and that the debt on which it is founded has not been paid, secured or compounded, the court can make the bankruptcy order.

If the court makes an order adjourning the hearing of the bankruptcy petition, the petitioning creditor must, subject to any order made by the court to the contrary, send the debtor a notice of the adjournment stating the new time, date and venue for the hearing. In *Re Williams (a bankrupt) The Times,* July 16, 1997, the court held that where a bankruptcy petition had been presented and the debtor had indicated that he could repay his debt by instalments, as it was found there was no reasonable prospect that repayment could be made within a reasonable time, it was not open to the court to grant repeated adjournments of the bankruptcy proceedings.

If an order is made dismissing the bankruptcy petition, or the court allows the petition to be dismissed with leave, then an order must also be made allowing the registration of the petition to be vacated from the register of pending actions.

Once made, the court will send a sealed copy of any such order to the debtor.

What date does the bankruptcy commence?

14–57 By virtue of IA 1986, s.278, the commencement date of the bankruptcy is now the date on which the bankruptcy order is made.

What is the impact of a bankruptcy order on the enforcement of a judgment debt?

14–58 The commencement date of the bankruptcy will be the relevant date in determining whether a creditor may continue to receive or retain money obtained following execution by the High Court Enforcement Officer.

After the making of the bankruptcy order, no creditor who has a debt provable in the bankruptcy may commence an action without the consent of the court (IA 1986, s.285).

The High Court Enforcement Officer's duties after the order is made are clearly defined under IA 1986, s.346 and in the Insolvency Rules. Where any of the debtor's goods have been taken in execution, and *before the completion* of the execution notice is given to the High Court Enforcement Officer or other officer charged with the execution that the debtor has been adjudged bankrupt, then the High Court Enforcement Officer or the officer must deliver to the Official Receiver or trustee of the bankrupt's estate the goods or any money seized or recovered in part satisfaction of the execution.

14–59 Where no request is made to deliver up the goods, the High Court Enforcement Officer's duty remains to proceed with the execution and sell the goods, but the proceeds, less expenses, must be handed over to the trustee (see *Woolfords Estate v Levy* (1892) 66 L.T. 812). The rights conferred on the Official Receiver and the trustee may, to such extent, and on such terms as it thinks fit, be set aside by the court in favour of the creditor who has issued the execution.
The costs of execution become a first charge on the goods or money delivered and the Official Receiver may sell the goods or part of them for the purpose of satisfying the charge (IA 1986, s.346(a) and (b)).

Execution is "completed" by the seizure and sale of the goods and the proceeds of sale, or a payment made to avoid sale, being held by the High Court Enforcement Officer for 14 days before the commencement of the bankruptcy. As to the rights of a creditor during this period, see *Marley Tile Co v Burrows* [1978] Q.B. 241; [1977] 3 W.L.R. 641, CA.

14–60 Insolvency Rules 1986, r.12.19 requires that the notice to the High Court Enforcement Officer or other officer charged with execution confirming that a bankruptcy petition has been presented, or that a debtor has been adjudicated bankrupt, should be in writing and should be delivered by hand or sent by recorded delivery to the office of the High Court Enforcement Officer or other officer charged with the execution when the execution comes from the county court.

Insolvent partnership orders—general considerations

14–61 The Insolvent Partnerships Order 1994 (SI 1994/2421) governs insolvent partnerships. This Order will be referred to as the IPO 1994 throughout the remainder of this chapter.

A reminder—what is a partnership?

14–62 A partnership is a relationship that exists between two or more persons carrying on business together with a view to making a profit. A partner can be an individual or a company (known as a corporate member), and is personally liable (usually without limit) for the debts of the partnership. Therefore, a creditor of a partnership can pursue one or more of the partners personally, as well as the partnership itself, for a partnership debt.

What insolvency options are available in relation to partnerships?

14–63 It is possible for a judgment creditor to pursue the partnership and yet not the partners individually, which allows the partners to continue to trade in other businesses that may generate profits to allow outstanding liabilities to be settled. The form of petition in this scenario closely follows the form of a petition against a company.

Alternatively, a judgment creditor can pursue the individual assets of the partners, together with their partnership property. The only ground upon which a partnership may be wound up in this scenario is if the partnership is unable to pay its debts.

The circumstances in which a partnership is deemed to be unable to pay its debts are outlined in s.222(1) of the IA 1986, as modified by the IPO 1994.

An individual partner will be unable to pay his or her debts if:

- the partnership owes a debt in excess of £750.00; and
- a statutory demand has been served on both the partnership and the individual partner; and

- payment has not been forthcoming as provided under the IA 1986, subject again to modifications made by the IPO 1994.

How can a judgment creditor wind up a partnership that has an outstanding judgment debt?

14–64 Because the partners are personally liable for the debts of the partnership, a partnership can be wound up and bankruptcy orders also made against the individual partners.

The IPO 1994 has been periodically amended to take account of changing circumstances; for example, in 1996, SI 1996/1308 amended Art.7 to broaden the list of possible petitioning creditors when it comes to the winding up process.

A full discussion on insolvent partnerships is outside the scope of this text, so the reader is directed to a leading text such as Berry, Bailey, Miller *Personal Insolvency: Law and Practice*, 3rd edn. (London: Butterworths, 2001), ch.16 on the finer points of handling an insolvent partnership problem.

Again, as with any other enforcement procedures, it is necessary to identify the exact nature of the debtor, be that a sole trader, limited company or partnership.

14–65 The IPO modifies the IA 1986 in relation to insolvent partnerships so that an insolvent partnership can be dealt with under the provisions of the IPO 1994 as follows:

The partnership itself can be wound up	This involves presenting a winding–up petition, which will need to be prepared/served and presented against the insolvent partnership. The form of petition is the same as a petition to wind up an unregistered company and can be used with the necessary modifications (see Form 4.2 in Sch.4 to the Insolvency Rules)
The partnership itself can be wound up and the individual partners made bankrupt	The ground for presenting a petition in these circumstances is that the partnership is unable to pay its debts. Evidence of that fact will be the failure to pay a debt in excess of £750 following service of a statutory demand served both on the partnership and the individual partners
One or more of the individual partners can be made bankrupt without making all the partners bankrupt and without winding up the partnership	Individual partners can be made bankrupt and a creditor has the choice of also winding up the partnership.

Which courts have jurisdiction?

14–66 In the High Court, a petition to wind up an insolvent partnership as an unregistered company may be presented if the partnership has or at any time has had either:

- a principal place of business; or
- a place of business at which business is or has been carried on in the course of which a debt arose, which forms the basis of a petition for winding up a partnership.

In the county court, provided the court in question has bankruptcy jurisdiction, then a petition may also be presented.

Petitions presented in either the High Court or county court are required to show that the partnership carried on its business in England and Wales within a three-year period, ending with the day on which the petition is presented to the court.

What are the necessary grounds for an IPO petition?

14–67 The various grounds on which an insolvent partnership may be wound up are set out in s.221(7) of the IA 1986, as amended by Sch.3(3) Pt 1 of the IPO 1994. However, for the purpose of this book, the only ground which is relevant is the inability of the partnership to meet its liabilities.

14–68 A partnership will be deemed unable to pay its debts in the same way that an unregistered company cannot meet its liabilities, for example:

- where a creditor has served a statutory demand in the proper form and no payment has been forthcoming;
- where an action or proceedings have been instituted against a member of the partnership for a debt or demand, or a sum has been claimed as due from either the partnership or the partner and written notice has been served on the partnership of the commencement of proceedings, yet payment has not been made and the debt remains unpaid (see s.222 of the IA 1985 as modified by Sch.3(5), Pt 1 of the IPO 1994);
- execution or other process issued following a judgment against the partnership has been returned unsatisfied;
- it is proved to the court's satisfaction that the partnership is unable to pay its debts as they fall due;

- a court is satisfied that the value of partnership assets outweighs its liabilities.

What happens at the hearing of the petition?

14–69 The hearing of the petition to wind up the partnership will be heard before the hearing of the petition to bankrupt the individuals.

It should be noted that a creditor may only withdraw the petition at the hearing if notice is given to the court three days prior to the hearing of the petition of the intention to do so.

As in other insolvency procedures, the court has power to substitute creditors in respect of both the partnership and individual partners.

A petition against an individual partner follows the same basic procedure as an ordinary bankruptcy application. As stated above, the hearing will take place after the hearing to wind up the partnership.

What happens after the partnership is wound up?

14–70 Where a winding up order has been made against the partnership, the partnership affairs are dealt with in the same way as a limited company.

Chapter 15

Debt Management in Post Judgment

Introductory comments

15–01 It is widely accepted that the government is committed to supporting debtors who become over-indebted. As we go to publication in 2010 we find ourselves in the midst of an economic storm, with austerity measures soon to be announced. In these difficult times, there is also no doubt that the government has laudable aims in ensuring that debtors are protected where possible from the impact of enforcement procedures and are allowed to shelter under a variety of schemes to enable them to rehabilitate their financial position.

The 2007 Tribunals Courts and Enforcement Act included a series of new measures to help the public affected by enforcement under Pt 5. However, with the government now having to take radical action to reverse the UK balance sheet, cuts in public spending threaten the likelihood of some of these measures ever seeing the light of day.

15–02 In the area of debt management and relief, a recent consultation paper published by the Ministry of Justice, *Administration and Enforcement Restriction Orders: Setting The Parameters* (MoJ, 2008) acknowledged that due to the need to support IT changes in the courts it would not be possible to introduce either the reformed administration order (AO) scheme or the Enforcement Restriction Order (ERO) until April 2011 at the earliest.

Nonetheless, as AOs and EROs come under Pt 5 of the TCEA 2007, we will look at these two measures along with debt relief orders (DROs) and debt management schemes (DMSs) so that the reader has a complete understanding of the extent to which government is prepared to go to rehabilitate people in debt within the enforcement process.

Administration orders

How does the new Act amend existing law?

15–03 To begin with, the government intends to exclude specifically from the current regime of administration orders those debts classed as non-provable in bankruptcy. These include fines, sums due under orders made in family proceedings and maintenance assessments made under the Child Support Act 1991. The government also intends to exclude student loans. These changes will provide consistency with current insolvency practice and the Insolvency Service's Debt Relief Order (DRO) scheme introduced by Ch.3 of Pt 5 of the TCEA 2007 in April 2009.

Additionally, provision has been made in the TCEA 2007 to allow debts that cannot be brought into either the administration order or enforcement restriction order schemes to be defined. For example, all secured debts (i.e. debts secured against an asset where the loan came into being), along with business debts, are excluded from both schemes by statute.

Regulations may exclude other types of debt, for which consultation has been carried out and responses published. Additionally, under the new provisions, orders must be revoked where a business debt has been incurred during the currency of the order or where it is shown that any of the entry criteria were not, or are no longer, met.

15–04 The TCEA 2007 also gives the Lord Chancellor the power to review and set a limit for the total amount of debt that can be included in an AO by secondary legislation. As stated in Parliament, the government intends to set this at £15,000 initially.

For the statutory basis of an administration order, reference should be made to the TCEA 2007 Pt 5 Ch.1 in which, under s.106(1), a new Pt 6 of the County Courts Act 1984 is substituted, which in turn amends s.112 of the 1984 Act.

What value of debt can be subject to an administration order?

15–05 A county court can make an administration order on behalf of an individual who is a debtor where there are two or more qualifying debts. The definition of "qualifying debt" relates to all debts which are unsecured. It is possible that further exclusions may be made by the regulations when these are produced.

Administration orders are not designed to assist the debtor to shelter from business creditors. The Act provides a definition of this in the term "business debt", which is defined as "(whether or not a qualifying debt) which is incurred by a person in the course of the business" (see County Court Act 1984, s.112AB, as amended by the TCEA 2007).

When can an administration order be made?

15–06 The debtor must have at least two qualifying debts and be unable to pay at least one of them. An order can only be made where the debtor's qualifying debts are less than the minimum amount prescribed, which at present is £5,000.

One of the more controversial areas of the TCEA 2007 is that the new Act will prescribe a higher limit for the amount that can be subject to the order. We wait to see what the new limit will be. The outcome of a consultation paper in September 2009 has been that in view of support for the proposal of a minimum repayment this will now be set at £50 per month. This was supported by 57 per cent of respondents to the consultation exercise.

Can an administration order be made in proceedings?

15–07 CCR Order 39, r.1 allows an administration order (AO) to be made by a district judge, who in reality may well delegate this authority to a member of his court staff.

Rule 2 of CCR Order 39 requires a judgment debtor to file a request on Form N92 in the court where he or she resides, or to carry on business to seek the shelter of the AO procedure.

It is also possible for an AO to be made following the examination of the judgment debtor under an Order to Obtain Information application (see CPR Pt 71). If the judgment debtor provides sufficient information to enable the court to make an AO, then the court may proceed with the AO procedure as if it was originally made by the judgment debtor. However, to enable the court to proceed in this way, the judgment debtor must have provided to the court, on oath, a list of his creditors and the amounts he owes to each, along with sufficient details of his resources and needs. The form for listing creditors is Form N93.

If the court orders the judgment debtor to furnish it with a list under s.4(1)(b) of the Attachment of Earnings Act 1971, then that list must be filed within 14 days after the order is made, unless the court makes an order to the contrary.

Any statement made by the judgment debtor must, under CCR Order 39, r.3, be verified on oath.

What is the decision making process for ordering an AO?

15–09 The question as to whether an AO order should be made, and the terms of the AO, may be decided by the court officer in accordance with the provisions of CCR Order 39, r.5.

Once the court receives the judgment debtor's request or list of creditors, the court officer will consider the debtor's means. If he considers that these are sufficient to discharge the total amount of the debts in the judgment debtor's list (within a reasonable time), the court officer can determine the amount and frequency of the payments to be made under an AO (referred to as the "proposed rate" under CCR Order 39, r.5(2)).

The court officer will then:

- notify the judgment debtor of the proposed rate and require the judgment debtor to give written reasons outlining any objection to the proposed rate within 14 days of service of the notification upon him;
- also send to each creditor mentioned in the list provided by the judgment debtor a copy of the debtor's request on Form N92, or of the list on Form N93, together with the proposed rate;
- the court will require any creditor on the list to similarly give written reasons for any objection he may have to the making of an AO within 14 days of service of the debtor's request and/or list—the creditor's objections may include an objection as to the making of the AO, the proposed rate or the inclusion of the creditor's debt in the debtor's list;
- ideally, all creditors and the debtor should be notified of the proposed rate as part of this procedure. In the case of *Re Chancery plc* [1991] B.C.L.C. it was held that where the company in respect of which the AO was sought was a bank, the circumstances may justify making the AO without prior service.

If no objections are received within the time stated, the court officer may then make an AO providing for a full payment of the total amount of the debts included in the debtor's list.

15–10 If the debtor or a creditor notifies the court of any objection within the time stated, the court officer must fix a date for a hearing so that the district judge can decide whether the AO should be made. The court officer must give not less than 14 days' notice of the hearing date to the debtor and to each creditor mentioned in the debtor's list. Neither the Act nor the Rules expressly prescribe the circumstances in which such objections should be upheld. It seems that the issue of handling objections is a matter of judicial discretion.

It should be noted that whether or not a particular debt is included, the court's jurisdiction to make an order depends on the total value of the debtor's indebtedness and not on the value of the debts included in the order.

What happens if the court cannot fix a proposed rate?

15–11 Under CCR Order 39, r.5(5) if the court officer is unable to fix a rate, whether because he considers that the debtor's means are insufficient or for some other reason, he must refer the request for an AO to the district judge.

CCR Order 39, r.5(6) allows the district judge to fix the proposed rate without the attendance of the parties at court on terms that are practicable. If this happens, the proposed rate fixed by the district judge is then notified to the parties for them to list their objections as set out above. If the district judge does not fix a proposed rate, he must direct the court officer to arrange a date for the hearing of the debtor's request at which he will decide whether an AO should be made. The court officer must again give not less than 14 days' notice of the date of the hearing to both the debtor and to each creditor mentioned in the list provided by the debtor.

Where an AO is made under para.(3) of CCR Order 39, r.5, the court officer may exercise the power of the court under s.5 of the Attachment of Earnings Act 1971 to make an order to secure the payments required by the AO.

What is the time limit for any objection by a creditor?

15–12 Under CCR Order 39, r.6(1) any creditor who has received notice of the proposed rate, and who objects to any debt being included in the list prepared by the debtor, must, not less than 7 days before the date of hearing for the AO, give notice of his objection, setting out the grounds of that objection to both the court officer, the debtor and the creditor. Unless this procedure is followed, a creditor cannot proceed with the objection to a debt unless he gives notice under this part of the rule.

What happens at the hearing?

15–13 Under CCR Order 39, r.7 on the day of the hearing:

- any creditor, whether or not he is mentioned in the list prepared by the debtor, may attend and prove his debt or, subject to r.6 above, object to any debt included in that list;
- every debt included in that list must be taken to be proved unless it is objected to by a creditor, disallowed by the court or required by the court to be supported by evidence;
- any creditor whose debt is required by the court to be supported by evidence must prove his debt;
- the court may adjourn proof of any debt and, if it does so, may either adjourn consideration of the question of whether an AO should be made or proceed to determine the question, in which case, if an AO is made, the debt, when proved, must be added to the debts scheduled to the order;
- any creditor will be entitled to be heard as to the terms of any AO that is to be made.

Can the court order the review of the AO?

15–14 The court may on making an AO, or at any time in the future, direct that the AO must be subject to review at times and intervals as directed by the court. If a time for review is given, then the court officer must give notice of the hearing date of any review hearing at least 7 days prior to the fixed date.

How is the AO served?

15–15 Under CCR Order 39, r.9 once the AO is made, the court officer must send a copy of it to the debtor, along with every creditor whose name is included on the list prepared by the debtor, and any other creditor who has proved his debt. In addition, the court must serve notice of the AO on every other court in which, to the knowledge of the district judge, judgment has been obtained against the debtor or proceedings are pending in respect of any debt scheduled to the order.

Can a creditor who missed the original hearing still object?

15–16 Provision is made under CCR 39, r.10 for a creditor who did not receive notice under CCR Order 39, r.5 to be able to object to either a debt scheduled to the AO or to the manner in which payment was directed to be made by instalments. Such a creditor must give notice to the court officer of his objection and the grounds of that objection.

When this is received by the court, the court officer must consider the objection and either allow it, dismiss it or adjourn it for hearing. Security for costs may also be ordered. The court has the power to dismiss an objection if it is not satisfied that the creditor gave notice within a reasonable time of his becoming aware of the AO.

Can additional creditors add their debt to the AO?

15–17 CCR Order 39, r.11 provides for a creditor whose debt is either:

- not scheduled to an administration order; or
- after the date of the AO became a creditor of the debtor

to prove his debt by sending particulars of his claim to the court officer, who must then give notice of it to the debtor and to every creditor whose debt is scheduled to the AO.

Provided there is no objection to the debt, it will be taken as proved and added to the AO. If either the debtor or any other creditor wishes to object, they have seven days after receipt of the notice of the new debt to object to the court.

If an objection to the new debt is received within the seven-day period, or the court requires the claim for the new debt to be supported by evidence, the court officer must fix a date for the court to consider the claim and give notice of that hearing to the debtor, the creditor of the new debt and any creditor making an objection. At the subsequent hearing, the court may either allow the claim in full or in part, or may disallow the claim for the new debt to be added to the AO schedule.

If added to the schedule, a copy of the order adding it must be then sent to the creditor who made the claim.

Can a creditor present a bankruptcy petition against a debtor who has an AO?

15–18 Section 112(4) of the County Courts Act 1984 precludes a creditor scheduled to an AO from presenting or joining in a bankruptcy petition without the permission of the court. Under CCR Order 39, r.12 an application by a creditor under s.112(4) of the 1984 Act for permission to present or join in a bankruptcy petition must be made on notice to the debtor in accordance with CPR Pt 23, but the court may, if it thinks fit, order that notice be given to any other creditor whose debt is scheduled to the administration order.

What about the conduct of the AO?

15–19 Under CCR Order 39, r.13 court staff are responsible for the conduct of the order and must take all proper steps to enforce it (including exercising the power of the court under s.5 of the Attachment of Earnings Act 1971 to make an attachment of earnings order to secure payments required by the AO) or to bring to the attention of the court any matter which may make it desirable to review the order.

Without prejudice to s.115 of the Act, any creditor whose debt is scheduled to the order may take, with the permission of the court, proceedings to enforce the order.

The debtor or, with the permission of the court, any such creditor may apply to the court to review the order.

What happens if the debtor defaults in making a payment(s)?

15–20 Provision is made under CCR Order 39, r.13A for the court to take a series of steps where it appears that the debtor is failing to make payments in accordance with the AO. If this happens, the court officer must (either of his own initiative or on the application of a creditor whose debt is scheduled to the AO) send a notice to the debtor informing him of the amounts outstanding and requiring him (within 14 days of service of the notice upon him) to either:

- make the payments as required by the order; or
- explain his reasons for failing to make the payments; and
- make a proposal for payment of the amounts outstanding; or
- make a request to vary the order.

If the debtor does not comply with the notice regarding the defaulting payments within the time stipulated, then the court officer must revoke the AO.

15–21 Under s.429 of the Insolvency Act 1986, where a person fails to make any payment required under an AO, the court administering that person's estate under the AO may revoke the order and direct that s.429 of the Insolvency Act 1986 (dealing with the limit of credit) and s.12 of the Company Directors Disqualification Act 1986 (dealing with the appointment as either a director or liquidator in the promotion, formation or management of a company) will not apply to the debtor for a specified period not exceeding two years.

If, however, the debtor comes back with reasons for failing to make payments, or a proposal to pay the amount outstanding, or a request to vary the AO, then the court officer must refer that matter to the district judge, who may then either deal with the response without requiring the attendance of the parties, and either revoke the AO or suspend it, or alternatively require the court officer to fix a date for the review of the AO.

All parties must be given notice of any order made by the court, and given an opportunity to attend any hearing. At the hearing, the district judge may either confirm the AO or set it aside and make a new order on terms as he thinks fit.

What powers does the court have in reviewing an AO?

15–22 Under CCR Order 39, r.14 on the review of an AO the court may either:

- suspend the operation of the order for such time and on such terms as it thinks fit, if satisfied that the debtor is unable to pay the amounts due under the order; or
- if satisfied that there has been a material change in any relevant circumstances since the order was made, vary any provision of the order made by virtue of s.112(6) of the Act; or
- if satisfied that the debtor has failed without reasonable cause to comply with any provision of the order, or that it is otherwise just and expedient to do so, revoke the order, either forthwith or on failure to comply with any condition specified by the court; or
- make an attachment of earnings order to secure the payments required by the administration order, or vary or discharge any such attachment of earnings order already made.

The court officer must send a copy of any order varying or revoking an AO to the debtor and to every creditor whose debt is scheduled to the AO and, if the AO is revoked, to any other court to which a copy of the AO was sent pursuant to CCR Order 39, r.9.

What other points are applicable to AOs?

15–23 Under CCR Order 39, r.16 on the revocation of an AO, any attachment of earnings order made to secure the payments required by the AO must be discharged.

The method of payment to creditors of sums paid by the debtor is by way of the declaration of a dividend. Under CCR Order 39, r.17 the court officer with responsibility for the conduct of the AO must from time to time declare dividends and distribute them among entitled creditors. When a dividend is declared, notice must be sent by the court officer to each of the creditors.

A debtor who changes his residence must inform the court immediately of his new address under CCR Order 39, r.19. Where the debtor becomes resident within the district of another court in England and Wales, the court in which the AO is being conducted may arrange to transfer the proceedings to the new court.

Registering an administration order

15–24 Any debtor against whom at least one County Court Judgment is registered can make an application to the court for an AO. If granted, this provides protection from further action by creditors in respect of any debts listed under the terms of the order. Creditors not included in the AO cannot pursue their debt separately through the court, and if they try, these debts will automatically be added to the AO in place.

Registry Trust Limited is contracted to the Ministry of Justice to maintain a statutory public Register of Judgments, Orders and Fines in England and Wales, one section of which includes details of AOs. The register contains:

- the name and address of the debtor;
- the court name and order number;
- the total amount payable;
- the date of order;
- the date of any varied order, notice of satisfaction or revocation of the judgment.

Orders registered after April 6, 2006 will also include the judgment debtor's date of birth (if this is known) and their address which will include the mandatory postcode.

If the AO is varied, courts must notify Registry Trust and the register will be updated. Where an AO has been paid in full, the court must also notify Registry Trust so that the register can be amended. The debtor can also apply to the court for a certificate of satisfaction, available for a court fee of £15 (at the time of preparing this book).

15–25 It is also possible that the debtor will be unable to continue payments for a period; where the reason for this is accepted by the court, Registry Trust will not be notified and the register will not be updated.

Despite the government's clear commitment to the administration order procedure as a way to help alleviate over-indebtedness, statistics from Registry Trust show that in the first quarter of 2009 only 620 administration orders were actually made—resulting in a 9 per cent drop on the figures for the previous quarter.

It remains to be seen whether, with new technology and a new impetus to promote administration orders as a way of alleviating indebtedness, these will actually become more prevalent when the relevant parts of the TCEA 2007 become operational.

What is a debt relief order?

15–26 The Tribunals, Courts and Enforcement Act 2007 introduced into Pt 5 of the Act a new form of debt relief called the debt relief order (DRO). The policy idea was to create a further form of shelter for people in debt from their creditors. The DRO is designed to give people in debt, who owe small amounts of money and have little or no disposable income and no assets, a way to be able to repay what they can afford whilst sheltering from their creditors.

In essence, DROs create a partnership between the Insolvency Service and the debt advice sector in England and Wales. Advisors act as "approved intermediaries" and will help the debtor to apply for a DRO, which can be done using an online application form. When this is filled out and subsequently submitted, the official receiver and not the court will consider the debtor's application.

Debt relief orders

Who is eligible for a debt relief order?

15–27 To be eligible for a DRO, the debtor must meet all of the following conditions:

- the debtor must be unable to pay his or her debts;
- the debtor must owe up to a maximum of £15,000 (not including un-liquidated or excluded debts);
- the debtor's total gross assets must not exceed £300;
- after deducting tax, National Insurance contributions and the usual household expenses, the debtor's disposable income must not exceed £50 a month;

- the debtor's place of domicile must be in England and Wales, or at any time in the last three years the debtor must have been resident or carried on a business in England and Wales;
- the debtor must not have been subject to a previous DRO within the last six years;
- the debtor must not be involved in any other formal insolvency procedure at the time the application for the DRO is made, which includes:
  - any undischarged bankruptcy order;
  - a current individual voluntary arrangement;
  - any current bankruptcy restrictions order (BRO);
  - any current debt relief restriction order or undertaking (DRRO or DRRU);
  - an interim order.

15–28 The definition of "gross assets" as mentioned above is defined as the value of the debtor's combined assets before all charges and other fees requiring repayment have been deducted. Excluded from the definition are:

- Motor vehicles up to a value of £1,000.
- Clothing.
- Bedding.
- Furniture.
- Household equipment.
- Other basic items needed by the debtor and his or her family in the home.

Can the judgment debtor apply for bankruptcy at the same time?

15–29 It is not possible for a debtor to petition for bankruptcy and apply for a DRO at the same time. If the creditor is petitioning for the debtor's bankruptcy, the debtor must get the creditor's permission before applying for a DRO.

If the debtor has given away any property or sold it for less than its true value in the previous two years before applying for the DRO, the Official Receiver may not approve the debtor's application.

If the debtor has preferred any creditors over other creditors by making payments to them within the last two years the Official Receiver again may not approve the debtor's application for a DRO.

How does the debtor apply for a DRO?

15–30 The debtor can apply for a DRO via an approved intermediary, i.e. a debt advisor. The application form for a DRO is only available online, but once it has been submitted it must be printed and sent to the Debt Relief Order Unit at The Insolvency Service in Plymouth.

On applying for a DRO the debtor will have to pay a fee, which at the time of writing this book is currently £90. The fee is non-refundable, whether or not the Official Receiver approves or rejects the debtor's application.

The fee for the DRO must be paid in cash, unless a charity has agreed to pay the fee on the debtor's behalf, in which case payment can be made by cheque. The approved intermediary will provide the debtor with a unique barcoded letter, which can be presented at a number of outlets in order to pay the fee, and the intermediary will be able to give details to the debtor of approved agents in the area.

Who will deal with the debtor's case for a DRO?

15–31 The debtor's case for a DRO will be dealt with by an approved intermediary drawn from the skilled debt advisers who have been authorised by a competent authority as being able to advise and assist individuals with the completion and submission of their DRO application. An Official Receiver who is appointed by the Secretary of State and is an officer of the court would be responsible for assessing the application for a DRO and administering it afterwards.

The Official Receiver is responsible for looking into the debtor's financial affairs, both before and during the time a DRO is made. The Official Receiver may report to the court and notify creditors of their findings, and must also report any evidence when they find that a debtor has committed criminal offences in connection with the DRO that has been made, find that the debtor's behaviour has been dishonest or that the debtor has in some way been to blame for the DRO, perhaps by making transfers at an undervalue.

What are the duties of a debtor when considering applying for a DRO?

15–32 When a debtor applies for a DRO, certain duties must be fulfilled. If a debtor applies for a DRO, he or she must:

- provide the Official Receiver with a full list of his or her assets and liabilities, together with the names of any creditors;
- comply with the Official Receiver's request to provide information about his or her financial affairs, so that the Official Receiver can consider the debtor's application. The debtor needs to be prepared to co-operate fully with the Official Receiver, as and when required to do so.

When the debtor's application for a DRO has been approved, the debtor is under a continuing responsibility to comply with the Official Receiver's request to give further information about his or her financial affairs. The debtor must also inform the Official Receiver of any assets which he or she obtains or whether the debtor sees increases in his or her income whilst subject to a DRO, including lump-sum cash payments, windfalls and property and inheritance money.

15–33 The debtor must also not try to obtain credit of £500 or more from anyone without first telling them that a DRO has been made against them. They must not make payments direct to creditors included in the DRO and they must be aware that if they leave out information required in the application form, the Official Receiver may refuse to grant a DRO if he finds information was left out while considering the debtor's application. Indeed, the Official Receiver may decide to cancel the DRO if he later learns that information was deliberately left out, which could mean that the debtor would be at risk of actions from creditors. If the Official Receiver thinks the information that was left out was very serious, then the debtor could be charged with a criminal offence and/or be subject to a civil action such as a Debt relief restriction order (DRRO).

How does the debt relief order affect a debtor?

15–34 The main effect of a DRO will be to place a "moratorium" period on the debts listed in the debtor's DRO. This means that creditors cannot take any action to recover or enforce their debts against the debtor during a 12-month period, which usually lasts from the date of the order, although there may be exceptions, and after that time the listed debts will be discharged.

If the debtor's circumstances change enough for the debtor to be able to make payments to his or her creditors, the Official Receiver will need to consider whether or not to terminate the DRO. If circumstances change close to the end of the 12-month moratorium, the Official Receiver can extend it for up to three months to allow the debtor to come to an arrangement with his or her creditors.

During this time the debtor is subject to the same limitations and receives the same protection as during the first 12 months of the DRO.

How are payments made to creditors under a DRO?

15–35 If the Official Receiver approves the debtor's application and grants the DRO, all the creditors listed in the order will be notified that a DRO has been made, which means they cannot recover the debts which are owed to them. Furthermore, the debtor must not make any further payments to the creditors included in the DRO. If creditors ask for a payment to be made to them during the period of the DRO, the debtor needs to tell them that he or she is subject to a DRO, but may wish to seek independent advice regarding certain debts such as rent arrears.

As in bankruptcy, the debtor will also remain liable for certain debts which include:

- Student loans, which remain the responsibility of the debtor to repay within the terms of the loan agreement.
- Any obligation arising under a confiscation order made under s.1 of the Drug Trafficking Offences Act 1986 or s.1 of the Criminal Justice (Scotland) Act 1987 or s.71 of the Criminal Justice Act 1988 or Pts 2, 3 or 4 of the Proceeds of Crime Act 2002.
- Court fines and any other obligations arising from an order made in family proceedings or under a maintenance assessment made under the Child Support Act 1991.
- Any secured debt—the DRO does not affect the rights of secured creditors to deal with their security. However, it is unlikely that a debtor who owns secured property can qualify for a DRO, as this would mean that the debtor's gross assets were likely to exceed £300.

During the period of the DRO the debtor must carry on paying monthly commitments such as rent and utility bills, and will be responsible for any debts incurred after a DRO has been made.

To what restrictions is the debtor subject under a DRO?

15–36 Under a DRO the debtor is placed under the following restrictions:

- If the debtor carries on a business either directly or indirectly in a name that is different from the name under which the DRO was granted, the debtor must first tell all those with whom he or she does business the name under which the debtor was granted a DRO.
- A debtor subject to a DRO must not be involved (directly or indirectly) with the promotion, management or formation of a limited company, and must not act as a company director, without the court's permission.
- If the debtor wishes to obtain credit of £500 or more, either alone or jointly with another person, the debtor must first tell the lender that he or she is subject to a DRO. This restriction applies to borrowing money, and also to getting credit by acting with the intention of getting it, even though he has not entered into a specific agreement for it. This would include, for example, ordering goods without requesting credit but then failing to pay for the goods when they were delivered.
- A debtor who applies for a DRO is not eligible to apply for a DRO again for six years.

That said, the debtor is permitted to open a new bank or building society account after the DRO is granted. The bank or building society may require the debtor to disclose that he or she is subject to a DRO, and may then decide whether or not to permit the debtor to open an account or to impose any conditions or restrictions on the use of the account.

What is clear is that the debtor must tell the bank or building society that he or she is subject to a DRO before applying for any overdraft facilities. In addition, if the debtor is subject to a DRO, then he or she must not write any cheques which are likely to be dishonoured.

What happens if the debtor has been dishonest?

15–37 If, as part of the enquiry into the debtor's affairs, the Official Receiver decides that the debtor has been dishonest before or during the DRO, or that the debtor is otherwise to blame for his or her position, then the Official Receiver may apply to the court for a debt relief restriction order (DRRO). The court may make an order against the debtor for between two and 15 years, the issuance of which will mean that the debtor will continue to be subject to the restrictions of a DRO, as set out above. A debtor may also give a debt relief restriction undertaking (DRRU), which has the same effect as a DRRO but means that the matter will not go before the court.

What is the position in relation to debts incurred after the granting of a DRO?

15–38 After the date of the DRO it is the responsibility of the debtor to manage his or her finances more carefully. The DRO itself only deals with debts at the date the DRO is approved. If the debtor incurs new debts after this date, this could result in:

- either a bankruptcy order being made against the debtor;
- prosecution if, when the debtor incurred debts, he or she did not disclose that they were subject to a DRO.

As a result, the debtor must think very carefully and seek proper financial advice on managing budgets after a DRO is made against him or her.

Enforcement restriction orders

15–39 Although still in the consultation stage at the time of producing this text, it is generally thought that enforcement restriction orders will be introduced in April 2011.

EROs were introduced under Pt 5 of the TCEA 2007 to provide a short-term method of relief to a judgment debtor who finds him or herself unable to meet their obligations through a sudden and unforeseen change in their financial circumstances, but from which they are likely to recover.

What are the key points?

15–40 A number of key factors need to be borne in mind when faced with a judgment debtor applying for an ERO. These include:

- there is actually no need for there to be a judgment debt in existence, so one must not make the mistake in thinking that an ERO only applies post judgment—but for the purposes of this book we will refer to the person subject to an ERO as the "judgment debtor";
- the ERO will be limited to a period of 12 months, during which time a judgment creditor cannot enforce the debt without the leave of the court;
- consideration must be given to judgment creditors' objections to any order, but the grounds for these objections are not yet defined;

- the court can require the judgment debtor to update the court with details of his or her finances and any disposal of assets;
- a repayment programme will be set up under the ERO if the debtor has sufficient surplus income to do so;
- the judgment debtor will be under an obligation to make the court aware of any changes in his or her occupation, marital status or anything which affects his or her monthly income and expenditure;
- the judgment debtor will need to inform the court of any windfall or money gain in excess of £500.

15–41 To seek the protection of an ERO, a judgment debtor:

- cannot have any "business debts";
- cannot be subject to an individual voluntary arrangement (or an interim order pursuant to the Insolvency Act 1986 s.252);
- cannot be subject to a bankruptcy order or a bankruptcy petition;
- cannot be subject to an existing ERO;
- must also have two or more qualifying debts which do not include business debts or debts secured against assets (see the County Courts Act 1984 s.117B).

What is the impact of an ERO?

15–42 If the debtor's application for an ERO is successful, the following provisions shall apply:

- Utility companies will not be able to stop the supply of gas or electricity or the supply of associated services (see s.117E TCEA 2007).
- If any other debt management arrangements are in place, these will cease to be effective when the ERO is made—including any AO which is in place, debt relief order or debt repayment plan.
- Any county court proceedings will be stayed once the ERO is made in respect of a qualifying debt (see s.117L of the TCEA 2007).

- A creditor will not be able to present a bankruptcy petition in respect of a qualifying debt without the court's permission (see s.117C TCEA 2007).
- A creditor will not be able to pursue any remedy for the recovery of a qualifying debt without the court's permission.

For how long will the ERO last?

15–43 The maximum period of an ERO will be 12 months beginning from the day on which the order is made (see s.117H TCEA 2007). When the order is made, the court will specify the day on which it will come to an end and set the period if less than twelve months.

How does the debtor make repayments?

15–44 EROs allow repayments to be made over a period of time. The ERO may expressly impose a repayment requirement on the judgment debtor, although this is not an absolute requirement. It cannot alter the amount which is to be repaid and the ERO will not in itself reduce the debt, because the ERO anticipates that there is a realistic prospect that the debtor's financial circumstances will improve (see s.117B(7) TCEA 2007).

Who can make the application for an ERO?

15–45 Only the judgment debtor will be able to make an application for an ERO, which can be made whether or not he or she is a person with a judgment against them.

What is the duty on the debtor?

15–46 Under s.117J of the TCEA 2007 a judgment debtor has to provide information at prescribed times in relation to earnings, income, assets and outgoings. Failure to comply with the requirements to provide information will be an offence under s.117K of the TCEA 2007. If the judgment debtor fails to provide the court with details of any disposals of property or assets, or other information as required, he or she will be committing an offence, which will attract a fine of up to £250 or imprisonment for a period of up to 14 days.

The TCEA 2007 provides the mechanism for supporting regulations to be made to underpin the ERO regime.

Debt management schemes

15–47 In September 2009, the Ministry of Justice and the Business, Innovation and Skills executive agency, along with Insolvency Service, published the consultation paper *Debt Management Schemes—delivering effective and balanced solutions for Debtors and Creditors*.

The consultation paper was written in conjunction with the government's White Paper *A Better Deal for Consumers: Delivering Real Help Now and Change for the Future*, which was issued by the Department for Business, Innovation and Skills. The consultation paper looks at the way in which debtors deal with their indebtedness, and asks for evidence on whether government should use its powers contained in Ch.4 of Pt 5 of the TCEA to improve the operators of debt management schemes.

In the interim, while government works through its consultation process it intends to publish guidance on what to expect from non-court-based debt management scheme operators, to help debtors better understand the benefits and pitfalls of current debt management plans.

The Insolvency Service's guide *In debt?—Dealing with Your Creditors* was published on July 2, 2009 and provides details of the range of current measures available to assist debtors, regardless of whether or not they have the ability to repay their debts.

15–48 The government's objectives up until the change of administration in May 2010 were:

- helping people who could, but who were struggling, to repay their debts;
- ensuring that fees charged by debt management scheme operators were reasonable and consistent;
- ending the practice of some creditors adding interest to debts included in their repayment plan;
- preserving the best features of the current debt management industry;
- ensuring that the needs of debtors, creditors and other operators were correctly balanced; and
- ensuring that debtors were aware of the range and options available to them, and were advised on the most appropriate and sustainable solutions for their circumstances.

In addition to these objectives, the stated aim of government was to take tough action against operators of non-court-based debt management plans which failed to comply with OFT guidance.

In its response to the government's consultation paper, the Citizens Advice Bureau (CAB) pointed out that it continued to see consumer detriment arising from the practices of some debt management plan providers, which included examples of poor advice, poor service and excessive charging.

15–49 The CAB believes that a key function of the statutory debt management plan regime would be to provide breathing space to people in financial difficulties. The CAB did not believe it would be difficult to put in safeguards to ensure that this regime was not abused or used inappropriately, but it could prevent,

> "a lot of the pain, cost and confusion that can turn a period of financial difficulty into an unbearable and unmanageable debt problem".

The CAB made the point in its response that many of the people seeking help in relation to debt problems are (with some advice) able to pay something to their creditors.

Statutory debt management plan provisions in the TCEA from the CAB's point of view contain the possibility of a new form of non-court-based debt relief. The CAB welcomed this and believed that the Ministry of Justice should bring these proposals forward, stating that the current system of remedies allows debt relief through IVAs for those debtors that have sufficient available income to meet the requirements of IVA providers, but many people seen by the CAB do not have the level of income needed to be able to repay under an IVA plan.

15–50 In certain circumstances the CAB sees the requirements of IVA providers and some creditors setting "hurdle rates", where a debtor is required to have available income in the region of perhaps £150 to £200 a month to be able to enter into a plan.

The CAB makes the point that many of the people it sees through its doors do not have this level of income, which then leaves those debtors with the option of bankruptcy or the DRO, neither of which may be suitable or indeed available. According to CAB research, many of their advisors see people who have more than £50 a month available or debts over £15,000 a month that would put them outside of the DRO provisions. Bearing in mind that the upgraded administration order is not now likely to be introduced before 2012—if at all—this leaves people with more than £50 of surplus income but not enough income to enter into an IVA with no choice at all as to how they manage their debts. Many of these people would also have debts over £15,000, putting them outside the scope of the proposed new administration order.

Citizens Advice estimates that over 18,000 of its clients per year in the debt arena have non-priority debts alone of more than £15,000 and money for non-priority creditors of between £50 and £200 a month.

How can the government's objectives on a DMP be met?

15–51 A statutory debt management plan scheme gives a guarantee of fair protection to debtors who try to deal with their debts in a reasonable way. Section 124(1) of the TCEA 2007 states that "the operator of an approved scheme may recover its costs by charging debtors or affected creditors (or both)". The CAB certainly believes strongly that any scheme should be non-profit making if the scheme is to be fair to both debtors and creditors. In fact, it goes further and states that the only feature of the current debt management industry worth preserving is the fair share approach to debt management, which is currently used by the Consumer Credit Counselling Service and Payplan. These schemes ensure that the creditor rather than the debtor pays for debt advice and support, by returning a percentage of the payment made by the debtor to the debt management plan operator.

The debt management plan solution has arisen to meet the demand of those consumers for whom the current suite of insolvency options available is not appropriate for their financial situation. DMPs are therefore a non-statutory method for providing help and assistance for those who need structured support to repay their debts.

15–52 Although there are no firm figures for the number of DMPs currently in existence, industry estimates vary between 300,000 to over 700,000. Research by the Money Advice Trust in the government's consultation paper suggests there could be 400,000 to 560,000 plans across the whole debt management industry. It is generally accepted, though, that between 100,000 and 150,000 new DMPs come in to existence every year, which means that the total numbers set up each year are at least equal to and more likely exceed the number of debtors using the current suite in statutory schemes.

Current debt management plans

15–53 Where a DMP is the chosen course, the operator establishes income and expenditure in order to calculate the surplus income before negotiating repayment terms with creditors, which often involves the freezing or lowering of interest and other charges. This in turn allows debtors to repay their debts over time by making a single monthly repayment to the operator from disposable income. The payment is then distributed amongst the creditors until the debtor's debts are paid in full.

An indebted person can have multiple debts and may be pursued by several creditors at the same time. An agreed DMP can help to prioritise repayments and ensure that the debtor is able to pay his or her most pressing debts such as secured debts and mortgage payments.

Ideally, for the long-term sustainability of individual plans, monthly repayment offers should be made from verified surplus income which debtors can afford.

It is recognised that a suite of statutory measures already exist to support debtors who do not have the ability to repay what they owe.

In response to meeting its objectives we can expect government to push on at some point with the commencement of powers in Ch.4 of Pt 5 of TCEA 2007 to introduce statutory debt repayment plans.

15–54 If, following a consultation process, the government decides to move ahead with its proposals, the TCEA 2007 provides the statutory framework for debt repayment plans to be set up under approved debt management schemes. These schemes must:

- be open to non-business debtors (s.109(2) TCEA 2007);
- specify all of the debtor's qualifying debts (s.110(2) TCEA 2007);
- require the debtor to make repayments in respect of each of the specified debts (s.110(3) TCEA 2007);
- exclude secured debts, e.g. mortgages, hire purchase agreements (s.132 TCEA 2007);
- restrict a creditor presenting a bankruptcy petition against the debtor while the statutory debt repayment plan is in operation, unless specified in regulations or the creditor has the permission of a county court (s.115 TCEA 2007);
- restrict creditor enforcement action from the date the debtor has asked the operator of an approved debt management scheme to arrange a statutory debt repayment plan, unless specified in regulations or the creditor has the permission of a county court (s.116 TCEA 2007) and;
- stop the addition of any additional charges, for example making payment penalties, and interest from the date the debtor asked the operator of an approved debt management scheme to arrange a statutory debt repayment plan, unless specified in regulations or the creditor has permission of a county court (s.117 TCEA 2007).

15–55 In addition, statutory debt repayment plans may:

- be registered in the Register of Judgments, Orders and Fines (s.120 TCEA 2007); and
- be subject to a right by creditors to appeal to a county court about the statutory debt repayment plan being arranged, their debt being included therein or the terms of the plan (s.122 TCEA 2007).

15–56 If introduced where an approved debt management scheme operator recommended that a statutory debt repayment plan was the correct course of action, a proposal showing the date that the plan would come into force would be sent to creditors to consider. This would include details of income and expenditure and any assets the debtor might have. Enforcement action and interest would be frozen from the date that the debtor requested a statutory debt repayment plan be arranged. However, creditors would be able to take bankruptcy proceedings against the debtor until the date that the plan first came into effect.

Individual creditors will then be given time to confirm balances, discuss the terms of the plan and/or raise objections with the operator. Assuming no objections were raised, the statutory debt repayment plan would automatically come into force on the date fixed in the notice sent to creditors. At that point a notification could be sent to the Register of Judgments, Orders and Fines.

Any objections to a plan would be considered by the operator. Where a creditor's objection was rejected, the creditor would have the right to appeal to the court about the existence of a statutory plan, their debt being included therein or the terms of the plan. As with any proceedings where an appeal is made, a court fee would be payable by the creditor and it would be for the court to decide who should meet any costs incurred by the debtor, creditor and the approved debt management scheme operator. This would provide a certain amount of assurance against frivolous challenges by creditors and would also act as a further incentive for operators to ensure that the correct process had been followed and the correct decision made.

15–57 The powers set out in the TCEA 2007 would allow the legislation to prescribe the mechanism the operators could use to assess a debtor's eligibility for such a scheme. For example, this could include requiring the operator to discuss all available options (including their effects) with debtors before plans were suggested or came in to operation and that debtors would be encouraged to choose the option(s) that best met their circumstances.

A statutory scheme could also include capping fees of specified levels (though it should be recognised that this would have an impact on competition) and operators could be required to adopt specified mechanisms for assessing the ability to pay.

Taken together, these measures would provide assurance to creditors that, if adopted, a regulated debt repayment plan was the best option for a particular type of debtor and that they would as a result be repaying the maximum sustainable sum towards their debts.

15–58 Government anticipates that if such a scheme commenced, existing schemes would continue to operate as now—it would not be mandatory for operators to apply for approval and, even where they did, they would still be able to offer non-statutory plans alongside regulated plans.

In addition to the mandatory features for approved debt management schemes, the TCEA 2007 provides that further provision could be made in regulations on any or all of the areas explored in the consultation paper.

We now wait to see the outcome of the consultation by a variety of important stakeholders in the debt advice arena and to see whether government is still prepared to introduce its statutory management plan scheme as a further alternative for debtors to manage their over-indebtedness.

Chapter 16

Enforcement of Orders for Possession to Recover Land

Introductory comments

16–01 The enforcement of orders for possession to recover land is an important area of enforcing a judgment, which is now dealt with under CPR Pt 55 "Possession Claims" and Schs 1 and 2 of the old RSC and CCR Rules, where these still apply. CPR Pt 55 came in to force on October 15, 2001. This is important, as claims issued prior to October 15, 2001 are governed by the old Rules, which were in force immediately prior to the introduction of CPR Pt 55 (see Civil Procedure (Amendment) Rules 2001 (SI 2001/256) para.31).

Whether against tenants who have failed to pay their rent, squatters illegally occupying a property or eco-warriors who invade a site to protest against development, the CPR offers a response to a claimant looking to enforce the judgment or order of the court, as well as mechanisms for the defendants to ensure access to justice.

16–02 The approach to be taken in enforcing an order for possession will be defined by the nature of the proceedings for possession. Much will depend on the legislation under which possession is sought, as well as the forum in which proceedings are taken.

Again, at this point in time, the CPR has duality between business in the High Court and the county courts, which can be confusing and unhelpful to someone using the courts on an infrequent or one-off basis.

What is clear is that proceedings for possession involving a residential tenant can rarely be commenced in the High Court, and as such most court users will start proceedings in the county court local to where the property is located.

What is less clear is when the High Court can be used as a forum for proceedings. Both the Chancery and Queen's Bench Divisions have well defined procedures, and where proceedings can be brought and used in the High Court, it is likely that, due to the much lower levels of business, the way forward to an order granting possession will be swifter.

In essence, the person wishing to seek a possession order from the courts must establish the legislative basis for the action for possession, and consider whether they would like any future enforcement of the possession order to be carried out by either county court bailiffs or High Court Enforcement Officers.

Devising a checklist to enforce a possession order

16–03 To help establish how a possession action might be started, and then any order enforced, a series of questions can be devised:

Is the possession action in respect of a tenancy, licence or mortgage?	The action for possession will need to be commenced under either ss.8 or 21 of The Housing Act 1988 or The Rent Act 1977 (or previous Rent Acts) and see generally CPR Pt. 55.4.3–5	Proceedings to be commenced in the county court—with potential to transfer to the High Court for enforcement, depending on the wording of the Pt 8 claim.
Is the possession action in respect of squatters?	The action for possession will need to be commenced under CPR Pt 55 and see generally CPR 55.4.5.	Proceedings can be commenced in the county court or the High Court if the requirements of CPR Pt 55, r.3 are met. Enforcement proceedings can be transferred from the county court to the High Court under CPR Sch.2 CCR Ord. 22 r.8(1A)(b).
Is the possession action in respect of travellers?	The action for possession will need to be commenced under CPR Pt 55, as above.	Proceedings can be commenced in the county court or the High Court if the requirements of CPR Pt 55, r.3 are met. Enforcement proceedings can be transferred from the county court to the High Court under CPR Sch.2 CCR Ord. 22 r.8(1A)(b).
Is the possession action in respect of eco-warriors by way of protest?	The action for possession will need to be commenced under CPR Pt 55, as above.	Proceedings can be commenced in the county court or the High Court if the requirements of CPR Pt 55, r.3 are met. Enforcement proceedings can be transferred from the county court to the High Court under CPR Sch.2 CCR Ord. 22 r.8(1A)(b).

What is meant by a "possession claim"?

16–04 A "possession claim" is defined in CPR Pt 55.1(a) as "a claim for the recovery of possession of land (including buildings or parts of buildings)".

CPR Pt 55.1(b) goes on to define a "possession claim against trespassers" as,

> "a claim for the recovery of land which the claimant alleges is occupied only by a person or persons who entered or remained on the land without the consent of a person entitled to possession of that land, but does not include a claim against a tenant or sub-tenant whether his tenancy has been terminated or not".

The definition under CPR Pt 55 therefore includes as a trespasser a former licensee whose licence has expired or which has been validly determined.

However, the definition of "trespasser" under CPR Pt 55 *does not* include a claim against a tenant or sub-tenant, regardless of whether the tenancy has been terminated or not (CPR r.55.1(b)). The position has therefore changed since October 15, 2001, because prior to the introduction of the new Pt 55, CCR Order 24 and RSC Order 113 could be used as mechanisms to evict unlawful subtenants (see *Moore Properties (Ilford) Ltd v McKeon* [1976] 1 W.L.R. 1278, Ch D).

The meaning of "mortgage" in terms of possession claims is also defined at CPR Pt 55.1(c) to include both a legal or equitable mortgage as well as a legal or equitable charge, and "mortgagee" is interpreted accordingly.

So, Pt 55 must be used where court proceedings include a possession claim brought by a landlord, a lender or a licensor (CPR r.55.2).

Is the possession action in respect of a tenancy, licence and mortgage?

16–05 All tenancies created on or after January 29, 1989 in respect of dwellings are governed by the Housing Act 1988. Consequently, there are now relatively few tenancies governed by the Rent Act 1977 or its predecessors, so the first step is to decide if the occupier was a former tenant, licensee or mortgagee, and then decide on which procedure to follow under the CPR Pt 55 to regain possession.

The granting of a possession order always requires the exercise of judicial discretion.

In which court should a claim for possession be commenced?

16–06 In some ways this question is outside the scope of this book, which is concerned with the enforcement of the resulting order for possession. However, as will become apparent, the forum chosen for the issue of the claim for possession will influence the eventual enforcement of the order for possession, so a short rehearsal of the rules under CPR Pt 55 for the issue of the claim can be important.

The basic rule is that the claim for possession must be started in the county court for the district in which the property is situated (CPR r.55.3(1)).

However, a claimant may start a possession claim in the High Court if there are exceptional circumstances (see the Practice Direction to CPR Pt 55 at para. 2.1), e.g. where:

- there are complicated disputes of fact;
- there are points of law of general importance; or
- there is a claim against trespassers in the case of a substantial risk of public disturbance or of serious harm to persons or property that requires immediate determination.

16–07 The value of the property and the amount of the financial claim may be relevant circumstances, but they alone will not normally justify starting the claim in the High Court. The Practice Direction points out the consequences of issuing in the High Court when it is not justified. In such circumstances, courts will normally either strike out the claim or transfer it to the county court on its own initiative, which is likely to result in delay and the court will normally disallow the costs of starting the claim in the High Court and of any transfer.

High Court claims for the possession of land subject to a mortgage will be assigned to the Chancery Division of the High Court (see CPR PD55, para. 1.6).

Many court users are confused as to how the High Court can be used as a forum to adjudicate on a claim for possession, which means that many applications for claims against trespassers, or claims which involve complex issues of fact and law, can be started and then enforced in the High Court. In devising a strategy for either a single claim or a series of claims, a claimant seeking possession can take advantage of the duality of approach created within the present rules, resulting in efficiencies in time from the point of view of listing a claim, the hearing and then the eventual enforcement.

Proceedings involving persons whose occupation of the buildings or land is causing serious harm to other persons or to the land itself, or whose presence is creating a disturbance which requires immediate determination, are all potential claims which could be issued in the High Court forum.

16–08 The White Book Service deals extensively with the various statutes and types of possession proceedings at para. 45.3.4. The court user must identify the legislation governing the occupation of the premises or land, as well as reading the tenancy and/or other agreement, allowing occupation to assess how possession proceedings can be commenced and subsequently enforced.

The next sections of this chapter look at the enforcement of orders for possession in either the High Court or the county court.

High Court business—writs of possession

16–09 CPR Sch.1, RSC Order 45, r.3 is the main reference used when dealing with High Court writs of possession. References to permission are also included in RSC Order 46. All three Rules must be consulted when issuing a High Court writ of possession.

Is permission to issue a writ of possession required?

16–10 By virtue of RSC Order 45, r.3(2), a writ of possession to enforce a judgment or order for the giving of possession of any land must not be issued without the permission of the court, except where the judgment or order was given or made in proceedings by a mortgagee or mortgagor, or by any person having the right to foreclose or redeem any mortgage, being proceedings in which there is a claim for one or more of the following:

- payment of monies secured by the mortgage;
- sale of the mortgaged property;
- foreclosure;
- delivery of possession (whether before or after foreclosure, or without foreclosure) to the mortgagee by the mortgagor or by any person who is alleged to be in possession of the property;
- redemption;
- re-conveyance of the land or its release from the security;
- delivery of possession by the mortgagee.

The reasoning behind why a mortgage action does not require permission is that the position of every person in occupation is known before the order for possession is made (see *Leicester Permanent Building Society v Shearley* [1950] 2 All E.R. 738). A definition of "mortgage" follows similar wording to that set out in CPR Pt 55 at RSC Order 45, r.3(2A).

16–11 For permission for leave to issue a writ of possession, it is important to bear in mind that the following points must be dealt with in the application to seek leave for permission to issue a writ of possession. Unless shown, the court will not be willing to give its permission. It must therefore be shown that:

- "every person"—so this issue needs to be covered by the appropriate form of service,
- "in actual possession of the whole or any part of the land"—which needs to be dealt with by accurate reference to a plan of the area,
- "has received notice of the proceedings"—the rules on service need to be followed carefully,
- "to satisfy the court that the person served had sufficient information to be able to apply to the court for any relief to which he may have been entitled".

Permission to issue a writ of possession cannot be given on an interlocutory application. It can only be given to enforce a final judgment or order for possession (see All E.R. *Manchester Corp v Connolly* [1970] 2 W.L.R. 746; [1970] 1 All E.R. 961, CA).

16–12 In the Queen's Bench Division the application for permission to issue the writ of possession is made without notice, supported by evidence which must comply with the requirement of para.(3) of RSC Order 45 and see Form PF91.

Where (as often happens) the property consists of a house, of which various parts are sublet to, or in the occupation of, different persons, the evidence should show the nature and length of the notice that has been given to the various occupiers. Where the defendant or any other person is in actual possession of the premises, the evidence must contain, amongst other things, the following information:

- whether the premises or part of the premises are a dwelling house;
- if the premises are a dwelling house, what is the rateable value of the dwelling house and is it let furnished or unfurnished;
- if the dwelling house is let as furnished, what is the amount of furniture within the property;
- and include any other matters which will assist the Master in determining whether any occupier is protected by the Rent Acts (*Practice Direction (Q.B.D. Writ of Possession)* [1955] 1 W.L.R. 1314; [1955] 3 All E.R. 646).

Permission is required to issue a writ of possession on a suspended order for possession.

Does notice of the proceedings for permission need to be given?

16–13 Basically, the answer is "yes". Where the defendant is the only person in possession of the premises, the claimant must give the defendant notice of the judgment or order, and "call upon him" to give up possession under that judgment or order.

Does notice of the proceedings need to be served?

16–14 Where the defendant is the only person in possession of the premises, the claimant will be required to give the defendant notice of the judgment or order.

Where there are other people who are not parties to the proceedings in actual possession of the premises or land, then it is also necessary to serve them with written notice, which will give them a reasonable opportunity to apply to the court.

The combined effect of RSC Orders 45 and 46 is that notice of an application for a writ of possession must be given to a tenant, and the writ of execution should not be issued without the tenant having an opportunity to apply to the court for relief (see *Leicester City Council v Aldwinkle, The Times*, April 5, 1991, CA).

However, the need to serve notice of the claimant's intention to seek possession does not confer any new rights on a tenant or other occupier. The only effect of the notice is to give those who may apply for relief an opportunity to do so.

Can a writ of possession enforce a money judgment?

16–15 A writ of possession may include provision for enforcing the payment of any money adjudged or ordered to be paid by the judgment or order which is to be enforced by the writ—see RSC Order 45, r.3(4).

How is a county court order for possession transferred to the high court for enforcement?

16–16 A county court order for possession against trespassers can be transferred to the High Court for enforcement using HCEOs as the court officers responsible for the enforcement of the writ of possession.

The transfer procedure follows a process similar to that used for a money judgment, in that the claimant applies to the local county court, which made the order for possession, for a certificate of judgment on form N.293A, seeking confirmation that the order for possession is still outstanding. The county court staff complete and seal the form, which is then returned to the claimant who must complete the reverse which then becomes the praecipe to the actual writ of possession.

The writ of possession form is then completed using Form 66A and is sent to the High Court or District Registry for sealing and onward transmission to the local HCEO. A court fee will be payable on the sealing of the High Court writ of possession.

There is no requirement to seek leave to transfer the enforcement of the writ of possession to the High Court.

How is a High Court writ of possession prepared following a High Court judgment?

16–17 Where the claim was issued in the High Court, the resulting judgment or order is enforceable by a High Court writ of possession. The claimant must complete Form 66 together with the form of praecipe in Form 86. A court fee will be payable on the sealing of the writ of possession. Current court fees can be found at *http://www.hmcs.gov.uk* [Accessed October 19, 2010]. A writ of possession can be combined with the enforcement of a money judgment by way of a combined writ of fi fa and possession.

Once issued, the claimant needs to deliver the sealed writ of possession to the HCEO of choice, ready for enforcement.

As a matter of best practice, if the enforcement is likely to require planning, police support and has health and safety considerations, it is better to plan the eviction with the HCEO of choice to ensure time in planning the expulsion is minimised. Police support can be called upon under The Courts Act 2003, Sch.7, para.5, which provides assistance to an Authorised High Court Enforcement Officer in the execution of a writ.

How does a writ of restitution aid a writ of possession?

16–18 Turning to the note to RSC Order 46 at para.46.3.1, in practice the writ of restitution is the most commonly used writ "in aid of any other writ of execution". Permission to issue a writ "in aid of" another needs to be applied for without notice supported by evidence, usually in the form of an affidavit sworn by someone with knowledge of the relevant facts.

The old RSC Order 113 was, of course, repealed with the introduction of CPR Pt 55. The only remaining provision is RSC Order 113, r.7, which provides for the issue of writs of possession to enable landowners to evict trespassers who have moved back in to premises or on to land after the execution of a writ of possession. This procedure can only be used if there is a "close nexus" between the new occupiers and any people who were dispossessed in the earlier proceedings. If the further occupation is "part and parcel of the same transaction" (see *Wiltshire CC v Frazer* (Writ of Restitution) [1986] 1 W.L.R. 109; [1986] 1 All E.R 65 per Simon Brown J.), the landowner is entitled to apply—without notice—for a warrant of restitution in the county court or a writ of restitution in the High Court.

The effect of a writ of restitution is most commonly used to enable the High Court Enforcement Officer to evict any person in unlawful occupation of premises—again, without the landowner having to issue new proceedings. A writ of restitution may be issued even though not all of the new occupiers of the land were among the original defendants.

16–19 Where, after entry of the enforcement officer under a writ of possession, or after the claimant has been put in possession by the enforcement officer, the defendant resumes possession of the property, either by force or some other strategy, the claimant may apply for a writ of restitution (*Pitcher v Roe* (1841) 9 Dowl 971) to be issued. This is the normal procedure and not an application to commit for contempt (*Alliance Building Society v Austen* [1951] 2 All E.R. 1068). Application for the writ should be made without notice to a Master supported by evidence such as a witness statement or affidavit of facts, after which an order will be made for the writ to be issued. The writ then needs to be directed to the HCEO of choice to ensure that the subsequent eviction can take place as soon as practicable.

Conversely, where a claimant has evicted a defendant under a writ of possession, and the underlying order for possession is subsequently set aside but the defendant is unable to regain possession, the defendant can apply to the Master for an order setting aside the writ of possession and ordering possession to be given by the claimant to the defendant. Permission may be given at the time of this hearing or subsequently, on a without notice application, to issue a writ of restitution.

Similarly, where possession has been obtained under an irregular writ of possession, or of more land than is properly covered by the writ of possession, then the defendant can apply for an order to set aside the writ of possession and, if unable to restore possession, to make an application for possession to be given and for a writ of restitution to be issued.

What costs are allowed on the issue of a writ of possession?

16–20 Under CPR Pt 45.5 fixed costs are allowed on the issue of a writ of possession as set out in the rules, which should be consulted by reference to an up-to-date reference such as *http://www.hmcs.gov.uk* [Accessed October 19, 2010] or *http://www.justice.gov.uk/rules* [Accessed October 19, 2010].

Is an order for possession enforceable by way of committal or sequestration?

16–21 A judgment or order to give possession of land will not be enforceable by an order of committal or by way of sequestration, unless it specifies the time within which the possession is to be given and the defendant refuses or neglects to give possession within that time. Therefore, as a judgment or order to give possession of land will not in practice specify the time within which the act of possession is required to be done (see RSC Order 42, r.2(2)), a judgment or order for possession will not usually be enforceable by an order of committal or by writ of sequestration, leaving just the better known writ of possession as the standard course of action to enforce the order for possession.

If the situation does arise, however, in a severe case of non-compliance, and a claimant wishes to enforce the order for possession against a recalcitrant defendant by an order of committal or order of sequestration, then the claimant will need to apply to the court under RSC Order 45, r.6 for an order to fix the time for possession, with which the defendant must comply to avoid being subject to either committal or sequestration. Such an order will need to be served on the defendant under RSC Order 45, r.7, followed by a further application under RSC Order 45, r.5 for an order of committal under RSC Order 52.

What form does the writ of possession need to be in?

16–22 The writ of possession takes two forms:

- a writ of possession to recover land—Form 66—set out in the Appendix;
- a writ of possession combined with a writ of fieri facias—Form 53—to recover land and any connected judgment for the payment of money—usually in the form of rent arrears or dilapidations.

The writ of possession contains a recital of the judgment or order that the defendant "do give" to the claimant possession of the land which is the subject of the order. The writ itself must therefore contain a description of the property of which possession is to be given. The wording of the description of the land needs to be specific, as the rules warn against generality. Essentially, a plan is the best way to describe the land for which possession is required, perhaps linked to a title number held at H M Land Registry, or an Ordnance Survey map reference so that the land can be staked out where it consists of open land such as a field, heath or common (and see *Thynne v Sarl* [1891] 2 Ch. 79).

Is a form of "return" required for a writ of possession?

16–23 There is no requirement on a High Court Enforcement Officer to make a "return" to the outcome of the execution of a writ of possession, but an HCEO is directed within the writ of possession to,

> "endorse it immediately after execution with a statement of the manner in which he has executed it and to send a copy of such statement to the claimant".

In practice, HCEOs will require a representative of the claimant organisation to be present at the time possession is handed over, to "sign off" possession of the land and to confirm that possession has been given to the satisfaction of the claimant.

The endorsement of the writ of possession is a mere formality of procedure and is not necessary in order to complete a seizure under the writ (*Rea v Hobson* [1886] 33 Ch. D. 493).

How is a writ of possession issued in the Queen's Bench Division of the High Court?

16–24 An application for permission to issue a writ of possession in the Queen's Bench Division is made without notice supported by evidence which must comply with the requirements of para.(3) of Practice Form 91.

Where (as often happens) the property to be repossessed consists of a house which has been sublet, the claimant will need to set out in evidence the nature and length of each occupant's occupation and the length of notice given to each occupier.

Where the defendant or any other person is in actual possession of the premises, the evidence must also contain the following information:

- whether the property or any part of it is a dwelling house;
- if the property is a dwelling house, the rateable value of the dwelling house and whether it is let furnished or unfurnished, and, if furnished, the amount of furniture within the property—for a site giving details of how to calculate rateable values, see *http://www.ofwat.gov.uk/faq/watercompanieschargesfaqs/prs.faq.watercharge.co.uk* [Accessed November 16, 2010]
- any other matters which will assist the Master in determining whether any occupier is protected by the Rent Acts (*Practice Direction* (*QBD; Writ of Possession*) [1955] 1 W.L.R. 1314; [1955] 3 All E.R. 646).

Can a writ of possession be stayed?

16–25 The court has no power to grant a stay of execution to a writ of possession, as against a trespasser. A stay of execution against a former tenant or service occupier will normally be limited to between four to six weeks (see *McPhail v Persons, Names Unknown* [1973] Ch. 447, CA). However, in a serious and substantial dispute between the parties, a period of three months or even longer may be granted (see *Bain & Co v Church Commissioners for England* [1989] 1 W.L.R. 24).

What is the position in relation to a claim for possession against a company?

16–26 In the course of winding up proceedings, the Companies Court has jurisdiction to make an order for possession against a company where there is no defence to the claim for the forfeiture of the lease.

However, the Companies Court has no jurisdiction to entertain an application by a sub-tenant or mortgagee for relief and forfeiture under s.146 of the Law of Property Act 1925, as the winding up proceedings are not an "action", and therefore applications for relief and/or forfeiture have to be applied for by separate proceedings (see *Re Blue Jean Sales Limited* [1979] 1 W.L.R. 362).

What is the position if there is a wrongful or irregular execution of a writ of possession?

16–27 HCEOs executing a judgment by evicting the occupiers, however wrong the judgment or however they may be mistaken as to its effect, are not liable in an action for damages.

A landlord will also not be rendered liable by simply being present at the time of the eviction (see *Williams v Williams* [1937] 2 All E.R. 559, CA).

What happens if the defendant is in the armed forces?

16–28 If the defendant is a member of the armed forces, and the case is covered by the Reserve and Auxiliary Forces (Protection of Civil Interests) Act 1951, a judgment or order for recovery of possession of land in default of payment of rent can be enforced without the leave of the court (see s.2(3) of the 1951 Act). As stated in the White Book Service 2010, this section may be of particular relevance given the Government's policy of using the Territorial Army on active service.

County court business—warrants of possession

16–29 County court warrants of possession are far more prevalent than their High Court counterparts. As in the High Court, a claimant has to identify the nature of the defendants against whom an order for possession is sought. Are they tenants/licensees/mortgagors, or are they squatters/travellers or eco-warriors? Depending on the nature of the trespasser, the county court rule which applies will either be:

- CPR Sch.2, CCR Order 24 dealing with summary possession proceedings involving land; or
- CPR Sch.2, CCR Order 26 dealing with ordinary possession actions and which supplements the possession rules prescribed under CPR Pt 55.

Is leave needed to issue a warrant of possession?

16–30 The county court rules follow RSC Order 46 in providing for cases in which permission to issue a warrant of possession is required. The issue of a warrant without the necessary permission is an abuse of process (see *Hackney London Borough Council v White* (1995) 28 H.L.R. 219, *The Times*, May 17, 1995, CA).

Where is the starting point for county court rules on the enforcement of orders for possession?

16–31 CPR Sch.2, CCR Order 26, r.17 is the starting point for enforcement rules remaining in the county court for the enforcement of orders for possession.

A judgment or order of the county court for the recovery of land is enforceable by a warrant of possession (CCR Order 26, r.17(1)).

A person requiring a warrant of possession to be issued needs to make a request for a warrant on form N325, which must certify that the land that is the subject of the order has not been vacated, in accordance with the judgment or order directing that possession be given (CCR Order 26, r.17(2)).

A judgment creditor in issuing a warrant of possession is entitled by the same warrant or separately to execution against the judgment debtor's goods for any sum payable under a money judgment (CCR Order 26, r.17(3)).

If the request for the warrant for possession includes enforcement of a money judgment, or where an order for possession has been suspended on terms as to the payment of a sum of money by instalments (such as payment of rent arrears), the judgment creditor when making his request for a warrant of possession must certify:

- the amount of money remaining due under the judgment or order; and
- the whole or part of any instalment due remains unpaid.

(See CCR Order 26, r.17(3A)).

16–32 Overall, this rule may be compared with RSC Order 45, r.3. The rule does not repeat a former provision that a warrant of possession might be issued after the expiration of the day on which the defendant was ordered to give possession or, if no day had been fixed for this purpose, after the expiration of 14 days from the day on which judgment was given.

In practice, except in squatters' cases, a judgment for possession always specifies the day on which possession is to be given (which is to be contrasted with the High Court procedure).

What is the usual form of judgment?

16–33 The usual form of judgment in a claim for the recovery of land is that the claimant do recover possession of the land and that the defendant gives possession on a specified day. This is so, even in a mortgage action, where the claimant has never been in possession of the land. In cases under CCR Order, 24 however, unless the court exercises any power it has to order possession to be given on a specified day, the order will simply be that the claimant recovers possession of the land, and in that event a warrant of possession may be issued at any time after the making of the order (see CCR Order 24, r.6(1)).

If, of course, a day is specified, a warrant cannot be issued until after that day (see CCR Order 24, r.6(3)).

Is leave required in the county court?

16–34 A county court warrant for possession may not be issued without leave more than six years after the order for possession. The obtaining of a warrant after this time without leave is an abuse of process, which cannot be cured by the application of CPR 3.10 and entitles the defendant to have the warrant set aside under the principles set out in *Hammersmith and Fulham London Borough Council v Hill* (1995) 27 H.L.R. 368, CA and *Hackney London Borough Council v White* (1996) 28 H.L.R. 219, *The Times*, May 17, 1995 CA. It is not necessarily an abuse of process to apply for and execute a warrant of possession when the defendant is absent from the premises because of ill health (see *Leicester City Council v Aldwinkle* (1992) 24 H.L.R. 40, CA).

A warrant of possession obtained and executed without fault on the part of the landlord or the court could not properly be set aside as an abuse of process or an oppressive act within the *Aldwinkle* principle—see *Jephson Homes Housing Association v Moisejevs* [2001] 2 All E.R. 901; 33 H.L.R. 594, CA (where Simon Brown L.J. observed that the advancing of the European Convention on Human Rights contentions added "nothing of substance to the appellant's case").

What form is used for a county court warrant of possession?

16–35 Form N325 is the request for the warrant of possession, and N49 is the actual form of warrant of possession. N50 completes the trio as the warrant of restitution, which may still be used. It should be noted that in both the High Court and county court forums the direction "forthwith" means "as soon as practicable" (see *Six Arlington Street Investments Ltd v Persons Unknown* [1987] 1 W.L.R. 188 involving the execution of a writ of possession by a Sheriff).

What happens if an eviction is carried out without a warrant of possession?

16–36 By virtue of CCR Order 26, r.17(3), a claimant cannot enforce an order for the recovery of land other than by a warrant of possession issued under CCR Order 26 in the county court. Therefore, a statutory tenant against whom an order for possession has been made cannot lawfully be evicted other than by execution of a warrant by the bailiff (see *Haniff v Robinson* [1993] Q.B. 419; [1993] 1 All E.R. 185, CA.

Does CCR Order 26 cover any order for possession?

16–37 CCR Order 26 appears to enable any order for possession to be effected by the issue of a warrant of possession, which requires the defendant to give possession of land to a claimant including, for example:

- an order under Pt IV of the Family Law Act 1996 terminating a spouse's rights of occupation;
- prohibiting the exercise by either spouse of his or her right to occupy the matrimonial home;
- an order excluding a spouse from the matrimonial home.

(See also *Danchevsky v Danchevsky* [1975] Fam. 17; [1974] 3 All E.R. 934, CA, *Larkman v Lindsell* [1989] Fam. Law 229, CA, and *C v C (Contempt: Committal)* [1989] Fam. Law 477).

For the authority of the court's general jurisdiction in actions for the recovery of land, see s.21 County Courts Act 1984.

If an order for possession is made which is found to be totally indeterminate, as was the position in the case of *Kidder v Birch* (1981–82) 5 H.L.R. 28; (1983) 46 P. & C.R. 362; CA, then it is likely the order will be amended so that it can be carried out. In the case of *Kidder v Birch* the order read that "the claimant do recover possession but that the warrant do lie in the office until the death of a named person". The order was amended so as to become operative only if the named person died within 12 months.

What notice has to be given regarding the issue of a warrant for possession?

16–38 The issue of a warrant of possession is an administrative, not a judicial act and the issue of a warrant without prior notice to the tenant does not amount to a breach of the tenant's rights under the European Convention of Human Rights.

It was found in the case of *St Brice v Southwark London Borough Council* [2001] EWCA Civ 1138; [2002] 1 W.L.R. 1537, that it was important that the tenant should receive notice of the eviction in Form N54 in time to enable an application to be made to the court. However, the imposition on the tenant of the burden of making the application did not amount to a breach of the tenant's ECHR rights.

In respect of a mortgagee seeking possession of a property via a warrant of possession, the Mortgage Repossessions (Protection of Tenants etc) Act 2010 shall apply. This act is described in its preamble as:

> "An Act to protect persons whose tenancies are not binding on mortgagees and to require mortgagees to give notice of the proposed execution of possession orders".

16–39 The court can seek to postpone the delivery up of possession on the application by a tenant for a period not exceeding two months (see s.1(2)), when a mortgagee under a mortgage is seeking possession of a dwelling house of the mortgaged property, and there is an unauthorised tenancy relating to that property (see s.1(1)). An unauthorised tenancy is defined as an assured tenancy (within the meaning of the Housing Act 1988) or a protected or statutory tenancy (within the meaning of the Rent Act 1977), see s.1(8).

A mortgagee is required to give notice to the tenant of the unauthorised tenancy of the execution of the order for possession; the notice period is governed by the Dwelling Houses (Execution of Possession Order by Mortgagees) Regulations 2010 and is currently 14 days. The notice should be given upon application by the mortgagee for a warrant of possession (see s.2 of the Mortgage Repossessions (Protection of Tenants etc.) Act 2010 and regs 2 and 3 of the Dwelling Houses (Execution of Possession Order by Mortgagees) Regulations 2010). The commencement date for the Mortgage Repossessions (Protection of Tenants etc.) Act 2010 and the Dwelling Houses (Execution of Possession Order by Mortgagees) Regulations 2010) is October 1, 2010.

How is a county court warrant for possession executed?

16–40 The execution of a warrant of possession issuing from the county court differs somewhat from the execution of a writ of possession issuing from the High Court, under which it is considered that the writ is not completely executed until all persons and goods on the premises have been removed.

Section 111(1) of the County Courts Act 1984 provides that, for the purpose of executing a warrant to give possession of any premises, it is not necessary to remove any goods or chattels from the premises which are the subject of the warrant.

The bailiff enforcing a warrant of possession is entitled to evict any person found on the premises, even though that person was not a party to the proceedings for possession (see *R v Wandsworth County Court, Ex p. Wandsworth LBC* [1975] 1 W.L.R. 1314; [1975] 3 All E.R. 390, DC). This decision would appear to apply whether the proceedings have been brought under CCR Order 24 or in the usual way (and see also *Wiltshire County Council v Frazer* [1986] 1 W.L.R. 109; [1986] 1 All E.R. 65, where it was held that a warrant of restitution will issue to recover land from occupants who were neither parties to the original proceedings nor dispossessed by the order, provided that there was a plain and sufficient nexus between the order for possession and the need to effect further recovery of the same land. This decision was followed in the case of *Lambeth London Borough Council v Guyt* [1986] C.L.Y. 464).

If a person on the premises claims to have some right against the claimant to remain there, he should apply to be added as a defendant under CPR 19.3, and if he fails to take this step after being given a reasonable opportunity to do so, the bailiff may evict him. Although the warrant requires the bailiff to give possession of the land to the claimant "forthwith", his duty is to execute "as soon as reasonably practicable" (see *Six Arlington Street Investments Ltd v Persons Unknown* [1987] 1 W.L.R. 188, involving the execution of a writ of possession by a Sheriff).

How long does a county court warrant of possession last?

16–41 By s.111(2) of the County Courts Act 1984:

> "The duration of any warrant of possession issued by a county court to enforce a judgment or order for the recovery of land or for the delivery of possession of land shall be such as may be fixed by or in accordance with county court rules."

CCR Order 26, r.6 provides for an unexecuted warrant to remain in force for one year, and then subject to renewal, year by year, by leave of the court.

There is special and separate provision in relation to a warrant of possession against trespassers in proceedings to which CPR Pt 55 applies. No warrant of possession shall be issued after the expiry of three months from the date of the order (see CCR Order 24, r.6(2)).

What is the county court equivalent of a writ of restitution?

16–42 CCR Order 26, r.17(4) and (5) make provision for the recovery of possession of land where wrongful re-entry on the land has been made following eviction by warrant of possession, whether in an ordinary claim or in proceedings under CCR Order 24. The procedure by warrant of restitution is analogous to the writ of restitution available in the High Court.

What power of committal does the county court have?

16–43 Where a defendant resists the execution of a warrant for possession by a bailiff, the most appropriate step would be for a contempt application to be issued based on the defendant's obstruction of the bailiff. However, in some cases, it would be right for a contempt application to be based on the non-compliance with the possession order itself. In such a case, it would be sensible for a copy of the possession order to be served endorsed with a penal notice, although the court has power to dispense with such a service (see *Bell v Tuohy* [2002] EWCA Civ 423; [2002] 1 W.L.R. 2703; [2002] 3 All E.R. 975, CA).

What is the effect of setting aside a warrant of possession?

16–44 An order for possession and any warrant issued thereunder may be set aside by the court, even after execution of the warrant, if:

- the order on which it is based is also set aside (see *Peabody Donation Fund Governors v Hay* (1987) 19 H.L.R. 145, CA; or
- the warrant has been obtained by fraud; or
- there has been an abuse of process or oppression in its execution: *Hammersmith and Fulham London Borough Council v Hill* (1995) 27 H.L.R. 368, CA.

In the case of *Cheltenham and Gloucester Building Society v Obi* (1996) 28 H.L.R. 22, CA, the entitlement of a former tenant to housing benefit may be a relevant consideration on an application for the suspension of a warrant for possession (also see *Haringey LBC v Powell* (1996) 28 H.L.R. 798, CA).

Once a warrant of possession has been executed it was found to be too late for the borrower's wife to apply for reinstatement (see *Mortgage Agency Services v Bal* [1998] 95 (28) L.S.G. 31, CA).

16–45 In the case of *Circle 33 Housing Trust Ltd v Ellis* [2005] EWCA Civ 1233; [2006] H.L.R. 7 a housing association that obtained a possession order on the grounds of arrears of rent, and issued a warrant for eviction, was not found guilty of "oppressive" conduct due to a number of factors peculiar to the case. Although in the case it subsequently appeared that the tenant should have been entitled to housing benefit throughout the period of the tenancy, the court rejected the argument that the order and warrant should be set aside because the landlord's conduct had been "oppressive". The statutory guidance directing a housing association to liaise with the housing benefit department before taking enforcement action, a direction that was deemed to be an express term of the tenancy agreement, was found to have been satisfied given that the landlord had been told by the housing benefit department that entitlement to benefit had ceased, and given also that the tenant failed to attend a pre-eviction meeting with his housing officer.

What are the issues surrounding "oppression" and "human rights" in the execution of county court warrants of possession?

16–46 The case law and examples of a changing political climate for the enforcement of these types of judgments and orders is apparent in the county court, where the numbers of cases are far greater than the High Court.

The issue of oppression has been the subject of a number of cases in recent years. "Oppression" itself has been defined as the insistence of a public authority on its strict rights in circumstances which make that insistence manifestly unfair (see *Southwark LBC v Sarfo* [1999] CLY 3705, CA, following *Barking and Dagenham LBC v Saint* (1999) 31 H.L.R. 620). However, even if oppression is proved it does not make the setting aside of the warrant of possession mandatory, as the court has to exercise its discretion.

Oppression may take the form of the giving by the court staff of misleading information which deprives a defendant of the opportunity to have the execution of a warrant stayed (see *Hammersmith and Fulham LBC v Lemeh* (2001) 33 H.L.R. 23; (2000) 80 P. & C.R. D25, CA).

However, there is no "oppression" to justify setting aside unless there is some unfair use of court procedures, so a reduction of the arrears made by the tenant in the mistaken belief that it would prevent eviction under the order is insufficient ground for setting aside a warrant (see *Jephson Homes Housing Association v Moisejev* [2001] 2 All E.R. 901; (2001) 33 H.L.R. 54, CA).

16–47 On the issue of human rights, the issue of the warrant for possession is no more than an administrative act to give effect to a judicial decision. The tenant's rights under the ECHR are considered at a trial, and separate determination of those rights arises on the issue of the warrant (see *St Brice v Southwark LBC* [2001] EWCA Civ 1138; [2002] 1 W.L.R. 1537).

How is a county court order for possession set aside?

16–48 The case of *Leicester City Council v Aldwinckle* (1992) 24 H.L.R. 40, CA set out the circumstances in which a county court order for possession could be set aside. That case set the precedent that notice of the application for a warrant of possession must be given to the tenant, and the warrant or writ of possession (in the case of the High Court) cannot be issued without the tenant having an opportunity to apply to the court for relief.

In the case of *Hammersmith and Fulham LBC v Hill* (1995) 27 H.L.R. 368; (1994) 91 (22) L.S.G. 35, CA, where a tenant was evicted from a secure tenancy without notice of a warrant for possession, it was held that the warrant of possession could only be suspended or set aside in the circumstances set out in *Leicester City Council v Aldwinckle* (1992) 24 H.L.R. 40, CA.

How is a warrant of possession stayed in the county court?

16–49 In the High Court there is no provision for the stay of a writ of possession.

In the county court, where mortgagees obtain a warrant for possession to enforce their security by sale "forthwith" and the mortgagor proposes to apply to the High Court under the Law of Property Act 1925, s.91(2) to enable him to sell the property in due course, on an application by the mortgagor a county court has no jurisdiction to stay the execution of the warrant (*Cheltenham and Gloucester Plc v Krausz* [1997] 1 W.L.R. 1558; [1997] 1 All E.R. 21, CA). In light of the Mortgage Repossessions (Protection of Tenants etc.) Act 2010 and the Dwelling Houses (Execution of Possession Order by Mortgagees) Regulations 2010) a tenant will be served with a notice in the prescribed form set out in the Dwelling Houses (Execution of Possession Order by Mortgagees) Regulations 2010, which will enable the tenant an opportunity to apply for a stay of the warrant of possession.

16–50 Where the court has power, under s.36 of the Administration of Justice Act 1970 and s.8 of the Administration of Justice Act 1973, to allow the mortgagor a "reasonable period" to pay sums due under the mortgage, in the absence of unusual circumstances the outstanding term of the mortgage is the starting point in determining how long it would be reasonable to keep a mortgage (see *Western Bank Ltd v Schindler* [1977] Ch. 1 and *Cheltenham and Gloucester Building Society v Norgan* [1996] 1 W.L.R. 343). There is no rule that, for example, all arrears must be paid off within four years. Neither is there a rule that, where the mortgage is to be repaid by reselling the property, a warrant can only be suspended if a sale will take place within a short period of time. Thus, if there is evidence that completion of a sale could take place in six or nine months or even a year, the court may conclude that the mortgagor was "likely to be able within a reasonable period to pay any sums due under the mortgage" as per *National and Provincial Building Society v Lloyd* [1996] 1 All E.R. 630). However, where there is insufficient evidence to show that either the mortgagor could sell the property within three to five years or that the proceeds would be sufficient to discharge the mortgage debt, a warrant should not be suspended, as per *Bristol and West Building Society v Ellis* (1997) 29 H.L.R. 282; (1997) 73 P. & C.R. 158, CA).

What is the procedure for summary possession of land in the county court?

16–51 Under CPR Sch., CCR Order 24 r.6, a warrant of possession to enforce an order for possession in a possession claim against trespassers under CPR Pt 55 may be issued at any time after the making of the order and subject to the provisions of Order 26, r.17, (as above), a warrant of restitution may be issued in aid of the warrant of possession.

A warrant of possession cannot be issued after the expiry of three months from the date of the order without the permission of the court. An application for permission may be made without notice being served on any other party unless directed otherwise by the court.

However, a warrant for possession cannot be issued before any date for possession is given in the court's order.

The form to be used is form N52 (warrant of possession), and N51 (warrant of restitution) may still be used.

16–52 The warrant of possession under CCR Order 24 is effective against all occupiers, and it is not incumbent on a landlord to bring proceedings against every occupier of the premises, even if one such occupant is the husband or wife of the tenant (see *Thompson v Elmbridge Borough Council* [1987] 1 W.L.R. 1425, CA). In *R v Wandsworth County Court, Ex p. Wandsworth LBC* [1975] 3 All E.R. 390 it was held that the bailiff enforcing the warrant of possession was entitled to evict anyone he found on the premises, even though that person was not a party to the proceedings for possession.

A warrant of restitution is permissible subject to the rules in CCR Order 26 r.17.

Chapter 17

Ecclesiastical Executions

Introductory comments

17–01 In essence, this chapter deals with the enforcement of a judgment against a clergyman. It is an extremely rare procedure.

Despite its rarity, the CPR provides for the possibility that every so often a member of the clergy may owe a judgment debt which has to be enforced, with a writ being directed to the Bishop of the diocese.

The procedure is set out in Sch.2 to the Civil Procedure Rules under RSC Order 47, r.5, which refers to a "*Writ of Fieri Facias De Bonis Ecclesiastics*, etc".

The Tribunals, Courts and Enforcement Act 2007 does refer to this form of writ in Pt 3 at s.62, where reference is made to enforcement by taking control of goods. However, in relation to writs of fieri facias de bonis ecclesiasticis, the commentary to the Act describes these forms of writ as "unique", and due to the special role of the bishop in the enforcement process they are not to be renamed or to be the subject of the new unified procedure detailed in Sch.12 of the TCEA 2007.

History of this type of enforcement

17–02 An examination of the history of canon law sheds light on the approach taken to enforce against a member of the clergy or, as properly termed, a "beneficed clergyman", better known as a "vicar" or "rector".

The enforcement of a writ against a member of the clergy continues to be the responsibility of the clergyman's Bishop. For that reason there has to be a mechanism within the Civil Procedure Rules (as there has under the previous rules of court to allow a Bishop to handle the execution of a writ against a clergyman should the need arise).

A beneficed clergyman has a freehold in a parish and lives in the freehold for at least nine months of the year, unless he chooses to resign or is removed from office by due process of law for his disability or for a specified offence. He may live outside of the parish if he gets a licence from the Bishop to do so, and his widow may remain in the parsonage house for two months after his death. Parochial clergy fall into two categories: beneficed and unbeneficed. A beneficed position is a freehold office, the holder of which is known as the "incumbent", who may also be styled "rector" or "vicar". The incumbent is said to be a corporation sole and has a freehold interest in the emoluments of the benefice until retirement or vacation of the benefice.

Initial steps to enforce a judgment

17–03 To initiate enforcement, the judgment creditor issues a writ of fi fa against the judgment debtor—in this instance the beneficed clergyman or woman. It is possible that the status of the clergyman or woman will not be known at the outset of the execution when the writ of fi fa is sent to the High Court Enforcement Officer.

If the judgment debtor is then found to be a beneficed clergy, i.e. a rector or a vicar, or the judgment creditor knew that the judgment debtor held such a position, the High Court Enforcement Officer must make a special return. This follows the form of a no goods return (widely known as a *nulla bona*). This special return also certifies that the judgment debtor has no "lay fee" and gives the full status of the beneficed clergy, i.e. that he is a rector, vicar, etc. (the name and position of the beneficed clergy must be stated in the return (see *Regina v Powell* (1836) 1 M&W 321)). Obviously, the High Court Enforcement Officer will need to make full enquiries with the church authorities to establish the position of the judgment debtor for the purposes of making the return. The website of the Anglican Church at *http://www.cofe.anglican.org* [Accessed October 19, 2010] may well provide a starting point for verifying whether a judgment debtor is a bona fide member of the clergy in England and Wales.

If the clergyman is in receipt of a lay fee or is not the incumbent of the benefice, then execution must proceed by way of ordinary writ of fi fa and not the *writ of fieri facias de bonis ecclesiastics*.

Application for leave to issue a writ of fieri facias de bonis ecclesiastics

17–04 Once the High Court Enforcement Officer has made the special return as outlined above, the judgment creditor will need to seek leave to issue the *writ of fieri facias de bonis ecclesiastics* so as to renew the execution against the benefice clergy. The application is made under CPR Pt 23, without notice to a Practice Master, together with a witness statement in support as provided under RSC Order 46, r.4. The application need not be served on the beneficed clergy unless directed by the court.

17–05 In the application in support of permission to issue the writ, RSC Order 46, r.4 sets out a series of requirements for the witness statement or affidavit, which need to be included as follows:

- the judgment or order to which the application relates needs to be identified;
- if the judgment or order is for the payment of money, the evidence must state the amount originally due under the judgment or order and the amount due at the date the application notice is filed (i.e. allowing for interest, costs, etc.);
- the evidence must also set out other information necessary to satisfy the court that the applicant (i.e. the judgment creditor) is entitled to proceed with the execution of the judgment or order in question;
- and finally, it must be established that the person against whom it is sought to issue execution is liable to execution as a beneficed clergy.

If satisfied with the evidence, the court may grant permission in accordance with the application or it may order that any other issue or question which requires a decision to determine the rights of the party be tried, and may impose other terms as to costs, interest, etc. as it thinks just.

However, once leave is granted, the *writ of fieri facias de bonis ecclesiastics* will be issued in the Action Department of the Central Office. A *praecipe* will be required. The form of writ is Form No.58. As required under RSC Order 47, r.5(2) the writ must be delivered to the Bishop, to be executed by him within the diocese where the beneficed clergy is situated.

If the benefice is vacant, then the writ to the Bishop has to be directed to the Archbishop of the relevant province.

Execution of the writ by the Bishop

17–06 A Bishop will execute the *writ de bonis ecclesiastics* in the same manner as a High Court Enforcement Officer would execute a corresponding lay writ of fi fa. Warrants are issued to the Bishop's enforcement officers. The Bishop, who probably does not have enforcement officers at his immediate disposal, may well delegate the enforcement to appointed Authorised High Court Enforcement Officers.

As provided under RSC Order 47, r.5(3) the Bishop is only entitled to take such fees, or allowed by or under any enactment including any measure of the General Synod of the Church of England.

Following the execution of the writ, the Bishop must make a return, which sets out an account of the sums received. There is provision for the incumbent to make an application for a Master to deal with deductions made in the Bishop's account (see *Dawson v Symonds* [1848] 12 Q.B. 830).

Effect of changes to High Court enforcement

17–07 The High Court Enforcement Officers Regulations 2004, which came into force on March 15, 2004, expressly state under para.2(2)(b) that a writ of execution does not include a writ relating to ecclesiastical property.

In the Government's review of enforcement, and in particular the review in relation to High Court enforcement published by the Department of Constitutional Affairs in July 2003, the enforcement of ecclesiastical writs was discussed. It was stated that the enforcement of these special writs against clergyman, which were very rare, would continue to be the responsibility of the clergyman's Bishop.

Chapter 18

Enforcement in Family Matters

Introductory comments

18–01 Perhaps one of the most sensitive areas relating to enforcement is where there is a breakdown in the family relationship and the system of enforcement is relied upon to compel payment. The enforcement process can take place between spouses, partners in a relationship and between spouses/partners and their children.

At the time of writing this book, the jurisdiction of the courts in England and Wales is experiencing the effect of a severe economic recession, which has hit the whole of the United Kingdom. As a result, the need to compel payments to either spouse or child maintenance is going to be more relevant, and for this reason we aim to address this new area of enforcement law within the current edition of this book.

The aim of this chapter is to therefore identify when the enforcement of an agreement or order involving a family matter may be necessary, and how this will impact on the parties to the action.

The nature of family proceedings

18–02 Under the Matrimonial Causes Act 1973, the court has power to make financial orders in relation to both the income and capital of the parties. Ultimately, either spouse may be looking for an ancillary relief order to meet their financial requirements in accordance with this well established legislation. The basis of the criteria for such an order is outside the scope of this book; however, ultimately, an order will be made by the court based on the evidence before it as to how the assets of the marriage are to be divided. That order may lead to reliance on one of the court based enforcement methods to bring it to fruition for payment of either capital and/or income.

The form of application for family enforcement proceedings

18–03 Under Pt VII of the Family Proceedings Rules 1991 (SI 1991/1247) (FPR 1991) detailed guidance on how to enforce the various types of ancillary relief order is set out.

In any application, an affidavit must be filed under r.7.1 of the FPR 1991. This needs to be done for any process issued in relation to the enforcement of an order made in family proceedings for the payment of money. The affidavit will need to verify the amount due and must show how that amount has been calculated.

A writ of fieri facias or warrant of execution cannot be issued, without the permission of the court, under the rules, to enforce either a sum due under an order for ancillary relief or an order made under the provisions of s.27 of the Matrimonial Causes Act 1973 if there is already an application pending to vary the current order.

18–04 The rules provide for enforcement by way of writ of fieri facias, warrant of execution, attachment of earnings and order to obtain information.

The rules also provide for an application for committal and injunctive relief to be made as part of family proceedings. These rules are subject to the main rule on committal, which is set out in CPR Pt 52, r.6. Should it become necessary to enforce an order for committal in relation to family proceedings, then by virtue of these rules, where the application is being dealt with in the Royal Courts of Justice, the Tipstaff shall be deemed an officer of the court. The Tipstaff as an officer of the High Court of England and Wales is appointed under s.27 of the Courts Act 1971. Although appointed and operating from the Royal Courts of Justice, the Tipstaff's authority extends across England & Wales when it comes to enforcing the orders of the High Court. They are authorised to force entry if necessary and will have a police officer present to prevent breach of the peace. They are also the only people who can make an arrest within the precincts of the Royal Courts of Justice. The majority of the Tipstaff's modern duties involve taking children into custody (i.e. a place of safety), including cases of child abduction abroad.

The rules also provide that orders made in a divorce county court as part of family proceedings can be transferred to the High Court by the party wishing to transfer filing the necessary affidavit and stating the sum outstanding. That said, this does not apply where the sum involved is for outstanding periodical payments or the recovery of arrears of periodical payments. However, once an order that can be transferred is in the High Court, it is treated for enforcement as if it were an order of the High Court.

Limitation issues

18–05 In other enforcement proceedings, the ability to enforce an order for the payment of a lump sum that is more than six years old will not be automatically barred by the Limitation Act 1980.

As in the case of *Lowsley v Forbes* (*T/A LE Design Services*) [1999] 1 A.C. 329; [1998] 3 W.L.R. 501 HL, enforcement proceedings were held to be proceedings by way of execution rather than a "fresh action", and therefore could be commenced after the six year period had expired from the date of the order.

In relation to maintenance order proceedings or proceedings to enforce payment of a lump sum by installments, there is no limitation as to when those proceedings can be commenced.

18–06 Payments of arrears more than 12 months old, however, become unenforceable without the leave of the court. Sage advice from solicitors to their clients should be that if there is any default in relation to such orders, their client should contact them immediately so they can contact the other party or their legal representatives and start the process of reminding the other party that payment is due and in the absence of co-operation an application will be made to compel payment.

Of course, as in all enforcement proceedings, the client should be advised as to the likely cost of enforcing any order. It should be explained clearly that even in the event that judgment is obtained, or has been obtained, if that party has no money, then recovery becomes a wasted and expensive exercise. Hopefully, the answer to this question will have been addressed before the main action is commenced. Even in matrimonial proceedings, there is a need to really focus on the likely assets of the paying party and to evaluate what any success will mean in monetary terms for a client.

The available methods of enforcement in family proceedings

18–07 As in mainstream civil court enforcement proceedings, the main methods of enforcement available in family proceedings include:

- attachment of earnings order;
- order for sale;
- judgment summons;
- charging order;
- third party debt order;
- warrant or writ of execution.

Attachment of earnings orders in family proceedings

18–08 The rules for attachment of earnings applications in family proceedings follow the rules set out in the earlier chapter in this book dealing with such an application. The respondent to the application must be in employment, and if he or she is self-employed or unemployed, the order cannot be enforced.

Charging orders in family proceedings

18–09 Again, the same rules apply to charging orders in family proceedings as they do in ordinary civil proceedings. However, in family proceedings this method of enforcement can be the most suitable form of enforcement for payment of a lump sum. Charging orders can also be used to enforce any accumulated arrears of maintenance under an order for payment.

The procedure used to apply for a charging order in a family dispute is the same as in ordinary proceedings. If a final order is obtained, the court can exercise its discretion as to whether to order a sale of the property under s.24A of the Matrimonial Causes Act 1973.

Orders for sale in family proceedings

18–10 Under s.24A of the Matrimonial Causes Act 1973, the court can make an order for the sale of any property in which the respondent is beneficially entitled under this legislation. Such an order is only suitable for enforcing a lump sum ordered to be paid, or to secure a periodical payments order or property adjustment order.

An order in these terms can be made either at the time of the original order, as a precaution should there be a later default, or after a period of time if the respondent subsequently defaults in meeting the terms of the original order.

There is a risk that in making an application for some time in the future the value of the matrimonial home may fall, making it difficult to sell the property and then realise the amount outstanding.

However, the court does have power to order any consequential or supplementary provisions as it thinks fit, for example that the sale should only take effect at the expiry of a specified period of time (see s.24A), as above.

18–11 In exercising its discretion, the court will take into account the relative value of the debt and the value of the property that is to be the subject of the order. The court is unlikely to make an order where either the value of the debt or the value of the property is small and there is no real benefit in ordering a sale.

However, if a respondent fails to comply with any order for sale which the court is minded to make, then he or she will be in contempt of court, for which committal proceedings can be the remedy. It should be noted that in the 1975 case of *Danchevsky*, any such committal proceedings should only be issued if there is no alternative.

Judgment summonses in family proceedings

18–12 The rules on when to use judgment summonses in the context of family enforcement proceedings are set out in Ch.2 of Pt VII of the FPR 1991. A judgment summons can be made in relation to outstanding maintenance payments, as well as to orders which include lump sums and orders for payment of school fees where the obligation is to pay direct to the school in question a sum equivalent to the fees not specified in monetary terms (see *L v L (School Fees: Maintenance: Enforcement)*) [1997] 2 F.L.R. 252.

To make an order, the applicant must be entitled to enforce a judgment or order under s.5 of the Debtors Act 1869.

The sanction is severe and, if it is proved that the debtor has defaulted and yet had the means to pay the order but refused or neglected to do so, he or she can find themselves committed to prison for up to six weeks or until the amount owing is paid. Any such order may, however, be suspended under r.7.4(10) of the FPR 1991.

An application for enforcement in these terms should be made on Form N16, together with a supporting affidavit verifying the amount due. A copy of the order should be attached to the affidavit.

18–13 Following the case of *Mubarak v Mubarak* No.1 [2001] 1 F.L.R. 698, the burden of proof is on the applicant to show beyond reasonable doubt that the respondent has defaulted and has the means to pay.

One of the advantages to this method of enforcement is that committal to prison does not extinguish the debtor's liability, so it is possible to subsequently issue other methods of enforcement to recover the outstanding arrears.

Enforcement in the Family Proceedings Court

18–14 If a maintenance order was originally made in the Family Proceedings Court rather than the county court or High Court, as discussed above, the two main ways of enforcing it are either:

- through an attachment of earnings order as discussed above; or
- registration of the order in the High Court or county court.

A maintenance order may be registered in one of the above courts under s.2(3) of the Maintenance Orders Act 1958 (MOA 1958). The application for registration does not need to be in writing or an oath (see The Magistrates' Maintenance Orders Act 1958).

When registered, this enables the applicant to adopt one of the enforcement methods available under the Civil Procedure Rules. The drawback to doing this is one of cost, as it is seen to be more expensive to take action in the civil courts rather than the Family Proceedings courts. Moreover, there may not be sufficient monies within the family to make this option worthwhile.

There is the third possibility of committal to prison, but this is a very rare application and should only be used as a method of enforcement as a last resort.

The option to register in the Family Proceedings Court

18–15 It is also possible for orders of maintenance made in the county court or High Court to be registered in the Family Proceedings Court under s.1 of the Maintenance Orders Act 1958.

Under r.7.23 of the Family Proceedings Rules, the procedure for making an application is carried out by the solicitor applying to the original court for registration, by providing a certified copy of the maintenance order, two copies of the application in Form M33 and a fee.

Solicitors should be aware that some judges will only permit such registration if there are arrears of maintenance.

Once registered, all payments must be made to a designated court officer, which results in the advantage of all payments being recorded. Once this is done, it also becomes possible to apply for a variation of the order, which is also available in the county court.

Variation proceedings

18–16 The court has the power under s.31 of the Matrimonial Causes Act 1973 to vary, discharge or suspend certain orders for financial relief.

The power is not available in relation to orders for payment of a lump sum unless the payment is to be by installments or ordered in relation to a pension.

The procedure for applying to vary an order for financial relief is very similar to the procedure for the original order, which means using Form A to apply.

18–17 If both parties agree to a variation, the procedure for a consent order is governed by r.2.61 of the FPR 1991. The court itself has several options when discharging or varying a periodical payments order, which include:

- ordering the payment of a lump sum;
- making one or more property adjustments orders;
- making one or more pension sharing orders; and
- extending the period to which the original order is limited.

When making such an order under s.31(7) of the Matrimonial Causes Act 1973, the court must have regard to all the circumstances of the case, with its first consideration being to the welfare of any child of the family who has not yet reached the age of eighteen. Additionally, any side letter to the original order should be drawn to the court's attention on the variation application, and although it is not binding, the court may decide to uphold its terms.

18–18 If the parties can settle their differences by agreement in a consent order (e.g. when one party's earning capacity has reduced), this is clearly a sensible economic benefit and the respondent should be less likely to default in future. Nevertheless, if an agreement is not adhered to, the added cost of pursuing another enforcement method should be borne in mind.

However, an applicant may also apply to vary an order where, for example, the respondent has won the lottery or received a redundancy payment and yet is still refusing to make regular payments to the applicant.

In such a situation, the court is unlikely to make a variation of the original order and may discharge the periodical payments order by putting a lump sum order in its place.

Enforcement of child maintenance

18–19 Another alternative to the other methods of enforcement where there are children involved is utilising the Child Maintenance and Enforcement Commission (CMEC), formally referred to as the Child Support Agency (CSA).

If a parent's income changes, he or she can inform the CMEC/CSA, which can result in a change to the amount of maintenance that they are paying.

If the parent with care is simply not receiving payments from the non-resident parent, then CMEC/CSA have the power to take enforcement action. It is important to note that the court has jurisdiction to make an order for 12 months after the making of a maintenance order. Only after this date may an applicant apply to the CMEC/CSA for further support.

The court can then make a deduction from earnings order (DEO), which is virtually the same as an attachment of earnings order discussed at the beginning of this chapter. It is interesting to note that it was announced in the House of Commons that the CMEC intends to pilot the use of DEOs as a primary method of collection for employed non-resident parents.

If such an order then becomes ineffective because the parent becomes unemployed, then CMEC/CSA can take court action against the non-resident parent. This can be extremely costly for the non-resident parent and could result in additional penalties, including the loss of a driving licence for up to two years or access to a bank account being frozen.

18–20 A non-resident parent who fails to provide information, or gives information that he knows to be false, can end up being taken to court by the CMEC/CSA, resulting in a court fine.

Of course, the problems that CMEC/CSA have experienced with compliance have been well publicised. According to the CSA's website, more enforcement action is now being taken. In total, 18 per cent more enforcement actions were taken in 2007/2008 as compared to 2006/2007, but still 31 per cent of parents are not complying with their obligations to pay for their children under maintenance orders.

Using the CMEC/CSA's route remains a far more cost-effective method of enforcing maintenance orders for parents with care than going to court themselves.

Where does this leave enforcement in family proceedings?

18–21 The more difficult it becomes for a party to pay, the more difficult it is to enforce. The amount to be enforced needs to be worth the cost of compelling enforcement through the court system, and whilst this is true in relation to any type of enforcement proceedings, it is perhaps more acute in family proceedings where emotions are often heightened by a need to protect loved ones.

It must be understood that one of the least upsetting and cost effective ways to enforce maintenance orders is to apply for an attachment of earnings order between the parties. Of course, this may become useless if the respondent is or becomes unemployed, and is certainly unsuitable for lump sum orders. However, where there is a salary available from the paying party from which deductions can be made, then the process should be automatic.

18–22 If there are children involved, the CMEC/CSA route may be a cost effective way for a parent with care to enforce maintenance obligations, although this does not guarantee results and the applicant must wait a year after any court order to apply to the agencies for maintenance.

For lump sum orders, a charging order or an order for sale may be the best available means of enforcement.

Agreements to vary a maintenance order may be successful if the parties are amenable and intend to adhere to it. In cases where one party simply refuses to pay, the only option may be to make the application to the court to vary an existing order or to make an order for sale. In the worst scenario, the ultimate option is to order a judgment summons.

In a nutshell, various enforcement options are available to judgment creditors in family proceedings, but practitioners need to consider the costs and the processes before jumping in feet first.

Chapter 19

Sequestration

Introductory comments

19–01 Sequestration is a form of contempt, and a party against whom it is issued is referred to as the contemnor. It is available only where the person is already in contempt for disobeying an existing order of the court. It has to be said that sequestration is a drastic remedy involving four sequestrators, who take control of the contemnor's property until the contempt is purged.

Nowadays, it is most frequently encountered in matrimonial cases, although there was a flurry of reported cases on the enforcement procedures of sequestration in the early days of the National Industrial Relations Court—although the procedure differed to the rules on sequestration found in court rules today.

As sequestration can only be used in respect of orders in the nature of an injunction, it rarely involves the enforcement of money judgments.

How is the application for a writ of sequestration made?

19–02 If sequestration is to be pursued, an application in accordance with CPR Pt 23 is made to a judge seeking permission to issue a writ of sequestration, a form of writ appointing four sequestrators, which directs them to take possession of all the real and personal property of the contemnor (being a person in contempt) and to keep that property until the contempt is cleared.

The court may apply the property for the benefit of the judgment creditors; for example, see *Mir v Mir* [1992] Fam.79, involving wardship proceedings the care of an order was made for the sale of land previously sequestrated, in order to finance further litigation overseas.

Which rules within the CPR apply?

19–03 In the county court the jurisdiction to order sequestration falls within the ancillary jurisdiction of the court (see County Courts Act 1984, s.38 and the case of *Re Rose* (Fanny) [1989] 3 W.L.R.873, [1989] 3 All E.R. 306, which confirm the county court's jurisdiction).

The formal application for a warrant of sequestration directs and authorises the sequestrator to take possession of the assets of the person in contempt, as per High Court Rules. The county court format directs and authorises the sequestrator to take possession of the assets of the person in contempt, as per the High Court rule. In making the application in the county court it is desirable to submit a draft order for a judgment to be settled (see CCR Order 13, r.6(6)).

In the High Court the rules on sequestration are found in CPR Sch.1, RSC Order 45, r.12(4) and RSC order 46, r.5. A praecipe for a writ of sequestration is completed using Form PF87, and the form of a writ of sequestration is made on Form 67.

What is the effect of sequestration?

19–04 As sequestration is a form of contempt (see *Pratt v Inman* [1890] L.R. 43 Ch.D. 175) the rule requires that a writ of sequestration can only be issued with permission of the court, when granted by a judge on an application duly served and supported by evidence.

Where disobedience to the order of the court is not obstinate and the breaches have been remedied, the court may impose a fine in lieu of the sequestration of the assets of a company or other corporate body, especially where sequestration would adversely effect the livelihood of innocent parties (see *Steiner Products Limited v Willy Steiner Limited* [1966] 1 W.L.R. 986, [1966] 2 All E.R.387).

Which judgments are enforceable by sequestration?

19–05 Judgments or orders which may be enforced by a writ of sequestration include:

- those which require a person "to do an act" within a specified time, extended where necessary;
- those which require a person to abstain from "doing an act".

and see CPR Sch.1, RSC Order 45, r.5(1). Negative orders are now enforced for a sequestration by virtue of the expressed provision of RSC Order 45, r.5(1)(b).

19–06 The overriding condition under which a positive judgment or order may be enforced by sequestration is that it *must* specify the time limit within which the required act must be done. Usually, time for compliance will not be specified expressly in a judgment or to pay money to some other person, to give possession of land or to deliver goods. The time for compliance will not generally be specified *unless* the person is required to do that act and can be shown to be wilfully refusing or neglecting to do it.

It is therefore likely to be as rare in the future as it has been in the past for the writ of sequestration to be available or issued in the case of orderly common law judgments for the payment of money to another person, or for the delivery of land or goods.

Similarly, it is not the practice of the courts to limit the time for payment of costs, and therefore sequestration is unlikely to be used as a method of enforcing an order for these payments.

Despite this, CPR Sch.1, RSC Order 45, r.5 refers to the power of the court to grant permission to issue a writ of sequestration where a party refuses or neglects to comply with, or disobeys, a coercive order of the court. The court has an inherent power to ensure that its orders are carried out where the interests of justice demand that they can be complied with. Therefore, in the case of a declaratory order, where a party knowingly adopts and continues a policy of refusing, neglecting or disobeying to comply with its terms, the court has power under its inherent jurisdiction to give permission to issue a writ of sequestration (see *Webster v Southwark* LBC [1983] Q.B.698; [1983] 2 W.L.R. 217).

19–07 For examples where an order to pay money or costs has been enforced by sequestration, the following cases (which are not modern day) should be referred to:

- *Knill v Dumergue* [1911] 2 Ch.199 (where the facts are inaccurately stated, but which involves a vendor's action for specific performance)
- *Re Slade* [1881] 18 Ch.D. 653 (damages and costs)
- *Willcock v Terrell* [1878] 3 Ex.D. 323 (an order to pay by instalments)
- *Capron v Capron* [1927] W.N. 178 (a case involving alimony)

Sequestration may also be used to enforce a judgment or order for the payment of money into court, which must specify the time limit over which the payment is to be made.

A writ of sequestration may also be used to enforce an order against a child (see CPR Pt 21), or against the defendant who has become a patient since the date of the order (see *Robinson v Galland* [1889] W.N. 108).

Sequestration is not available to enforce a judgment against the Crown (RSC Order 77, r.15(1)); it is also not available against third persons who are not parties to the action (*Per* Gorell Barnes J. in *Craig v Craig* [1896] P.171 at 174).

Can a writ of sequestration be issued against a company director?

19–08 If the person required by the judgment to do, or restrain from doing, the act is a company, then original sequestration may be issued against the company's property or (with the expressed leave of the court) against the property of any director or any other officer of the company (see RSC Order 45 r.5(1)(ii)).

However, an officer of a company will only be liable to have his property sequestrated if he is responsible for the company's breach of the order in the sense that it is required under the general law of contempt. Mere knowledge of the order without the mens rea or actus reus is insufficient to find action for committal or a sequestration (see *Director General of Fair Trading v Buckland* [1990] 1 W.L.R.920).

How is sequestration used as a method of enforcement in family proceedings?

19–09 Where there have been repeated contempt of court orders to safeguard the welfare of children, the courts have been prepared to allow a writ of sequestration to be issued, to deal with the issue of the contempt. The use of the writ seems to be particularly prevalent where there may be reciprocal enforcement provisions with another country, or where funding to finance litigation needs to be liquidated.

In the case of *Richardson v Richardson* [1989] Fam.95; [1990] 1 F.L.R. 186 the mother had moved her children to the Republic of Ireland leaving behind a property in England and Wales. A writ of sequestration against that property was granted, and leave was given to the sequestrator to raise money against the security of the property to enable the father to fund litigation in Ireland to secure the return of the children.

In *Mir v Mir* [1992] 1 F.L.R. 624 an order was made for the respondent to transfer his interest in the family home to sequestrators, who could then finance litigation in Pakistan.

Who can be appointed as sequestrators?

19–10 The sequestrators are chosen by the person presenting the judgment or order. Four people are named as sequestrators, but they are not required to be professional persons and are not required to give security for what they may receive.

Often, accountants in large firms are nominated to be appointed sequestrators. In *Romilly v Romilly* [1964] P.22, the court on hearing the application by a sequestrator, who apparently would have been placed "under an intolerable conflict of duty", discharged him and appointed a substitute.

What are the duties of the sequestrators?

19–11 Sequestrators are officers of the court and subject to its control, although they also have a duty of care to the owner of the property that has been sequestrated (see *Inland Revenue Commissioners v Hoogstraten* [1985] Q.B. 1077; [1984] 3 All E.R. 25).

Immediately on the issue of the writ, the sequestrator must take physical possession of the real property and personal chattels of the person or body in contempt.

What is the effect of a writ of sequestration?

19–12 The writ "binds" real property (see *Re Lush* [1870] L.R. 10 Eq. 442) and personal property in possession from the time the writ is issued (see *Burdett v Rockley* [1682] 1 Vern 58 and *Dixon v Rose* [1876] 35 L.T. 548). However, the issue of the writ does not create a charge to the land unless it is registered (see Land Charges Act 1972, s.6(1)(a) or Land Registration Act 2002).

The issue of the writ, and the service of it on the party indebted to the judgment debtor, is not enough to create a charge on the "chosen action" (see *Ex p. Nelson* [1880] 14 Ch.D. 41 and *Re Pollard* [1903] 87 L.T. 61); instead, an order for payment must be obtained. As to the effect and operation of the sequestration, this is set out in detail in the judgment of Roma L.J. in *Re Pollard Ex p*. [1903] 2 K.B. 41 at 47 and 48, CA.

The position of a third party in relation to a writ of sequestration is that said party is under a duty to not knowingly take any action which would obstruct the compliance of the terms of the writ of sequestration, which in turn requires the sequestrators to take possession of the assets of the contemnor (see *Eckman v Midland Bank Limited* [1973] Q.B. 519; [1973] 1 All E.R. 609, NIRC, not following *Re Pollard* above).

Can a person be punished for preventing the sequestrator from carrying out their duties?

19–13 When a sequestration of a contemnor's assets has been ordered, anyone who prevents the sequestrators from carrying out their duty will be treated as obstructing a court order, and therefore may be technically found in contempt of court.

Any proper or necessary request made by the sequestrators to the contemnor's accountants to give information concerning details of the contemnor's assets must be answered, and the accountants must divulge the information even in the absence of a contemnor's consent, which is irrelevant (see *Messenger Newspaper Group v National Graphical Association* [1984] 1 All E.R. 293, CA).

What type of property is liable to be sequestrated?

19–14 Reported cases involving writs of sequestration over the years have involved the sequestration of:

- rents and profits from real estate and/or personal estate;
- the pension of a retired naval officer;
- the pension of a civil servant;
- money received in commutation of a pension;
- a deposit on appeal, ordered to be returned;
- a rent charge;
- a person under the East India Annuity Funds Act 1874;
- a positive bank balance.

Interestingly, the pension of an officer in the Army was excluded.

How is the application made for permission to issue a writ of sequestration?

19–15 The application for permission to issue a writ of sequestration must be made to a judge in accordance with CPR Pt 23. The application notice must state the grounds of the application and be accompanied by a copy of the witness statement or affidavit in support of the application.

It is not necessary on the application for leave to issue a writ of sequestration to indicate that there is any specific property which may be available for sequestration. However, it should be remembered that the remedy itself is discretionary and the court must be satisfied that the application is reasonable (see *Hulbert and Crowe v Cathcart* [1896] A.C. 470).

Once the application for leave to issue the writ of sequestration is made, then the application can only be withdrawn with the permission of the court (see the judgment of Edmund Davis J. in *Showerings v Fern Vale Brewery Co* [1958] 9 C.L. 287A).

The difference between High Court and county court proceedings is the forms that are used, as both applications start using CPR Pt 23.

How is notice of the application served?

19–16 The application must be served personally on the person against whose property it is sought to issue the writ. The court may dispense with service of the application notice under this rule if it thinks it is just to do so. Substituted service may also be ordered (see *Suarez v Suarez* [1980] Ch. 176, CA).

Service of the application may be dispensed altogether if the court thinks it is just to do so.

What is the format of the hearing of the application?

19–17 The hearing for the application for permission to issue a writ of sequestration will be a public hearing unless the judge would be entitled to hear the application in private, because the case satisfies the criteria under CPR Sch.1, RSC Order 52, r.6). This deals with the provisions of committal (although it applies in this instance), and provides that a court hearing an application for an order may sit in private in the following cases:

- Where the application arises out of proceedings relating to the wardship or adoption of an infant, or relates wholly or mainly to the guardianship, custody, maintenance or upbringing of an infant or rights of access to an infant.
- Where the application arises out of proceedings relating to a person suffering, or appearing to be suffering, from a mental disorder within the meaning of the Mental Health Act 1983.

- Where the application arises out of proceedings in which a secret process, discovery or invention was, or is, an issue.
- Where it appears to the court that in the interest of the administration of justice, or for reasons of national security, the application should be heard in private.

How is the writ of sequestration executed?

19–18 A writ of sequestration directs the sequestrators to sequestrate all property of whatever nature of the contemnor (being the person in contempt).

Sequestrators may break open inner doors and boxes in executing the writ to sequestrate assets. However, they do not enjoy the same power equivalent to a High Court Enforcement Officer in asking for police assistance under the Court Act 2003, Sch.7, para.5.

Once inside the property, the sequestrators must detain and keep any property taken until the court's order is obeyed or the contempt is otherwise purged. The person in contempt is not physically seized!

The mention in a writ of sequestration of a money judgment of the total amount due from the person in contempt is, presumably, only intended as a guide to the sequestrators in order that they may check whether the judgment has been obeyed. In principle, this would not seem to limit their authority in a case under the rules. In contrast some orders of the old National Industrial Relations Court authorised the levy of particular amounts to cover fines (see *Goad v AUEW* [1972] I.C.R. 429 and *Com Mech (Engineers) Ltd v Same* [1973] I.R.L.R. 33).

Are the sequestrators liable for their acts?

19–19 In sequestrating, the sequestrators are deemed to act under the creditor's instructions, and accordingly they are liable in trespass to a third party who is injured.

Although a sequestrator appointed under a writ of sequestration is an officer of the court, he is not immune from liability for negligence in respect of anything done or committed by him in the course of the sequestration. He owes an ordinary duty of care to the owner of the sequestrated property (see *Inland Revenue Commissioners v Hoogstraten* [1985] Q.B 1077; [1984] 3 All E.R. 25).

Sequestrators have no automatic power or authority to sell the assets of the person in contempt (unlike a writ of fi fa), although a sale of property (other than land) may be ordered by the court.

Although there is doubt as to whether a sale of land can be ordered, if the person in contempt has already contracted to sell the land, the court may be persuaded toward the benefit of any contract for sale to be "released" to the sequestrators, so that they in effect sell the land, with one of them being appointed under the Trustee Act 1925, s.50, to execute the conveyance (see *Hipkin v Hipkin* No.1 [1962] 1 W.L.R. 491).

Property of which the person in contempt is a "mere trustee", as well as property which would be protected under a writ of fi fa, is exempt from seizure.

What happens if a person interferes with the sequestrator?

19–20 Any resistance or interference with the sequestrators is a further contempt, as they are the officers of the court. An injunction against such interference may be granted (see *Hipkin v Hipkin* (No.1) [1962] 1 W.L.R. 491).

What is the effect of a third party claim to goods seized by sequestrators?

19–21 There is no interpleader procedure available in relation to a writ of sequestration, but a third party whose goods have been seized may apply to the court for leave to be examined, and an enquiry may be ordered as to whether the applicant has any interest in the property that has been sequestrated.

Is a "return" to a writ of sequestration available?

19–22 No form of "return" to a writ of sequestration is provided under the rules, as is the case in relation to a writ of fi fa. Once the contempt has been purged, an order for the dissolution of the sequestration is applied for by the sequestrator.

The order discharges the sequestration, directs the sequestrators to withdraw from possession of the sequestered property and then to pass their final accounts, from which they will retain their costs, charges and expenses for any payments properly made by them. This then leaves a balance to be paid to the person in contempt, and the order then discharges the sequestrators from all liability in respect of their office.

In the case of *Coles v Coles* [1956] 3 W.L.R. 861; [1956] 3 All E.R. 542 it was held that where a writ of sequestration had been issued and the person in contempt became bankrupt but had not purged his contempt, the trustee in bankruptcy was not entitled to have the writ of sequestration discharged.

What is the position of a disposition of assets where a writ of sequestration has been issued?

19–23 The court may set aside any transaction entered into by the debtor before the sequestration, where the debtor, in collusion with any other person, has disposed of property belonging to him to avoid his creditors, or in which he attempts to prefer one creditor over another. Indeed, any person who is found to have been a party to such a disposition will be liable to make good any loss caused to the insolvent's estate (see *Fourie v Roux* [2005] EWHC 922 [Ch]).

Chapter 20

Court's Power to Appoint a Receiver CPR Part 69

Introduction

20–01 The history of this method of enforcement evolved through the law of equity, which over the centuries added a "gloss" to common law, and "equitable execution" was developed to cure defects in the common law arrangements for enforcement. As to the nature of the remedy in the nineteenth century, see *Levasseur v Mason & Barry* [1891] 2 Q.B. 73 and *Re Shepherd* [1889] 43 Ch.D. in which Bowen L.J. on page 137 describes the position: "It is not execution but a substitute for execution".

In more modern times, the previous rules under RSC Order 51 (Receivers: Equitable Execution) and CCR Order 32 were revoked by the Civil Procedure (Amendment) Rules 2002 (SI 2002/2058), which introduced the new Pt 69 to the Civil Procedure Rules on December 2, 2002.

20–02 CPR Pt 69, and its accompanying Practice Direction, now covers the rules and procedures in both the High Court and county courts. The new rule provides a comprehensive procedural code to deal with the appointment by the court of receivers and managers, which includes provisions relating to:

- the application for appointment;
- the evidence required in support of that appointment;
- security and remuneration of the receiver which is strictly controlled by the court;
- the receiver's accounts and discharge;
- the termination of the receiver's appointment.

It should be borne in mind that the power to appoint a receiver is discretionary, and accordingly the court will do so whenever it appears to be just and convenient to do so in handling any application.

When should the appointment of a receiver be considered?

20–03 Part 69 is designed to cover both the appointment of receivers appointed for the purpose of preserving property during the course of litigation, as well as the appointment of receivers by way of equitable execution, a procedure which is said to be "comparatively rare" nowadays because of the availability of charging orders.

It was said in the case of *Morgan v Hart* [1914] 2 K.B. 183 that the jurisdiction will not normally be exercised where there is no impediment to legal execution (i.e. warrant or writ) or attachment of debts (i.e. attachment of earnings, third party debt order), not where there is a property against which such execution could be issued (charging order). So, in effect, this method of enforcement, although rare, should be considered when none of the more usual methods of enforcement is available.

Types of property which may require the appointment of a receiver

20–04 Firstly, the application to appoint a receiver needs to relate to a specific item(s) of property. The application is not confined just to the equitable estates or interests of the debtor.

Examples include:

Examples of cases where property has been the subject of a successful application	Examples of cases where property has not been the subject of a successful application
The debtor's reversionary interest in the proceeds of sale of realty (*Tyrrell v Painton* [1895] 1 Q.B. 202).	Solicitor's costs untaxed
The debtor's share of rent and profits of freehold and leasehold property held on a joint tenancy subject to mortgages (*Hills v Webber* (1901) 17 T.L.R. and see also *Hart v Emelkirk Ltd* [1983] 3 All E.R. 15—and see *Bank of Australasia v Whitehead* (1898) 24 V.L.R. 308 and *Cadogan v Lyric Theatre Ltd* [1894] 3 Ch. 338 (rents and profits of theatre subject to a mortgage)	Monies receivable from patents before licence granted

Examples of cases where property has been the subject of a successful application	**Examples of cases where property has not been the subject of a successful application**
Rents accruing but not accrued	Salary of a public office not yet due and not assignable (*Cooper v Reilly* (1892) 2 Sim 560)
Pensions (except pensions of HM Forces personnel)	
Income of a trust fund (*Oliver v Lowther* (1880) 42 L.T. 47	
An interest in pure personality subject to a mortgage	
Property subject to a lien (*Levasseur v Mason & Barry* [1891] 1 Q.B. 73)	
Debts where a third party debt order is inappropriate e.g. *Moloney v Cruise* (1892) 30 L.R. Ir. 99 (civil servant's pension) and see the more modern case of *Soinco S.A.C.I. and anor v Novokuznetsk Aluminium Plant and ors* [1988] Q.B. 406	
Fund in the High Court, where the judgment is a county court judgment (see *London County Council v Monks* [1959] Ch. 239	
A reversionary interest under wills—*Fuggle v Bland* (1883) 11 Q.B.D. 711	
Note: In the case of *Crowe v Price* [1889] 22 Q.B.D. 429, the sums in question were moneys received on behalf of the debtor in commutation of part of his retired Army pay, and moneys received on behalf of the debtor for his retired pay. A receiver was appointed in respect of the first but not of the second!	

20–05 In practice, the appointment of a receiver by way of equitable execution is designed to enable a judgment creditor to obtain payment of his debt when legal execution (which is explained in the preliminary chapter to this work) is not available because of the nature of the judgment debtor's interest in the property. In *Maclaine Watson and Co Ltd v International Tin Council* [1988] Ch. 1 it was stated clearly by the court that such an order can only be made where:

- it is impossible to enforce using any of the other methods of enforcement; and
- the appointment of a receiver will be effective.

Both the Queen's Bench and the Chancery Divisions have explanatory guides relating to the procedure under CPR Pt 69, and a summary of these guides in table form is set out in the appendix under "Resources For CPR Pt 69—Court's Power to Appoint a Receiver" along with template documents [Forms PF30CH].

What is the scope of the rule?—CPR part 69.1

20–06 The court's powers to appoint a receiver are set out in the following statutory powers:

- High Court—s.37 of the Supreme Court Act 1981 (dealing with the powers of the High Court in respect of injunctions and receivers)
- County Court—s.38 of the County Courts Act 1984 (remedies available in county courts) and s.107 of the County Courts Act 1984 (dealing with receivers by way of equitable execution

What are the court's powers to appoint a receiver?—CPR part 69.2

20– 07 The court's powers to appoint a receiver are wide-ranging in order to include appointment before proceedings have started or in existing proceedings, or on or after judgment—so they are not limited to just a post-judgment remedy. However, the appointment of a receiver before proceedings have started is only possible where it can be shown that the application has been properly served. In practice this means that an application under the CPR Pt 23 application in the intended claim will need to be served on the persons identified in CPR 69.4. CPR 25.2(2) contains provisions about the grant of the order appointing the receiver before proceedings are started.

The receiver must be an individual—as opposed to a company. By virtue of CPR 69.1(2) the definition of a "receiver" includes a "manager". The court has power at any time to terminate the appointment of the receiver, or replace the receiver with a new appointee. The rule which provides for the appointment to be terminated (CPR 69.2(3)) provides for the termination of an appointment and for a replacement to be appointed. However, this rule must be read in conjunction with CPR 69.9.

If the application for the appointment of a receiver is joined with an application for an injunction, for example for the detention, custody or preservation of relevant property, then the second practice direction which supplements Pt 2 (Allocation of Cases to Levels of Judiciary) sets out who may grant the injunctive relief. By virtue of PD 69.3 this includes a Master or district judge, where the injunctive relief is related to the appointment of a receiver by way of equitable execution.

How is the application made to appoint a receiver?—CPR part 69.3

20–08 An application for the appointment of a receiver may be made without notice (CPR 69.3(a)) and must be supported by written evidence (CPR 69.3(b)). The application is made using an application notice. The Master or district judge may grant an injunction relating to an order appointing a receiver by way of equitable execution. Usually, the application needs to be served on the person to be appointed and every other party to the claim.

A without notice application may be possible if the matter is urgent, or special circumstances warrant an urgent application. In these cases any order made is likely to be only of an interim nature, which then allows the parties to come back before the court to apply to vary or discharge any of the interim order's terms.

What are the requirements for evidence in support of the appointment of a receiver?

20–09 The accompanying Practice Direction sets out the requirements for evidence in support of the application, and clearly careful attention must be given to these evidential issues. This evidence needs to be rehearsed in a witness statement referred to in the CPR Pt 23 application notice. The witness statement must contain a statement of truth, as one might expect.

The evidential requirements set out in PD69.4 include:

(1) evidence explaining the reasons why the appointment is required;

(2) details of the property which it is proposed that the receiver should get in or manage, including estimates of:

  (a) the value of the property; and
  (b) the amount of income it is likely to produce;

(3) additional details including:

  (a) the judgment which the applicant is seeking to enforce
  (b) the extent to which the debtor has failed to comply with the judgment
  (c) the result of any steps already taken to enforce the judgment; and

(d) why the judgment cannot be enforced by any other method; and

(4) if the applicant is asking the court to allow the receiver to act:

(a) without giving security; or
(b) before he has given security or satisfied the court that he has security in place, to explain the reasons why that is necessary.

In addition, the written evidence should deal with the identity of the individual whom the court is being asked to appoint as receiver ("the nominee"), and should: **20–10**

(1) state the name, address and position of the nominee;

(2) include written evidence by a person who knows the nominee, stating that he believes the nominee is a suitable person to be appointed as receiver, and the basis of that belief; and

(3) be accompanied by written consent, signed by the nominee, to act as receiver if appointed.

If the applicant does not nominate a person for the position of receiver, the court has power to order the appointment of a suitable person or direct a party to nominate a person who can be appointed.

What is the form of order?

When an order has been made appointing a receiver, it will, in the usual case, be necessary to apply thereafter for directions by a PF23 application notice. Paragraph 6 of the PD to Pt 69 lists the matters on which directions will be usually given. A draft order should accompany the application. This will not be the case if the original order appointing the receiver gives comprehensive directions. **20–11**

Does the order appointing a receiver need to be served?

The order appointing the receiver must be served by the party who applied for it on the person appointed, every other party to the proceedings and any other persons who the court directs needs to be served with the order. **20–12**

What are the courts powers in relation to security?—CPR 69.5

20–13 The court has a range of powers to direct the level and timing of security from the receiver under CPR 69.5 and the accompanying Practice Direction at PD 69, para. 7. Ultimately, the court may terminate the receiver's appointment in the absence of security. In making the application it is good practice to make a draft order available to the judge, together with details of the bond to be given to the court by the receiver along with a draft guarantee with a clearing bank or the insurance company. A form of draft guarantee is listed in Appendix 2 to "A Guide for Receivers in the Chancery Division (amended 2003)".

Generally, the court is likely to require security from the receiver by way of guarantee or bond. Paragraph 7.2 of the PD is important in connection with situations where the person to be appointed is a licensed insolvency practitioner. If the receiver is an insolvency practitioner, the issue of security will be dealt with by a form of bond provided under the Insolvency Practitioner Regulations 1990. A form of guarantee is Form PF30CH. In the Chancery Division the executed guarantee is signed by the receiver and sealed by the bank, and then is lodged in Room TM 7.09, Royal Courts of Justice, WC2A 2LL. It will then be produced to the Master and placed on the court file.

What are the court's powers to make directions?—CPR 69.6

20–14 This rule provides flexibility to either the court to make directions, or to the receiver to apply for directions throughout the period of the receiver's appointment.

In relation to the court's powers, obviously issues of security will be dealt with by directions (see above).

Other matters which may be the subject of directions include:

- the receiver's remuneration;
- the preparation and service of account;
- the payment of money into court;
- authorising the receiver to carry on an activity or incur an expense.

The receiver may also apply to the court at any time for directions to assist him in fulfilling his duties and function as a receiver. The procedure and requirements for the receiver's application are set out in the PD 69.8. There is provision for the receiver to apply to the court for permission by letter when a formal application is not appropriate.

How is the receiver remunerated?—CPR 69.7

20–15 This rule makes it clear that a receiver may only charge for his services if the court has authorised the amount to be charged. The rule controls the amount to be charged, along with power to the court, to specify who is responsible for the receiver's charges and to identify the fund or property from which the receiver's remuneration is to be deducted. Rule 69(3) provides that if the amount of a receiver's remuneration is to be determined by the court, then the receiver will not be paid or entitled to recover any costs until after such determination.

Rule 69.7(4) and para. 9.2 of the PD provide a list of the matters to be taken into account in determining the remuneration to be authorised on the basis of what is reasonable and proportionate. Rule 69.7(5) provides that the court may refer the determination of a receiver's remuneration to a costs judge. This course may be taken if the remuneration is substantial and it is felt that the costs judge is best placed to determine amounts.

There is also power available at PD 69.9(5)(2) to the court to appoint an assessor under CPR 35.15 to assist the court in determining a receiver's remuneration.

Expenses incurred by a receiver in carrying out his functions are not part of his remuneration. Instead, these are treated as part of the accounts and set against the assets recovered (PD 69 para. 9.6).

There is provision for a receiver to apply for an interim order authorising his remuneration, which may also deal with who is responsible for paying the remuneration and from which fund the remuneration should be paid.

What accounts should the receiver prepare?—CPR 69.8

20–16 As might be expected, the court may order a receiver to prepare and serve accounts. Again, the accompanying Practice Direction (PD 69.10) contains directions.

The court's powers extend to the preparation and service of accounts by a specified date(s) and on whom those accounts need to be served. If the accounts can be agreed between the parties, then the court will not become involved—provided no objection is raised to any accounts which are served on any party.

What is the sanction in the event of non-compliance by a receiver?—CPR 69.9

20–17 If a receiver fails to comply with either the rules of court or the order or direction of the court, then he may be ordered to attend a hearing to explain his non-compliance.

If such a hearing becomes necessary, the court has flexibility to make any order it considers appropriate including terminating the appointment of the receiver, reducing the receiver's remuneration or perhaps even disallowing it altogether, and ordering the receiver to pay the costs of any party.

If the court has ordered a receiver to pay a sum into court and the receiver has failed to do so, then the court may order him to pay interest on that sum for the period of default and at a rate it considers appropriate.

How is a receiver discharged?—CPR 69.10

20–18 Either a receiver or any party to the proceedings may apply for an order from the court to discharge the receiver once his duties have been completed. The same persons served under CPR 69.5 must be served with the application seeking the discharge.

What is the form of order discharging or terminating the appointment of a receiver?—CPR 69.11

20–19 An order discharging or terminating the appointment of a receiver may require him to pay monies into court, or specify another person to whom the receiver must pay monies or transfer assets, and provide for the discharge/cancellation of any guarantee given by the receiver to the court as security.

In practice, an order will be made at the conclusion of the receivership on the application by the receiver, supported by a witness statement made by him, and it will deal with the monies held by him, the assets of the receivership and the cancellation of any bond or guarantee given by him. The order itself must be served on the persons who were required under CPR 69.4 to be served with the order appointing the receiver.

After the order is made, the guarantee and a duplicate order will be endorsed to that effect for return to the bank or insurance company for cancellation.

Chapter 21

Committal in the Context of Enforcement

Introductory comments

21–01 Committal proceedings in the context of enforcement are undoubtedly expensive, and therefore can be off-putting to a court user who needs to use the machinery of contempt to ensure that the court order is observed. However, the rules on committal are important, as they provide the ultimate sanction for a party who either ignores or refuses to comply with the court's order.

The previous rules of enforcing a judgment to do or abstain from doing an act are preserved for all High Court business in CPR Sch.1, RSC order 45, r.5 and in CPR Sch.2, CCR 29.

The breach of a court judgment which directs a defendant to do something will be referred to as a "positive order." Where the court judgment directs a defendant to abstain from doing something, then this will be referred to as a "negative order."

High Court business

Where is the starting point in the rules of the Supreme Court?

21–02 RSC order 45, r.5 is the starting point in understanding the rules on contempt of procedure in the High Court. This rule governs the methods of the enforcement by the court of its judgments or orders in circumstances amounting to a contempt of court. It applies to both positive and negative judgments or orders.

It is important to note that coercive methods of enforcement (see para. 21–04) under the rule *cannot* be used to enforce a judgment or order to do an act *unless* the act to be done has not been done within a specified time which has been fixed by the court either with its original judgment or by a subsequent judgment. Naturally, the time may have been abridged, as provided under CPR, r.3.1(2)(a), or fixed under RSC Order 45, r.6.

Are irregular judgments or orders subject to the rules on contempt?

21–03 Even though a judgment or order may be found to be irregular by the court, it must still be obeyed unless, and until, it is set aside. Disobedience to even comply with an irregular interlocutory injunction has been found to amount to a contempt of court (see *Isaacs v Robertson* [1985] A.C. 97; [1984] 3 All E.R.140, PC).

How can a party be coerced into complying with the court's order?

21–04 The "coercive" methods of enforcement (which in effect mean compelling a person to behave involuntarily in a certain way, by using some other form of pressure or force) and which are referred to above, include:

- the use of a writ of sequestration against available assets (see RSC Order 46, r.5); and
- an order of committal under RSC Order 52 (as detailed below), which is additional to the powers of the court under the Debtors Acts 1869 and 1878 (although these powers were curtailed by s.11 of the Administration of Justice Act 1970).

The provisions under RSC Order 45, r.5 must be read in conjunction with the provision of RSC Order 45, r.7, which sets out the stringent rules of personal service of the order on the person in default. The requisite form or penal notice must be endorsed on the reverse of any order of the court which requires compliance.

It should be noted that a "declaratory order" is not the same as a coercive order, and therefore the refusal by a party to comply with its terms does not amount to a contempt of court (see *Webster v Southwark LBC* [1983] Q.B. 698). Such orders are enforced by a party returning to court and seeking an injunction to enforce the order.

How is a judgment enforced where a positive act is required to be done?

21–05 Under RSC order 45, r.5(2) a judgment or order which requires an act to be done must state the time within which the act is to be completed, before it can be enforced by the methods provided by this rule. The time of completion of the act to be done may be specified either:

- by the original judgment or order (see practice direction (judgment and orders) para.8.1 (40B PD.8)); or
- as time extended or abridged under CPR r.3.1(2)(a); or
- by agreement of the parties under CPR r.2.11; or
- by a supplemental order made subsequently under r.6.

Who is required to comply?

21–06 The act required to be done under the judgment or order may be directed to be done by the party by whom a judgment or order was obtained or by some other person appointed by the court, and at the expense of the disobedient party (RSC Order 45, r.8).

A person practicing as a solicitor but who is not qualified as a solicitor, and who has been ordered to deliver up documents and to pay money, may be committed for a breach of the order under this rule (*Re Hulm & Lewis* [1892] 2 Q.B. 261).

How can a company be made to comply?

21–07 Under CPR Sch.1, RSC Order 45, r.5 the remedies for enforcement of a judgment or order against a company are:

- by writ of sequestration against the company's property;
- by writ of sequestration against the personal property of any director or other officer of the company;
- by an order of committal against any director or other officer of the company.

The position of ensuring compliance in relation to a director's undertaking was dealt with in *Biba Ltd v Stratford Investments* [1973] Ch. 281.

Where a company disobeys an injunction, a director or other officer of the company becomes liable for that contempt under the general law of contempt, if it can be shown there was criminal intent to disobey the injunction (see *Director General of Fair Trading v Buckland* [1990] 1 W.L. 920; [1990] 1 All E.R. 545).

21–08 Where a company is restrained from doing certain acts, a director is under a duty to take reasonable care to secure compliance of the judgment or order. If the director is then found to have failed to take adequate steps to ensure compliance from to whom he delegated such a restraint, and the company then breaches the order, the director will find himself liable for contempt, even though he has not personally participated in the breach.

How is "refuses" or "neglects" or "disobeys" defined in the rule?

21–09 Under RSC Order 45.5.5, where a person "refuses or neglects" to do an act within the time specified by the judgment or order, or where he "disobeys" a judgment or order requiring him to abstain from doing an act, case law has developed to help define what amounts to "refusal", "neglect" or plain "disobedience" so that:

- An "intention to do a prohibited act knowing the consequences" as opposed to "a wilful intention to disobey a court order" has been held to constitute contempt (*P v P (Contempt of Court: Mental Capacity)* [1999] 2 F.L.R. 897).
- The refusal, neglect or disobedience must be sufficient to constitute a contempt of court (see *Heatons Transport (St Helens) Ltd v Transport and General Workers' Union* [1972] 3 All E.R. 101 per Lord Wilberforce at p.117).
- Acts excluded for amounting to a breach include acts found to be "casual or accidental and unintentional."
- A "lack of intention to disobey" may affect any penalty imposed by the court (*Chelsea Man Menswear Ltd v Chelsea Girl (No.2) Ltd* [1988] F.S.R. 217).
- In relation to companies, "disobedience" has been found to mean refusal by the corporation or its services *(Attorney General v Walthamstow UDC* [1895] 11 T.L.R. 533), or neglect by servants (*Stancomb v Trowbridge UDC* [1910] 2 Ch. 190), to do the things which the corporation has been ordered to do.

The standard proof is that defendants' acts must be proved "beyond reasonable doubt." It was held in *Chelsea Man Menswear Ltd v Chelsea Girl (No.2) Ltd* [1988] F.S.R. 217 that the standard may involve the question of the impression given to the court as to whether the facts surrounding the alleged breach amounts in law to a breach of the court order.

What is the costs position in pursuing an action for contempt?

21–10 Costs may be awarded on an indemnity basis (see *Attorney General v Walthamstow UDC* [1895] 11 T.L.R. 533, and *Lee v Aylesbury UDC* [1902] 19 T.L.R. 106, and *Stancomb v Trowbridge UDC* [1910] 2 Ch. 190). This may be a sufficient punishment where there have been minor breaches of the order because the defendants did not take sufficient care to comply with its term (see *GCT (Management Ltd) v Laurie Marsh Group Ltd* [1973] R.P.C 432).

How can a judgment or order required in delivery of goods be enforced?

21–11 If the judgment or order is for the delivery of goods, the defendant has the option either to deliver the goods or to pay their assessed value. Under RSC order 45, r.6 an order may be obtained requiring the defendant to deliver the goods within the specified time, and failure to comply with that order may then be enforced by an order for committal. Such an order can only be obtained by application to the master, and that application must be served on the defendant.

How is a time fixed for compliance?

21–12 In relation to judgments for the payment of money, recovery of land or delivery of goods, whilst the initial judgment may not specify a time to comply with a judgment, RSC Order 45, r.6 allows the court to make a supplemental order fixing the time for compliance.

An application to fix a time under this rule must be made in accordance with CPR Pt 23 with an application notice being served on the person required to do the act in question (RSC Order 45, r.6(3)).

It is normal practice to specify both the date and the time on which the act is to be done (CPR, r.2.9) so there is no ambiguity as to the deadline for compliance, for example "on or before (or not later than) the 31st May 2006," or "before noon (or 4:00 pm or as maybe) on—day, of the—day or—, 2007."

However, the court's power to fix a supplemental date for compliance does not apply to orders which merely prohibit acts from being done (*Selous v Croydon Rural Sanitary Authority* [1885] 53 L.T. 209) or to orders made under the Inheritance (Provision for Family and Dependents) Act 1975, see *Jennery (Deceased)* [1967] 1 All E.R. 691, CA).

What conditions need to be fulfilled as a prerequisite to enforcement under RSC order 45, r.7?

21–13 The conditions which need to be fulfilled as to the enforcement of a judgment or order, either by a writ of sequestration or by an order of committal under this rule, are explicit and must be strictly followed.

By virtue of sub-para. (6) RSC Order 45, r.7 the court has the power to proceed to the enforcement of a negative order by writ of sequestration or by order of committal to preserve the status quo, even if the original order has not yet been served.

The court must be satisfied that the person or party in question has had notice of the negative order, either by being present when the order was made or by being notified of his terms by telephone, fax or in "such other manner as the court may deem sufficient."

What documents need to be served?

21–14

- a copy of the order;
- copy of the judgment, whether or not it specifies a time within which the act is to be done; and
- copy of any order extending or shortening time under CPR r.3.1 (2)(a), or any written agreement to extend the time limit and made under CPR r.2.11; and
- any order under RSC Order 45, r.6 to fix additional time for the enforcement of the order (see *Re Seal* [1903] 1 Ch. 87).

Special rules under RSC Order 45, r.7 apply in respect of serving an order on a company in these circumstances.

What is the required method of service?

21–15 In every case the required document(s) must be served personally on the person required to do or abstain from doing the act in question. The court has flexibility by virtue of CPR r.6.8 to order an alternative method of service.

What are the warning notice requirements on the order?

21–16 The order to be served must display on the front page a clear warning to the recipient that disobedience of the terms of the order will amount to a contempt of court punishable by imprisonment or (in the case of an order requiring a company to do or abstain from doing an act) sequestration of the assets of the company and the imprisonment of any individual responsible.

The form of warning notice must be endorsed on the copy for the service of all orders which are required to be served, whether personally or not (see *Hampden v Wallis* [1884] 26 Ch. D. 746) and regardless of the fact that the "defendant" is a limited liability company (see *Benabo v William J and Partners Ltd* [1941] Ch. 52).

A similar warning notice must also be endorsed on orders in divorce proceedings requiring a person to do an act under RSC Order 45, r.7(4), or CCR Order 29, r.1 (being county court cases).

21–17 The endorsement on the front of the order, warning of the consequences of disobedience, must follow the examples below:

Individual	"If you, the within named A.B., neglect to obey this judgment (or order) by the time stated (or in the case of an order to abstain from doing an act, "if you, the within named A.B., disobey this judgment (or order)), you may be held to be in contempt of court and liable to imprisonment."
Company	"If you, the within named A.B. Ltd, neglect to obey this judgment (or order) by the time stated (or in the case of an order to abstain from doing an act, "if you, the within named A.B. Ltd disobey this judgment (or order)), you may be held to be in contempt of court and liable to sequestration of your assets."
Company Director (where enforcement proceedings are going to be sought against the director or other Officer of the company).	"If A.B. Limited neglect to obey this judgment (or order) for the time stated "or in the case of an order to abstain from doing an act, "if A.B. Limited disobey this judgment (or order), U, X.Y. a director or Officer of the said A.B. Limited may be held to be in contempt of court and liable to imprisonment."

The court does have discretion under RSC Order 45, r.7(6) to dispense with the failure to incorporate a penal notice in a judgment order requiring a person to *abstain* from doing an act. However, this discretion does not extend through a judgment or order which requires the recipient to *do* a positive act. (see *Dempster v Dempster, Independent,* November 9, 1990, CA). However, as a person's liberty is involved, strict compliance with the rule is desirable, and it is unwise to rely on the court's discretion.

What are the requirements on time for the service of documents?

21–18 Where a specified time is limited for doing the act required, the order must be served within the time (see *Iberian Trust Ltd v Founders Trust and Investment Co Ltd* [1932] 2 K.B.87).

If the order is not served within that time, then the remedy is to apply for a supplemental order giving a new time for compliance (see *Treherne v Dale* [1884] L.R. 27 Ch. D. 66 and *Re Seal* [1903] 1 Ch. 87).

Who must be served?

21–19 The following rules apply:

Individual	Documents must be served personally on that individual.
Persons "Jointly and severally liable," e.g. trustees/ partners.	If only one person can be served, that will be sufficient to found a committal against him (*Re Ellis* [1906] 54 W.R. 526)
Company	Documents must be served on the company in order to found an application for a writ of sequestration against the company's property.
Property of a Company Director	Documents must be served personally on a director or other Officer.

Can service be dispensed with?

21–20 An order of committal for a person who disobeys the court order to do an act within the given time will not be made unless a copy of the order, with the proper endorsement in the form of a warning notice (as set out above), has been personally served upon a person within the required time, or unless he has had notice of the order and is evading the service.

The fact that the person was present in the court when the order was made is not sufficient to dispense with service of the order (see *Re Tuck: Century Insurance Co v Larkin* [1910] 1 IR 91). However, in the case of *Haydon v Haydon* [1911] 2 K.B. 191, CA, involving an application under the debtor's acts, an order for committal was made, although the debtor had not been personally served with the order but he was in court when it was made and was present when the order was made for his committal.

What are the High Court powers to punish any contempt?

21–21 Under RSC Order 52, the court has power to punish contempt of court by an order of committal to prison or by other means. These may be by ordering a payment of a fine or by the issue of writ of sequestration. Committal applications under RSC Order 52, r.4 are always dealt with by a High Court Judge, and the following points apply to applications made under the rule:

- if proceedings are in progress, the application for committal is made by application notice;
- if proceedings are not in progress, a Pt 8 claim form must be issued (see Powers 2.1 and 2.2 of the Practice Direction—committal applications);
- evidence in support of a committal application must be by an affidavit and, together with a Pt 8 claim form or application notice, must be served personally on the person sought to be committed;
- a day for the hearing must be obtained from the Listing Office, Room WG5 of the Royal Court of Justice, Strand, London WC2A 1LL and endorsed on, or served with, the claim form or application notice.

Paragraphs 2.5, 2.6 and 3.1 to 3.4 of the Practice Direction deal with the content of the evidence and serving and filing, while para. 4 deals with the hearing date and management of the proceedings.

The proceedings are normally heard in public, but under RSC Order 52, r.6 certain cases may be heard in private (and see para.9 of the Practice Direction).

21–22 Where the court makes a finding of contempt, details of the contempt and of the order or undertaking breached (where appropriate) must be set out in the order. The term or any period of committal must be stated in the order and cannot exceed a two-year period.

Any fine must be expressed as payable to "Her Majesty The Queen" and the order must state the amount of the fine and the date and time within which it must be paid. A contemnor and his solicitors will be notified separately as to how the fine should be paid. A precedent of the order is in Form No. 85 and will normally be drawn by the court.

When an order for committal to prison is made, the court will issue a warrant to the Tipstaff authorising him to convey the contemnor to the appropriate prison. A copy of the order should be served on the prison governor.

RSC Order 52, r.8 deals with the discharge of the person committed.

County court business

Where is the starting point in the county court Rules?

21–23 The mirror provision in the county court to Order 45 is CCR Order 29. Once again, where a person is required:

- by judgment or order of the county court to do an act and then refuses or neglects to do it within the time fixed by the judgment or order or any subsequent order; or
- where a person disobeys a judgment or order requiring him to abstain from doing an act.

Then, subject to the Debtors Acts 1869 and 1878 in the provisions of CCR Order 29, the judgment or order may be enforced, by order of the judge, by a committal order against that person or, if that person is a company, against any director or other Officer of the company.

21–24 Subject to paras (6) and (7) of the CCR Order 29, a judgment order must not be enforced under para.(1) unless:

- a copy of the judgment or order has been served personally on the person required to do or abstain from doing the act in question;
- in addition, where that person is a company, on the director or other Officer of the company against whom a committal order is sought;
- in the case of a judgment or order requiring a person to do an act, the copy has been so served *before* the expiration of the time within which he was required to do the act and was accompanied by a copy of any order, made between the date of the judgment or order and the date of service, fixing that time.

Where a judgment or order enforceable by a committal order under this rule has been given or made, the court officer must, if the judgment or order is in the nature of an injunction, at the time when the judgment or order is drawn up, and in any other case on the request of the judgment creditor, issue a copy of the judgment or order, endorsed with or incorporating a notice as to the consequences of disobedience.

If the person served with the judgment or order fails to obey it, the judgment creditor can issue a claim form or, where appropriate, an application notice seeking the committal for contempt of court of that person, and the claim form or application notice must be served on that person personally.

This notice is usually referred to as a "penal notice," (see Form N77).

The claim form or application notice must identify the provisions of the injunction or undertaking, which it is alleged have been disobeyed or broken, by listing the ways in which it has been done.

21–25 Evidence in support of the application (or claim form) must be in the form of an affidavit stating the grounds on which the application is made, and unless service is dispensed with under para.(7) of CCR Order 29, a copy of the affidavit in support must be served with the claim form or application notice.

If a committal order is made, a follow-up order must be produced for the issue of a warrant of committal. Unless the judge states otherwise, a copy of that order must be served on the person to be committed, either before or at the time of the execution of the warrant.

Where the warrant has been signed by the judge, the order for issue of the warrant may be served on the person to be committed at any time within 36 hours after the execution of the warrant.

A warrant of committal must not, without further order of the court, be enforced more than two years after the date on which the warrant is issued.

21–26 A judgment or order requiring a person to abstain from doing an act may be enforced under para. (1) of the CCR Order 29, regardless of the fact that service of the copy of the judgment or order has not been effected in accordance with para. (2) CCR Order 29. The judge must be satisfied that, pending such service, the person against whom it is sought to enforce the judgment or order has had notice of the judgment or order either requiring him to do something, or to abstain from doing something, by being:

- present when the judgment or order was given or made; or
- notified of the terms of the judgment or order whether by telephone, telegram or otherwise (telegram is probably a rarity—so fax and email should be considered).

As in the High Court arena, the county court may dispense with service of a copy of a judgment or order or a claim form or application notice if the court thinks it just to do so.

Where service of the claim form or application notice has been dispensed with, a committal order is made in the absence of the respondent, the judge may take the initiative and fix a date and time when the person to be committed is to be brought back to court. The maximum sentence is two years (Contempt of Court Act 1981).

Does CCR Order 29 apply to family proceedings?

21–27 CCR Order does apply to family proceedings as varied by the Family Proceedings Rules 1991 (SI 1991/1247), rr. 3.9A and 4.21A.

How can contempt be committed in relation to a warrant of possession?

21–28 A person may be in contempt of court if he fails to comply with an order for possession requiring him to deliver up possession on a particular date. A person may be guilty of contempt of court if he obstructs a bailiff seeking to execute a warrant of possession (see *Bell v Tuohy* [2002] EWCA Civ 423; [2002] 1 W.L.R 2703.)

If the application for committal is based on a failure to comply with an order for possession, then, generally, the order will have to give a date and time for compliance and be endorsed with a penal notice.

How is a committal action started in the county court?

21–29 If there are existing proceedings before the court, the committal application should be made within those proceedings, and an application for breach of an undertaking order must be made in the proceedings in which the undertaking was given or made on Form N244 (see also CCR Practice Direction 29, para.2.2).

Where no existing proceedings are underway, the committal application must be started by issue of a Pt 8 claim form on Form N208 (see CCR Practice Direction 29, para.2.1).

21–30 The claim form or application (depending on which one is applicable) must:

- identify the provision of the injunction or undertaking which is alleged to have been disobeyed or broken;
- list the ways in which it is alleged that the injunction has been disobeyed or the undertaking broken, which is set out in a supporting affidavit stating the grounds on which the application is made—see generally CCR Practice Direction 29 paras 2.5 and 2.6;

- if the proceedings are by application notice and proceedings which already exist, then the notice must quote the title and reference number of those proceedings.

A copy of the affidavit must be served with the application form unless service is dispensed with.

A word of warning is that old Form N78 should not be used without the considerable adoption necessary to make it Human Rights Act 1998-compliant.

It should be noted that the court has jurisdiction to institute committal proceedings itself, without any application being made, but if it does so, another judge should hear the committal application (see *Re A Minors, The Times*, December 31, 1988 CA).

What are the rules on the service of proceedings/ an application?

21–31 If the application is made by the issue of a claim form, Pt 8 applies and the claim form together with copies of all original evidence must be served personally on the respondent. In line with High Court procedure, written evidence must contain a prominent notice of the possible consequences of the court making a committal order, and of the respondent's failure to attend, unless the court directs otherwise (see CCR Practice Direction 29, para. 2.5 (v)).

If the committal application is started by an application notice under CPR Pt 23, requirements as to the personal service and a prominent notice apply, and the application cannot be dealt with without a hearing (see CCR Practice Direction 29, para. 4.1).

Only in exceptional circumstances will service be dispensed with. A form of warning notice is annexed to the Practice Direction at CCR Practice Direction 29.

What evidence is required at the hearing?

21–32 Evidence in support of the application would have been served with the application, which in turn will have been filed. Written evidence in opposition to the application must be given by affidavit and filed, unless the court directs the contrary (see CCR Practice Direction 29, para.3.2).

Even if the respondent has not filed or served written evidence, he may give oral evidence at the hearing if he wishes. If he does, he may be cross-examined. The respondent may, with the permission of the court, call a witness to give oral evidence, notwithstanding the fact that the witness has not filed an affidavit (see CCR Practice Direction 29, para.3.4).

It should be noted that an amendment to the claim form or application notice can only be made if the court gives permission.

21–33 The hearing date of the committal application must not be less than 14 days after service of the application. The hearing date must be specified in the claim form and application notice, or in a separate notice served at the same time. The court may certainly also decide to give directions as part of its case management function and convene a directions hearing (see CCR Practice Direction 29, paras. 4.2 and 4.3).

If the matter is adjourned, the notice giving the date of the adjourned hearing must be personally served, unless the respondent was present to hear the new date or was remanded in custody. On an application to commit, the court would not exercise its power to cure procedural defects that affect the essential rights of the defendant (see CCR Practice Direction 29, para.10).

If, at the hearing, the defendant is unrepresented, he should be asked by the judge if he wishes to be legally represented, and in appropriate cases informed of the availability of assistance from the Community Legal Service (see *http://www.clsdirect.org.uk* [Accessed October 19, 2010]*)*. The defendant should be offered contact details. As to the request for an adjournment to exercise the right given by the Human Rights Act 1998, see *Berry Trade Ltd v Moussavi* (No.1) [2002] EWCA CIV 477; [2002] 1 W.L.R. 1910, CA.

21–34 The burden of proof is higher than "on the balance of probabilities" in view of the fact that the defendant may be sent to prison, and so it is at the higher standard of "beyond reasonable doubt." (see s.1 of the Human Rights Act 1998 and see CCR 29, r.1 [22]).

The committal hearing will normally be in public but if it is in private and the respondent is found guilty of contempt, the judge must make an announcement in open court containing the particulars set out in his findings.

A committal application cannot be discontinued without the permission of the court, but there are provisions to strike out a committal application contained in CCR Practice Direction 29, paras 8 and 5.

Except where under an enactment, a Master or district judge has power to make a committal order, which may only be made by a Circuit Judge or a person authorised to act, or capable by virtue of his office, so acting (see CCR Practice Direction 29, para. 11).

It should be remembered that committal is a remedy of the last resort, and the court will expect the claimant to have exhausted any other available remedy (see *Danchevsky v Danchevsky* [1975] Fam. 17 CA).

What is the effect of a committal order?

21–35 If a committal order is made, it will be for the issue of a warrant of committal, and unless the judge orders otherwise:

- a copy of the order will be served on the person to be committed before or at the time of the execution of the warrant; or
- where the order has been signed by the judge, the order for the issue of the warrant may be served on the person to be committed any time within 36 hours after the execution of the warrant. For a form of warrant of committal see Form N80.

It should be noted that imprisonment is not an automatic result of a breach. Further guidance can be gleaned from the note to CCR Order 29, r.1 [23] Civil Court Practice 2006, Vol. 1.

Does the court have powers to suspend a committal order?

21–36 The court has power to suspend a committal order and to impose consecutive census in respect of separate contempt (see *Lee v Walker* [1985] Q.B. 1191; [1985] 3 W.L.R. 170; [1985] 1 All E.R. 781). The court may suspend a committal order for an indefinite period, for example until further order (see *Griffin v Griffin* [2000] 2 F.C.R 302, CA).

Any suspended sentence must be for a fixed term (see *Re C (A minor)* (Wardship:Contempt) [1986] 1 F.L.R. 578), as must the period for which the order is suspended (see *Pidduck v Molloy* [1992] 2 F.L.R. 202). The period should be entered on Form N79A. The terms and conditions of the suspension should be set out in the order. Needless to say, suspension will not be appropriate if the terms of the original order have already been complied with.

Is there any time limit for the enforcement of a warrant?

21–37 A warrant for arrest, or a committal, should not be enforced more than two years after the date it was issued (see CCR Order 29, r.1 [5A]).

How is the party discharged from prison?

21–38 A person wishing to apply for discharge from prison can apply in writing, showing he has purged his contempt or wishes to purge his contempt. The application should be attested by the governor or other officer not below the rank of "principal officer."

CCR Order 27, r.8 relates to the discharge of a person committed with failure to obey an order or to attend and adjourn an application for an attachment of earnings order. CCR Order 28, r.4 relates to the discharge of a person committed under the judgment summons procedure. CCR Order 28, r.14 relates to the discharge of a person committed under s.5 of the Debtor's Act 1869.

21–39 A format for the application of discharge is not in the prescribed form, but the following may be used:

> "Take notice, that I intend on _____ day of ________ 2002 apply to the judge of this court (or to the District Judge of this court, as the case may be) [state to place] to discharge within custody. I have purged [or being desirous of purging] my contempt as follows [give detail] dated _____ day of ________200____.
>
> To ________ [address] etc."

The Secretary of State is required by s.258 of the Criminal Justice Act 2003 to release anyone in prison for contempt of court once half of the sentence has been served. The Secretary of State is empowered by the same section to grant earlier in exceptional circumstances on "compassionate grounds." The notice must be served not less than one day before the hearing on any party whose instance of warrant or order was issued.

Appendices

Request for Warrant of Execution

to be completed and signed by the claimant or his solicitor and sent to the court with the appropriate fee

1 Claimant's name and address

TOM GOOD
3 THE CLOSE
SURBITON
WARWICKSHIRE
CV4 6DF

In the COVENTRY **County Court**

Claim Number 10CV123456

2 Name and address for service and payment (if different from above)
Ref/Tel No.

LAW ONE SOLICITORS
THE HIGH STREET
COVENTRY
CV1 6FF

TG1/024 76 987654

for court use only

Warrant no.
Issue date:
Warrant applied for at o'clock
Foreign court code/name:

3 Defendant's name and address

MARGOT LEDBETTER
5 THE CLOSE
SURBITON
WARWICKSHIRE
CV4 6DF

4 Warrant details

(A) Balance due at date of this request	1233.54
(B) Amount for which warrant to issue	1233.54
Issue fee	100.00
Solicitor's costs	2.25
Land Registry fee	
TOTAL	1335.79

If the amount of the warrant at (B) is less than the balance at (A), the sum due after the warrant is paid will be

I certify that the whole or part of any instalments due under the judgment or order have not been paid and the balance now due is as shown

Signed

Claimant (Claimant's solicitor)

Dated 18.06.10

IMPORTANT
You must inform the court immediately of any payments you receive after you have sent this request to the court

You should provide a contact number so that the bailiff can speak to you if he/she needs to:
Daytime phone number: Evening phone number (if possible):
Contact name (where appropriate):
Defendant's phone number (if known):
If you have any other information which may help the bailiff or if you have reason to believe that the bailiff may encounter any difficulties you should write it below.

N323-w3-Request for warrant of execution (4.99) *Produced on behalf of The Court Service*

Combined certificate of judgment and request for writ of fieri facias or writ of possession

In the COVENTRY County Court	
Claim No.	10CV123456t
Creditor's/ Claimant's Ref.	TOM GOOD
Debtor's/ Defendant's Ref.	MARGOT LEBETTER
Date	01.04.10

Creditor/Claimant

TOM GOOD

Debtor/Defendant

MARGOT LEDBETTER
5 THE CLOSE
SURBITON
WARWICKSHIRE
CV9 8GG

Part 1

Date of judgment or order 23.03.10

Total amount of judgment *including any costs* £1223.76

or

Details of order for possession *including any costs*

Total amount of interest accrued at the rate of ____per day to date (*if any*)

I certify that the details I have given are correct and that to my knowledge there is no application or other procedure pending.

I request an order for enforcement in the High Court by

☑ Writ of Fieri Facias

☐ Writ of Possession

I intend to enforce the judgment or order by execution against goods, and/or against trespassers in the High Court and require this Certificate for this purpose.

....

signed – (Creditor/Creditor's solicitor)
(Claimant/Claimant's solicitor)

01.04.10
.... date

Part 2 ***(for court use only)***

I certify that this is a true extract of the court record in this case.

Order for enforcement in the High Court by

☐ Writ of Fieri Facias

☐ Writ of Possession

made on (date) ....

.... An Officer of the Court

Please Note:

This judgment or order has been sent to the High Court for enforcement by (Writ of Fieri Facias) (Writ of Possession against trespassers) only.

The county court claim has not been transferred to the High Court. Applications for other methods of enforcement or ancillary applications must be made to the county court in which the judgment or order was made, unless the case has since been transferred to a different court, in which case it must be made to that court.

The court office at

is open between 10 am and 4 pm Monday to Friday. When corresponding with the court, please address forms or letters to the Court Manager and quote the claim number.

THE ACTION DEPARTMENT of the High Court is open between 10am and 4.30pm. All correspondence should be sent to the Court Manager, Action Department, Royal Courts of Justice, Strand, London WC2A 2LL

N293A Combined certificate of judgment and request for writ of fieri facias or writ of possession (04.04) continued overleaf

Part 3

In the High Court of Justice
Queen's Bench Division
(Sent from the COVENTRY County Court by Certificate dated the day of)

High Court Enforcement Number

County Court Claim Number
10CV123456

Address of (Debtor)
(property of which possession is to be given)

5 THE CLOSE
SURBITON
WARWICKSHIRE
CV9 8GG

Seal a Writ of (Fieri Facias)(Possession) directed to the: To: "CLAIRE LOUISE SANDBROOK, an enforcement officer authorised to enforce writs of execution from the High Court'.

Or,

'The enforcement officers authorised to enforce writs of execution from the High Court who are assigned to the district of[1]_______in England and Wales'.

Note: If you have chosen this option you must send this writ to the National Information Centre for Enforcement for allocation.

against MARGOT LEDBETTER

for: *(Complete A, B, C as appropriate)*

A. the sum of:

(a) debt	£1233.76
(b) costs and interest	£
(c) Subsequent costs *(if any)*	£

B. and interest thereon at ...8...% per annum from the date of transfer and costs of execution

C. possession of

and £ for costs.

Signed
Address for service Law One Solicitors, The High Street, Coventry, CV1 1DD
Date 01.04.10

Guidance Notes

Enforcement in the High Court of county court judgments or orders.

The practice for the enforcement in the High Court of those county court judgments or orders to which Article 8(A) and (B) of the High Court and County Court Jurisdiction Order 1991 applies shall be as follows:

1. The applicant shall present to the judgment counter clerk a certificate of judgment of the county court sealed with the seal of that court, setting out details of the judgment or order to be enforced, together with a copy of the same. There is no fee payable on registration.
2. The judgment counter clerk will check that the certificate has been signed by an officer of the issuing court (a rubber stamp is not sufficient), dated and that the certificate complies with CCR 0.22, r8 (1A) (Sched. 2 to the CPR), and in particular with the requirement that on its face it states that it is granted for the purpose of enforcing the judgment or order by execution against goods or for possession against trespassers in the High Court.
3. Provided that paragraphs 1 and 2 have been complied with, the counter clerk will:-
   (a) Allocate a reference number, and year and endorse that on the top right hand corner of the certificate and copy.
   (b) Date and seal the certificate and copy. Return the original to the applicant who should send the writ to the appropriate enforcement officer or the National Information Centre for Enforcement for allocation and retain a copy for the court records.
4. The Certificate shall be treated for enforcement purposes as a High Court judgment or order and interest at the appropriate rate shall run from the date of the certificate. Such interest as claimed on the judgment in the county court should be incorporated in the judgment as above.
5. The title of all subsequent documents shall be as follows:-

   IN THE HIGH COURT OF JUSTICE High Court No.
   QUEEN'S BENCH DIVISION County Court Claim No
   (Sent from the County Court by Certificate dated the day of .)

   A.B.
   Claimant
   C.D.
   Defendant
6. When the appropriate fee is paid and a writ of *fieri facias* or possession is issued, the Certificate of Judgment retained by the applicant shall be date sealed by the counter clerk on the bottom left hand corner.
7. **Any application for a stay of execution should be made by application notice in the High Court returnable before a Queen's Bench Master. All other applications for enforcement or ancillary relief must be made to the county court in which the judgment or order was made, unless the case has since been transferred to a different court, in which case that court.**

R L Turner, Senior Master
Queen's Bench Division

[1] This should reflect the Districts as set out in the High Court Enforcement Officers Regulation 2004

Application for order that debtor attend court for questioning

In the	Claim No.
COVENTRY COUNTY COURT	10CV123456
	Appn. No.

TOM GOOD Claimant

MARGOT LEDBETTER Defendant

The [claimant] [defendant] ('the judgment creditor') applies for an order that the [defendant] [claimant] ('the judgment debtor') attend court to provide information about the judgment debtor's means and any other information needed to enforce the judgment or order given on 7TH MARCH 2010 [by the in claim no.].

1. Judgment debtor
The judgment debtor is MARGOT LEDBETTER
whose address is 5 THE CLOSE, SURBITON, WARWICKSHIRE

Postcode CV9 8GG

2. Judgment debt or order

[The judgment or order required the judgment debtor to pay £ 1223.76 (including any costs and interest). The amount now owing is £ 1223.76 [which includes further interest payable on the judgment debt]].

[The judgment or order required the judgment debtor to]

Note:
Questioning and documents
Questioning will be by a court officer unless a judge agrees there are compelling reasons for questioning to take place before a judge. Normally the court officer will ask the questions set out in Form EX140 and the judgment debtor will be told to produce all relevant documents including:

- pay slips
- bank statements
- building society books
- share certificates
- rent book
- mortgage statement
- hire purchase and similar agreements
- court orders
- any other outstanding bills
- electricity, gas, water and council tax bills for the past year.

and in the case of a business
- bills owed to it
- 2 years' accounts
- current management accounts.

Complete sections 3,4 and 5 only if applicable
The statement of truth overleaf must be completed.

3. [Attached is a list of questions which the judgment creditor wishes the court officer to ask the judgment debtor in addition to those in Form EX140.]

4. [Attached is a list of documents which the judgment creditor wishes the judgment debtor to be ordered to produce in addition to those listed in the note above.]

5. [The judgment creditor requests that the judgment debtor be questioned by the judgment creditor before a judge. The reason for this request is

Statement of Truth

*(I believe)(The judgment creditor believes) that the facts stated in this application form are true.

*I am duly authorised by the judgment creditor to sign this statement.

signed________________ date 15.04.10 ________________

*(Judgment creditor)(Litigation friend *(where judgment creditor is a child or a patient)*) (Judgment creditor's solicitor)

**delete as appropriate*

Full name JOSEPH BLOGGS

Name of judgment creditor's solicitor's firm LAW ONE SOLICITORS

position or office held SOLICITOR

(if signing on behalf of firm or company)

Judgment creditor's or judgment creditor's solicitor's address to which documents should be sent.

LAW ONE SOLICITORS
THE HIGH STREET
COVENTRY

Postcode CV1 1DD

Tel. no. 024 76 998565

	if applicable
Ref. no.	JB/TG
fax no.	024 76 122554
DX no.	
e-mail	

Application for charging order on land or property

In the	Claim No.
COVENTRY COUNTY COURT	10CV123456
	Appn. No.

TOM GOOD — Claimant

MARGOT LEDBETTER — Defendant

The [claimant] [defendant] ('the judgment creditor') applies for an order imposing a charge on the interest of the [defendant] [claimant] ('the judgment debtor') in the land or property mentioned below to secure payment of the amount owing under the judgment or order given on 7TH MARCH 20 10 [by the in claim no.].

1. **Judgment debtor**
   The judgment debtor is MARGOT LEDBETTER
   whose address is
   5 THE CLOSE, SURBITON, WARWICKSHIRE

   Postcode CV9 8GG

2. **Judgment debt**
   The judgment or order required the judgment debtor to pay £ 1223.76 (including any costs and interest). The amount now owing is £ 1223.76 [which includes further interest payable on the judgment debt].

   ☐ £ of the instalments due under the judgment or order has fallen due and remains unpaid.

   ☑ The judgment or order did not provide for payment by instalments.

3. **The land or property**
   The address of the land or property upon which it is sought to impose a to charge is
   5 THE CLOSE, SURBITON, WARWICKSHIRE, CV9 8GG

   [the title to which is registered at H.M. Land Registry under Title No. CV987654
   An Office Copy of the Land Register entries for this title is attached.]

4. **Judgment debtor's interest in the land or property**
   The judgment debtor is:
   ☐ the sole owner ☑ a joint owner ☐ a beneficiary under a trust

   ☑ This is shown by the Office Copy Land Register entries attached.

   ☐ The judgment creditor believes this to be so because

N379 Application for charging order on land or property (03.02)

5. Other creditors

☐ The judgment creditor does not know of any other creditors of the judgment debtor.

☑ The judgment creditor knows of the following other creditors of the judgment debtor: *(names and addresses and, if known, nature of debt and amount)*

MR JERRY LEDBETTER, 5 THE CLOSE, SURBITON, WARWICKSHIRE, CV9 8GG—SPOUSE AND JOINT PROPRIETOR

MONEY BANK PLC, 222 THE HIGH STREET, BROMLEY, KENT,—MORTGAGE COMPANY

6. Other persons to be served

☐ No other person has an interest in the property (including any co-owners, trustees and persons with rights of occupation).

☑ The following persons have or may have an interest in the property: *(name and address and, if known, nature of interest)*

MR JERRY LEDBETTER, 5 THE CLOSE, SURBITON, WARWICKSHIRE, CV9 8GG—SPOUSE AND JOINT PROPRIETOR MONEY BANK PLC, 222 THE HIGH STREET, BROMLEY, KENT,—MORTGAGE COMPANY

7. Further information

The judgment creditor asks the court to take account of the following:

8. Sources of information *(Complete only where the judgment creditor is a firm or a company or other corporation)*

[The information in this application is given [by me] [by of who is the of the judgment creditor] after making proper enquiry of all persons within the judgment creditor's organisation who might have knowledge of the facts.]

Statement of Truth

*I believe (the judgment creditor believes) that the facts stated in this application form are true.

*I am duly authorised by the judgment creditor to sign this statement

signed__________ date 11.05.10

*(Judgment creditor)(Litigation friend *(where judgment creditor is a child or a patient)*(Judgment creditor's solicitor)

**delete as appropriate*

Full name JOSEPH BLOGGS

Name of judgment creditor's solicitor's firm LAW ONE SOLICITORS

position or office held SOLICITORS *(if signing on behalf of a firm or company)*

Judgment creditor's or judgment creditor's solicitor's address to which documents should be sent.

LAW ONE SOLICITORS
THE HIGH STREET
COVENTRY

Postcode CV1 1DD

if applicable

Ref. no.	JB/TG
fax no.	024 76 122554
DX no.	
e-mail	
Tel. no.	024 76 998565

Application for third party debt order

In the	Claim No.
COVENTRY COUNTY COURT	10cv123456
	Appn. No.
TOM GOOD	
MARGOT LEDBETTER	Claimant
FIRST ABC BANK	Defendant
	Third Party

The [claimant] [defendant] ('the judgment creditor') applies for an order that the third party pay to the judgment creditor the debt which the third party owes to the [defendant] [claimant] ('the judgment debtor') (or so much of it as is necessary to discharge the amount owing under the judgment or order given on 7TH MARCH 20 10 [by the in claim no.]and the costs of this application).

1. Judgment debtor

The judgment debtor is MARGOT LEDBETTER
whose address is
5 THE CLOSE, SURBITON, WARWICKSHIRE

Postcode CV9 8GG

2. Judgment debt

The judgment or order required the judgment debtor to pay £ 1223.76 (including any costs and interest). The amount now due is £1223.76[which includes further interest].

☐ £ of the instalments due under the judgment or order has fallen due and remains unpaid.

☑ The judgment or order did not provide for payment by instalments.

3. Third party

The third party is within England and Wales and owes money to (or holds money to the credit of) the judgment debtor.

The third party is a bank or building society.
Its name is FIRST ABC BANK
Its head office address in England and Wales is:
3MONEY OFFICE VILLAGE
BANKERS DRIVE, LONDON, SW1 2DD

The branch at which the account is held is

☐ not known

☑ the COVENTRY BRANCH
whose address is 111 HIGH STREET, COVENTRY, CV1 2AA

The account number is	The sort code is
☐ not known	☐ not known
☑ 00235644	☑ 11–22–33

N349 Application for third party debt order (03.02) *Printed on behalf of The Court Service*

[The third party is not a bank or building society.

☐ the third party is

whose address in England and Wales is

4. Other persons' interests

The persons (in addition to the judgment debtor) who have a claim to the money owed by the third party are

☑ None

☐ The following: *(names and address(es))*

Information known about each person's claim:

5. Sources and grounds of information

The judgment creditor knowns or believes that the information in section 3 and 4 is correct because:

COPY CHEQUE PREVIOUSLY RETAINED IN RESPECT OF EARLIER PAYMENTS MADE BY THE DEBTOR

6. Other applications

In respect of the judgment debt,

☑ the judgment creditor has made no other applications for third party debt orders.

☐ the judgment creditor has already made the following application(s) for third party debt order:

Details of application(s)

Third party's name

Address

Postcode

Statement of Truth

*I believe (the judgment creditor believes) that the facts stated in this application form are true.

*I am duly authorised by the judgment creditor to sign this statement

signed______________________date__________

*(Judgment creditor)(Litigation friend (*where judgment creditor is a child or a patient*)(Judgment creditor's solicitor)

**delete as appropriate*

Full name JOSEPH BLOGGS

Name of judgment creditor's solicitor's firm LAW ONE SOLICITORS

position or office held SOLICITOR (*if signing on behalf of a firm or company*)

Judgment creditor's or judgment creditor's solicitor's address to which documents should be sent.

LAW ONE SOLICITORS
THE HIGH STREET
COVENTRY

Postcode CV1 1DD

if applicable

Ref. no.	JB/TG
fax no.	024 76 122554
DX no.	
e-mail	
Tel. no.	024 76 998565

Application to enforce an award of an Employment Tribunal and request a Writ of Fieri Facias

Name of court COVENTRY COUNTY COURT
Claim number (To be completed by the court)
Applicant TOM GOOD
Respondent ABC (123) LIMITED

Please give details of the Employment or Employment Appeal Tribunal award you are seeking to enforce under section 15 of the Employment Tribunal Act 1996:

Name of the Tribunal: COVENTRY

Award number: 122287/011

Date of award: 15/01/2010

Please attach the original award to this application.

1. Applicant's details

Name of applicant

TOM GOOD

Applicant's address

3 THE CLOSE
SURBITON
WARWICKSHIRE

Postcode CV9 8GG

Telephone no. 024 76 987654

Ref.

Email address

tg@yahoo.com

Address for service (*if different from above*)

Law One Solicitors
The High Street
Coventry

Postcode CV1 6FF

2. Respondent's details

Name of respondent

ABC (123) LIMITED

Respondent's address

UNIT 3
THE WORKS
COVENTRY
WARWICKSHIRE

Postcode CV3 4DF

N471 Application to enforce an award of an Employment Tribunal and request a Writ of Fieri Facias (04.10)

3. The amount now owing and the costs claimed

The amount of the award including costs awarded by the Tribunal	£ 16,745.98

To claim interest on the award please complete this section.
You must show details of your calculations.

[Interest on £ (as per the amount above)

from ☐☐/☐☐/☐☐☐☐ to ☐☐/☐☐/☐☐☐☐

at %]

or

[As shown in the attached calculation]	£
sub-total	£
Solicitor's costs	£
Less amount paid	£
Total now owing	£ 16,745.98

4. Requests

I request that the award be filed with the county court for enforcement and that an order be made for its enforcement in the High Court by Writ of Fieri Facias.

I intend to enforce the award by execution against goods in the High Court and require a certificate for that purpose.

5. Statement of truth

☐ I believe ☑ The applicant believes

that the facts stated in this application are true and to (my own) (the applicant's) knowledge there are no applications or other procedures pending.

Signed ______________________ Dated ☐☐/☐☐/☐☐☐☐

*(Applicant) (Litigation friend *(where applicant is a child or a Protected Party)*) (Applicant's solicitor or solicitor's agent)

* *delete as appropriate*

Full name JOSEPH BLOGGS

Name of applicant's solicitor's firm MASONS SOLICITORS

Position or office held SOLICITOR

(if signing on behalf of firm or company)

6. To be certified by the court ***(for court use only)***

I certify that the award, the original of which is attached, has been filed at the court and order enforcement in the High Court by Writ of Fieri Facias.

Dated ☐☐/☐☐/☐☐☐☐

Seal

An Officer of the Court

Please Note:

The award has been sent to the High Court for enforcement by Writ of Fieri Facias **only**.

The award **has not been transferred** to the High Court. Applications for other methods of enforcement or ancillary applications **must** be made to the county court in which the award was filed, unless it has since been transferred to a different court, in which case it must be made to that court.

7. Request for Writ of Fieri Facias

In the High Court of Justice

Queen's Bench Division

(Sent from the COVENTRY County Court by

Certificate dated the —— day of ————)

High Court Enforcement Number

[ ]

County Court Claim Number

[ ]

Address of (Debtor)

UNIT 3
THE WORKS
COVENTRY
WARWICKSHIRE
CV3 4DF

Seal a Writ of Fieri Facias directed to:
CLAIRE LOUISE SANDBROOK

an enforcement officer authorised to enforce writs of execution from the High Court.

against ABC (123) LIMITED

for:

A. the sum of:

(a) debt	**£** 16,745.98
(b) costs and interest	**£**
(c) Subsequent costs (*if any*)	**£**

B. and interest thereon at 8 % per annum from the date of transfer and costs of execution.

Signed [ ]

Address for service

MASONS SOLICITORS
122B BAKER STREET
COVENTRY
CV1 7GF

Date ☐☐/☐☐/☐☐☐☐

Rule 6.1

Notes for Creditor

- If the creditor is entitled to the debt by way of assignment, details of the original creditor and any intermediary assignees should be given in part C on page 3.
- If the amount of debt includes interest not previously notified to the debtor as included in the debtor's liability, details should be given, including the grounds upon which interest is charged. The amount of interest must be shown separately.
- Any other charge accruing due from time to time may be claimed. The amount or rate of the charge must be identified and the grounds on which it is claimed must be stated.
- In either case the amount claimed must be limited to that which has accrued due at the date of the demand.
- If the creditor holds any security the amount of the debt should be the sum the creditor is prepared to regard as unsecured for the purposes of the demand. Brief details of the total debt should be included and the nature of the security and the value put upon it by the creditor, as at the date of the demand, must be specified.
- Details of the judgment or order should be inserted, including details of the Division of the Court or District Registry and court reference, where judgment is obtained in the High Court.
- If signatory of the demand is a solicitor or other agent of the creditor the name of the his/her firm should be given

* Delete if signed by the creditor himself

Form 6.2

Statutory Demand under section 268(1)(a) of the Insolvency Act 1986. Debt for Liquidated Sum Payable Immediately Following a Judgment or Order of the Court

Warning

- This is an **important** document. You should refer to the notes entitled "How to comply with a statutory demand or have it set aside".
- If you wish to have this demand set aside you must make application to do so **within 18 days** from its service on you.
- If you do not apply to set aside **within 18 days** or otherwise deal with this demand as set out in the notes **within 21 days** after its service on you, you could be made bankrupt and your property and goods taken away from you.
- Please read the demand and notes carefully. If you are in any doubt about your position you should seek advice **immediately** from a solicitor, a Citizens Advice Bureau, or a licensed insolvency practitioner.

Demand

To **Margot Ledbetter**

Address 5 The Close, Surbiton, Warwickshire, CV9 8GG

This demand is served on you by the creditor:

Name **Tom Good**

Address 3 The Close, Surbiton, Warwickshire, CV9 3GG

The creditor claims that you owe the sum of **£1223.76**, full particulars of which are set out on page 2, and that it is payable immediately and, to the extent of the sum demanded, is unsecured. By a Judgment/Order of the **Coventry County Court** in proceedings entitled (case) Number **10CV123456** between **Tom Good** Claimant and **Margot Ledbetter** Defendant it was adjudged/ordered that you pay to the creditor the sum of **£1223.76**.

The creditor demands that you pay the above debt or secure or compound for it to the creditor's satisfaction.

[The creditor making this demand is a Minister of the Crown or a Government Department, and it is intended to present a bankruptcy petition in the High Court in London.] [Delete if inappropriate]

Signature of individual

Name **Joseph Bloggs**
(BLOCK LETTERS)
Date **15.04.2010**

* Position with or relationship to creditor **Solicitor**

* I am authorised to make this demand on the creditor's behalf.

Address **Law One Solicitors, The High Street, Coventry, CV1 1DD**

Tel. No. **02476998565** Ref. **JB/TG**

N.B. The person making this demand must complete the whole of pages 1, 2 and parts A, B and C (as applicable) on page 3

Form 6.2 contd.

Particulars of Debt

(These particulars must include (a) when the debt was incurred, (b) the consideration for the debt (or if there is no consideration the way in which it arose) and (c) the amount due as at the date of this demand.

1. The creditor obtained a judgment in the Coventry County Court in Claim No. 10CV123456 dated 7th March 2010 making a total judgment of £1223.76.

2. Despite attempts to recover the payment, the Debtor has failed to pay the judgment amount, or any part thereof.

3. The amount now due from the Debtor is £1223.76.

Notes for Creditor
Please make sure that you have read the notes on page 1 before completing this page.

Note:
If space is insufficient continue on page 4 and clearly indicate on this page that you are doing so.

Form 6.2 contd.

Part A
Appropriate Court for Setting Aside Demand

Rule 6.4(2) of the Insolvency Rules 1986 states that the appropriate court is the court to which you would have to present your own bankruptcy petition in accordance with Rule 6.40(1) and (2).

Any application by you to set aside this demand should be made to that court, or, if this demand is issued by a Minister of the Crown or a Government Department, you must apply to the High Court to set aside if it is intended to present a bankruptcy petition against you in the High Court (see page 1).

In accordance with those rules on present information the appropriate court is **Coventry County Court** of **140 Much Park Street, Coventry West Midlands, England CV1 2SN**

Part B

The individual or individuals to whom any communication regarding this demand may be addressed is/are:

Name **Joseph Bloggs**

(BLOCK LETTERS)

Address **Law One Solicitors, The High Street, Coventry, CV1 1DD**	
Telephone number **02476998565**	
Reference **JB/TG**	

Part C

For completion if the creditor is entitled to the debt by way of assignment

	Name	Date(s) of Assignment
Original creditor		
Assignees		

THERE ARE IMPORTANT NOTES IN THE NEXT PAGE

Form 6.2 contd.

How to comply with a statutory demand or have it set aside (ACT WITHIN 18 DAYS)

If you wish to avoid a bankruptcy petition being presented against you, you must pay the debt shown on page 1, particulars of which are set out on page 2 of this notice, within the period of **21 days** after its service upon you. However if the demand follows (includes) a judgment or order of a County Court, any payment must be made to that County Court (quoting the Case No.). Alternatively, you can attempt to come to a settlement with the creditor. To do this you should:

- inform the individual (or one of the individuals) named in part B above immediately that you are willing and able to offer security for the debt to the creditor's satisfaction; or
- inform the individual (or one of the individuals) named in part B immediately that you are willing and able to compound for the debt to the creditor's satisfaction.

If you dispute the demand in whole or in part you should:

- contact the individual (or one of the individuals) named in part B immediately.

If you consider that you have grounds to have this demand set aside or if you do not quickly receive a satisfactory written reply from the individual named in part B whom you have contacted you should **apply within 18 days** from the date of service of this demand on you to the appropriate court shown in part A above to have the demand set aside.

Any application to set aside the demand (Form 6.4 in Schedule 4 to the Insolvency Rules 1986) should be made within 18 days from the date of service upon you and be supported by a witness statement (Form 6.5 in Schedule 4 to those Rules) stating the grounds on which the demand should be set aside. The forms may be obtained from the appropriate court when you attend to make the application.

Remember!—From the date of service on you of this document
(a) you have only 18 days to apply to the court to have the demand set aside, and
(b) you have only 21 days before the creditor may present a bankruptcy petition.

Debt Management Relief Table

	Creates moratorium on enforcement action	Available for consumers or businesses	Requirements on repayment	Duration of scheme	Creditors' support needed	Discharge	Debt Limit	Income
Administration Orders	Yes	Consumer only	Repayment terms possible and flexible as to proportion	5 years maximum	No	Discharge available following payment of the proportion of the debt ordered	Currently £5000—likely to increase to £15,000	Must be above prescribed minimum
Enforcement Restriction Orders	Yes	Consumer only	Repayment terms possible but no reduction in debt level	1 year maximum	No	Discharge not possible	No limit	Must be realistic prospect income will improve within 6 months
Debt Relief Orders	Yes	Consumer and business	No requirement to repay	1 year maximum + 3 months (with extension)	No	Discharge available at end of moratorium	There will be a prescribed limit	No surplus income available to repay
Debt Management Schemes	Yes	Consumer only	Repayment depends on terms of scheme	Duration depends on terms of scheme	Depends on terms of scheme	Discharge available after payment under the debt repayment plan	Depends on terms of scheme	Depends on terms of scheme
IVAs	Yes	Consumer and business	Repayment depends on terms of arrangement	Flexible	Yes + 75% in value	Discharge if IVA complied with	No limit	Flexible

Flow Chart For Application For An Attachment Of Earnings Order – CCR Order 27

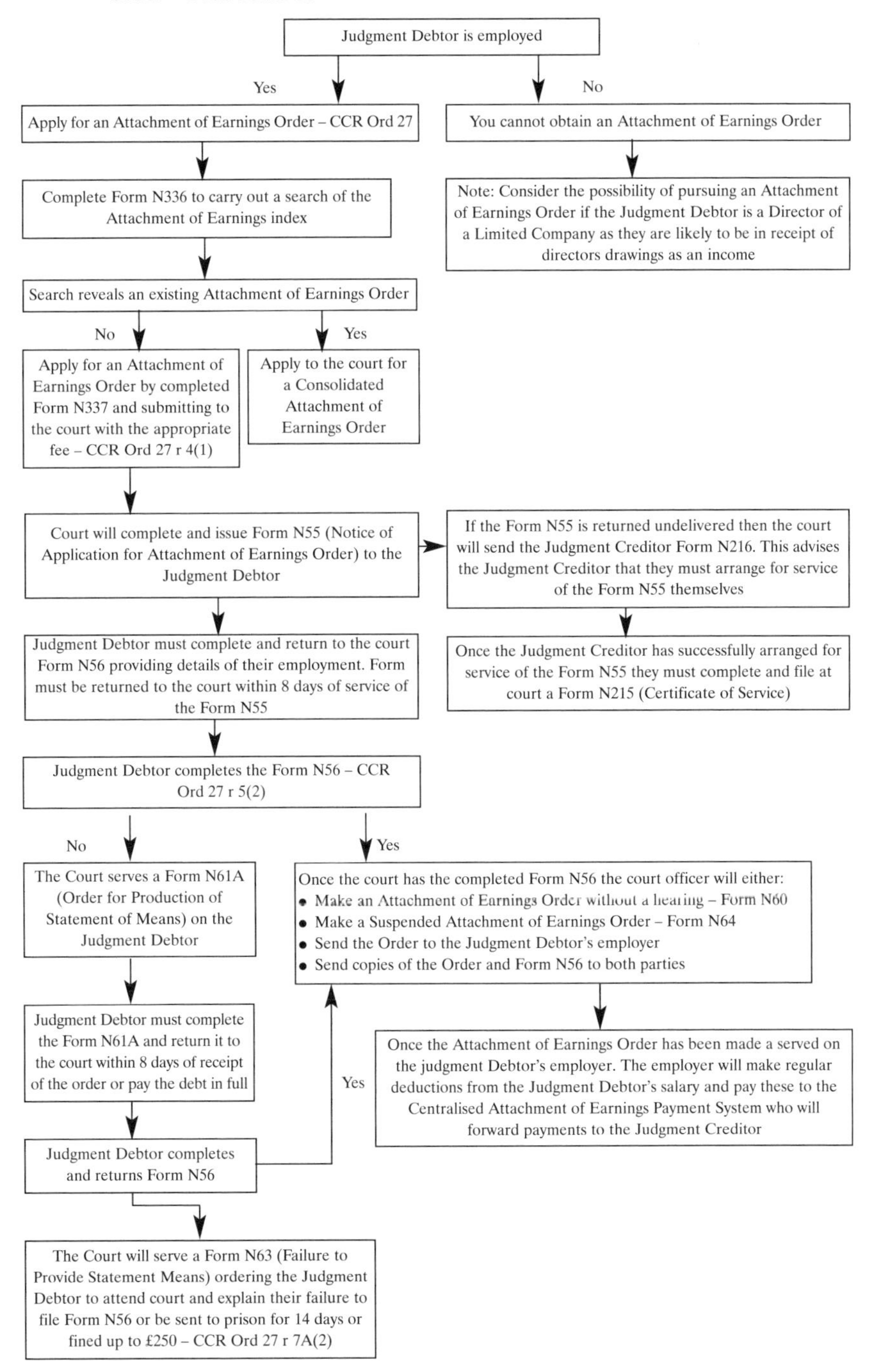

Flow Chart To Apply For A Charging Order Against Land – CPR 73

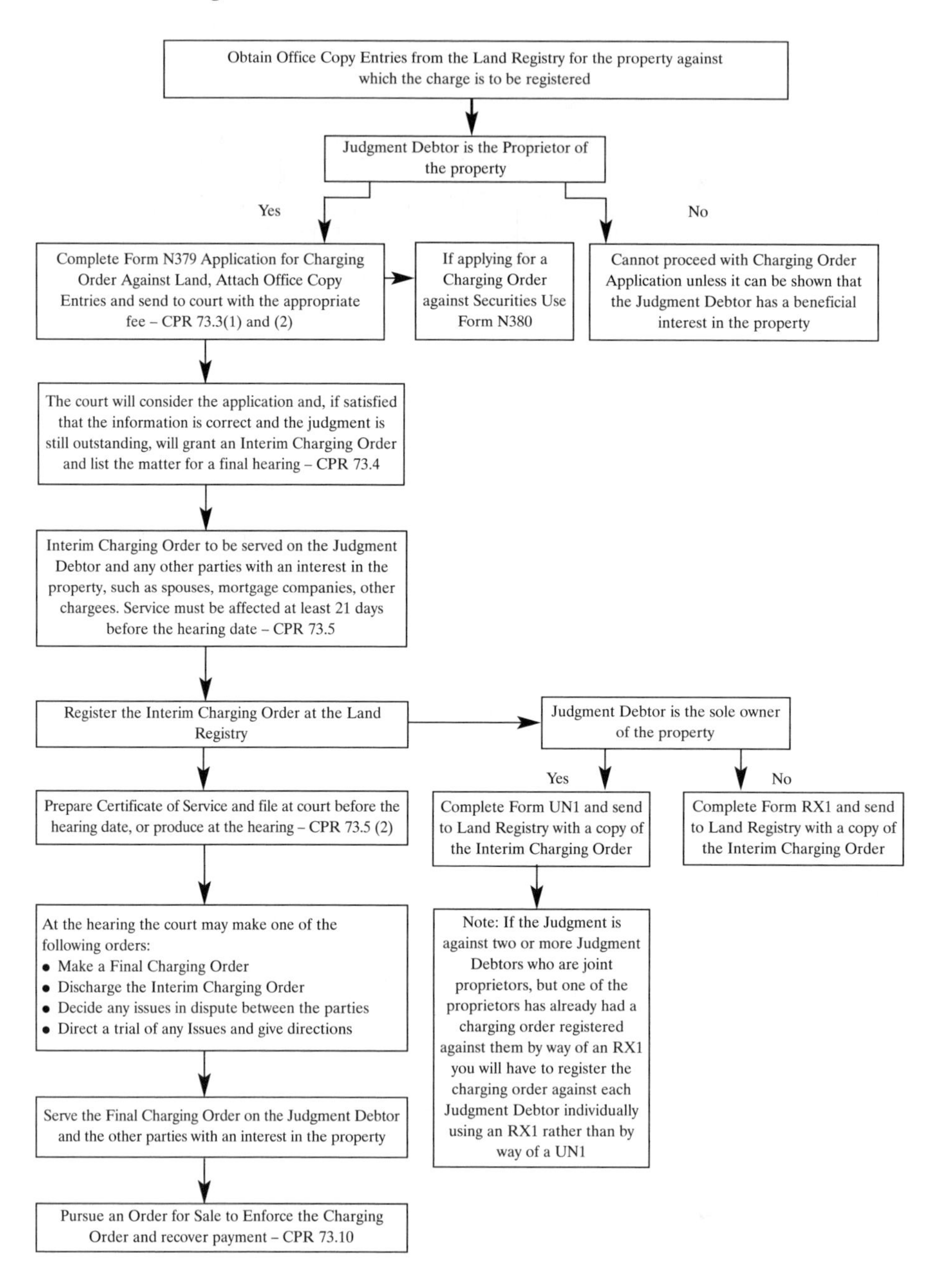

Flow Chart For Execution Against Goods By Way of Warrant of Execution (CCR Order 26) Or Writ of Fieri Facias (RSC Order 47)

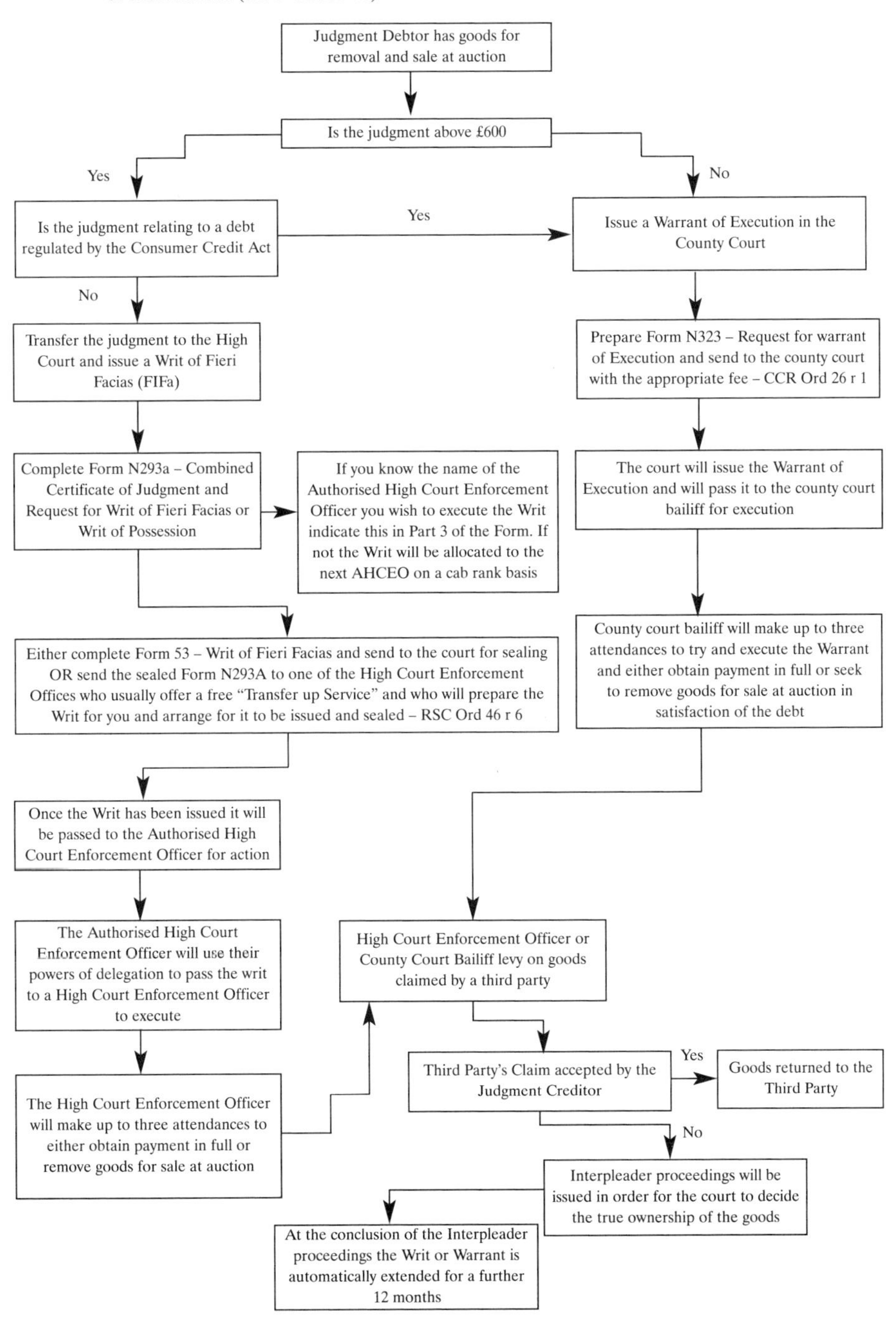

Flow Chart To Pursue Insolvency Against a Limited Company

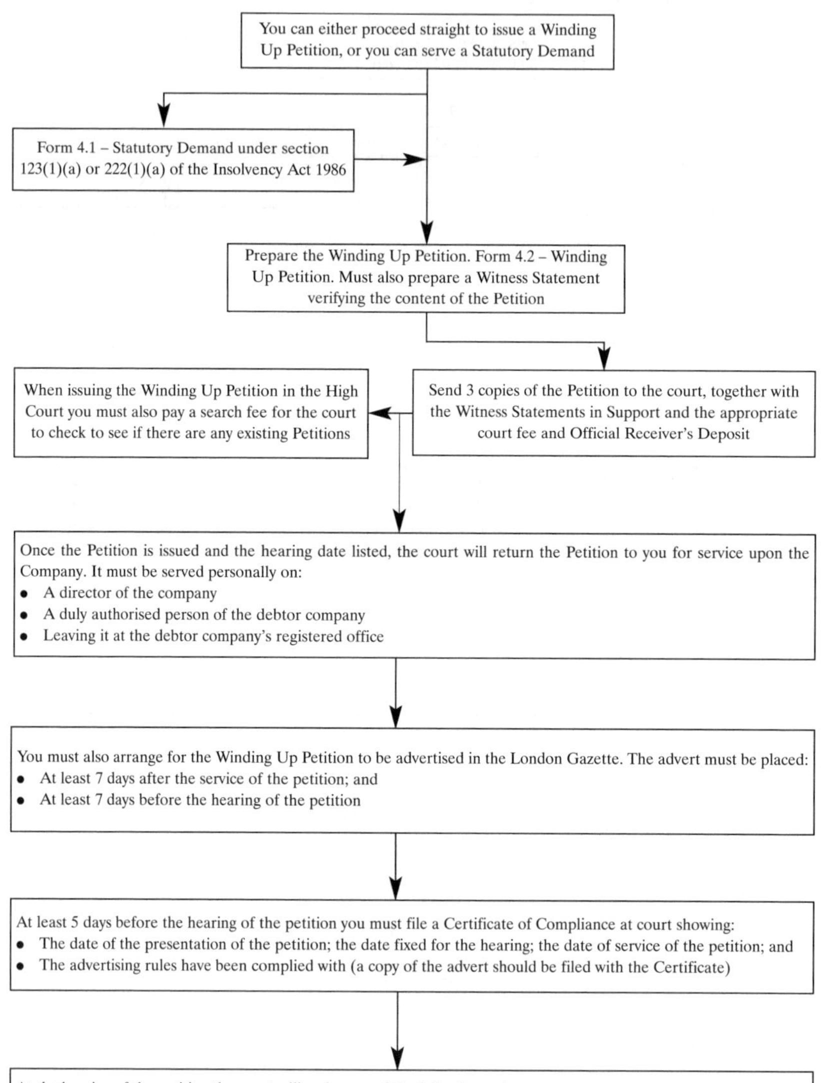

Flow Chart To Pursue Insolvency Against An Individual

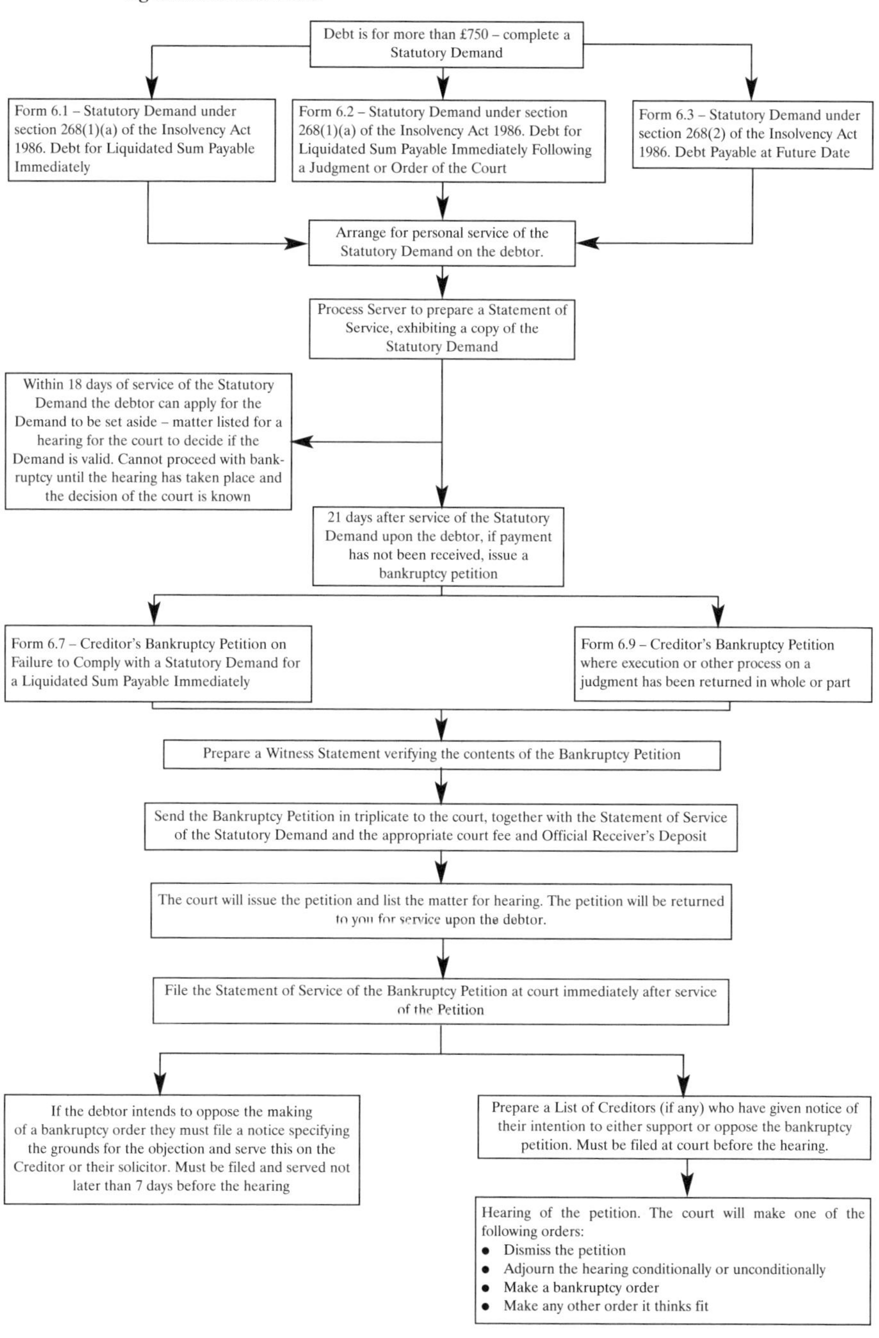

Flow Chart To Apply For An Order To Obtain Information – CPR 71

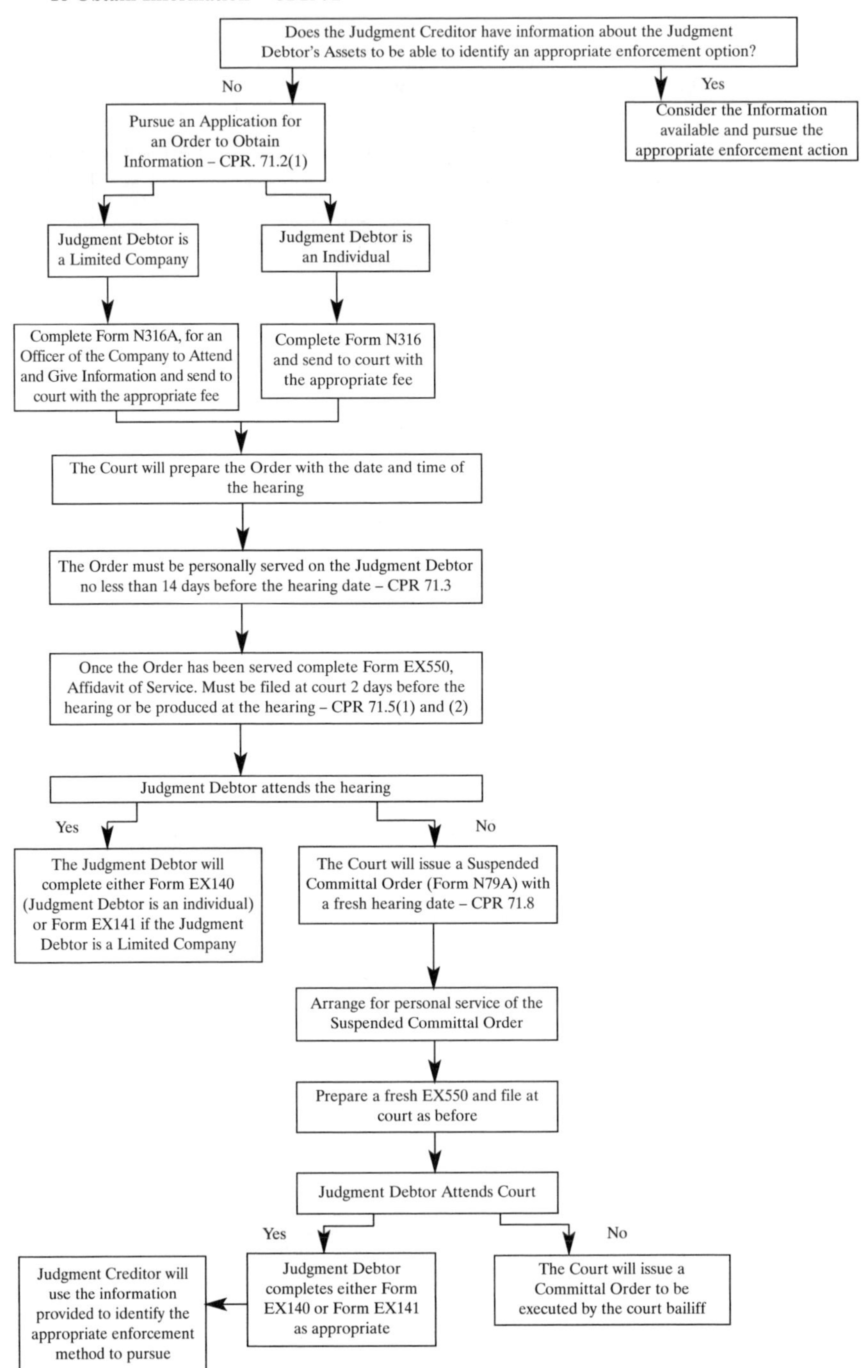

Flow Chart To Apply For A Third Party Debt Order – CPR 72

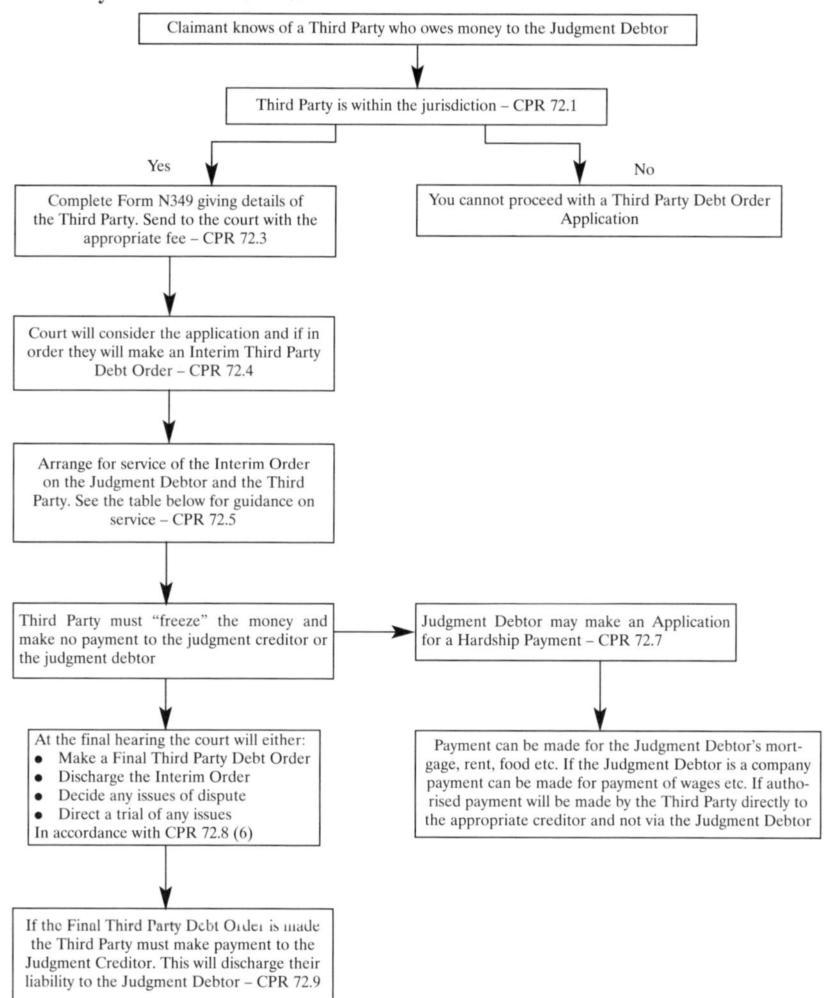

Third Party Debt Order Table For Service – CPR 72.5

Application for TPDO is made	Interim TPDO is made by the court	Final hearing is set not less than 28 days ahead	Third Party is served not less than 21 days before the final hearing date	Judgment Debtor is served not less than 7 days after a copy of the Interim TPDO has been served on the Third Party and 7 days before the final hearing	Final hearing takes place with all service requirements having been met
1st June	**4th June**	**4th July**	**Service on Third Party to be completed by 14th June**	**Service on Judgment Debtor to be completed not earlier than 21st June and before 28th June**	**Final hearing takes place on 4th July**

Look Up Table For Foreign Judgment Enforcement

Country	Reciprocal Treaty	Form of Certificate For Outgoing Judgment	Explanatory Notes
Anguilla	The Administration of Justice Act 1920	Form 110	
Antigua and Barbuda	The Administration of Justice Act 1920	Form 110	
Bahamas	The Administration of Justice Act 1920	Form 110	
Barbados	The Administration of Justice Act 1920	Form 110	
Belize	The Administration of Justice Act 1920	Form 110	
Bermuda	The Administration of Justice Act 1920	Form 110	
Botswana	The Administration of Justice Act 1920	Form 110	
British Indian Ocean Territory	The Administration of Justice Act 1920	Form 110	
British Virgin Islands	The Administration of Justice Act 1920	Form 110	
Cayman Islands	The Administration of Justice Act 1920	Form 110	
Christmas Island	The Administration of Justice Act 1920	Form 110	
Cocos (Keeling) Islands	The Administration of Justice Act 1920	Form 110	
Dominica	The Administration of Justice Act 1920	Form 110	
Falkland Islands	The Administration of Justice Act 1920	Form 110	
Fiji	The Administration of Justice Act 1920	Form 110	
The Gambia	The Administration of Justice Act 1920	Form 110	
Ghana	The Administration of Justice Act 1920	Form 110	
Grenada	The Administration of Justice Act 1920	Form 110	
Guyana	The Administration of Justice Act 1920	Form 110	
Territory of Norfolk Island	The Administration of Justice Act 1920	Form 110	
Jamaica	The Administration of Justice Act 1920	Form 110	
Kenya	The Administration of Justice Act 1920	Form 110	
Kiribati	The Administration of Justice Act 1920	Form 110	
Lesotho	The Administration of Justice Act 1920	Form 110	
Malawi	The Administration of Justice Act 1920	Form 110	
Malaysia	The Administration of Justice Act 1920	Form 110	

Mauritius	The Administration of Justice Act 1920	Form 110	
Montserrat	The Administration of Justice Act 1920	Form 110	
New Zealand	The Administration of Justice Act 1920	Form 110	
Nigeria	The Administration of Justice Act 1920	Form 110	
Papua New Guinea	The Administration of Justice Act 1920	Form 110	
Republic of Cyprus	The Administration of Justice Act 1920	Form 110	
Seychelles	The Administration of Justice Act 1920	Form 110	
Sierra Leone	The Administration of Justice Act 1920	Form 110	
Singapore	The Administration of Justice Act 1920	Form 110	
Solomon Islands	The Administration of Justice Act 1920	Form 110	
Sovereign Base Area of Akrotiri and Dhekelia in Cyprus	The Administration of Justice Act 1920	Form 110	
Sri Lanka	The Administration of Justice Act 1920	Form 110	
St Christopher and Nevis	The Administration of Justice Act 1920	Form 110	
St Helena	The Administration of Justice Act 1920	Form 110	
St Lucia	The Administration of Justice Act 1920	Form 110	
St Vincent and the Grenadines	The Administration of Justice Act 1920	Form 110	
Swaziland	The Administration of Justice Act 1920	Form 110	
Tanzania	The Administration of Justice Act 1920	Form 110	
Tasmania	The Administration of Justice Act 1920	Form 110	
Trinidad and Tobago	The Administration of Justice Act 1920	Form 110	
Turks and Caicos Islands	The Administration of Justice Act 1920	Form 110	
Tuvalu	The Administration of Justice Act 1920	Form 110	
Uganda	The Administration of Justice Act 1920	Form 110	
Zambia	The Administration of Justice Act 1920	Form 110	
Zimbabwe	The Administration of Justice Act 1920	Form 110	
Denmark	The Civil Jurisdiction & Judgment Act 1982	Form 110	
Gibraltar	The Civil Jurisdiction & Judgment Act 1982	Form 110	
Iceland	The Civil Jurisdiction & Judgment Act 1982	Form 110	

Northern Ireland (simplified procedure)	The Civil Jurisdiction & Judgment Act 1982	Form 111	
Norway	The Civil Jurisdiction & Judgment Act 1982	Form 110	
Scotland (simplified procedure)	The Civil Jurisdiction & Judgment Act 1982	Form 111	
Switzerland	The Civil Jurisdiction & Judgment Act 1982	Form 110	
Austria	Council Regulation (EU) 44/2001 and now Council Regulation 805/2004	Form N219/219A	
Belgium	Council Regulation (EU) 44/2001 and now Council Regulation 805/2005	Form N219/219A	
Czech Republic	Council Regulation (EU) 44/2001 and now Council Regulation 805/2006	Form N219/219A	
Estonia	Council Regulation (EU) 44/2001 and now Council Regulation 805/2007	Form N219/219A	
Finland	Council Regulation (EU) 44/2001 and now Council Regulation 805/2008	Form N219/219A	
France	Council Regulation (EU) 44/2001 and now Council Regulation 805/2009	Form N219/219A	
Germany	Council Regulation (EU) 44/2001 and now Council Regulation 805/2010	Form N219/219A	
Greek Cyprus	Council Regulation (EU) 44/2001 and now Council Regulation 805/2011	Form N219/219A	
Hungary	Council Regulation (EU) 44/2001 and now Council Regulation 805/2012	Form N219/219A	
Italy	Council Regulation (EU) 44/2001 and now Council Regulation 805/2013	Form N219/219A	
Latvia	Council Regulation (EU) 44/2001 and now Council Regulation 805/2014	Form N219/219A	
Lithuania	Council Regulation (EU) 44/2001 and now Council Regulation 805/2015	Form N219/219A	
Luxembourg	Council Regulation (EU) 44/2001 and now Council Regulation 805/2016	Form N219/219A	
Malta	Council Regulation (EU) 44/2001 and now Council Regulation 805/2017	Form N219/219A	
Netherlands	Council Regulation (EU) 44/2001 and now Council Regulation 805/2018	Form N219/219A	
Poland	Council Regulation (EU) 44/2001 and now Council Regulation 805/2019	Form N219/219A	
Portugal	Council Regulation (EU) 44/2001 and now Council Regulation 805/2020	Form N219/219A	

Republic of Ireland	Council Regulation (EU) 44/2001 and now Council Regulation 805/2021	Form N219/219A	
Slovakia	Council Regulation (EU) 44/2001 and now Council Regulation 805/2022	Form N219/219A	
Slovenia	Council Regulation (EU) 44/2001 and now Council Regulation 805/2023	Form N219/219A	
Spain	Council Regulation (EU) 44/2001 and now Council Regulation 805/2024	Form N219/219A	
Sweden	Council Regulation (EU) 44/2001 and now Council Regulation 805/2025	Form N219/219A	
Australia	The Foreign Judgments (Reciprocal Enforcement) Act 1933	Form 110	
Canada	The Foreign Judgments (Reciprocal Enforcement) Act 1933	Form 110	The Federal Court of Canada and any court to the province of British Columbia, Manitoba, New Brunswick, Nova Scotia, Ontario, Prince Edward Island, Saskatchewan, or the Yukon Territory Northwest Territories, Newfoundland, Alberta
Island of Guernsey	The Foreign Judgments (Reciprocal Enforcement) Act 1933	Form 110	
Isle of Man	The Foreign Judgments (Reciprocal Enforcement) Act 1933	Form 110	The courts in this jurisdiction will only recognise a High Court judgment which includes a County Court judgment transferred to the High Court for enforcement
Israel	The Foreign Judgments (Reciprocal Enforcement) Act 1933	Form 110	
Jersey (Bailiwick of)	The Foreign Judgments (Reciprocal Enforcement) Act 1933	Form 110	
Pakistan	The Foreign Judgments (Reciprocal Enforcement) Act 1933	Form 110	
Republic of India	The Foreign Judgments (Reciprocal Enforcement) Act 1933	Form 110	Territories named in schedule to Order in Council—SI 1958 No 425
Suriname	The Foreign Judgments (Reciprocal Enforcement) Act 1933	Form 110	
Tonga	The Foreign Judgments (Reciprocal Enforcement) Act 1933	Form 110	

Index